Mobsters, Unions, and Feds

JAMES B. JACOBS

Mobsters, Unions, and Feds

The Mafia and the American Labor Movement

New York University Press • *New York and London*

2560656

NEW YORK UNIVERSITY PRESS
New York and London
www.nyupress.org

Library of Congress Cataloging-in-Publication Data
Jacobs, James B.
Mobsters, unions, and feds : the Mafia and the American labor
movement / James B. Jacobs.
p. cm.
Includes bibliographical references and index.
ISBN-13: 978-0-8147-4273-0 (cloth : alk. paper)
ISBN-10: 0-8147-4273-4 (cloth : alk. paper)
1. Labor unions—United States—History. 2. Racketeering—United
States—History. 3. Mafia—United States—History. 4. Organized
crime—United States—History. 5. Organized crime investigation—
United States—History.   I. Title.
HD6490.R32U653 2006
364.1'06'0973—dc22   2005022953

New York University Press books are printed on acid-free paper,
and their binding materials are chosen for strength and durability.

Manufactured in the United States of America
10 9 8 7 6 5 4 3 2 1

To Herman Benson

Racketeering is the cancer that almost destroyed the American trade-union movement.

—DAVID DUBINSKY, president of the International
Ladies Garment Workers (1932–1966), David Dubinsky
and A. Raskin, *David Dubinsky: A Life with Labor*
(New York: Simon and Schuster, 1977), 145

American labor had better roll up its sleeves, it had better get the stiffest broom and brush it can find, and the strongest soap and disinfectant, and it had better take on the job of cleaning its own house from top to bottom and drive out every crook and gangster and racketeer we find, because if we don't clean our own house, then the reactionaries will clean it for us. But they won't use a broom, they'll use an ax, and they'll try to destroy the labor movement in the process.

—WALTER REUTHER, president of the United
Automobile Workers (1946–1970), opening address
of the sixteenth constitutional convention of the
United Automobile, Aircraft and Agricultural
Implement Workers of America, Atlantic City, NJ
(April 7, 1957), reprinted in Henry Christman, ed.,
Walter P. Reuther: Selected Papers (New York:
Macmillan, 1961), 192

Contents

Preface

Labor racketeering is an important example of American exceptionalism. No other country has a history of significant organized crime infiltration of its labor movement, and no other country has an organized crime syndicate with a power base in labor unions. The interrelationship, over most of the twentieth century, between organized crime and organized labor has political, social, and economic consequences that have hardly begun to be explored.

This book is not an exposé. From the early twentieth century, labor racketeering has been an important source of organized crime's power, prestige, and wealth. By "labor racketeering," I mean the exploitation of unions and union power by organized crime. By "labor racketeers," I mean Cosa Nostra* (mafia) bosses who wield influence over union officeholders and treasuries, Cosa Nostra *capos, soldiers,* and *associates* who hold union offices, and union officials who are closely allied to, and do the bidding for organized crime members. Labor racketeers treat unions like cash cows that generate money via salaries, perks, embezzlement, extortion, bribes, and fraud. They regularly use union power to establish and enforce employer cartels that fix prices, allocate contracts, and suppress competition. For these services they extract payoffs ("dues") from employer associations. Moreover, they routinely

---

* Joseph Valachi, an organized crime member who became a cooperating witness in the 1960s, first reported that members of the Italian-American organized crime families referred to their organization as "Cosa Nostra," which translates as "Our Thing." This was consistent with the usage of organized crime members themselves, as revealed in conversations intercepted during the 1950s. Somehow, the FBI and the media came to use the term "La Cosa Nostra" ("The Our Thing"), often abbreviated as "LCN." That name makes no grammatical sense and is not used by organized crime members. Nevertheless, because it is so widely used in journalistic and scholarly writings, I sometimes refer to Cosa Nostra as LCN.

take full or partial ownership in one or more of the firms that constitute the cartel.

In their exploitation of unions, labor racketeers commit numerous criminal offenses, e.g., *extortion* of employers by threatening unlawful strikes, work stoppages, picketing, and sabotage (labor peace extortion); *soliciting and receiving bribes* (labor bribery) from employers in exchange for advantageous contract terms and for allowing the employer to ignore the terms of a collective bargaining agreement ("sweetheart deal"); *thefts and embezzlements* from the union and its pension and welfare funds; *murder, assault and battery, arson,* and other violent crimes against rank-and-file "dissidents" and uncooperative employers; and *antitrust* violations by means of price fixing, contract allocations, and preventing competitors from entering a market.[1]

Despite the fact that labor racketeering has often been exposed by congressional and other hearings, investigative journalists, and in criminal and civil racketeering cases, it has not attracted much interest from university-based scholars. Students of crime, law and society, American history, and even American labor history have largely ignored this disturbing story.

While there is a large subfield in criminology devoted to corporate crime, there is no corresponding subfield of *union crime.* Even though Edwin Sutherland invented the field of *white-collar crime,* Sutherland's and Cressey's best-selling general criminology text does not even mention labor corruption or labor racketeering. Even organized crime scholars, of whom there are very few, fail to recognize that the Mafia's unique political and economic position in American society derives from its base in the labor movement.

Academic labor lawyers do not view labor racketeering as part of their bailiwick. Their courses give short shrift to the 1957–1959 U.S. Senate (McClellan Committee) labor racketeering hearings, the most extensive congressional investigation in U.S. history.* Most law students finish their labor law course unaware that the 1959 Landrum-Griffin Act

---

* The McClellan Committee (Senate Select Committee on Improper Activities in the Labor or Management Field) hearings lasted almost three years, 1957–1959. They gave labor racketeering unprecedented attention. Following the hearings, Senator John L. McClellan (D.-Ark.) published *Crime Without Punishment* and the committee's chief counsel, Robert F. Kennedy, published *The Enemy Within.* Both books warned that the misuse of union power constituted a threat to the nation.

was passed to remedy the labor racketeering problems exposed by the McClellan Committee. Students of employment rights and benefits are unaware that ERISA (Employee Retirement Insurance Security Act) was in part a legislative response to revelations of organized crime's infiltration and misuse of union pension and welfare funds.

No labor law casebook mentions *United States v. International Brotherhood of Teamsters,* perhaps the most ambitious organizational reform case in American history. The Department of Justice filed its civil racketeering complaint in the IBT International case in 1988. The case was settled in 1989, but the remedial phase of the litigation, i.e., the enforcement of the settlement, continues to this day (fall 2005) with no end in sight.[*2]

While there has been much academic writing about the decline of the American labor movement since approximately 1960, I don't know any scholarly article or book that even suggests that the corrosive impact of labor racketeers on union organizing and administration might have undermined the labor movement's attractiveness and strength. Rather than attributing labor's decline to internal factors like bad tactical decisions and the mechanization of the workplace or to external factors like globalization or governmental policy, this book offers organized crime penetration and exploitation as both an external and internal contributor to organized labor's dwindling power.

With just one or two exceptions, labor historians have not sought to document or explain how organized crime elements took over union locals, regional or area-wide councils, and even international unions,

---

[*] Despite the fact that most casebooks provide brief 75–100-page histories of the labor movement, they do not mention the long, deep, and complex twentieth-century relationship between organized labor and organized crime. For example, in Michael Harper and Samuel Estreicher's *Labor Law: Cases, Materials and Problems* (4th ed., 1996) there is no mention of the McClellan Committee hearings or the federal government's twenty civil RICO suits and resulting court-appointed trusteeships over international, regional, and local labor unions. Many labor law casebooks devote a chapter to the Landrum-Griffin Act, but without mentioning that Landrum-Griffin embodies an anti-racketeering strategy based on a belief that racketeering can best be opposed by an informed rank and file that can speak out against, organize to overthrow, and vote to oust labor racketeers. Clyde Summers et al.'s *Labor Law, Cases and Materials* (2d ed., 1998) is one of the few casebooks to provide a thorough discussion of union democracy, but the authors do not relate union democracy to organized crime exploitation. In fact, they do not mention organized crime.

looted their pension and welfare funds, sold out union members' interests, and made a mockery of union democracy.* No labor historian has sought to document and analyze the government's efforts to punish and prevent labor racketeering.

Perhaps scholars of American labor wear ideological blinders. A number of people have suggested to me that it is *antilabor* to focus on labor racketeering.** Perhaps lack of attention is explained by a general loss of interest in unions. Contemporary labor scholars seem to have turned their attention to the social and economic history of workers and the working class and away from labor organizations.

Despite the dearth of scholarship on labor racketeering, I am hardly writing on a blank slate. I owe a debt to many journalists and few scholars who have created a small but strong edifice of labor racketeering studies on which this book can build. One of the best scholars of labor racketeering was one of the first, Chicago sociologist John Landesco. In his classic *Organized Crime in Chicago*[3] (prepared as part of the massive 1929 Illinois Crime Survey), Landesco provided a great deal of description and commentary on labor racketeering before the emergence of LCN. Landesco recognized the importance of labor racketeering to organized crime. He described the connection between labor racketeering and what he called "industrial racketeering." According to Landesco, gangsters parlayed their control of unions into control over businesses and whole industries.

> In "racketeering," the gunman and the ex-convict have seized control
> of business associations and have organized mushroom labor unions
> and have maintained or raised price and wage standards by violence,

* Irving Bernstein's two-volume *History of the American Worker* (1970 and 1983) devotes only three pages per volume to labor racketeering. Melvyn Dubofsky's *The State and Labor in Modern America* (1994) and Christopher Tomlins's *The State and the Unions* (1960) do not contain an index entry for labor racketeering or organized crime. See Irving Bernstein, *The Lean Years: A History of the American Worker, 1920–1933* (Perseus Book Group, 1983), 338–41; Irving Bernstein, *Turbulent Years: A History of the American Worker, 1933–1941* (Houghton Mifflin, 1970), 123–24, 710–12. Melvyn Dubofsky, *The State and Labor in Modern America* (Chapel Hill: University of North Carolina Press, 1994); Christopher Tomlins, *The State and the Unions* (New York: Cambridge University Press, 1960).
** I strongly disagree. There is nothing prolabor about organized crime penetration and exploitation of the labor movement. Moreover, studying racketeering in the labor movement is no more antilabor than studying family violence is antifamily.

and have exploited these organizations for personal profit. . . . The
gunman and gangster are, at the present time, actually in control of
the destinies of over ninety necessary economic activities. Al Capone,
overlord of organized crime in the Chicago region, now a stock-
holder in a business enterprise, ensures it "the best protection in the
world."[4]

Landesco identified twenty-three racketeer-controlled trades including window cleaning, machinery moving, paper stock, cleaning and
dyeing, laundries, candy jobbers, dental laboratories, ash and rubbish
hauling, grocery and delicatessen stores, garage owners, physicians,
drugstores, milk dealers, glaziers, photographers, florists, bootblacks,
restaurants, shoe repairers, fish and poultry, butchers, bakers, and window shade men.[5] He observed that, in some "cut-throat industries,"
gangsters provided businessmen important assistance by organizing and enforcing profitable employer cartels that fixed prices, allocated contracts, and generally stifled competition. Racketeers used the
union's monopoly over labor to force businesses to join employer associations. The employers paid "dues" that were passed along to the
crime bosses. In exchange they obtained protection from business competitors and from union problems. They also obtained relief from enforcement of collective bargaining agreements and sometimes immunity from union organizing in the first place. Landesco's insight into
the functional role that labor racketeers played in curbing business
competition presaged the more systemic analysis of law professors
G. Robert Blakey and Ronald Goldstock in the 1970s,[6] economist Peter
Reuter in the 1980s,[7] and the New York State Organized Crime Task
Force (led by Goldstock) in the 1990s.

Harold Seidman's *Labor Czars: A History of Labor Racketeering* (1938)
appeared a decade after Landesco's book. Seidman, then a journalist
and later an academic, chronicled the careers of late nineteenth- and
early twentieth-century gangster-type *labor czars,* like Joey Fay (Chicago) and Robert Brindell (New York). Brindell dominated and exploited the New York City building trades for years, frequently enlist-
ing gangsters to intimidate and extort employers and workers. Brindell
and Fay treated union members' rights as commodities, which, in
exchange for bribes, they sold to employers. Seidman's book clearly
showed that labor racketeering preceded the dominance of Italian-
American organized crime and that gangsters gained control of union

locals at a time when law enforcement was weak or corrupt or both. Like Landesco, Seidman argued that (usually small) employers preferred to deal with gangsters than with politically and socially radical labor officials.

In 1931, Louis Adamic, a Chicago-based journalist, novelist, and political activist, published *Dynamite: The Story of Class Violence in America* and devoted several chapters to racketeering. He provided examples of how labor unions recruited gangsters (even "dynamiters") to help them fend off employer repression. Adamic, who was a contemporary of Al Capone's in Chicago, saw that once organized crime had its foot in the union's door, it often sought to take over. He wrote:

> We need not be shocked when we realize how close the relationship is between organized labor and organized crime. Nor need we be shocked by the thought that organized labor was a vital factor in the early history of modern racketeering, that, indeed, organized labor, perhaps more than any other economic group, started the professional criminals whose names now shriek in the headlines of their amazing careers. One should bear in mind that gangsterism was a vital factor early in the American class struggle, first on the capitalist side and then on the side of labor; and that its history is inextricably bound up with the history of organized labor.[8]

In January 1940, conservative journalist Westbrook Pegler (*Chicago Daily News* and the *Washington Post*) exposed the connection of organized crime figures, especially Arthur Flegenheimer ("Dutch Schultz") to George Scalise, president of the Building Services Employees International Union (BSEIU).[9] Early in his career, Scalise moved from union to union. He used his connections with Dutch Schultz to obtain a Teamsters charter for a union of parking garage workers.[10] David Witwer, an historian writing many decades later explained:

> Scalise, and others of his type, went into the labor movement to make money; they came from outside the ranks of the workers in the industry, with whom they did not really identify. Nor did they depend upon those workers to organize the union through mass picketing and long strikes. Instead, they used selective acts of violence committed by a few individuals, probably with links to organized crime. Free from

having to depend on a mobilized, united membership, the Union's leadership could safely ignore the members' needs, or sacrifice them to the interests of the employers. As a result, unskilled workers scattered across a wide area and labored in small shops, [they] had little knowledge of their union, and often no say in its affairs.[11]

Later, with the backing of Chicago's organized crime syndicate, Scalise took over a Chicago BSEIU local.[12] Then via a rigged election, Al Capone assured Scalise's victory for BSEIU eastern vice-president. Eventually, Scalise became the BSEIU's international president.[13]

After World War II, investigative journalists continued to outperform university-based scholars in documenting and analyzing labor racketeering. In 1949, a *New York Sun* reporter, Malcolm Johnson, wrote a Pulitzer Prize–winning series of articles on "gangsterism" in the International Longshoremen's Association (ILA). A year later he published *Crime on the Labor Front,* a book that provided a wealth of detail about labor racketeering in the ILA, the Building Services Employees, the Waiters Union, the Cafeteria Workers Union, the International Alliance of Theatrical and Stage Employees, the International Brotherhood of Teamsters, and several construction unions. Johnson explained how mobsters take over unions and establish employer cartels.

[A] gangster can break into a union by threats and violence or he can "fix" an election so that one of his stooges becomes a key official. Once in power, he can bribe his opposition into cooperation, or he can sew them in sacks and drop them into the river. As for carrying away the loot, almost every gangster resorts to the same tried-and-true rackets to swindle the members and coerce the company.[14]

Johnson provided many examples of how labor racketeers violate the rights and subvert the interests of union members in order to line their own pockets and the pockets of their organized crime partners. However, he insisted that employers were not just the labor racketeers' victims but, in many cases, their coconspirators: "In permitting themselves to become extortion victims they [the employers] nearly always were seeking some advantage for themselves, usually at the expense of the workers."[15] Johnson's articles and book later provided the basis for

Budd Schulberg's screenplay for Elia Kazan's Academy award–winning film *On the Waterfront*.

In 1951, Daniel Bell (then a journalist, later a renowned Harvard sociologist) published his classic article "Last of the Business Rackets"[*] in *Fortune Magazine*. Bell provided a rich description and trenchant analysis, incorporating geographical, economic, political, ethnic, and other sociological variables to account for rampant racketeering on the New York City docks. In part, Bell attributed waterfront corruption and racketeering to geographic and economic variables. New York City was the nation's most important port. Yet, there were no railroad connections to the docks; everything had to be loaded onto and unloaded from trucks. New York City's narrow streets ensured constant bottlenecks and long queues of truckers trying to pick up or set down ship cargo. Because delay was so expensive to shippers, racketeers could manipulate the loading and unloading process to extort and/or solicit bribes.

The abundance of casual laborers in the port suited both the union bosses and the shippers. The union bosses controlled the longshoremen through their power to hire and blacklist. The stevedoring companies did not maintain a permanent workforce. Gangsters, who controlled each pier, decided who would work when ships needed loading and unloading. Men who cooperated with the racketeers were rewarded with work. Those who complained were blacklisted.[16] The racketeers also controlled all sorts of criminal enterprises that flourished on the docks, including thievery and usury.

Abused and exploited workers had no place to turn for assistance except to Father John M. Corridan, the heroic "waterfront priest." Joseph Ryan, the ILA's boss for decades, delivered votes to local politicians; in exchange the politicians turned a deaf ear to reformers' demands for improving conditions on the docks. Ryan was closely allied with William J. McCormick, business mogul, czar of the port, and one of the silent powers in New York's Democratic Party.

Bell's sophisticated analysis explained why labor unions exerted so much power over workers and so much leverage over shippers; why control of the ILA was so attractive to professional criminals; how a corrupt relationship between business and labor enriched the labor rack-

[*] Bell reworked the article and retitled it "Racket-Ridden Longshoremen" for his book, *The End of Ideology* (1960).

eteers at the expense of the workers; and how politicians and law enforcement officials were corrupted Ethnic politics were also important. Ryan and most longshoremen were Irish. However, Italian-American gangsters like Albert Anastasia and his brother, Anthony Anastasio, controlled some ILA locals and eventually took the union away from Ryan. In 1954, the brutal exploitation of ordinary ILA members was brilliantly dramatized in the movie *On the Waterfront*, starring Marlon Brando, Eva Marie Saint, Karl Malden, Lee J. Cobb, and Rod Steiger. A spectacular success, the movie generated public and political sentiment for reforming the dockworkers' plight.

Despite at least a half century of journalistic exposés of labor racketeering, no mainstream labor historian addressed the subject until 1958, when Professor Philip Taft (Brown University) published a small (sixty-page) monograph, *Corruption and Racketeering in the Labor Movement* based on three lectures delivered at Cornell University.[18] Despite the title, Taft was not familiar with organized crime's role in the labor movement or, if he was, he chose not to write about it. Instead, he offered some vague bromides. For example, he attributed union corruption to "the avaricious creed of the larger society." He observed that "[r]acketeering in labor unions appears to flow from a general slackness in American society, an emphasis upon material gain, and practices prevalent in many areas of the business community."[19] Many labor scholars who followed Taft defended or opposed "business unionism" as the nonideological basis for the American labor movement without noting that, in some unions, so-called business unionism was essentially organized crime exploitation of workers.

In 1959, Sidney Lens, a left-wing peace and labor activist, socialist, director of CIO Local 329, occasional political candidate, and a leading American radical intellectual from the 1930s to the 1960s,* published *The Crisis of American Labor,* a remarkable book that seems to have been almost completely ignored. (Lens, like many left-wing intellectuals, got his start as a labor organizer. When his union career was stymied for political reasons, he gravitated into journalism.) Drawing on his personal experience, Lens documented and analyzed the methods by which

---

* In his autobiography *Unrepentant Radical* (Boston: Beacon Press, 1980), Lens said that his "true occupation was full-time revolutionary." A one-time Trotskyite, he served as secretary of Branch 26 of the Workers Alliance, Department Store Employees Union Local 291, and later as full-time director of Local 329 (the only staff member).

organized crime figures obtained influence in the labor movement. Although he didn't cite Louis Adamic, his conclusions echo Adamic's:

> [Once the employers took to hiring thugs as strike breakers,] the unions . . . took to hiring their own muscle men, men like "Big Jack" Zelig, "Joe the Greaser" Rosensweig, "Dopey Bennie" Fein. . . . [By] 1920 the gangsters had learned that it was possible to pursue the racket further. The men who came to dinner decided to stay on. They muscled themselves into a few local unions as partners. The next stage in labor racketeering was a broader effort not only to take over key local unions but international unions as well. In New York, the gambler Arnold Rothstein not only supplied thugs to the furriers and garment unions but bribed police not to molest pickets. His successors . . . Louis "Lepke" Buchalter and "Jacob the Gurrah" Shapiro built this business into a fortune.[20]

Although Lens was a labor activist, not a criminologist, he fully grasped the importance of labor racketeering for the empowerment of organized crime. "Labor racketeering is not only a source of income for the syndicate but a means of rounding out its empire; it is a not-too-hidden persuader, an integral part of a criminal trust that stretches across many fields."[21]

A decade passed before the appearance of another book on U.S. labor racketeering, but it was worth the wait. UCLA historian John Hutchinson's 1972 book, *The Imperfect Union: A History of Corruption in American Trade Unions*,[22] was the first professional history of U.S. labor corruption and racketeering. Drawing heavily on the U.S. Senate's 1957–1959 McClellan Committee hearings, it covered the period from the early twentieth century up to 1960. Hutchinson presented descriptive chapters on the "building trades," "the racketeers" and "the intervention of Congress." However, like Philip Taft, he did not distinguish ordinary corruption from Cosa Nostra labor racketeering.* In other words, despite the McClellan Committee's revelations, he did not identify organized crime's penetration of and influence over union lo-

---

* In addition to the small number of works on labor corruption and racketeering, there are a number of studies that touch tangentially on labor racketeering. Among these, Virgil Peterson's *100 Years of Organized Crime in New York City* is particularly useful, as is Mary Stolberg's *Fighting Organized Crime: Politics, Justice and the Legacy of Thomas E. Dewey*.

cals, regional unions, and national/international unions as a special sociopolitical problem. However, the wealth of information about the influence of criminal elements in the labor movement that he unearthed must be the starting place for any subsequent study of labor racketeering.

The next important building block in the creation of the scholarly corpus on American labor racketeering was the 1990 New York State Organized Crime Task Force (OCTF)'s *Final Report on Corruption & Racketeering in the NYC Construction Industry,* published by New York University Press.[23] (I was principal draftsman.) Utilizing informants, grand juries, cooperating witnesses, union dissidents, and brainstorming sessions with various industry participants, the OCTF documented the persistence and pervasiveness of organized crime racketeering in New York City's construction unions from the early twentieth century through the late 1980s. Among other things, the report explained how the organized crime families converted their control over construction unions into a large revenue stream.

Expanding on an analysis first developed by G. Robert Blakey, Ronald Goldstock, and Gerard Bradley,[24] the OCTF investigation elaborated the concepts of *racketeering susceptibility* and *racketeering potential.* The former referred to the strategic importance of a union for an entire industry; the latter referred to the potential revenue and other advantages that could be derived from a particular union's exploitation. The OCTF report hypothesized that labor racketeers target or at least are successful in penetrating unions where both racketeering susceptibility and racketeering potential are high. It also made clear that in the past successful criminal prosecutions had little, if any, impact on LCN's influence over labor unions because other LCN members and associates simply assumed the authority and responsibilities of their incarcerated comrades. The report offered a number of recommendations, including new criminal laws, a construction industry–specific regulatory agency, and a new institute for union democracy.

There are many authors whose work, though not focusing directly on labor racketeering, does touch on the subject. For example, Stephen Fox's *Blood and Power* (1989), a history of organized crime, devotes a chapter to "gangsters, unions and employers"; Virgil Peterson's *The Mob* (1983) includes the chapters on "The Rise of Jimmy Hoffa" and "The New York State Waterfront hearings";[25] and Howard Abadinsky's *Organized Crime* text has a chapter on labor racketeering. Professor

Abadinsky points out that "[a]lthough labor-related business racket-eering can be conducted by anyone, the history of the labor movement shows that the most substantial corruption of unions is conducted by organized crime"[26] and that "[l]abor and business racketeering distinguish traditional organized crime from other forms, making traditional OC more influential than the others."[27] Gus Russo's recently published history of Chicago organized crime, *The Outfit: The Role of Chicago's Underworld in the Shaping of Modern America*, provides extremely useful information about the Capone gang's labor racketeering activities in the 1920s and 1930s.[28] Peter Reuter's *Racketeering in Legitimate Industries* (1987) provides important insight into organized crime's methods of creating employer cartels.[29] He explains how Cosa Nostra used Teamsters Local 813 to establish and police a cartel in New York City's commercial waste hauling industry.

As for biographies, while we do not yet have a biography of an organized crime figure who specialized in labor racketeering, such as Johnny Dioguardi, Anthony Scotto, Tony Provenzano, and Ralph Scopo, there are various biographies of criminals, labor leaders, and law enforcement officials that shed some light on labor racketeering. Among these are John Kobler's biography of the Chicago organized crime boss Al Capone; Peter Maas's biography of New York City's Gambino crime family underboss Sammy "the Bull" Gravano; James Neff's biography of Teamsters General President Jackie Presser (who was simultaneously an ally of Cosa Nostra and an FBI informant!); Mary Stolberg's biography of New York City prosecutor (later governor and Republican presidential candidate) Thomas E. Dewey, and several biographies of Teamsters President Jimmy Hoffa.[30]

The International Brotherhood of Teamsters (IBT) has attracted far more journalistic and scholarly attention than any other U.S. union.[31] Two recent books on the Teamsters are among the best: historian David Witwer's *Corruption and Reform in the Teamsters Union* (2003) and Stier, Anderson & Malone's *The Teamsters: Perception and Reality* (2002).

Although academic scholarship on labor racketeering is thin, there is an enormous amount of information to be mined from congressional hearings and reports, and more recently, from court decisions and the reports of court-appointed trustees. Throughout this book, I draw on the work of the Senate Select Committee on Improper Activities in the Labor or Management Field (the McClellan Committee) and on a number of hearings and reports by the U.S. Senate Subcommittee on Investigations. Two hearings—(1) Federal Government's Use of Trusteeships under the RICO Statute (April 4, 6, & 12, 1989), and (2) Federal Government's Use of the RICO Statute and Other Efforts Against Organized Crime (August 1, 1990)—are especially valuable because they are devoted to the propriety and usefulness of civil RICO union trusteeships for combating labor racketeering. The 1986 President's Commission on Organized Crime's volume *The Edge: Organized Crime, Business and Labor Unions* synthesizes many congressional reports and adds new material.[32] Admittedly, these governmental sources reflect a certain perspective (e.g., labor racketeering is a serious problem), but they provide a great deal of information. The hearings provide a forum for law enforcement officials, union leaders, and union democracy proponents to express their views on the problem and its strategies for remediation.

With a few exceptions, the efforts of rank-and-file union members to oust racketeers from their unions have gone undocumented. The most important exception is the tiny but dogged Association for Union Democracy's (AUD) newsletters, *Union Democracy in Action* (1959–1972) and *The Union Democracy Review* (1972–present), which provide valuable information and commentary on "dissidents'" and rank-and-file insurgents' struggles for justice.[33]

So far we have been surveying what has been written about the history and dynamics of labor racketeering. But what of academic work and journalism on governmental, judicial, and labor *responses* to labor racketeering? On this, there is even less scholarship. Remarkably, although the litigative efforts of the U.S. Department of Justice (DOJ) over the past twenty years to purge organized crime from the labor movement constitute one of the most ambitious attempts at court-ordered and -supervised organizational reform in our history,* it generated little legal scholarship. There are no books and just a few law review articles.

---

* I don't mean to slight the ambition of court-supervised school desegregation and prison reform but, as hard as those goals were to achieve, they did involve geographically fixed institutions run by state and local employees. In the labor racketeering context, we are dealing with massive unions (Teamsters has 1.4 million members) organized into hundreds of locals spread across North America. Some of the officials of these unions wield political influence at the very highest level of American society. Some of the organized crime figures involved are among the most ruthless and influential power brokers in American history.

In 1980, building on previous work by their Cornell Institute of Organized Crime, Professors G. Robert Blakey and Ronald Goldstock published "On the Waterfront: RICO and Labor Racketeering,"[34] advocating use of the federal civil racketeering statute, Racketeer Influenced and Corrupt Organizations Act of 1970 (RICO), to combat labor racketeering. In addition to its draconian criminal provisions, RICO provided the federal courts with authority to use injunctions and other "equitable remedies" to *prevent* racketeering. Blakey and Goldstock argued that "control of syndicate crime and labor racketeering will not be achieved by standard law enforcement practices," and that "RICO provides the flexibility required to implement a comprehensive strategy in the labor racketeering area. To the extent that it is used appropriately and with discretion, it offers significant potential to affect what is clearly a national problem."[35] This book shows the prescience of their prediction and also how difficult it is to purge organized crime from and reform the governance and administration of heretofore "captive" labor organizations.

From the standpoint of the union democracy movement, Professor Michael Goldberg (Widener Law School) published the most important law review article in 1989. Unfortunately, the article was published too soon to take account of the government's pathbreaking civil RICO suit against the IBT's general executive board and the Mafia's "commission" of organized crime bosses.[36] Goldberg was able to draw on the complaints and settlements (and in one case the trial transcript) from three RICO suits against union locals. However, his main goal was normative: to argue that civil RICO suits and resulting court-ordered or court-supervised trusteeships are justified because they are the only way to liberate racketeer-ridden unions. He is joined in this conclusion by Herman Benson, the founder and driving force of the Association for Union Democracy, a shoestring nongovernmental organization that has fought valiantly since 1969 to protect the rights of union members against labor racketeers.

My own (with student coauthors Christopher Panarella and Jay Worthington III) 1994 book *Busting the Mob: United States v. Cosa Nostra* sought to document and analyze the DOJ's all-out attack on organized crime triggered by the murder of Jimmy Hoffa in 1975. Toward that end, Part II of that book consists of five chapters, each a case study of an important 1980s organized crime case. One chapter is devoted to the DOJ's (federal Newark, New Jersey, Organized Crime Strike Force) 1982 civil

RICO suit against Teamsters Local 560 and another chapter to the DOJ's (Southern District of New York, headed by U.S. Attorney Rudy Giuliani) 1989 suit against the IBT's general executive board. My coauthors and I drew on the formal legal complaints, the trial and decree (in the Local 560 case), the consent decree (in the IBT case), and numerous court opinions and trustee reports. Nevertheless, when we were writing the book, the remedial phases of both cases were in their early days. At that time, it was unclear how long court monitoring would last or whether, ultimately, either trusteeship would be successful. A decade has passed; the Local 560 trusteeship has been declared successful and terminated, but the Independent Review Board in the IBT case continues, with no end in sight, to bring disciplinary actions against organized crime–connected union officials.

As the 1990s progressed, a nascent law review literature began to grow around the question of whether it is justifiable and desirable for the government to seek to reform mobbed-up unions through court-appointed and -supervised trusteeships established by civil RICO suits. Critics of the DOJ/FBI offensive against labor racketeering pointed to the unsavory history of governmental and judicial interventions in nineteenth and early twentieth century labor disputes. The critics emphasized that even well-intentioned government initiatives threatened the labor movement's independence. On the other side, Professor Michael Goldberg and University of Pennsylvania Law Professor Clyde Summers, the nation's leading legal scholar of union democracy, argued that although RICO-triggered union trusteeships carry certain dangers, there is no other way to purge organized crime from racketeer-ridden unions.

In the 2000s, my students and I published two case studies of union trusteeships and one overview of DOJ's effort to purge organized crime from the labor movement. The first case study focused on the IBT Local 560 case, which was terminated in 1999, after the DOJ and the court were persuaded that the trustee's remedial efforts had successfully purged organized crime, produced fair elections, and established a viable union democracy.[37] The second case study focused on a regional union, the New York City District Council of Carpenters, which comprised some twenty-two Carpenter union locals.[38] That trusteeship began in 1994 and was terminated in 1999, the judge declaring success and folding the trusteeship's tent. However, upon closer inspection, and in light of events that occurred after the trusteeship ended, we could not call that trusteeship a success. Finally, in a 2004 article, two law students and I attempted to bring together what is known about all twenty civil RICO-generated union trusteeships up to that time.[39] We found only three trusteeships that could unequivocally be declared successes. Since the 2004 article, no new civil RICO union lawsuits have been filed, but it is likely that, in the years to come, there will be many more.* Certainly, criminal indictments involving organized crime and labor racketeering continue to be handed down. The on-going investigations of LIUNA, IBT, ILA, and other union locals also continue to expose corruption and racketeering.

The twenty civil RICO union lawsuits and resulting trusteeships constitute an extraordinarily important chapter in both American labor history and American law enforcement history. They inform our understanding of why the U.S. labor movement evolved the way it did and what its possible future might look like. They also inform our understanding of the potential and limits of organized crime control, and of purging organized crime from organizations dominated by intimidation and patronage. Moreover, a close look at these lawsuits and trusteeships ought to interest students who study the capacity of courts to reform corrupted or unconstitutional organizations and institutions.

---

* In the summer of 2005, while this book was in press, DOJ (Eastern District of New York) filed a civil RICO complaint against the leaders of the International Longshoremen's Association and several organized crime figures.

Acknowledgments

The origins of this book date back to the mid-1980s when I served as principal draftsman of the New York State Organized Crime Task Force's (OCTF) investigation and analysis of corruption and racketeering in the New York City construction industry. Our Final Report focused on labor racketeering as the basis of Cosa Nostra's immense power and influence in the construction industry. Indeed, we identified several dozen local construction unions that were strongly influenced, even controlled, by Cosa Nostra. I am indebted to the then-OCTF Director, and longtime friend, Ronald Goldstock and his excellent staff for educating me about organized crime generally and labor racketeering specifically. All the members of the OCTF were my teachers, but I want to take this opportunity to again especially thank Martin Marcus, Thomas Thacher III, Robert Mass, and Wilda Hess.

During my stint with OCTF, I came to know Herman Benson, Executive Director of the Association for Union Democracy, editor of its journal *Union Democracy Review,* and a lifetime crusader for union members' democratic rights (to speak, vote, run for office, have fair hiring halls, and fair grievance procedures). Herman, who is nearly ninety years old as this book goes to press, is a force of nature. He has encyclopedic knowledge of the struggle for union democracy. Over the many years that I have known him, he has never hesitated to share his knowledge and insights with me. His own memoir, *Rebels, Reformers, and Racketeers: How Insurgents Transformed the Labor Movement* (2004), is required reading for anyone interested in union democracy and the efforts of union members to achieve basic political rights.

When several academic publishers shied away from publishing OCTF's *Final Report on Corruption & Racketeering in the NYC Construction Industry* because of fear of displeasing some union officials (and those who claimed to speak on behalf of organized labor) who did not wish to have labor racketeering discussed in public, NYU Press agreed to publish the report as an academic book. For that I thank Colin Jones and Niko Pfund, then president and editor in chief.

My next step on the road to this current volume was *Busting the Mob: U.S. v. Cosa Nostra* (NYU Press, 1994) (*BTM*), a volume documenting the government's attack on organized crime in the 1970s and 1980s. Two cases highlighted in *BTM* were the 1982 civil RICO cases against IBT Local 560 and the 1988 civil RICO suit against the IBT's general executive board. For helping me to bring that work to completion, I acknowledge the excellent assistance of two NYU student coauthors, Christopher Panarella and Jay Worthington III.

In the course of researching and writing *BTM*, I got to know two remarkable public servants: Robert Stewart, the career federal prosecutor who brought the IBT Local 560 suit and steadfastly enforced the court's decree during more than ten years of litigation, and Edwin Stier, the court-appointed trustee who ultimately succeeded in reforming Local 560 and later went on to play an historic role in the effort to reform the International Brotherhood of Teamsters. Our country and its labor movement owe a great debt of gratitude to these two men. So do I.

In 1998, NYU Press published my third volume on the government's campaign against organized crime. *Gotham Unbound: How New York City Was Liberated from the Grip of Organized Crime* focused on how NYC's five Cosa Nostra organized crime families came to play such an important role in the city's economic power structure, especially in construction, the garment center, the Fulton Fish market, cargo operations at JFK airport, and the Jacob Javits Exhibition Center. Labor racketeering was not the whole story in Cosa Nostra's infiltration and exploitation of these economic sectors, but it was the most important part. Again, I was ably assisted by two NYU law student coauthors, Coleen Friel and Robert Radick, now both assistant U.S. attorneys, and by a number of research assistants including Alex Hortis, with whom I coauthored a case study of the IBT Local 560 trusteeship.

By the time we finished *Gotham Unbound,* it was clear to me that labor racketeering warranted a book in its own right. I was familiar enough with the scholarly literature to know that criminal law professors and criminologists had written very little about labor racketeering and that labor historians and legal scholars had written practically nothing about it. I began the current project. My strategy included organizing and teaching an NYU School of Law seminar (Labor Racketeering and Union Democracy) in fall 2002 and fall 2003. It was tremendously valuable for me to have Bob Stewart as coprofessor of the seminar in 2002. The students and I were enriched in so many ways by his unique experiences and encyclopedic knowledge. But that wasn't my only good fortune. Carl Biers, Executive Director of the Association for Union Democracy, sat in on and participated in the seminar. What's more, a number of key players in the struggle to reform "mobbed-up unions" came to the seminar as guest speakers and submitted to our relentless questioning. All of them deserve my thanks: Herman Benson, Susan Jennick, Robert Luskin, Kurt Muellenberg, Edwin Stier, and Patrick Syzmanski. Of course, thanks are also due to my students, whose participation and papers were a very important part of my education.

Over two academic years, from 2000 to 2002, I was fortunate to have NYU law student Ellen Peters working with me on a wide-ranging review of labor racketeering as a crime problem. Our article, "Labor Racketeering: The Mafia and the Unions," appeared in *Crime and Justice: A Review of Research* (2003). In summer 2002, two law student research assistants, Eileen Cunningham and Kimberly Friday, worked with me on assessing all of DOJ's civil RICO labor racketeering cases. They kept hammering away on drafts until they graduated in May 2004. Our research was published in the *Labor Lawyer* (spring 2004). I want to thank Syracuse University's Professor Robert Rabin and Jeff Philp, respectively faculty and student editor of that journal, for their patience and assistance. Several other research assistants also deserve my heartfelt thanks. Stephanie Greene provided outstanding assistance on the AFL-CIO's response to labor racketeering. Kristin Stohner did a great job on a case study of the NYC District Council of Carpenters litigation, which was published in the *California Criminal Law Review*. Sarah Marcus was an enormous help as my full-time research assistant over the 2003 summer; and likewise Adam Dressner over the 2004 summer.

In October 2004, David Garland convened an all-day workshop on the first draft of my manuscript. The participants gave me penetrating and comprehensive critiques and suggestions. This was the epitome of collegiality. In addition to David, my deep thanks to Rachel Barkow, Ron Goldstock, Susan Jennick, Bill Kornblum, John Monahan, Peter Schuck, Jerry Skolnick, Bob Stewart, and Joe Viteritti.

The final revision of the manuscript began on October 16, the day after the workshop. For the next four months Dave Sacks, working under the auspices of an NYU Center for Research in Crime & Justice fellowship served as full-time research assistant. He was simply invaluable. I could not have met the March 1, 2005 deadline without him; indeed, I almost didn't make it with him. Finally, I want to thank Bill Nelson and the NYU Legal History Colloquium for giving me an opportunity in January 2005 to workshop the revised manuscript; I benefited from many astute comments.

Throughout this project, my secretarial assistant, Marni Brand, has been a splendid right hand. She has assisted me with the preparation and logistics of the manuscript and with the multitude of administrative details of running a research project and administering a small research center. All this she does with intelligence, good humor, and professionalism. Cristina Alger provided excellent proofreading assistance at the final stage. I also received very helpful suggestions from Oscar Chase, Brandon Garrett, Deborah Malamud, and NYU Press editor Deborah Gershenowitz.

The NYU School of Law has been my professional home for more than twenty years. If there is a better place to work in academia, I haven't heard about it. I have flourished under three splendid deans—Norman Redlich, John Sexton, and Ricky Revesz—who have done more than their part in supporting and encouraging this work. I am stimulated and sustained every day by David Garland, Jerry Skolnick, and a terrific group of criminal law colleagues.

List of Acronyms

AAGCU: (AFL-CIO's) Americans Against Government Control of Unions

AFL: American Federation of Labor

AFL-CIO: American Federation of Labor-Congress of Industrial Organizations

AIW: Allied Industrial Workers of America

AUD: Association for Union Democracy

BSEIU: Building Service Employees International Union

CIO: Congress of Industrial Organizations

CSPF: (IBT's) Central States Pension Fund

DOJ: (U.S. government's) Department of Justice

DOL: (U.S. government's) Department of Labor

EO: Elections Officer (one of original three trustees in IBT case)

ERISA: Employee Retirement Income Security Act

FER: Final Election Rules

FBI: Federal Bureau of Investigation

GEB: General Executive Board

HERE: Hotel and Restaurant Employees

HEREIU: Hotel and Restaurant Employees International Union

IA: Independent Administrator (one of original three trustees in IBT case)

IATSE: International Alliance of Theatrical Stage Employees

IBT: International Brotherhood of Teamsters, Chauffeurs, Warehousemen & Helpers of America

IHC: Independent Hearing Committee

ILA: International Longshoremen's Association

ILGWU: International Ladies' Garment Workers' Union

IO: Investigations Officer (one of original three trustees in IBT case)

IRB: Independent Review Board (post-1993 investigating/ disciplinary office in IBT case)

IRO: Investigations and Review Officer

IRS: (U.S. government's) Internal Revenue Service

IUOE: International Union of Operating Engineers

IWW: Industrial Workers of the World

LMRA: Labor Management Relations Act (Taft-Hartley Act)

LCN: La Cosa Nostra ("our thing"), the Mafia, or the mob

LIUNA: Laborers' International Union of North America

LMRDA: Labor Management Reporting and Disclosure Act (Landrum-Griffin Act)

MITA: Metropolitan Import Truckmen's Association

MTA: Master Truckmen of America

NEMF: New England Motor Freight

NLRA: National Labor Relations Act (Wagner Act)

NLRB: National Labor Relations Board

OCRS: Organized Crime and Racketeering Section, U.S. Department of Justice

OCTF: (New York State) Organized Crime Task Force

OLMS: Office of Labor-Management Standards, U.S. Department of Labor

OLR: Office of Labor Racketeering, U.S. Department of Labor

PCOC: President's Commission on Organized Crime

RICO: Racketeer Influenced and Corrupt Organizations Act of 1970

TDU: Teamsters for a Democratic Union

TFL: Teamsters for Liberty

UBC: United Brotherhood of Carpenters

UNIRAC: FBI's acronym for its investigation of union racketeering

UTWA: United Textile Workers of America

WPPDA: Welfare and Pension Plan Disclosure Act

1

Introduction

The public must not be allowed to believe that organized labor is represented by those few unions in which union delegates have become criminals, or criminals have been made into union delegates. Unless they are purged, labor unions which have been thus taken over by criminals will, just as certainly as night follows day, wreck the cause of organized labor in this country and set back its progress many years. The officers of these unions are all too frequently the willing tools of professional criminals who direct their activities and keep them in office by means of force and fear.
—Special NYC Prosecutor Thomas E. Dewey, July 30, 1935, radio address, quoted in Dewey's autobiography, *Twenty against the Underworld*

We thought we knew a few things about trade union corruption, but we didn't know the half of it, one-tenth of it, or the one-hundredth of it. We didn't know, for instance, that we had unions where a criminal record was almost a prerequisite to holding office under the national union. . . .
—AFL-CIO President George Meany reacting to the McClellan Committee hearings, as reported by the New York Times on November 2, 1957

Labor racketeering, the exploitation of unions and union power by organized crime, has been an unpleasant fact of life since the late nineteenth century. It thrived practically unopposed until the last quarter of the twentieth century and continues, albeit under relentless government attack, into the twenty-first century.

The racketeers' basic *modus operandi* includes looting union treasuries and pension funds by theft, fraud, and bloated salaries; selling out union members' rights and interests in exchange for employers' bribes and kickbacks; exploiting union power to extort employers, and conspiring with employers to operate employer cartels that allocate contracts and set prices. Labor racketeering serves the organized crime families as a bridge to the power structure in many American cities. For much of the early and mid-twentieth century, corrupt politicians provided labor racketeers protection from the criminal justice system in exchange for campaign contributions, campaign workers, votes, manipulation of elections and corrupt opportunities for personal enrichment.[1]

In the late 1950s, the Senate McClellan Committee made labor racketeering a national issue. Over the next two decades, Congress created some special labor racketeering offenses and the Senate Permanent Subcommittee on Investigations held periodic hearings and issued reports criticizing the Department of Justice and the Department of Labor for failing to attack labor racketeering. Not until the mid-1970s, after the death of longtime FBI Director J. Edgar Hoover, did federal law enforcement make organized crime control a priority. When Teamsters president Jimmy Hoffa disappeared in 1975, apparently the victim of an organized crime assassination, the FBI made labor racketeering an important target in its campaign against organized crime. By contrast, the U.S. Department of Labor and the organized labor movement essentially ignored complaints by rank-and-file union "dissidents" about organized crime intimidation, fraud, mistreatment, and exploitation.

In the 1980s the FBI, the U.S. Department of Justice, and the U.S. Department of Labor launched investigations, criminal prosecutions, and civil racketeering lawsuits against racketeer-ridden union locals, regional councils, and even national/international unions. (*International unions* have local affiliates in Canada as well as the United States.) This campaign produced hundreds of prosecutions and at least 20 court-monitored trusteeships imposed on organized crime–dominated labor unions. Some of those trusteeships have been brought to conclusion, having achieved varying degrees of success, but as of late 2005, most of them remain works in progress. New organized crime and labor racketeering cases (criminal, civil, and administrative) continue to percolate.

This chapter previews the rest of the book. Chapters 2–4 provide background on the nature and extent of the problem. Beyond that, they seek to establish two fundamental points: first, that labor racketeering has been a central and defining activity of the Cosa Nostra (LCN) or-

ganized crime families; second, that labor racketeers have been a significant problem for the U.S. labor movement throughout the twentieth
century. More specifically, Chapter 2 documents and explains the extent
of LCN exploitation of labor unions and how that exploitation turned
organized crime figures into economic and political power brokers.
Chapters 3 and 4 document and explain the nature and extent of labor
racketeering in the labor movement circa 1980 (Chapter 3) and in New
York City in the post–World War II period (Chapter 4).

Chapters 5–7 deal with the response to labor racketeering by the
American Federation of Labor (AFL), the Congress of Industrial Organizers (CIO), and the combined AFL-CIO (Chapter 5), by rank-and-file
union members (Chapter 6) and by local, state, and federal law enforcement agencies (Chapter 7). Chapter 5 explains that the AFL-CIO,
the U.S. umbrella labor federation, took some halting steps against
labor racketeering in the 1950s, during and after the U.S. Senate's Mc-
Clellan Committee hearings. However, since then, the AFL-CIO has
more or less ignored the problem, apparently fearing that an attack on
labor racketeering would divide and weaken the labor movement. In
Chapter 6, we will see that although labor racketeers used intimidation,
violence, and economic power to thoroughly repress workers and rank-
and-file union members, reformers, often called "dissidents," have
courageously challenged this domination with protests, election challenges, and litigation. Sadly, these struggles almost always failed, frequently costing the reformers their economic livelihood, physical security, and sometimes even their lives. Chapter 7 argues that for most of
the twentieth century, local law enforcement was either too corrupt or
too weak to take on organized crime although, to be sure, there were
some important exceptions. Federal law enforcement remained aloof
from organized crime control. When federal law enforcement finally
took action, the labor racketeers suffered major defeats and momentum
passed into the hands of reformers.

Utilizing in-depth case studies, chapters 8–13 begin the monumen-
tal task of documenting and analyzing the federal government's campaign against labor racketeering. The campaign began in 1982 with
the filing of the first civil RICO (Racketeering and Corrupt Organizations Act) lawsuit against the racketeer-ridden Teamsters Local 560 and
continues to the present (fall 2005). Chapter 8 explains the way the
RICO law works in labor racketeering cases and provides an overview
of twenty years of antilabor racketeering investigations and litigation.

Chapter 9 presents a case study of the IBT Local 560 case, a remarkable success story. After twelve years of effort by the Department of Justice, the Department of Labor, a federal district court judge, a court-appointed trustee, and members of Local 560 purged the mobsters and voted a reform regime into office. The same cannot be said of the New York City District Council of Carpenters (Chapter 10), which, though subject to vigorous criminal and civil litigation and despite the best efforts of a savvy court-appointed trustee, has not been successfully liberated. In Chapter 11, we examine the RICO-spawned remediation of the four international unions that, for decades, have been most influenced by organized crime. Because of the immense size (geographically and numerically) of these unions, it is difficult to evaluate the RICO litigation, but we will identify some of the most important features of the reform efforts. Chapter 12 will draw some conclusions about the successes and failures of more than twenty years of anti–labor racketeering initiatives and suggest future strategies. The concluding chapter will attempt to place labor racketeering and its remediation in conceptual and theoretical perspective.

Having previewed the book's organization, we now turn to introducing the "characters."

COSA NOSTRA

The Italian-American organized crime groups that became Cosa Nostra did not invent labor racketeering. Members of Jewish and Irish organized crime groups were the earliest labor racketeers and established the basic patterns of labor racketeering.[2] The Italian-American organized crime groups became extraordinarily powerful during the period of national alcohol prohibition (1920–1933). By the 1940s, these crime "families" had more or less achieved their present-day form.[*] There were twenty-four crime families operating in twenty cities; five

[*] The history of Cosa Nostra has been often told. The bloody Castellamarese war of the late 1920s pitted two organized crime factions against each other. Salvatore Maranzano emerged the victor. But when he attempted to further consolidate his power, he was assassinated by Charles ("Lucky") Luciano, Vito Genovese, Meyer Lansky, and several other organized crime figures. Luciano assigned the major crime families territories and established a commission to mediate interfamily conflicts. See Thomas E. Repetto, *American Mafia: A History of Its Rise to Power* (New York: Henry Holt, 2004).

families coexisted in New York City. All were organized along the following lines: the boss was assisted by an underboss and a *consigliere* (counselor) chosen by the "capos" as a kind of ombudsman to whom they could bring problems that arose with other capos or even with the boss. The "made members" or "soldiers" who had gone through an initiation ritual and sworn fealty to Cosa Nostra were organized into "crews," each led by a "capo" or captain. Moreover, each crew included "associates" who worked with the capo and soldiers but who were not themselves "made members." Scholars disagree as to whether the twenty-four families were "ruled" or "coordinated" by a "commission" of large family bosses. My view is that there is little evidence of the existence of a Mafia commission that *ruled* in any meaningful sense of the word. No doubt crime family bosses met from time to time, and in different configurations, to "adjudicate" or negotiate interfamily disputes and discuss matters of mutual concern. The famous 1957 mass meeting at Apalachin, New York, is an example of a convention-type get-together.[3] From time to time there may have been a group (committee) of bosses who met as a kind of court, as occasions arose, to settle interfamily disputes. But there was never anything resembling national government of organized crime families that made "law" or issued and enforced policy. The crime families have always operated autonomously.

THE UNIONS

The history of the American labor movement can be traced back to the eighteenth century.[4] Nascent labor unions proliferated by the late nineteenth century with the growth and industrialization of the U.S. economy. Indeed, that period was marked by some extraordinarily bloody clashes between labor organizers and businesses determined to prevent their workers from organizing. Most often the police and the courts sided with the employers. Many union organizers were prosecuted in state courts for conspiracy and other offenses.[5] Many courts issued injunctions ordering union leaders and members to cease and desist from strikes and other disruptions of business.* This era of violence brought

---

* The Norris-LaGuardia Act (1932), 29 U.S.C. § 101, prohibited federal courts from enjoining most strikes.

gangsters into labor/management conflicts on both sides and laid the ground for permanent organized crime infiltration of the labor movement. Intervention by the police, prosecutors, and courts on the side of business established a legacy of suspicion and distrust of government involvement in labor matters that persists to this day throughout the labor movement.

The 1935 Wagner Act[6] recognized the right of private-sector workers to bargain collectively with their employers. The act established a National Labor Relations Board to administer a complex web of regulations governing union jurisdiction, recognition or election of the union that would serve as a given group of workers' exclusive bargaining agent, and the duties of both management and labor in negotiating in good faith with each other. Union membership soared, increasing from 3.8 million in 1935 to 12.6 million in 1945.[7]

By 1947, business leaders, Republicans and some Democrats in Congress, and some elements of the citizenry had become convinced that organized labor was too powerful. Over fierce opposition from the labor movement, Congress passed the Taft-Hartley Act,[8] which aimed to cut back labor's power by prohibiting secondary boycotts, allowing the president to temporarily halt certain strikes, prohibiting political contributions by unions, and prohibiting the closed shop. The act also included a provision outlawing labor bribery; it became a crime for an employer to give anything of value to a labor official and for a labor official to accept anything of value from an employer. President Harry Truman vetoed the law, but Congress overrode the veto with a two-thirds vote.

Labor unions were organized at the local, regional, and national/international levels. National unions granted charters to individuals to organize local chapters of their union among workers in a particular bargaining unit. Local unions typically included workers employed by a number of different businesses, usually but not always in the same industry. Thus, a local's membership could range from the low hundreds to more than ten thousand. The local's officers bargained with each of their members' employers to achieve collective bargaining agreements that governed the terms and conditions of employment. Beginning in the 1940s, union negotiators regularly sought to obtain employer contributions to worker pension and welfare funds. By the 1950s and 1960s some of these funds held immense deposits, thereby posing an irresistible target for organized crime.[9]

The constitutions of some national unions provided for regional councils comprising all the local unions in that council's geographical area. The officers of the councils were chosen by the leaders of the union locals that made up the council. The powers of the councils differed, but in many cases the councils engaged in collective bargaining with the various locals' members' employers. They also provided a level of insulation for the officers who were accountable to the locals' representatives, not to the rank and file.

LABOR RACKETEERING

The penetration of labor unions by professional criminals dates back to the late nineteenth century.[10] Not all unions were equally susceptible to being taken over by organized crime elements. The most susceptible unions were those whose members worked for numerous small employers in geographically dispersed locations. Such workers were unable to organize themselves to oppose gangsterism. Working alone or in small groups, they could be easily intimidated and subdued. Therefore, it is not surprising to find that some of the first unions to be captured by organized crime were made up of restaurant workers, coach and truck drivers, and construction workers. Other unions susceptible to takeover included construction and longshoring (loading and unloading seaborne cargo), where work was seasonal or sporadic and employers relied on union hiring halls to send them workers when needed. Racketeering susceptibility was very high when union officials could punish opponents and reward supporters by denying or awarding jobs. The craft unions, those with the highest susceptibility to racketeering, were mostly affiliated with the American Federation of Labor (AFL).

The racketeering susceptibility of so-called "industrial" unions composed of factory workers was much lower. Factory workers were organized much later than "craft" workers, in part because the large employers could resist more effectively. When factory workers were organized, it was along the lines of the whole plant, that is, in industrial unions. Workers who belonged to large industrial unions were more closely tied to their employers than were craft workers who often moved from job to job, and employer to employer. Therefore it was much more difficult for labor racketeers to intimidate and dominate them. The industrial unions also tended to be more ideological than the craft unions; socialist and even communist ideology commanded a great deal of support. The more ideologically minded labor officials were less attracted to corrupt opportunities for personal enrichment. The unions that represented the factory and mine workers were mostly affiliated with the Congress of Industrial Organizations (CIO). There have been very few examples of organized crime groups making any headway in these unions.

In 1955, the American Federation of Labor (AFL) and the Congress of Industrial Organizations (CIO) combined to form the AFL-CIO. In the late 1950s, the newly combined AFL-CIO took steps against labor racketeering in its affiliated unions, but by the 1960s these initiatives had completely dissipated. Thereafter, the AFL-CIO almost always excoriated congressional and law enforcement anti–labor racketeering hearings, legislation, and campaigns as sinister attacks on the labor movement.

EMPLOYERS

Up until passage of the Wagner Act in 1935, many employers, especially large employers, fought hard to prevent the unionization of their employees. When unionization proved inevitable, these employers sometimes sought to sign representational agreements with gangster-controlled unions, which they much preferred to left-wing labor organizations because the former were susceptible to bribes in exchange for sweetheart contracts.[11] Both the employers and the labor racketeers themselves used "red-baiting" (calling opponents communists) to smear dissidents who criticized or challenged them.[12] (Echoes of such tactics can be found right up to the present day.)* The gangsters who controlled these unions could be bribed—indeed, they were in the business of soliciting bribes—to make concessions in collective bargaining agreements and/or not to enforce the terms of the agreements.

Small employers in competitive industries had another reason for preferring to deal with unions controlled by racketeers. Where there are

---

* In his case study of the efforts of rank-and-file Teamsters reformers to take back their local from mobsters and their cronies, Professor Robert Bruno explains how the incumbents branded the reformist group, Teamsters for a Democratic Union (TDU), "socialist and slanderous." *Reforming the Chicago Teamsters: The Story of Local 705* (De Kalb: Northern Illinois University Press, 2003), 34.

large numbers of small employers in a competitive industry (for example, restaurants, laundry, trucking), the employers have a greater reason to accept, indeed to reach out to gangsters to "stabilize" cutthroat competition, neutralize labor unrest and opposition,[13] and not enforce collective bargaining agreements.[14] In addition, a strong gangster-controlled union could establish and enforce an employers' cartel that would restrict the number of employers, fix prices, and allocate contracts and customers to the cartel's members.* The union was in a position to do this because it could "discipline," even put out of business, an employer who refused to cooperate with the cartel.

POLITICIANS, POLICE, AND PROSECUTORS

For much of the twentieth century, urban law enforcement was laced with political influence and corruption. In most big cities, the police department, and often the prosecutor's office, was subservient to the party political machine, which, in turn, was frequently allied to organized crime. (This was dramatically illustrated by the 1951–1952 U.S. Senate hearings presided over by Senator Estes Kefauver.) By the 1940s, the local power structure in many cities was a quadripartite alliance of organized crime, elements of organized labor, elements of the business community and the Democratic Party political machine, including district attorneys and top police brass."[15] For example, Frank Costello, New York City organized crime boss, was a power in Tammany Hall, and Tom Pendergast, the Kansas City political powerhouse, was closely allied to organized crime in Chicago and New York.

Even when they were not corrupted, local police departments and county district attorneys' offices did not have the resources to conduct the lengthy and sophisticated investigations required in organized

---

* Under the 1935 National Labor Relations Act, 29 U.S.C. § 151 et seq., an employer can voluntarily agree to recognize an organization as the exclusive bargaining representative for the employer's workers. The employees have the right to petition the National Labor Relations Board for an election, but if they do not, the employer can sign a collective bargaining agreement with the union that he or she has recognized.

** Robert Cooley, a Chicago lawyer closely involved with both organized crime and city politicians and judges, in the 1970s and 1980s, provides an excellent description of such an alliance. See Robert Cooley and Hillel Levin, *When Corruption Was King: How I Helped the Mob Rule Chicago, Then Brought the Outfit Down* (New York: Carroll and Graf, 2004).

crime cases. Special NYS Organized Crime Prosecutor and then Manhattan District Attorney Thomas Dewey's antiracketeering investigations and prosecutions during the 1930s were the exceptions. However, before the days of legal electronic surveillance, witness immunity, witness protection programs, and methods to prevent juror intimidation, it was extremely difficult to investigate and convict organized crime figures. Moreover, individual convictions had no impact on deeply embedded systemic criminality.

HOOVER'S FEDERAL BUREAU OF INVESTIGATION (1924–1972)

Federal law enforcement had more resources and freedom than state and local law enforcement to deploy agents as it chose (rather than in response to citizen complaints), but FBI Director J. Edgar Hoover denied the existence of the Mafia and refused to devote investigative resources to organized crime.* Scholars and commentators still disagree about Hoover's motives. Some believe that he was being blackmailed by mobsters who knew about his (supposed) homosexuality.[16] Other scholars believe that Hoover did not regard organized crime as a national problem; did not believe that the FBI had jurisdiction to investigate local gangsters; feared that FBI agents would be corrupted if they became involved in investigating the vice crimes that the Mafia was engaged in (gambling, drugs, and so on); or perhaps, prior to the exposure of the organized crime conclave in Apalachin, New York, in 1957, he did not believe there was any connection or coordination among local organized crime families. Still other scholars emphasize that Hoover did not want to divert resources from investigating communists and political subversives.** Although we will probably never be able to choose

---

* Actually, Harry Argersinger, Director of the Federal Bureau of Narcotics and Dangerous Drugs, had much more interest in and knowledge of organized crime than Hoover, but he did not have the resources or the jurisdiction to act on this knowledge. After the McClellan Committee hearings, the FBI did engage in extensive wiretapping against organized crime, but such intercepted conversations could not be introduced in court until passage of Title III of the 1968 Omnibus Crime Control and Safe Streets Act.
** There was already precedent for cracking down on left-wing unionists but not labor racketeers when Hoover took over the FBI. The so-called Palmer Raids, carried out by

definitively among these explanations, the facts are indisputable: until after Hoover's death in May 1972, the FBI did not devote resources to investigating organized crime while assigning top priority to exposing and prosecuting communists (broadly defined).[17] The Industrial Workers of the World (IWW) and other left-wing labor groups were relentlessly suppressed but organized crime labor racketeers were hardly opposed. By pursuing "radicals" rather than Mafiosi, Hoover contributed to the emergence of an American labor movement heavily infiltrated and influenced by organized crime.

Teamster history provides a telling example of how government, specifically the FBI, contributed to a racketeer-ridden labor movement while repressing a left-wing labor movement. In the 1930s, the most powerful Teamster leader in Minnesota was Farrell Dobbs, a socialist and brilliant labor organizer. He organized over-the-road freight drivers, dock workers and warehousemen throughout the Midwest. His Teamster protégé and eventual rival was Jimmy Hoffa, who recruited thugs linked to organized crime to help him battle employers. The FBI attacked Dobbs, while leaving Hoffa to prosper. In the late 1930s and early 1940s, Dobbs and more than two dozen militant socialist trade unionists were indicted under the anti-Communist Smith Act. Dobbs himself was imprisoned until the end of World War II.* Jimmy Hoffa became the undisputed leader of the Teamsters in Minnesota and soon in the entire Midwest. Hoffa's connections with organized crime were instrumental in vaulting him to the IBT general presidency and figured prominently in his administration of the union.[18]

U.S. Attorney General Alexander Mitchell Palmer between 1919 and 1923, amounted to a violent repression of left-wing unionism. Palmer's agents sent hundreds of radical unionists to prison and destroyed their union headquarters. The suppression of radical unionists continued for decades, and not only by the FBI. California Attorney General Earl Warren, who was destined to be Chief Justice of the most liberal Supreme Court in history, prosecuted longshoreman Harry Bridges for subversion in the 1940s. Lawrence Fleischer, *Thomas E. Dewey and Earl Warren: The Rise of the Twentieth-Century Urban Prosecutor,* 28 *Calif. W. L. Rev.* 1 (1992).

* After his release from prison, Dobbs served as editor of "The Militant" and, in 1953, became national secretary of the Socialist Workers Party. He ran as the SWP's presidential candidate in 1960 but received only 60,166 votes. In the 1970s, he published several books about the Teamsters, including: *Teamster Rebellion* (New York: Pathfinder Press, 1972); *Teamster Power* (New York: Monad Press, 1973); *Teamster Politics* (New York: Monad Press, 1975); and *Teamster Bureaucracy* (New York: Anchor Foundation, 1977).

POST-HOOVER FBI

After Hoover's death in 1972, the FBI modernized and became an up-to-date law enforcement (rather than antisubversives) organization. It redefined organized crime as a serious problem and a top priority.[19] After Jimmy Hoffa's disappearance in July 1975, the FBI focused on labor racketeering as a key part of the organized crime problem.

The FBI defined labor racketeering first as an organized crime problem and second as a union corruption problem. Despite the employers' complicity with organized crime in exploiting their employees and corrupting their unions, investigators and prosecutors did not focus on labor racketeering as a problem of labor/management corruption.* The law enforcement agents and agencies treated corrupt employers as victims or, at worst, minor wrongdoers who could be recruited as cooperating witnesses against organized crime figures and corrupt union officials. Labor racketeers who engaged in violence, extortion, intimidation, and all sorts of crimes in addition to labor racketeering, fit law enforcement's (and the general society's) stereotype of criminals; employers did not. The labor racketeers also belonged to ethnic minority groups that, at the time, were widely believed to have a dangerous predilection for crime. Employers, on the other hand, fit law enforcement's stereotype of essentially law-abiding citizens or, at worst, minor white-collar offenders.

The post-Hoover FBI mobilized itself for a massive attack on organized crime. By the early 1980s there were three hundred FBI agents in New York City assigned to organized crime investigations. The New York City office formed separate squads for each of the city's Cosa Nostra crime families. With the urging of G. Robert Blakey and Ronald

---

* As Sidney Lens explained, "I'm not suggesting that corporate-racketeer collaboration was a rule in the labor movement, but neither was it an incidental aberration." Thomas E. Dewey, when he was Manhattan district attorney, denounced employers who "invite racketeers to organize their industries to increase profits at public expense." Sidney Lens, *Unrepentant Radical* (Boston: Beacon Press, 1980), 105–6.

New York Times writer A. H. Raskin detailed in a *Commentary* article "the sordid story of employer collaboration" with the Longshoremen's Association over a quarter century. He charged that they had "subverted the union . . . kept its president, Joseph P. Ryan, in automobiles and expensive clothes," and had subsidized the hooligans Ryan recruited from Sing Sing to hold the rank and file in subjection." A. H. Raskin, "Unions and the Public Interest," *Commentary* (February 1954), p. 103.

Goldstock, the FBI sought to dismantle each crime family by attacking its revenue sources as well as by convicting its leaders. Unions were among organized crime's most important revenue sources and power bases.

U.S. CONGRESS

Until the late 1970s, the most important opposition to labor racketeering came from Congress via hearings, reports, and legislation. Beginning in the 1930s, but especially from the 1950s, Congress held dozens of hearings on corruption and racketeering in the labor movement, some attracted national media attention.[20] Labor officials accused Congress of holding these hearings to weaken labor rather than to fight racketeering and, to an extent, they may well have been right. It is not possible to dissect the motivations of the many senators and congressmen involved in such hearings over several decades, but undoubtedly some of their motives were antilabor or, at best, self-aggrandizing. The senators who were most aggressive in investigating and denouncing labor racketeering were southern conservatives who represented states where unions were weak and unpopular. Federal legislation that attacked labor racketeering usually was part of a larger bill that weakened organized labor. For example, the 1947 Taft-Hartley Act made it a federal crime for a union official to receive anything of value from an employer and similarly for an employer to give anything of value to a labor official. But the act also contained wide-ranging provisions designed to curb union power.*

On August 12, 1953, in response to a devastating New York State investigation of racketeering in the Port of New York and New Jersey,[21] President Dwight Eisenhower signed the Waterfront Commission Act, an interstate compact that permitted New York and New Jersey to

---

* Taft-Hartley (the Labor Management Relations Act) made the closed shop illegal and permitted the union shop only after a vote of a majority of the employees. It forbade jurisdictional strikes and secondary boycotts. It prohibited unions from contributing to political campaigns and required union leaders to affirm their loyalty and lack of communist ties. The act also gave the U.S. attorney general the power to obtain an 80-day injunction when a threatened or actual strike that he/she believed "imperiled the national health or safety." 29 USC Sec. 141–97. [Title 29, Chapter 7, United States Code.]

establish the Waterfront Commission of New York Harbor in order to regulate waterfront business activity and labor relations.[22] The Waterfront Commission replaced the infamous "shape up" (whereby the union bosses picked out who would work that day from the men assembled on the pier) with a hiring system that licensed longshoremen, assigned them to jobs, and guaranteed them an annual wage. It also ended the "public loading"* racket, by which the International Longshoremen's Association (ILA) required truckers to make corrupt payoffs in order to have cargo loaded or unloaded from their vehicles at the piers, even if they did not need or desire the public loaders' service. The act (and the implementing legislation passed by both the New Jersey and New York legislatures) gave the Waterfront Commission power to register workers, deny registration and employment on grounds of felony and misdemeanor convictions, and bar former convicts from holding elective ILA positions. The ILA resisted the Waterfront Commission by, among other things, challenging a provision in the law that prohibited unions that employed former felons as officers from collecting members' dues.[23] In *De Veau v. Braisted*, the U.S. Supreme Court upheld the provision, observing:

> In disqualifying all convicted felons from union office unless executive discretion is exercised in their favor . . . [this law] may well be deemed drastic legislation. But in the view of Congress and the two States involved, the situation on the New York waterfront regarding the presence and influence of ex-convicts on the waterfront was not a minor episode but constituted a principal corrupting influence.[24]

The McClellan Committee (Senate Special Select Committee on Improper Activities in the Labor or Management Field), 1957–1959, eclipses all other legislative or commission investigations into labor racketeering. Its one hundred member staff still stands as the largest congressional investigative staff in American history. The committee called 1,525 witnesses; many high-ranking union officials and mobsters refused to answer on Fifth Amendment grounds. (These were the days before the federal immunity statute, so witnesses could not

---

* "Public loader" referred to a worker who loaded and unloaded trucks that took cargo to and from the docks. The term was commonly used in the early twentieth century.

be compelled to answer questions under an immunity grant.) The clash between the committee's chief counsel, Robert F. Kennedy, and Teamsters vice-president and then (during the course of the hearings) general president, Jimmy Hoffa, provided high drama to a national audience.

Senator John McClellan (D.-Ark.) asserted that powerful mob figures Anthony Corallo and John Dioguardi had assisted Hoffa's campaign for the IBT presidency. The committee also uncovered mob links with other unions, businesses, and industries. In his book about the McClellan Committee hearings, *The Enemy Within,* Kennedy used apocalyptic language to warn that organized crime's strategic position in the labor movement gave it the power to shake down or shut down the nation: "The point I want to make is this: If we do not on a national scale attack organized criminals with weapons and techniques as effective as their own, they will destroy us."[25]

The McClellan Committee's hearings led directly to the 1959 Labor Management Reporting and Disclosure Act,[26] known as the Landrum-Griffin Act, which, for the first time, enlisted union democracy as a key strategy in fighting labor racketeering. Senator McClellan and his colleagues argued that the best antidote to labor racketeering would be an active and informed union rank and file that would monitor its officers and throw them out if they acted contrary to the interests of the membership. Landrum-Griffin set out a federally guaranteed union members' bill of rights, including the right to speak and associate freely, run for office in free and fair elections, and have the opportunity to find out about (and, in some cases vote on) what the union's officers are doing.[27]

Congressional, usually Senate, hearings on organized crime and on labor racketeering continued through the 1960s, 1970s, and 1980s. There were several hearings on exploitation of the unions' pension and welfare funds, leading to the passage of the landmark Employee Retirement Insurance and Security Act of 1975 (ERISA). (Senator McClellan introduced the first version of the bill that eventually passed.) The Senate Permanent Subcommittee on Investigations held hearings on the four most racketeer-ridden national/international unions: Teamsters, Laborers, Longshoremen, and Hotel and Restaurant Workers. Other hearings focused on the Department of Labor's willingness and capacity to respond to evidence of labor racketeering and later on the efficacy and desirability of the RICO-spawned union trusteeships.

U.S. DEPARTMENT OF JUSTICE (DOJ)

The U.S. Department of Justice is a cabinet-level department head-quartered in Washington, D.C., and headed by the U.S. Attorney General. In addition to the DOJ attorneys who represent the United States in criminal and civil litigation, the FBI, Federal Bureau of Prisons, and several other agencies come under the DOJ's aegis. Importantly, however, the FBI is substantially independent of the lawyers' side of the department. The FBI director is a presidential appointee, requiring Senate confirmation, who serves a ten-year term. The DOJ criminal division's priorities are not necessarily the same as the FBI's priorities, so an organized crime control campaign required a great deal of coordination.

The DOJ's criminal division comprises twenty sections, including fraud, domestic security, asset forfeiture, money laundering, and drugs. In the mid-1950s, under the Eisenhower administration, the DOJ formed the Organized Crime and Racketeering Section (OCRS) to focus the department's anti–organized crime resources. OCRS remained a small, fairly inactive department until it was revitalized in 1961 by the new attorney general, Robert F. Kennedy. As we will see in later chapters, by the 1980s OCRS played a leadership role in organized crime control.

In addition to its central headquarters, the Department of Justice is represented by a United States attorney's office in each of the ninety-three federal judicial districts that cover the entire territory of the United States. (New York City, for example, has two judicial districts and two U.S. attorney's offices: the Southern District of New York (SDNY), which includes Manhattan, the Bronx, Westchester, and some other suburbs; and the Eastern District of New York (EDNY), which includes Brooklyn, Queens, Staten Island, and the Long Island suburbs.) The U.S. attorneys are appointed for four-year terms by the president of the United States and, like cabinet officers and certain other high governmental officials, they are subject to Senate confirmation. The budgets for the U.S. attorneys are set by central DOJ, but the U.S. attorneys have substantial autonomy and, to a large extent, choose their own investigative/prosecutorial priorities.

When Robert F. Kennedy, as U.S. attorney general (1961–1964), revitalized the Organized Crime and Racketeering Section (OCRS), he established the first federal organized crime strike force in Buffalo,

New York; other strike forces soon followed.* The strike forces allowed Kennedy to circumvent both the FBI (controlled, at that time, by Hoover) and the U.S. attorneys' offices. The strike forces reported directly to the head of the OCRS, who, in turn, reported directly to Kennedy. Each strike force consisted of agents from a number of different agencies including the Internal Revenue Service, Labor Department, and FBI, although Hoover was not enthusiastic about cooperating. The strike forces undertook some important investigations and initiated some important prosecutions before Robert F. Kennedy resigned as attorney general in 1964, several months after his brother, President John F. Kennedy, was assassinated. The OCRS was not abolished, but it lost the luster and prominence that it enjoyed under Robert F. Kennedy. Not until the mid-1970s was it fully resuscitated and the number and resources of the federal organized crime strike forces increased.**

The turning point in law enforcement's attack on organized crime generally, and labor racketeering specifically, was the disappearance (immediately assumed to be a mob "hit") of James R. (Jimmy) Hoffa in the summer of 1975. Hoffa disappeared while campaigning to regain the IBT general presidency from former protégé Frank Fitzsimmons, with whom LCN had become quite comfortable.*** Organized crime had never before murdered a national figure of Hoffa's stature (unless, as some people believe, it assassinated President John F. Kennedy).[28] Almost immediately, the FBI made organized crime control its top priority. The Hoffa assassination gave the post-Hoover FBI and the OCRS a

---

* Kennedy's top priority was to "get Hoffa." Victor Navasky, *Kennedy Justice* (New York: Atheneum, 1971); Arthur A. Sloane, *Hoffa* (Cambridge: MIT Press, 1978); Arthur Schlesinger, Jr., *Robert Kennedy and His Times* (New York: Ballantine, 1996); David Witwer, *Corruption and Reform in the Teamsters Union* (Urbana-Champaign: University of Illinois Press, 2003). Indeed, DOJ prosecutors did bring Hoffa to trial in 1962 for extortion, but the case ended in a hung jury. In 1964, the DOJ convicted Hoffa of obstruction of justice and pension fund fraud. His appeals exhausted, he began serving his prison sentence in 1967. However, President Richard Nixon commuted the sentence in 1971, apparently a quid pro quo for the IBT's endorsement of his candidacy in the 1972 presidential election.

** Attorney General Richard Thornburgh abolished the strike forces in 1989. They had always been unpopular with the U.S. attorneys, who resented the central DOJ's taking high-publicity cases out of their hands. Individual organized crime units were subsequent established in each U.S. Attorney Office.

*** The FBI now believes that Hoffa was assassinated by Anthony Giacalone, boss of Detroit's organized crime family, and Tony Provenzano, Genovese crime family capo and head of IBT Local 560.

successful rationale for launching and sustaining a campaign against the Cosa Nostra organized crime families.[29] It bears emphasizing that the FBI viewed the attack on labor racketeering as part of its strategy of crushing LCN; without this link, union corruption would not have triggered and sustained the massive federal law enforcement effort.

RACKETEER INFLUENCED AND CORRUPT
ORGANIZATION ACT (RICO)

In the late 1960s, Senator John McClellan held hearings on the organized crime problem. Witnesses and the senators themselves observed that when an organized crime figure was sent to prison, the Cosa Nostra bosses assigned another to replace him. To have any chance of eliminating or substantially weakening organized crime, the government would have to do something other than prosecuting, convicting, and punishing individuals for discrete crimes.[30] The solution was RICO, a complex statute that provided DOJ and the federal law enforcement agencies with a multifaceted remedial statute whose criminal and civil provisions were aimed at convicting organized crime members and eliminating their economic base.

The 1970 RICO statute, cosponsored by Senator McClellan, created three new federal crimes, and a fourth that made criminal a conspiracy to violate any of the three. Under RICO it is a crime to invest the proceeds of racketeering activity or collection of an unlawful debt in an enterprise (any legal entity or an association in fact); it is a crime to take an interest in any enterprise through a pattern of racketeering activity or collection of an unlawful debt; and it is a crime to conduct or participate in the affairs of an enterprise through a pattern of racketeering activity or collection of an unlawful debt. In other words, it is a federal crime, punishable by up to twenty years in prison, to buy into an enterprise with "dirty money," to use muscle or fraud to acquire an interest in an enterprise, or to use an enterprise as a vehicle for carrying out racketeering activity.

In addition to its criminal provisions, RICO contains two different civil remedies. One remedy, Section 1964(a), provides a private right of action (with treble damages) for the victims of racketeering. While prominent and controversial in the commercial litigation context, this provision has never been used by victims of organized crime to sue the

Mafia for compensation. Maybe such victims doubt they would succeed in collecting any money from the mobsters; certainly fear of retal-
iation is a likely explanation. In any event, it is the second civil RICO
provision that has proved to be an outstanding tool for attacking systemic criminality like labor racketeering. Section 1964(b) authorizes the
U.S. attorney general to seek wide-ranging equitable relief to prevent
continuing RICO violations. If the attorney general can persuade a federal judge (there is no right to a jury trial) of the need for extreme remedial action, the court is empowered to expel union officers, change
election and hiring hall procedures, install financial controls, and appoint a trustee to monitor and enforce the remedial decree. This provides for the possibility of ongoing federal court supervision supported
by continued FBI and DOJ investigations and enforcement.

In 1982, DOJ's Organized Crime Strike Force in Newark, New Jersey, brought the first civil RICO suit against a union, IBT Local 560, the
largest Teamsters local in New Jersey (35,000 members). For decades,
Local 560 had been the fiefdom of Tony Provenzano, a capo in the Genovese crime family and the local's top official. Union members who
dared to complain or challenge "Tony Pro" were threatened, beaten,
even killed; collective bargaining contracts were mocked by sweetheart deals with employers. When Tony Pro finally was imprisoned, he
handed off operational control of the union to one of his brothers (who
himself was later sentenced to prison) and then to another crony.[31] As
would also be true in the many later civil RICO suits against unions, the
government's complaint in the Local 560 case named both union officials and mobsters as defendants. After a lengthy trial, Judge Harold
Ackerman found in favor of the government and ordered broad relief,
including a court-appointed trustee whose assignment was to purge the
mob and establish union democracy—a task, as it turned out, that consumed more than ten years.

All told, there have been twenty civil RICO suits resulting in court-
appointed trustees tasked with eliminating organized crime and "restoring" union democracy. This litigation is one of the most ambitious,
perhaps *the most ambitious* effort at government-sponsored and court-
supervised institutional reform in American history. Government lawyers, federal judges, and court-appointed trustees have had to confront
two of the most powerful institutions in American society: organized
crime and organized labor. Consider that just before Rudy Giuliani,
then U.S. attorney for the Southern District of New York, filed the

first civil RICO suit against an international union (the International Brotherhood of Teamsters) in 1988, 264 members of Congress signed a petition to U.S. Attorney General Edwin Meese, demanding that the rumored civil RICO suit not be filed. The letter insisted that "[t]he imposition of trustees to administer an international union by the government is, on its face, inherently destructive of the ability of workers to represent and speak for themselves through their unions."[32] The suit, of course, was filed and ultimately resolved by a negotiated consent agreement that, among other things, provided for a type of trusteeship that, as of fall 2005, is still in effect.

What are the consequences of a century of labor racketeering? The American labor movement has been profoundly affected by organized crime infiltration and exploitation. For some unions, the consequences are obvious: treasuries looted, collective bargaining agreements unenforced, candidates for union office murdered, and union democracy rendered meaningless. Other unions have suffered indirectly by the erosion of organized labor's reputation in the eyes of workers, intellectuals, and young people.

There can be no doubt about the American labor movement's extraordinary decline since the 1950s.[33] The peak year (in terms of percentage) of Americans' membership in unions was 1953, when 32.5 percent of workers belonged to labor unions. In 2005, approximately 13 percent of the workforce was unionized; the percentage of public employees unionized is now higher than the percentage of private employees. Although there are a number of reasons for the decline, it seems a worthy hypothesis that labor racketeering has been an important contributing factor. Of course, there has been retrenchment and decline in many unions where there has never been a documented organized crime presence. Arguably, however, even those "clean" unions have been affected by the labor racketeering taint that tarnishes the reputation of organized labor generally. It is entirely possible that the labor movement as a whole would be much stronger if certain key unions had not been infiltrated and controlled by Cosa Nostra.

Another explanation for the decline of labor unions is that mob-dominated unions do not perform well for their members. Labor racketeers aim to maximize the wealth and power of their crime families and themselves. For them, participation in the labor movement is a racket, stealing from the unions and their benefit funds and soliciting bribes from employers. Labor racketeers are not good unionists; they exploit unions and union members. Labor racketeers are not interested in organizing workers or running unions efficiently. They appoint and promote union officials on the basis of patronage, not competence. Their unions' payrolls are loaded with relatives, friends, and organized crime associates. The history of labor racketeering is rife with examples of sweetheart contracts, double-breasted shops (allowing employers to hire nonunion as well as union employees), allowing employers to avoid required pension and welfare contributions, workers being shuttled from high-pay to low-pay locals, AFL-CIO affiliated unions taken "independent" and many other schemes that victimize rank-and-file union members in order to line the pockets of organized crime members and their corrupt union allies.[34]

What might America look like today if at least part of the American labor movement had not been hijacked by labor racketeers? Would we have a socialist or socialist-leaning labor movement along the lines envisioned by Eugene Debs, Norman Thomas, or perhaps Walter Reuther? Would labor have involved itself in politics or even become a political party as Reuther once advocated?[35] Would so-called business unionism, which defines a labor union as a business that sells labor, have been relegated to the scrap heap of history rather than to the reigning ideology of the American labor movement? We will never know, but we can be sure, given the importance of labor movements to contemporary Western democracies, that the current sociopolitical organization of the United States would be different.

We might also ask what might have been if organized crime had not been enriched and empowered by labor racketeering? Without its base in labor, the Italian-American organized crime groups would have been left to supplying illicit goods and services on the black market. Of course, LCN was, and to some extent still is, deeply involved in drugs, gambling, and loan-sharking. But these rackets do not generate the kind of access to politicians and businessmen that labor racketeering does. Fabulously wealthy drug dealers have obtained considerable political power in some South American countries but not in the United States where drug dealers remain sociopolitical outcasts. Drug dealers, at least in the United States, do not endorse and assist political candidates. They may corrupt law enforcement officials and politicians but not as systematically and extensively as LCN, and they are not nearly as able to protect themselves from arrest, prosecution, and punishment. In short, it is a fair hypothesis that if LCN had not been able to penetrate and control elements of the American labor movement, it would not have reached the pinnacles of power that it did reach in the 1970s and 1980s.

Finally, we need to ask whether the use of federal civil RICO suits, leading to court-enforced consent decrees, provides a model of organizational reform that will succeed in purging organized crime from the unions and that could be used to reform other types of corrupted organizations in the United States and other countries. There has been a long debate among political scientists and law professors about the capacity of courts to bring about sociopolitical change. This study takes that debate into a new venue and challenges us to reconsider the potential and limits of law enforcement, courts, and government to remediate deep flaws in the social fabric.

2

Organized Crime and Organized Labor

The meeting [of organized crime bosses in Apalachin, New York, in 1957] gave to millions of Americans their first clear knowledge that we have in this country a criminal syndicate that is obviously tightly organized into a secret brotherhood, which none of its members dare to betray, and which has insinuated itself into business and labor and public life at high levels. . . . One of the most significant results of this examination of the backgrounds of the Apalachin visitors was the revelation that twenty-three of them were directly connected with labor unions or labor-management bargaining groups. It was no coincidence that the names of these men and their cronies and associates kept cropping up during almost every investigation that was made of improper activities in labor and management. Hundreds of honest, decent union officials throughout the country, and perhaps millions of their hard-working members, are daily subjected to the manipulation of these racketeers and their henchmen.

—Senator John McClellan, *Crime without
Punishment* (1962), 116

The benefits a union officer's position gave to a La Cosa Nostra member included the ability to transform an ugly criminal caterpillar into a very dangerous but beautiful butterfly. It gave instant legitimacy, an unlimited expense account, legitimate income for income tax purposes, plus all the money you could steal from union dues, an entree into the business community and an entree to those aspiring for political office. Later, the unions developed Political Action Committees or PACs to use for even more political leverage. To me, the unlimited possibilities the organized crime professional criminals involved in the American labor movement had to control the American public's capitalistic and democratic society was frightening.

—James Moody, FBI official in charge of organized crime,
Testimony Before Senate Permanent Subcommittee
on Investigations, July 24, 1996

23

Labor racketeering has never been just a sideline activity for the Cosa Nostra organized crime families. The image that some scholars and observers have of organized crime moving into unions and industrial racketeering as a way of laundering funds obtained from gambling, prostitution, drugs, and other black market operations is not accurate. Labor racketeering was a defining feature of American organized crime from the first decades of the twentieth century. Ultimately, it was labor racketeering that made Cosa Nostra part of the sociopolitical power structure of twentieth-century America.

LAYING THE GROUNDWORK

During the first third of the twentieth century, it was relatively easy for organized crime groups to take over local unions, especially craft unions. In violent conflicts between workers and employers, professional criminals supplied goons to both sides.[1] Once the gangsters had a foot in a union's door, they could take over by means of violence, intimidation, and election fraud. The immigrant workers could be intimidated, coerced, and deceived, but nefarious techniques were not always necessary. Some labor racketeers were charismatic leaders whom workers admired. No doubt, some workers thought they would be better off being represented by individuals with a reputation for being tough and well-connected. According to Harold Seidman's study of early twentieth-century labor racketeering, *Labor Czars* (1938):

> Unionists continued to do their own slugging until the great strikes of 1909 necessitated a change in tactics . . . the unions engaged gangsters to protect women strikers and pickets against employer thugs. . . . The unions soon discovered that gangsters did not accept temporary work. Once hired, they remained permanently employed, whether the union liked it or not. . . .[2]

Sometimes gangsters became labor officials without any vote or other action by the workers whom they came to represent. Under the 1935 National Labor Relations Act (NLRA), an employer could voluntarily recognize a particular union as the exclusive bargaining agent for his workers.* That representation would be binding for three years and would continue unless the workers voted to be represented by a different union or not to be represented by any union. Some employers happily recognized practically nonexistent racketeer-constructed "unions" because, in effect, such unions were a scam allowing the racketeers to extract bribes and the employers to avoid having to deal with a real union. Indeed, employers could call upon these unions to establish and police an employers' cartel. To cite just one early example, John Landesco's 1929 study for the Chicago Crime Commission reported that racketeers controlled the laundry industry by dominating the union that represented the drivers.

In the 1920s, such Jewish organized crime figures as Arnold Rothstein (1882–1928), Jacob Orgen (1894–1927), Jacob Shapiro (1899–1947), and Louis Buchalter (1897–1944) infiltrated the International Ladies' Garment Workers' Union (ILGWU) and leveraged their union power into domination of New York City's garment district.[3] (Carl Sifakis, author of *The Mafia Encyclopedia*, calls Buchalter *the foremost labor racket czar in the United States*.)[4] The labor racketeers of this era were sometimes recruited by "honest" union leaders to help defeat rival unions; Sidney Hillman, head of the Amalgamated Clothing Workers Union, and a key FDR New Deal advisor, called upon Buchalter to suppress competing unions and recalcitrant employers who stood in the way of his union.[5] In the 1920s, Dutch Schultz (a.k.a. Arthur Flegenheimer (1903–1935)) forcibly took over and controlled the New York City Restaurant and Cafeteria Workers Union.

THE ORIGINS OF COSA NOSTRA LABOR RACKETEERING

The Italian American organized crime groups engaged in labor racketeering from the time they began to form in the United States. Joseph ("Socks") Lanza (1904–1968) founded the Seafood Workers Union in the late 1920s and, from this power base, dominated the Fulton Fish Market

---

* Under the National Labor Relations Act (Sec. 9), the employees have the right to petition the National Labor Relations Board for an election, but if they do not, the employer's choice of his or her workers' exclusive bargaining agent stands. National Labor Relations Act, 29 U.S.C. §§ 151–69.

in lower Manhattan, the largest wholesale fish market in the country. All the participants in the fish market made payoffs to Lanza.[6] Likewise, Anthony Anastasio (1906–1963), president of the International Long-shoremen's Association (ILA) Local 1814 and vice-president of the ILA International, dominated the Brooklyn docks on behalf of his organized crime group (later taken over by Carlo Gambino and thereafter known as the Gambino crime family) from the 1930s to the early 1960s.

In Chicago, in the 1910s and 1920s, Al Capone's (1899–1947) or-ganized crime group (later "the Outfit") dominated dozens of Chicago locals in the building trades, hotels and restaurants, and other sectors. Sometimes the Capone gang wrested control of a union from union leaders who themselves were gangsters. Harold Seidman recounts that

> [o]ne of Chicago's most powerful labor leaders was summoned to the presence of the "Big Fellow." Capone informed the unionist that the racketeers intended to take over control of his unions and, through his unions, capture many trade associations. He was advised that he could continue in nominal and titular control if he so desired. The labor leader elected to go along with the mob.[7]

Capone's gang took control of the Chicago-based Motion Picture Oper-ators Union (MPOU). At first, the gang just demanded a partnership, but within two years Capone ordered the union president killed.[8] The Chicago Outfit leveraged its control over the MPOU to extort the the-ater owners and Hollywood producers. The movie producers paid the mob $150,000 (the equivalent of about $2 million in 2003 dollars) for a seven-year no-strike contract.[9] According to investigative reporter Gus Russo, under Capone lieutenant Curly Humphreys's stewardship,

> labor racketeering was perfected, turning a modestly profitable con into a multi-million dollar operation, with the Outfit controlling as much as 70 percent of the city's unions. In 1928, the boys were see-ing an estimated $10 million [$107 million in 2003 dollars] a year in profit from Curly's rackets; by 1931, the estimated revenue escalated to $50 million [$604 million in 2003 dollars]—small by bootlegging standards, but with unlimited potential, since unlike Volstead [the National Prohibition Act], labor was never going to be repealed.[10]

Capone biographer, John Kobler, notes: "Toward the end of 1928 the [Chicago] state's attorney's office listed ninety-one Chicago unions and [employer] associations that had fallen under racketeer rule."[11] After National Alcohol Prohibition was repealed in 1933, labor racketeering became an even more important revenue source for organized crime.

When the International Alliance of Theatrical Stage Employees (IATSE) went on strike in 1933, the employers sought the Outfit's help. The Outfit sent thugs to keep the theaters open and thereby broke the strike.[12] Paul Ricca, Tony Accardo, and Curly Humphreys demanded that IATSE hire Outfit members and associates for positions throughout the union, ensuring organized crime's presence in the film business for decades.[13] When President Ronald Reagan appointed the President's Commission on Organized Crime in 1984, he explained that he was familiar with labor racketeering because of his experience as a leader in the Screen Actors Guild.*

Every Cosa Nostra crime family has a documented history of labor racketeering (see Table 2-1 at the end of the chapter). For decades, Al Capone's protégé and successor, Tony Accardo, longtime head of the Outfit,[14] controlled numerous Laborers' International Union of North America (LIUNA) locals in Chicago. That control enabled the Outfit to designate and control the national general presidents of the international union, Peter Fosco, later Peter's son Angelo, and then Arthur E. Coia.[15] Similarly, control over the Hotel and Restaurant Employees (HERE) enabled the Outfit to name and control General President Ed Miller and his successor, Edward Hanley.[16] The Outfit, through its associate Sidney Korshak, exercised enormous influence over the IBT Central States Pension and Welfare funds, as well as influence over the IBT itself.[17]

Angelo Bruno, LCN boss in Philadelphia, dominated the roofers' union, as well as several Hotel and Restaurant Employees (HERE) locals in Atlantic City. Kansas City's LCN boss, Nick Civella, controlled the powerful IBT Joint Council. He and several other organized crime figures, as well as corrupt union officials, treated the nation's largest pension and welfare fund (IBT Central States Funds) as a bank

---

* Reagan was well aware of organized crime's infiltration of the IATSE, the union that represented stage hands. He himself had served as president of the Screen Actors Guild, which represented movie actors. Available at http://www.cbsnews.com/stories/2003/09/17/earlyshow/leisure/books/main573799.shtml.

for organized crime.[18] (Las Vegas was first developed by loans from this fund to organized crime figures through their front men.) Angelo Lonardo, boss of the Cleveland LCN family, was also heavily involved in labor racketeering. William "Big Bill" Presser (1907–1981), an "associate" of Cleveland's Licavoli crime family, headed IBT Joint Council 41 and served as president of the huge Ohio Teamsters Conference. From this power base, he and Lonardo, with help from Civella, were able to orchestrate (Bill's son) Jackie Presser's career in several different unions, culminating in Jackie's 1983 succession to the IBT presidency.[19] Cosa Nostra bosses had a major role in choosing IBT general presidents Jimmy Hoffa, Frank Fitzsimmons, Roy Williams, Jackie Presser, and William McCarthy.

The Licavoli crime family in Cleveland controlled a number of labor unions, including ILA Local 1317 and Teamsters Locals 41, 410, and 416.[20] Moe Dalitz (1899–1989) was the crime family's chief labor racketeer. His connections to Hoffa and the Teamsters bore fruit when, later in his career, he used Teamsters' pension fund loans to build Las Vegas casinos in partnership with LCN.[21] The Cleveland organized crime family associate "Big Bill" Presser served as president of IBT Joint Council 41. For years, Presser was one of the most powerful figures behind the Teamsters Central States Pension Fund.[22] His power reached its pinnacle when son Jackie became IBT general president in 1983.[23]

Practically every major Cosa Nostra figure in the twentieth century can be linked to labor racketeering. To take a few examples: Anthony Corallo (1913–2000), a Johnny Dioguardi protégé who worked his way up to boss of the (New York City) crime family, was closely linked and, at one time or another, held office in the Painters and Decorators Union, the Conduit Workers Union, the United Textile Workers, and IBT Local 239.[24] He was convicted in the 1987 Commission Case and sentenced to one hundred years in prison.[25] Tony Accardo (1906–1992), head of the Chicago Outfit for several decades, maintained and even extended the Outfit's extensive labor racketeering interests in Chicago. Nicholas Civella (1912–1983) boss of the Kansas City crime family, through his control of IBT leader Roy Williams, was a major force in the IBT's Central States Pension and Welfare Fund and in the IBT Central States Joint Council. Angelo Lonardo, Cleveland crime family boss (who became a cooperating government witness) explained how he teamed up with Civella to get the approvals of the Chicago and New York City mobsters to make Roy Williams IBT general president. At a 1985 organized crime trial, Williams testified that, at Civella's insistence, he approved a $62.5 million pension fund loan ($107 million in 2003 dollars) to finance a mob associate's acquisition of two casinos.[26]

In the 1970s, Nicodemo "Little Nicky" Scarfo (1929–) was in charge of Philadelphia's Bruno crime family's Atlantic City interests, most importantly HERE Local 54. Later, Scarfo himself became boss of the family. Raymond Patriarca (1908–1984), for many years boss of the New England LCN family, exerted influence over New England LIUNA and IBT locals. Toward the end of his life, he was indicted for labor racketeering but was too ill to stand trial.[27] Vincent "Chin" Gigante (1926–), boss of the New York City Genovese crime family, used the family's control over Port of New York ILA locals to extort money from shipping companies. Although he began serving a life sentence in 1997, a 2003 indictment alleged continued Genovese crime family domination and exploitation of the ILA, stevedoring companies, and the New York port.

HOW MOBSTERS GAINED CONTROL OVER UNIONS

It was not difficult for organized crime figures to take over a union local. They could use threats and actual violence to drive off competing unionists and anyone else who opposed them. They could rig elections (using intimidation and fraud) to have themselves or their stooges elected to office. They could obtain employer recognition of their union by threats of violence and sabotage, or by promises of sweetheart deals. They were usually aided by widespread union members' apathy toward union governance and administration.[28]

Let us consider some examples:

LCN creates a union. Johnny Dioguardi, one of the century's most notorious labor racketeers and an early member of Al Capone's gang, moved to New York City where he became a capo in the Lucchese crime family. He and Jimmy Hoffa worked out a deal whereby Hoffa gave him a charter to organize seven so-called paper IBT locals. Hoffa needed the votes of these seven locals to assure the election of an ally to the top position in the NYC IBT Joint Council.*[29]

---

* Dioguardi was indicted for hiring a small-time hoodlum to throw acid in the face of crusading labor columnist Victor Riesel in 1956. (The charges against Dioguardi were dropped when the principal defendant was murdered and other witnesses refused to testify.)

New labor racketeer–dominated unions continued to be formed in the decades that followed. For example, writing in March 2005 about a labor racketeering case that has gone on for almost twenty-five years, Federal District Court Judge John Gleeson said:

> Local 530 [of the Operative Plasterers and Cement Masons' International Association] was founded in 1978 by gangsters for gangsters and the companies affiliated with them. Specifically, it was founded by Lou Moscatiello, who was then an associate of the Genovese Crime Family of La Cosa Nostra, to be an employer-friendly alternative to Local 1974 [of the Drywall Tapers and Pointers].[30]

LCN takes over a union through intimidation. In 1921, several Building Service Employees International Union (BSEIU) leaders were convicted of conspiracy. The union's officials managed to obtain pardons by appealing to the Outfit to use its political influence on their behalf. As a result, the BSEIU became indebted to organized crime. Within a short time, organized crime moved to take control of the union. They gave the union's officers an ultimatum: put mob cronies in top union positions or leave town. Given the mob's influence over Chicago's political machine, there was no one to whom the union could appeal.[31]

LCN obtains control through election intimidation and fraud. In 1938, George Scalise obtained a charter to create Local 94 of the Bowling and Billiards Academy Employees Union. Scalise called on organized crime to stuff union ballot boxes.[32] Not surprisingly, he "won" the election. The local was forced to transfer to the mob a large portion of its dues and control over certain decisions.[33] Using the same strategy of election intimidation and fraud, the mob later made Scalise the BSEIU's national president.

LCN labor organization voluntarily recognized by employer as collective bargaining agent. The mob took control of some unions simply by creating the union and "persuading" employers to recognize it as the workers' exclusive bargaining agent. A good example is New York City's parking garage workers. When garage owners were threatened with systematic vandalism to customers' cars, they "voluntarily" signed representational agreements with a mob-dominated sham union; the workers paid dues without receiving any benefits or representation.[34]

There is no historical record on when organized crime's infiltration of various unions began or when it matured into working control. There

is good reason to believe, however, that Cosa Nostra's influence continued to radiate into previously untainted unions throughout the later
half of the twentieth century. For example, as new LIUNA locals were
chartered in the New York area, they quickly succumbed to mob control. Because of international LCN domination, sometimes the establishment of new locals was dictated by the interests of LCN. Local 1030
in New Jersey is a prime example. It was set up nominally to deal with
asbestos removal, but it appears that 1030 was intended from the beginning to be a vehicle for the DeCavalcante group to get its share of the
action (since the NYC locals "belonged to" the Genovese and Lucchese
families).

Yet another strategy that began to be used more regularly when
civil RICO trusteeships started purging mobsters from the Teamsters,
Hotel and Restaurant Workers, Laborers, and Longshoremen's Association was for the labor racketeers to start so-called "independent"
unions, unaffiliated with any national/international union. For example, after being permanently expelled from the IBT in 1994 for embezzlement, dual unionism, and breach of other fiduciary duties, Vincent
Sombrotto, former president of IBT Local 966, and that union's former secretary treasurer, Edwin Gonzales, set up a new "independent"
union, Local 116 in Secaucus, New Jersey. Sombrotto and Gonzales en-
rolled current IBT Local 807 members into their new union. The Federal
Second Circuit Court of Appeals stymied that scheme by holding that
Sombrotto and Gonzales violated the district court's consent decree,
which prohibited them from having any further association with the
IBT. In other cases, however, racketeers successfully decertified the old
(now cleaned-up) union and reestablished mob dominance over the
same workers through a new independent union.

HOW ORGANIZED CRIME CONSOLIDATES
ITS UNION CONTROL

LCN achieved working control of a local union by placing one of its
members or an associate in the position of top union official or by in-
timidating or recruiting a union leader to do its bidding. The next step
was to consolidate control through a combination of sticks and carrots. Any union member who dared to challenge the mob faced loss
of employment and/or violent reprisals. There are many examples of

"dissidents" beaten at union meetings, their homes firebombed, and themselves murdered for criticizing the union's administration or seeking union office. (See Chapter 6, Table 6-1.)

Dissidents could be expelled from the union on some trumped-up grounds. If the dissident depended on the union for job assignments through a hiring hall, as is the case in the construction industry and in longshoring, he would find himself unemployed. In industries where employers do their own hiring, a mob figure who controlled the union could tell the employer that one of his employees had become a thorn in the union's side and that the union would like to see that employee fired. The employer would likely comply in order to avoid labor trouble. Obviously, the fired employee would not get the union's assistance in challenging the dismissal. Judge Harold Ackerman described organized crime's complete lock on IBT Local 560, pointing out that LCN capo and Local 560 president, Tony Provenzano, had created a reign of terror by, among other things, killing two "dissident" Local 560 members. The message to the membership could not have been clearer: one opposed the union's leadership at risk of life and limb.[35]

The mob figures who control a union local have many "carrots" to distribute. Friends and supporters can be appointed as business agents and shop stewards or assigned no-show or high-paying jobs or lucrative service contracts. Treating the union treasury as a trough, corrupt leader can offer supporters all sorts of perks, including high salaries, no-show jobs, cars, trips, union reimbursement of personal expenses, loans, and the like. If the union operates a hiring hall, friends and supporters can be assigned regular work and the easiest and most desirable jobs. For example, the New York City District Council of Carpenters Union used a special "pool" of workers designated by the Genovese crime family from which to choose carpenters for high-paying jobs at the Javits Exhibition Center.[36] Once the mob took hold of a union, it proved nearly impossible to overthrow.

HOW LCN USES THE UNION AS A CASH COW

Labor racketeering has proved very profitable to organized crime, especially since the 1940s, when unions began bargaining to have employers automatically deduct union dues from union members' paychecks.[37] With the "check-off" in place, unions received a monthly flow of revenue without lifting a finger. A corrupt union official and the organized crime family that controlled him could take advantage of the ever-replenishing union treasury. Dues could be increased without regard for rank-and-file opposition.

There were many legal and illegal ways for labor racketeers to pull money out of a union. First, they could draw bloated and multiple salaries, a kind of legalized graft. Some union constitutions require a membership vote on officers' salaries; however, LCN treated this rule as a formality or simply ignored it. In addition to their salaries, corrupt union officials enjoyed use of union-owned cars, planes, and boats. Frequently the union also provided overpaid jobs to family members, friends, and mistresses. They also handed out no-show jobs.

Second, mob leaders could embezzle union funds. "Their unions" either maintained no financial records or kept such sloppy records that even if financial chicanery were discovered, embezzlement was practically impossible to prove. Labor racketeering became much more lucrative in the 1940s and 1950s with the rise of multimillion- (and soon, multibillion-) dollar union pension and welfare funds.[38] It became commonplace for collective bargaining agreements to impose an obligation on the employer to make payments to such funds on behalf of the employees. According to federal law, the funds would be managed by equal numbers of union-designated and employer-designated trustees. In practice, the employer appointed trustees deferred to the union trustees because (in contrast with the union) having made the contributions, the employer had little interest in how the pension money was invested or spent. Racketeers embezzled the assets of pension and welfare funds by disguising thefts as "loans," payments for nonexistent goods and services, as inflated payments for goods and services.

Third, labor racketeers could use their union position to solicit bribes from employers who wished to obtain relief from expensive collective bargaining agreement provisions. For the right price, corrupt union officials would allow employers to operate a "double breasted shop" (one employing nonunion as well as union employees), or even to operate completely nonunion. Corrupt union officials typically sold their members' rights to overtime pay, pension and welfare contributions, and to jurisdiction over certain work.

Fourth, labor racketeers could rake in money by means of the "strike insurance racket" or labor peace extortion by threatening employers with labor problems. In many businesses, any disruption of operations is enormously expensive; prolonged disruption can mean bankruptcy.

Fifth, labor racketeers could make money by using the union to set up and police employer cartels. Once the union represented workers in all or most of the firms operating in a particular industry, the organized crime faction that controlled the union could organize an employers' association. Employers' dues were passed along to Cosa Nostra, but the employers got something important for their money: the union could effectively prevent firms that were not association members from participating in the industry. If a firm tried to challenge the cartel, it would find itself beset by labor troubles and/or sabotage.[39]

Sixth, from control of an employer cartel, it was only a small step for LCN members and associates to start up, buy, or strong-arm their way into a firm doing business in the cartelized industry. The LCN-owned firms would have a competitive advantage over other cartel members: they would not have to hire union employees or, if they did, they could pay them below union wages or fail to make required contributions to union pension and welfare funds. Another scheme was to have their employees represented by a low-wage local.

Seventh, LCN could direct employers to purchase certain goods and services from mob-owned or mob-controlled supply companies. An employer who refused might face labor troubles or worse.

THE VALUE OF LABOR RACKETEERING

There is no audit to tell us how lucrative labor racketeering has been for the mob, but there are bits of evidence here and there. For example, around the turn of the century, Robert Brindell was the highest paid union official in the country; his graft is said to have netted more than $500,000 a year ($5.2 million in 2003 dollars).[40] Thomas Dewey's 1930s investigation into corruption within the restaurant industry found that racketeers embezzled one-third of union members' dues as well as $75,000 ($1 million in 2003 dollars) from Restaurant Workers Local 6; $45,000 ($600,000 in 2003 dollars) from Local 322; and $120,000 ($1.6 million in 2003 dollars) from an employer association.[41] Additionally, the racketeers received about $150,000 ($2 million in 2003 dollars) from restaurant owners. In the 1960s, Genovese crime family capo Tony Provenzano was the nation's highest-paid union official. Additional pension and financial packages were provided for him after his murder conviction.[42] In Peter Maas's biography of Sammy "the Bull" Gravano (onetime Gambino crime family underboss), Gravano states that labor racketeering could double the profit margin on a construction contract, from 15 to 30 percent, because mob-owned contractors didn't have to pay union wages or benefits.[43] A 1986 *Fortune* magazine article listing the fifty wealthiest underworld figures in the United States identified *unions* or *construction* (always union related) as a key source of income for half of these individuals (see Table 2-2 at the end of chapter).

Labor racketeering has given Cosa Nostra its special character as an organized crime syndicate. Control over labor put LCN figures in close touch with businessmen who employed the captive unions' members. The businessmen did not have the option of refusing to meet with, deal with, and get along with union officials. Moreover, when businessmen ran into labor problems, they naturally reached out to the only individuals who could fix those problems: the local LCN bosses. Because an LCN boss had influence in a number of unions, he could solve jurisdictional disputes or rein in an obstreperous union official. Their union influence turned LCN bosses into power brokers.

Labor racketeering also put LCN bosses in touch with politicians. In most big cities, at least those in the East and Midwest, organized labor was a powerful political force for much of the twentieth century. Labor endorsements were avidly sought; in addition, a supportive labor union would provide campaign contributions and manpower to distribute campaign literature and make phone calls. Union support also provided corrupt opportunities for personal enrichment. By contrast, labor opposition would practically assure defeat. Moreover, labor problems that make city life unpleasant or inconvenient during an incumbent's term, especially near election time, could very much weaken a mayor's or other public official's appeal. For all these reasons, it was important for urban politicians to curry favor with organized crime figures who were influential in the labor movement.

CONCLUSION

Labor racketeering schemes were well established by the late nineteenth and early twentieth centuries. The early twentieth-century Italian American organized crime groups were drawn to labor racketeering just as were their Jewish and Irish counterparts. As the bridge between underworld vice rackets and upper-world businesses and politics, labor racketeering turned LCN bosses into urban, regional, and even national power brokers. Craft unions especially could easily be taken over by mobsters with the capacity and reputation for violence. The racketeering potential of labor unions was high. A regular revenue stream for organized crime could be generated by union salaries, perks, extortions, bribes, embezzlements, and frauds. By the 1940s, as Cosa Nostra emerged as the dominant American organized crime syndicate, labor racketeering was an important part of LCN crime families' operations. It also provided the route by which Cosa Nostra become part of the power elite in twentieth-century urban America. In fact, it is labor racketeering that distinguishes the Cosa Nostra organized crime families from other contemporary organized crime groups such as biker gangs, street gangs, and drug-trafficking organizations.

Table 2-1

A Sample of Unions Reputed to Have Been Infiltrated by LCN at Some Time

LCN Family	Sample of Unions Reputed to Have Been Infiltrated by LCN
Buffalo	HEREIU Local 66; IBT Local 398
Chicago (The Outfit)	HEREIU Locals 304 and 450; LIUNA Locals 1, 5, and 8; Motion Picture Operators Local 110; Laundry Workers Local 46
Cleveland	IBT Locals 41, 73, 293, 410, 415, 416, and 796; Ironworkers Local 17
Dallas	IBT Local 745
Detroit	IBT Locals 124 and 614
Kansas City	HEREIU Local 64; IBT Local 41
Los Angeles	HEREIU Local 30
Miami/Tampa (Traficante)	LIUNA Locals 767 and 797
Milwaukee (Balistrieri)	HEREIU Local 122
New Jersey (DeCavalcante)	35 IBT locals; LIUNA Locals 394 and 1030
Northeast Pennsylvania (Bufalino)	IBT Locals 693 and 326
New England	IBT Local 25; New England LIUNA
New York (Bonanno)	Newspaper and Mail Deliverers Union of New York and Vicinity
New York (Colombo)	International Union of Operating Engineers Locals 14 and 15; HEREIU Local 3
New York (Gambino)	ILA Locals 824, 1809, 1814, and 1909; LIUNA Local 342; IBT Locals 282 and 813; ILGWU Local 102
New York (Genovese)	Plasterers Local 530; United Brotherhood of Carpenters Locals 11, 17, 608, and 964; LIUNA Locals 21 and 958; Bricklayers Local 10

Table 2-1 (continued)

LCN Family	Sample of Unions Reputed to Have Been Infiltrated by LCN
New York (Lucchese)	LIUNA Local 66; IBT Locals 295, 805, 810, and 851; Painters and Decorators Union
Northern California	HEREIU Local 50; IBT Local 856
Philadelphia (Bruno/Scarfo)	Roofers Union; HEREIU Local 54; IBT Local 478
Rochester	IBT Local 398
St. Louis	LIUNA Locals 42 and 110

Table 2-2
"Top 50" Wealthiest Reputed U.S. Mafia Bosses

Rank	Name	Nickname	Age in 1986	Headquarters	Family	Source of Income
1	Anthony Salerno	Fat Tony	75	New York City	Genovese	Construction, *unions*, gambling, loan sharking
2	Anthony Accardo	Joe Batters	80	Palm Springs	Chicago	Gambling, *unions*, loan sharking
3	Anthony Corallo	Tony Ducks	73	Long Island	Lucchese	Garbage, extortion
4	Gerardo Catena	Jerry	84	Boca Raton	Genovese	*Construction*, gambling, casinos
5	Gennaro Langella	Jerry Lang	47	Brooklyn	Colombo	*Construction*, loan sharking, gambling
6	Carmine Perisco	Junior	53	Brooklyn	Colombo	*Construction*, loan sharking, gambling
7	Christopher Furnari	Christie Tick	62	New York City	Lucchese	*Construction, unions*, gambling, loan sharking
8	Salvatore Santoro	Tom Mix	70	New York City	Lucchese	*Construction, unions*, loan sharking
9	Philip Rastelli	Rusty	68	New York City	Bonanno	*Concrete, unions*, loan sharking, narcotics
10	Vincent DiNapoli	Vinnie	49	New York City	Genovese	*Construction, unions*
11	Ralph Scopo		57	Brooklyn	Colombo	*Construction, unions*
12	Russell Bufalino		83	Scranton	Bufalino	*Sweetheart contracts*
13	John Gotti		46	New York City	Gambino	Loan sharking, robbery, phonograph records
14	Joseph Bonanno	Joe	82	Tuscon	Bonanno	Narcotics
15	Santo Trafficante	Louis Santos	71	Tampa	Tampa	Gambling, loan sharking, narcotics
16	Carlos Marcello	Little Man	76	New Orleans	New Orleans	Gambling, real estate, nightclubs
17	Frank Balistrieri	Frankie Bal	68	Milwaukee	Milwaukee	Gambling, liquor, *Teamsters pension funds*
18	Michael Franzese		35	Long Island	Colombo	Movies, auto dealerships, bootleg gasoline

(continued)

Table 2-2 (continued)

Rank	Name	Nickname	Age in 1986	Headquarters	Family	Source of Income
19	Vincent Gigante	Chin	57	New Jersey	Genovese	Unions, gambling, loan sharking
20	Joseph Ferriola	Joe Nagall	59	Chicago	Chicago	Gambling, extortion
21	Joseph Aiuppa	Joey O'Brien	78	Chicago	Chicago	Gambling, casinos, unions
22	Gus Alex	Slim	70	Chicago	Chicago	Gambling, political fixing
23	Vincent Alo	Jimmy Blue Eyes	82	Miami	Genovese	Gambling, casinos, money laundering
24	Anthony Indelicato	Bruno	39	New York City	Bonanno	Narcotics
25	Michael Genovese	Mike	65	Pittsburgh	Pittsburgh	Gambling
26	Joseph N. Gallo		74	New York City	Gambino	Pornography, real estate
27	Philip Lombardo	Benny Squint	78	Miami	Genovese	Construction, gambling, loan sharking
28	Raymond Martorano	Long John	59	Philadelphia	Philadelphia	Narcotics, unions, vending machines
29	Anthony Provenzano	Tony Pro	69	New Jersey	Genovese	Unions
30	John Cerone	Jackie	72	Chicago	Chicago	Casinos
31	James Napoli	Jimmy Napp	75	New York City	Genovese	Gambling, loan sharking
32	Paul Vario Sr.		72	New York City	Lucchese	Gambling, robbery
33	Carl DeLuna	Toughy	59	Kansas City, MO	Kansas City	Gambling, casinos
34	Gennaro Angiulo	Jerry	67	Boston	Boston	Numbers, loan sharking, money laundering
35	Matthew Ianniello	Matty the Horse	66	New York City	Genovese	Unions, topless bars, loan sharking
36	James Failla	Jimmy Brown	67	New York City	Gambino	Unions
37	John Riggi Sr.		61	New Jersey	DeCavalcante	Construction, waterfront unions
38	Louis Manna	Bobby	57	New Jersey	Genovese	Construction, gambling, loan sharking
39	John DiGilio	Johnnie Dee	53	New Jersey	Genovese	Waterfront unions, gambling, loan sharking
40	William Cammisano	Willie	71	Kansas City, MO	Kansas City	Gambling, loan sharking, fencing
41	Vincent Meli	Little Vince	62	Detroit	Detroit	Steel hauling
42	Vincent Solano	Vince	67	Chicago	Chicago	Gambling, unions
43	Nicodemo Scarfo	Nicky	57	Atlantic City	Philadelphia	Gambling, numbers, unions

Table 2-2 (continued)

Rank	Name	Nickname	Age in 1986	Headquarters	Family	Source of Income
44	Tino Fiumara	George Grecco	46	New Jersey	Genovese *Age in*	*Waterfront Unions*
45	Donald Angelini	Don Angel	60	Chicago	Chicago	Gambling
46	Peter Milano	Pete	60	Los Angeles	Los Angeles	Gambling
47	Paul Schiro	Paulie	45	Pheonix	Chicago	Gambling
48	Chris Petti		47	San Diego	Chicago	Gambling
49	Angelo Tuminaro	Little Angie	81	Unknown	Lucchese	Narcotics
50	Frank Buccieri	The Horse	62	Palm Springs	Chicago	Loan sharking

Source: Fortune (November 10, 1986) compiled a list of the fifty wealthiest Mafia leaders from infor-mation provided by FBI agents, federal prosecutors, and local law enforcement officials. Available at http://www.fortune.com/fortune/mafia. Author's italics indicate income likely dervied from labor racketeering.

3

President's Commission on Organized Crime

My family [Genovese] made a lot of money from gambling and the numbers rackets. We got money from gambling, but our real power, our real strength, came from the unions. With the unions behind us, we could shut down the city, or the country for that matter, if we needed to get our way. Our brugad [crime family] controlled a number of different unions, some of which I personally dealt with, some of which I knew about from other amico nostra. In some cases, we got money from our dealings with the unions, in some cases we got favors such as jobs for friends and relatives—but, most importantly, in all cases, we got power over every businessman in New York. With the unions behind us, we could make or break the construction industry, the garment business, the docks, to name but a few.

—Vincent Cafaro, quoted from an affidavit filed with
Senate Permanent Subcommittee on Investigations,
April 1988, 16–17

The Commission believes that the first step in ending labor racketeering is a recognition that the problem is both persistent and pervasive throughout many areas of the United States. During the past 25 years, law enforcement agencies have often successfully used the tools available to them to prosecute individual labor racketeers. But . . . criminal prosecutions alone are insufficient. Because of its insidious and systemic nature, labor racketeering is not easily deterred by prosecutorial efforts that merely "count bodies" as a measure of success. Instead, a new strategy must be developed to bankrupt individual mobsters and to discourage union officers, employers, and public officials from accommodating organized crime.

—President's Commission on Organized Crime, *The Edge:
Organized Crime, Business, and Labor Unions, Section 1:
Overview and Summary of Recommendations,* President's
Commission on Organized Crime (1986), 5

How extensive has labor racketeering been in the United States? How extensive is it now? These are not easy questions. There are hundreds of national/international unions and thousands of local unions. New unions are established, old ones die, some combine—hence, the number of unions varies considerably over time. Moreover, the concepts of "controlled" or "influenced" by organized crime are not self-defining. In some local unions, labor racketeers (organized crime members or associates) have held high office and controlled day-to-day administration. In other unions, key officers, though not LCN members themselves, have been the pawns of organized crime members or associates. Ideally, students of labor racketeering would have an up-to-date list of all unions which, to some extent, have been controlled or influenced by organized crime. Unfortunately, there is no such list. We do not have accurate information on possible organized crime influence in even a substantial minority of unions. Moreover, even knowledge of a percentage of racketeer-ridden unions would not tell the whole story. We would surely want to know what percentage of all union members belong to mob-infected unions.

Suppose a national/international union is run by labor racketeers and allows those racketeers to dominate key regional and local affiliates, to plunder its treasury and its pension and welfare funds, and to compromise its collective bargaining and contract enforcement. For purposes of assessing the problem should we conclude that all locals of that international union, and all members of all those locals are victims of labor racketeering? For my purposes, it is not necessary to pinpoint the percentages of unions or union members who, at any time, have been dominated, controlled, or affected by Cosa Nostra labor racketeers. The purpose of this chapter and the next is to establish that the problem is widespread, deep, persistent, and significant. This chapter examines the extent of labor racketeering through the lens of the President's Commission on Organized Crime, which was appointed in 1983. The next chapter presents a snapshot of labor racketeering in New York City during approximately the same time period.

CREATION OF THE PRESIDENT'S COMMISSION ON ORGANIZED CRIME

In 1983, President Ronald Reagan charged his eighteen appointees to the newly established President's Commission on Organized Crime

(PCOC) to provide "a full and complete national and region-by-region analysis of the nation's organized crime problems, including information on its participants, an evaluation of applicable law and responses to the issue, and recommendations for future action." He named Irving Kaufman, a U.S. Second Circuit Court of Appeals judge, as chairman. The other commissioners included Senator Strom Thurman (R.-S.C.), Congressman Peter Rodino (D.-N.J.), law enforcement professionals with experience. Combating organized crime, a representative of organized labor, several academics, and the senior editor of *Readers Digest.* The commission heard testimony from FBI and Department of Labor investigators, Department of Justice lawyers, and labor leaders. The research staff undertook a comprehensive review of prior congressional investigations, hearings, and reports. The PCOC produced a series of reports, including volumes on gambling, drug trafficking, and money laundering. It devoted a thick volume, *The Edge,* to organized crime's exploitation of labor unions.

Released on March 1, 1986, *The Edge* focused mainly on four international unions with the most extensively documented history of labor racketeering: the International Brotherhood of Teamsters (IBT), the Hotel and Restaurant Employees International Union (HERE), the Laborers' International Union of America (LIUNA), and the International Longshoremen's Association (ILA). It also focused attention on labor racketeering within independent unions. Widespread labor racketeering, according to the PCOC, was distorting the nation's economy and making a mockery of union members' rights and collective bargaining agreements. Organized crime's influence over labor unions provided businesses owned, dominated, or favored by organized crime an edge over competitors.

THE TEAMSTERS

The PCOC charged that "corruption and the Teamsters [are] synonymous" and that, since the 1950s, the Teamsters had been "firmly under the influence of organized crime."[1] John Dioguardi, a capo in the Lucchese crime family, and a power broker with influence in several unions (including United Automobile Workers-AFL), was one of Jimmy Hoffa's key supporters in his rise to the IBT presidency. Hoffa gave Dioguardi charters for several New York area IBT "paper locals" (that is, locals without any members, but whose officials were either made-members or associates of the Mafia) in exchange for Dioguardi's using those locals to support Hoffa's efforts to control the important New York area IBT Joint Council, the support of which he needed to become IBT general president. According to the PCOC, organized crime has continued to maintain a firm grip on the IBT long after Hoffa's reign, using intimidation and occasional acts of violence "to quell all forms of dissent, criticism, and opposition."[2]

The Edge explained that IBT presidents "[Jimmy] Hoffa and [Roy] Williams were indisputably direct instruments of organized crime," and that [Frank] Fitzsimmons held his office by "establish[ing] a meas-ure of détente whereby he was allowed to head the union, while organ-ized crime stole the workers' benefit funds and used the union for numerous criminal ventures."[3] At the time of the Commission's inves-tigation, former IBT General President Roy Williams, was cooperating with the government. Having previously been convicted of attempting to bribe Senator Howard Cannon (D.-Nev.) to vote against trucking deregulation, Williams hoped to shorten his prison sentence by serving as a cooperating witness. He testified that "every big [Teamster] local union . . . had some connection with organized crime."[4] Williams him-self had been controlled by Kansas City Cosa Nostra boss Nick Civella, who had quarterbacked Williams's campaign for the IBT presidency by obtaining support from organized crime bosses around the country. Williams testified that incumbent IBT president, Jackie Presser (whose father, William Presser, was a Cleveland organized crime family associ-ate and an IBT Central States Pension Fund Trustee until he was forced to resign from the IBT in 1976), depended upon organized crime sup-port for his election.[5] Presser had also served as an FBI informant, help-ing the FBI to make cases against his political rivals in the union.

The most spectacular charge in *The Edge* was that Presser was controlled by organized crime. Presser was one of the nation's most powerful labor leaders and one of the only ones to have endorsed Rea-gan's presidential candidacy. The PCOC criticized Reagan's close ties with Presser: "[I]n the current administration, long delays in reaching a resolution of a DOJ investigation of Presser [could raise a concern] whether Presser's support of the administration in the 1980 and 1984 election campaigns influenced the conduct of the investigation."

The PCOC traced organized crime's control over the IBT interna-tional union to its control over key IBT locals. It documented a relationship between Cosa Nostra families and thirty-six IBT locals, one joint council, and a conference (a regional association of joint councils).[6] LCN converted control of locals into control of whole business sectors. For example, Gambino crime family associate Bernard Adelstein's decades-long control of IBT Local 813 was the key to the mob's domination of New York City's waste-hauling industry.

Mob-controlled union locals elected mob-controlled officers who chose mob-controlled convention delegates. The mob-controlled delegates ratified the decisions and proposals of mob-controlled international presidents, vice-presidents, and general executive board (GEB) members. Because the IBT's general president and GEB members were chosen by mob-controlled convention delegates and not by the rank-and-file members, the PCOC judged it "unlikely . . . that a reform-minded Teamster president can be elected in the near future."[7]

The PCOC explained how the Cosa Nostra organized crime families' influence in the IBT provided leverage over tens of thousands of businesses dependent upon truck deliveries; the leverage could be converted into cash through extortion, solicitation of bribes, and no-show jobs. The mobsters also enriched themselves by siphoning money from union coffers, taking kickbacks for sweetheart service contracts, and arranging loans from IBT pension and benefit funds. LCN associates like Allen Dorfman and Sidney Korshack (Chicago) and Bill Presser (Cleveland) managed the IBT Central States Pension Fund (CSPF) for the benefit of organized crime. A typical pension fund invested 5 to 10 percent of its assets in real estate; the CSPF invested more than 70 percent in real estate, much of it in mob-sponsored Las Vegas casinos. Despite the 1976 settlement of the government's challenge to the fund's governance that put control over its investments in the hands of an institutional fiduciary, organized crime continued to plunder the fund. Moreover, Dorfman continued to draw substantial fees for handling the fund's insurance business.[*]

The Edge concluded pessimistically that "no single remedy is likely to restore even a measure of true union democracy and independent leadership to the IBT."[8] It urged the Department of Justice to purge corruption and racketeering from the IBT through criminal prosecutions,

---

[*] Dorfman was murdered while awaiting trial on charges arising out of the FBI's STRAW-MAN investigation, which focused on a conspiracy to use the Central States Pension Fund to secure interests in, and skim profits from, Las Vegas casinos. (Jacobs, *Busting the Mob*, 25.)

civil actions, administrative proceedings, and civil RICO trusteeships. Even then, the PCOC foresaw only a "modest hope of success" in wresting the IBT from the grip of organized crime.[9]

HOTEL EMPLOYERS AND RESTAURANT EMPLOYEES INTERNATIONAL UNION

According to the PCOC, LCN had exerted powerful influence over HEREIU since National Prohibition (1920–1933). The murder of a union member at the union's 1936 national convention precipitated an investigation by New York City Special Prosecutor Thomas Dewey, who uncovered rampant racketeering in restaurant industry unions and employer associations. His investigation resulted in the criminal conviction of three union officials, the suspension of a union local, and the expulsion of several union officials.[10] The McClellan Committee's hearings (1957–1959) revealed organized crime's pervasive influence in Chicago's restaurant industry through control of three HEREIU locals. Thirty years later, the PCOC charged that HEREIU has "a documented relationship with the Chicago 'Outfit' of La Cosa Nostra at the international level and [is] subject to the influence of the Gambino, Colombo, and Philadelphia La Cosa Nostra families at the local level."[11]

The PCOC drew heavily on the Senate Permanent Subcommittee on Investigations 1981–1984 hearings. One of the subcommittee's reports stated:

> The Hotel and Restaurant Employees Union represents the converse of the International Brotherhood of Teamsters. In the Teamsters, the corruption and organized crime influence are a result of the massive infiltration of the local unions. The HEREIU, on the other hand, has been infiltrated from the top. This occurred as a result of the power wielded in the Chicago area locals and the joint executive board by Joey Aiuppa, the underboss of the Chicago Syndicate. Edward Hanley was elected president of [HEREIU] in 1973 because of the power and influence of Aiuppa and the Chicago mob. This is not to say that none of the locals are hoodlum controlled or that Hanley is the first corrupt president of the union. Nevertheless, Ed Hanley represents the classic example of an organized crime takeover of a major union.[12]

FBI officials told the Senate Permanent Subcommittee that HEREIU was forcing its locals to put their pension and benefit plans under the international's control to facilitate their exploitation. President Hanley reportedly said that he was "going to be able to loan out that money [pension and welfare funds] just like the Teamsters do."[13] HEREIU officials called to testify before the Senate Permanent Subcommittee repeatedly refused to answer questions. When Senator William Roth (R.-Del.) asked HEREIU Local 54 President Frank Gerace (an alleged associate of the Philadelphia Bruno/Scarfo crime family) whether he subscribed to the 1950s AFL-CIO Ethical Practices Committee's prohibition on labor officials taking the Fifth Amendment to avoid congressional scrutiny, Gerace refused to answer on Fifth Amendment grounds. The hearings also established that HEREIU officials had raised bail for Nicodemo Scarfo, boss of Philadelphia's Cosa Nostra crime family. The subcommittee's final report concluded that "many of the officers of HEREIU have consistently accorded a higher priority to their own personal and financial interests than to the interests of the rank and file membership."[14]

PCOC branded HEREIU corrupt to the core. It charged that HEREIU's president Edward Hanley had been handpicked by Tony Accardo, boss of the Chicago Outfit. Under Hanley's regime, mob figures obtained union loans and jobs and feasted on the union's assets. When the subcommittee called Hanley to testify about HEREIU's ties to organized crime, he invoked his Fifth Amendment right against compelled self-incrimination.[15]

Due to HEREIU's centralized organization, Cosa Nostra's control over Hanley provided significant influence over numerous HEREIU locals. For example, since 1978, Local 54 in Atlantic City had been dominated by different factions of Philadelphia's Bruno/Scarfo crime family. Several of Local 54's officers had criminal records for murder, arson, extortion, drugs, bribes, kickbacks, and racketeering. (The struggle for control of Local 54 led to the 1980 murder of John McCullough, president of Philadelphia Roofers Union Local 30. He was shot to death at his home allegedly for competing with HEREIU Local 54 to organize Atlantic City security guards.)[16] Local 54's dental and welfare funds were controlled by organized crime. The local also corrupted businesses and the local government in Atlantic City.

In 1982, the New Jersey Casino Control Commission prohibited Local 54 from collecting dues from casino employees because the influence of organized crime made the local unfit to represent the casino workers' interests. Ultimately, the U.S. Supreme Court upheld that decision, observing that "[t]he advent of casino gambling in New Jersey was heralded with great expectations for the economic revitalization of the Atlantic City region, but with equally great fears for the potential for the infiltration by organized crime. . . . Congress has indicated both that employees do not have an unqualified right to choose their union officials and that certain state disqualification requirements are compatible with [the National Labor Relations Act]."[17]

The PCOC found that HEREIU Locals 6 and 100 (New York City) had been chartered and governed for the convenience of the Colombo and Gambino crime families. What appeared to some observers as a jurisdictional dispute between these two unions, in fact represented the Colombo and Gambino crime families' conflict over the division of New York's restaurant workers into locals controlled by the two crime families. In an intercepted conversation, Paul Castellano, boss of the Gambino crime family, explained that the Chicago Outfit "own[ed] the international," and that the Colombo crime family controlled the other local.[18]

LABORERS' INTERNATIONAL UNION OF NORTH AMERICA (LIUNA)

The PCOC found that organized crime had a documented relationship with at least twenty-six Laborers' International Union locals, three district councils, and the international union. The mob defrauded the union's benefits funds, extracted no-show jobs from LIUNA employers, drew reimbursements for fictitious business expenses, and operated construction industry cartels in New York City and Chicago (and probably other cities as well). The commission complained that the federal government had never seriously attempted to attack this labor racketeering.[19]

According to the PCOC, "[O]rganized crime exerts its influence [in LIUNA] principally through top officers who are associates of organized crime."[20] Angelo Fosco, LIUNA's general president from 1968 to 1975 (whose father, Peter Fosco, was an Al Capone associate and Angelo's predecessor as general president) was closely associated with the Chicago Outfit. The PCOC charged that Fosco provided jobs to organized crime members and associates and generally followed organized crime's directions. In 1982, Fosco and Tony Accardo, boss of the Chicago LCN family were tried (and acquitted) for defrauding LIUNA's health and welfare funds.

The PCOC asserted that LCN also controlled LIUNA Vice-President John Serpico, an important LIUNA figure in Chicago. "Serpico admitted that he is a friend or personal acquaintance of virtually every important organized crime leader in Chicago."[21] He was also active politically. For example, he received successive gubernatorial appointments to serve as chairman of the Illinois International Port District. According to the PCOC, the Outfit used LIUNA's international officers to gain access to Chicago mayors and Illinois governors.[22]

The PCOC provided numerous examples of how labor racketeers act contrary to the interests of labor unions and members. When the commission questioned Vice-President Serpico about John Fecarotta's duties as a LIUNA business agent and organizer, Serpico could not name a single Fecarotta contribution to Local 8. Fecarotta himself could not remember having done anything for the union; did not know anything about the union's collective bargaining agreements or pension plans; did not know what information was on the union membership cards he supposedly distributed; and did not know the names of management employees or union officers with whom he supposedly worked. Clearly, Fecarotta was a "ghost employee" whose union position was a cover for his criminal career.[23]

Organized crime controlled LIUNA's Chicago Locals 1, 5, and 8. Local 1's president, Vincent Solano, territorial boss for the Outfit's north-side operations, used union headquarters as a "contact point for his criminal organization."[24] Local 5's president was also a high-ranking Cosa Nostra figure. The PCOC called Local 8, Serpico's home local, "ground zero for an organized crime-led LIUNA benefit plan scam."[25]

Organized crime members and their associates siphoned money from LIUNA's Central States Joint Health Board and Welfare Trust Fund. The dental plan was egregiously corrupt; 68 percent of its budget went to "administrative costs" rather than to services. LIUNA's treasury paid lawyers' fees on behalf of officials charged with looting the union as well as fees to private investigators for monitoring the federal government's investigation of LIUNA.[26]

According to the PCOC, the structure of LIUNA's governance facilitated organized crime's control. It was nearly impossible for an opposition candidate to be elected to a union office because LIUNA's executive board members were elected on a nationwide basis; no dissident could mount a nationwide campaign to defeat candidates put forward by the incumbent regime. When union offices became vacant, the mob-dominated executive board appointed replacements.

The PCOC found that Cosa Nostra used threats and intimidation to deter members from running for office against the ruling clique's candidates. It alleged that General President Angelo Fosco personally threatened to kill a potential challenger. In an intercepted conversation, LIUNA's international secretary-treasurer (and later its president), Arthur E. Coia, told a colleague that LIUNA would always be controlled by the "Italians."[27] At the 1981 LIUNA convention, a candidate who tried to speak in opposition to the ruling clique was assaulted on the spot. The PCOC pessimistically concluded that there was "little chance that the LIUNA membership will be able to eliminate organized crime's influence or control over their union as long as the governance structure remains intact. The commission believes that federal law enforcement agencies should give high priority to investigations of LIUNA and its locals."[28]

THE INTERNATIONAL LONGSHOREMEN'S ASSOCIATION

Drawing on FBI investigations, prosecutions, and legislative hearings, the PCOC called the International Longshoremen's Association "virtually a synonym for organized crime in the labor movement."[29] Ships entering harbors, day or night, need to be unloaded and reloaded quickly. Delay is expensive, even ruinous. Thus, the longshoremen have enormous leverage over shippers, who are extorted for labor peace payoffs. (The containerization of seaborne cargo since the late 1950s undermined this leverage.) Labor racketeers also enlisted port employees to facilitate cargo theft, solicited illegal labor payoffs, and extorted stevedores (companies that load and unload seaborne cargo). "Throughout its history, the international has done little, if anything, to disturb La Cosa Nostra influence in its locals."[30]

Cosa Nostra became the primary power on the New York harbor waterfront in 1937, when Anthony Anastasio (a.k.a. Anastasia) took control of the six New York harbor locals. (His brother, Albert Anastasia, was head of the infamous Murder Incorporated gang and boss of the crime group that later came to be known as the Gambino crime family.) "Under Anastasio, organized pilferage, strike insurance, kickbacks, and loansharking on the piers reached unprecedented levels."[31]

Anastasio delegated control of the New York City locals to various organized crime members and associates.

The 1953 New York State Crime Commission report on labor racketeering in New York City's harbor led to the creation of the New York–New Jersey Waterfront Commission. In a case involving the commission, the U.S. Supreme Court observed:

> For years the New York waterfront presented a notoriously serious situation. [The New York Crime Commission] reported that the skulduggeries on the waterfront were largely due to the domination . . . of the International Longshoremen's Association. . . . Its employment practices easily led to corruption, and many of its officials particpated in dishonesties. The presence on the waterfront of convicted felons in many influential positions was an important causative factor in this appalling situation.[32]

Despite the Waterfront Commission's efforts, the situation did not improve. The PCOC charged that Cosa Nostra completely controlled Thomas (Teddy) Gleason, the ILA's president from 1963 to 1986.[33] In the New York–New Jersey port, the Gambino crime family controlled the ILA international union.[*] The Gambinos controlled the New York side and the Genoveses controlled the New Jersey side. After Anastasio died in 1963, control of ILA Local 1814 passed to Anthony Scotto, a son-in-law who, until he was sent to prison in 1979, flourished in the union and as a capo in the Gambino crime family. Scotto was also influential in New York City politics, where he was a major fund-raiser for Democratic Party candidates.

In 1975, the FBI launched UNIRAC, an investigation of ILA racketeering in the ports of New York City, Miami, Wilmington, Charleston, and Mobile. Using undercover agents and electronic intercepts, the FBI uncovered extensive labor racketeering up and down the East Coast and on the Gulf Coast. Ultimately, UNIRAC led to the conviction of more than one hundred persons, including twenty ILA leaders, among them Anthony Scotto and Michael Clemente, both of whom held positions in the ILA and Cosa Nostra. In 1979, Scotto was convicted of taking more than $200,000 in payoffs from employers. New York's Gover-

---

[*] The PCOC report stated that the Genovese crime family controlled the Manhattan locals and the union's international. This is likely an error. The Gambino family was known to control these locals and the international.

nor Hugh Carey and two former New York City mayors, John Lindsay and Robert Wagner, testified on his behalf at the sentencing hearing. (Scotto raised $1 million for Carey's 1974 campaign and $50,000 for Mario Cuomo.) When Scotto was sent to prison, Anthony "Sonny" Ciccone succeeded him as Gambino capo and ILA vice-president.[34] The transition was seamless.

The PCOC complained that while UNIRAC was "a very successful operation demonstrating law enforcement skill and tenacity," subsequently there had been only sporadic investigations and prosecutions, leaving organized crime's influence intact all along the eastern seaboard. In February 1981, the Senate Permanent Subcommittee on Investigations held hearings on waterfront corruption. Its report stated:

> Witnesses testified that payoffs were a part of virtually every aspect of the commercial life of a port. Payoffs insured the award of work contracts and continued contracts already awarded. Payoffs were made to insure labor peace and allow management to avoid future strikes. Payoffs were made to control a racket in workmen's compensation claims. Payoffs were made to expand business activity into new ports and to enable companies to circumvent ILA work requirements.
>
> Organized crime exerted significant influence over the ILA and many shipping companies. Some companies learned how to prosper in the corrupt waterfront environment. They treat payoffs to LCN as a cost of doing business.
>
> The free enterprise system has been thrown off balance. Contracts were not awarded on the basis of merit. The low bid did not beat the competition. Profitability was not based on efficiency and hard work but rather on bribery, extortion and underworld connections. The combination of these corrupt practices was a recipe for inflationary costs and economic decline. Much of the corruption on the waterfront stemmed from organized crime's control over the ILA, a condition that has existed for at least 30 years.[35]

Pointing to the 1984 Senate Permanent Subcommittee on Investigations' findings, the PCOC concluded that, despite its successes, UNIRAC had not purged organized crime from the ports. "Corrupt practices . . . already have begun to return to the Atlantic and Gulf Coast docks. What is needed, then, is continued scrutiny of the maritime industry by government agencies."[36]

INDEPENDENTS AND OTHER UNIONS

Independent unions are labor organizations that are not affiliated with a national/international union or with the AFL-CIO. Therefore, they are free to "raid" AFL-CIO member unions. The McClellan Committee found that independent unions were particularly susceptible to organized crime's influence because their unaffiliated status made them especially difficult to monitor and police. The PCOC reached a similar conclusion: "Because such unions are not part of a larger organization that might provide supervision, labor racketeers are free to create and strategically maneuver them with complete freedom."[37] The PCOC cited Daniel Cunningham's control of the Allied Union of Security Guards and Special Police (Allied) as an example of how an independent union can become a "wholly-owned subsidiary of organized crime."[38]

Allied was founded in the 1960s by well-known racketeer Benjamin Ross and Genovese crime family soldier Joseph Agone.[39] After Ross's imprisonment, Allied presidents maintained the union's close ties to the Genovese family. In 1974, Cunningham literally purchased his position as head of Allied, using $90,000 to buy out the incumbent president's term. The Genovese crime family supported him and there was no rank-and-file vote. In return, he placed the union's pension and welfare funds at organized crime's disposal.

Cunningham ignored the union's constitution and federal labor law. No elections were held during his tenure. He appointed his cronies to top positions and increased his salary threefold. His methods for exploiting the benefit funds included reimbursing his associates for fake expenses, taking kickbacks from no-show employees and from employers and benefit providers, and making payouts to fictitious employees and service providers. In 1983, Cunningham was convicted of racketeering, bribery, embezzlement, and obstruction of justice. The PCOC concluded that the unskilled and unsophisticated workers who belong to independent unions face an especially high risk of exploitation by racketeers, exacerbated by the government's failure to investigate independent unions.

The PCOC devoted significant attention to racketeering within the New York City meat, fish, and poultry industry. Organized crime families controlled local unions affiliated with the Amalgamated Meat Cutters and Butcher Workmen of North America. They used that control to set themselves up in wholesale and retail businesses where they some-times profited from selling fraudulently dated or tainted meat. They also bribed government inspectors to falsely grade their meat products.

While the Bonanno and Lucchese families were also involved in the meat industry, the PCOC chose to focus on the Gambino family. Paul Castellano owned Dial Poultry, which distributed chickens throughout the New York City metropolitan area. His brother, Peter Castellano, op-erated Quarex, an even wider distributor.[40] Both of these businesses demonstrated how LCN can exploit its union power to achieve a com-petitive advantage for its own companies.

PCOC CRITICISMS OF THE GOVERNMENT AND THE AFL-CIO

The PCOC strongly criticized law enforcement's efforts to combat labor racketeering. It pessimistically noted that "the government's efforts to remove organized crime's influence over unions and legitimate busi-ness have been largely ineffective. This situation does not stem simply from too few laws or unavailable remedies. It arises from a lack of po-litical will, a lack of fixed responsibility, and a lack of a national plan of attack."[41] The PCOC concluded with a long list of recommendations.

The PCOC criticized the DOL for failing to embrace law enforce-ment goals, being susceptible to political interference, and failing to effectively enforce the Employee Retirement Income Security Act. It criticized the DOJ for failing to utilize civil RICO against labor racket-eering. In contrast, it praised some states (for example, Florida and Ari-zona) for aggressively using their own racketeering statutes. Finally, the PCOC criticized the National Labor Relations Board for not having a strategy to deal with corrupt institutions; the IRS for not giving signifi-cant priority to analyzing and investigating suspicious deductions and claimed expenses, and the AFL-CIO for abdicating responsibility.

THE PCOC'S RECOMMENDATIONS

The PCOC divided its recommendations into five parts: general na-tional strategy; protection of workers' rights; the private sector; admin-istration of justice; and state and local government.

General National Strategy

- A greater political will to attack labor racketeering, a national plan of attack, and an understanding of the need to confront entire organized cartels rather than individual criminals.
- An end to piecemeal division of resources and accountability.
- Task Forces able to carry out industry-by-industry campaigns.
- DOJ must take a more aggressive stance towards organized crime's labor racketeering.
- The DOL must play an active role in combating racketeering. It must consolidate enforcement and oversight of employee benefit plans and labor unions.

Protect Workers' Rights

- Labor Management Relations Act should be amended to make it an unfair labor practice for a union to be controlled by or to assist organized crime. The NLRB should view racketeering activity within the framework of violations which it recognizes. Because the NLRB lacks the resources for investigations, DOJ should provide investigative assistance.
- Congress should pass a statute specifically making illegal the sale of a union, union office or union members' right to work.
- Congress should give the Secretary of Labor power to act on behalf of union members when officers breach fiduciary obligations.
- Congress should make false reporting of union activities a felony.
- Congress should amend the Hobbs Act to prohibit violence regardless of whether a "legitimate union activity or objective" can be claimed.
- The DOL should computerize and more widely disperse its data.
- The Secretary of Labor should develop guidelines on unions' excessive administrative expenses.
- The Landrum-Griffin Act should be amended to permit the DOL to set aside union elections that clearly violate basic legal conduct (violence, destruction of ballots, etc.) regardless of whether (as current law requires) it can reach a finding that the violation would have changed the election's outcome.
- The IRS should reform its enforcement policies to confront labor racketeering. The IRS should step in to actively disallow excessive salaries agreed to in collective bargaining agreements for employees assigned to union business. Employee benefit reports should be processed more quickly to eliminate unreasonable delays and backlogs.

The Private Sector

- The labor movement needs to confront organized crime's influence in business and labor.
- The AFL-CIO needs to apply its code of ethical practices.
- The AFL-CIO should require that member unions file annual reports describing their measures to uphold and enforce the ethical practices codes. Reports should list all convictions and indictments of union officers and employees, fund trustees, consultants and service providers.
- AFL-CIO Ethical Practices Committee should become active and meet regularly.
- Unions not affiliated with the AFL-CIO should establish similar codes.
- Corporations should create and enforce codes of conduct that preclude doing business with organized crime.

Administration of Justice

- Tougher sentences for convicted labor racketeers.

State and Local Government

- State and local government should cooperate to protect the waterfront from labor racketeering.
- Local and state governments should not award government contracts to suspicious businesses. This is a low cost method for keeping organized crime out of the market place.

REACTION TO *THE EDGE*

The PCOC's book-length report, *The Edge,* was well received by the media, earning praise for having shone a light on organized crime, corrupted unions, and tainted businesses. The *New York Times* said:

> The report is not a how-to-do it manual. Its aim is to lift the consciousness of our citizens about what is going on around them, stealthily and adversely affecting their lives and fortunes. In the collision between society and organized crime, sunlight and the exposure that it generates are potent weapons. The Commission organized its affairs to generate as much light as possible with the resources put at its disposal.[42]

The AFL-CIO strongly criticized *The Edge*, especially its recommendation that the AFL-CIO take a more active role in ridding its affiliated unions of organized crime's influence. President Lane Kirkland stated, "If the labor movement is afflicted by racketeers, that points to a grievous failure by law enforcement authorities. . . . Corruption and criminality are attributes of individuals, not organizations." Kirkland denounced the commission's recommendations as "an Orwellian collection of proposals and in my view, a virtual blueprint for a police state."[43]

CONCLUSION

This chapter and Chapter 4 provide perspectives on the magnitude of the labor racketeering problem. I believe that a fair reading of the record would persuade an open-minded reader that the problem is significant. Over the course of the twentieth century, organized crime infiltrated and exercised influence, even control, over the nation's largest private-sector labor union and several other major unions. In addition, organized crime exerted control over hundreds of union locals. For example, approximately eighty Teamster locals (out of seven hundred) have had documented or alleged connection to organized crime.[*] Of course, in the great majority of Teamster locals, there was no organized crime presence. However, because of organized crime's influence over the IBT at the national/international level, over its largest pension and welfare fund, and over a significant number of its locals, labor racketeering almost certainly touched the lives of practically all Teamsters. In recent decades, the Teamsters have constituted roughly 9 percent of all U.S. union members.[**] If one were to add the percentage of union members in LIUNA, HEREIU, and ILA, it would be reasonable to conclude that at least as of the mid-1980s, racketeering was a substantial presence and problem in the U.S. labor movement.

[*] This figure was published by Project RISE, an internal Teamsters anticorruption program headed by Edwin Stier. See Stier, Anderson and Malone, LLC, *The Teamsters: Perception and Reality: An Investigative Study of Organized Crime Influence in the Union*, International Brotherhood of Teamsters, 2002.

[**] According to "Teamsters Online," the current IBT membership is 1.4 million members. According to the U.S. Department of Labor, there were 15.8 million union members in the United States in 2003.

4
Labor Racketeering in New York City

New York City is the home base of a large corps of sophisticated and ruthless racketeers who not only engage in traditional organized criminal activity (including loansharking, gambling, narcotics, and redistribution of stolen goods), but who also play a major role in numerous legitimate industries, including private sanitation, garment, cargo freight, and construction.

> —New York State Organized Crime Task Force (OCTF),
> *Corruption and Racketeering in the New York City*
> *Construction Industry: Final Report to Governor*
> *Mario M. Cuomo* (1990), 77

In the building trades, the key to nonunion labor was Cosa Nostra control of union shop stewards, many of whom were made members or sons or relatives of members. On average, a subcontractor using union labor might expect a profit margin of 15 percent. With nonunion workers, even with payoffs, the profit was 30 percent or more. If all else failed, there remained the Gambinos' control of IBT Local 282, so absolute that if all of the other New York families needed Teamster assistance, they had to share the proceeds with [Gambino boss] Paul Castellano. —Salvatore (Sammy) Gravano in Peter Maas,
> *Underboss* (1997), 116–17

This chapter, like Chapter 3, deals with the extent of labor racketeering. Here we focus just on New York City since approximately 1980. This is not an exposé. It does not draw on any confidential information. I am identifying only unions with publicly documented histories of organized crime influence. Almost certainly, there is unrevealed LCN influence in other New York City unions.

The labor racketeering problem in New York City is not qualitatively different than the problems in other U.S. cities with strong union traditions. It is likely that there was more labor racketeering in New York City circa 1980 than in any other U.S. city if only because New York City has the most unions (approximately 350 locals), the most union members, the most organized crime families (five), and the most organized crime members and associates. Since the mid-twentieth century, New York City has been home to the Genovese, Gambino, Lucchese, Bonanno, and Colombo Cosa Nostra crime families: Each of the five families has been heavily involved in labor racketeering.[1] In some cases, two or more families have exerted influence in a particular union. Although New York City is not typical, it is certainly not unique. Chicago's history of labor racketeering rivals New York's, and there is a documented record of labor racketeering for many other cities, including Atlantic City, Boston, Buffalo, Cleveland, Detroit, Kansas City, Miami, Philadelphia, Pittsburgh, and St. Louis.

In creating a snapshot of labor racketeering in New York City, I draw extensively on my 1990 collaboration with the New York State Organized Crime Task Force (OCTF), the *Final Report on Corruption and Racketeering in the NYC Construction Industry*, and on my 1999 study, *Gotham Unbound: How New York City Was Liberated from the Grip of Organized Crime.* The OCTF report documented and analyzed organized crime's penetration of the city's construction unions. *Gotham Unbound* illuminated Cosa Nostra's role in the political economy of the city, focusing on six commercial venues: the Garment District; the Fulton Fish Market; the Jacob Javits Convention Center; cargo operations at JFK Airport; the commercial-waste-hauling industry, and the construction industry. This chapter provides a picture of labor racketeering in those industries and several others. Because many unions are mentioned, the following preview may be useful:

The Garment District

- International Ladies Garment Workers Union (ILGWU) Local 102

Fulton Fish Market

- United Seafood Workers, Smoked Fish and Cannery Union Local 359

Air Cargo at JFK Airport

- International Brotherhood of Teamsters (IBT) Local 295
- IBT Local 851

Javits Convention Center

- IBT Local 807
- NYC District Council, International Brotherhood of Carpenters and Joiners (Carpenters)
- International Alliance of Theatrical and Stage Employees, Exhibition Employees Local 829

Waste-Hauling Industry

- IBT Local 813

Construction Industry

- IBT Joint Council 16
- IBT Local 282
- IBT Local 580
- Laborers (LIUNA) Blasters and Drill Runners Local 29
- LIUNA Cement and Concrete Workers Local 6A
- LIUNA Workers Local 20
- LIUNA Local 18A
- LIUNA Local 95
- LIUNA Local 66
- LIUNA Local 13
- LIUNA Local 23
- LIUNA Local 46
- LIUNA Local 59
- NYC District Council of Carpenters
- Carpenters Local 17
- Carpenters Local 608
- International Union of Operating Engineers (IUOE), Local 14
- IUOE, Local 15
- IUOE, Waterproofers Local 66
- Painters Union, District Council 9
- Plasterers Local 530
- Plumbers Union, Steamfitters Local 638

Seaborne Cargo in the Port of New York

- International Longshoremen's Association (ILA) Local 1814
- ILA Locals 824, 1809, and 1909 (collectively known as the West Side [of Manhattan] Locals)

- ILA Local 1804
- ILA Local 1588
- ILA Local 1

Other Industries

- Amalgamated Meat Cutters' Union Local 174
- Newspaper and Mail Deliverers Union of New York and Vicinity

THE GARMENT DISTRICT

Throughout most of the twentieth century, organized crime has been a major presence in the New York City Garment District (Manhattan, Seventh Avenue and mid 30s). In 1977, the garment industry's leading trade magazine, *Women's Wear Daily,* called ILGWU Local 102, which represented truck drivers carrying material and finished garments to and from the Garment District, "an active tool of labor racketeers." Sol C. Chaikin, the president of the ILGWU international union in the 1970s, admitted that "we have never been able to control [Local] 102."[2]

The Gambino crime family leveraged control over Local 102 to establish and police an employers' association, the Master Truckmen of America (MTA), which operated a cartel among truckers doing business in the Garment District. In effect, the cartel, backed by the union's power to shut down employers, determined which truckers could do business. Cosa Nostra enforced "marriages" between manufacturers and truckers; each garment maker was bound to a particular trucking company and, whether or not satisfied with the price it paid for the service it received, it could not switch. No other trucker would handle its business. Even if the manufacturer chose to do its own trucking, it still had to pay its assigned trucker as if that trucker had done the work. Failure to comply would invite labor problems.

If a trucker refused to join the association or to follow its rules, the MTA would order a Local 102 job action—for example, drivers would sit down on the job or otherwise stop or subvert the "rebel" trucking firm's operations. If that was insufficient to bring the maverick into line, its vehicles would be vandalized or stolen. Cartel members also blocked curbs or entire streets to prevent a rebel trucker from making pickups and deliveries.

An incident in the mid-1970s provides an example of how Local 102 enforced the employers' cartel. As soon as a government undercover agent running a sting operation purchased a trucking company, MTA President Frank Wolf (of the employer association) threatened a Local 102 strike (by the union) unless the new owner paid 10 percent of the purchase price to the MTA (the employers' association).

The mob's control over Local 102 ensured that Cosa Nostra's (mostly the Gambino crime family's) trucking companies enjoyed labor peace. It also gave them an opportunity to make even more profit by not enforcing the collective bargaining agreement. For example, Thomas Gambino operated his trucking firm as a "double-breasted" shop, employing both unionized and low-wage nonunionized drivers. There was, of course, no objection from the union.*

FULTON FISH MARKET

The Fulton Fish Market, the largest wholesale fish market in the United States, became a Cosa Nostra power base and profit center since the early twentieth century. The Genovese crime family's influence in the fish market was rooted in its control of the United Seafood Workers, Smoked Fish and Cannery Union.** As federal prosecutors noted in a 1981 sentencing proceeding involving several convicted officers of Local 359, "[I]n the wholesale [fish] industry, where competition is fierce and time is of the essence, it is crucial for businesses to maintain the good will of the union and the men who run it. Organized crime recognizes this power and knows how to use it."[3] The union had 850 to 900 members, including wholesalers, managers, supervisors, and the four hundred "journeymen" who set up the wholesalers' seafood

---

* Thomas Gambino agreed to withdraw from the Garment District and pay a $12 million fine as part of a 1993 plea bargain with the Manhattan DA's office. He was also convicted in 1993 on unrelated racketeering charges in Connecticut.

** "[Joseph 'Socks'] Lanza organized a local of the Seafood Workers Union in 1922. From that power base he turned the market into his own fiefdom, controlling every aspect of the trade, essentially by himself. . . . Under Lanza's regime the fishing boat crews were not allowed to unload their own catches. They sat by while Lanza's men took off the fish, for a fee. Lanza also charged each boat another ten dollars 'for the union's benevolent fund.' If a skipper balked at the surcharge, a five-hundred-pound bucket of fish might be accidentally dumped into the harbor." (Fox, *Blood and Power*, 176.)

displays, negotiated the sales, and delivered the fish to the retail purchasers' vans parked nearby.

Carmine Romano, a Genovese crime family associate, served as Local 359's secretary-treasurer (the union's de facto top position) from 1974 to 1980. In 1980, when Carmine became a trustee of the union's pension and welfare funds, his brother Peter succeeded him as the local's secretary-treasurer. Both brothers were later convicted of RICO, conspiracy to violate RICO, aiding and abetting violations of the Taft-Hartley Act, misusing union pension funds, and extortion of union members and employers.[4]

Local 359 officers coerced wholesalers into paying for various "services" that they did not desire or need, such as cardboard signs advertising their employment of union labor. The Romanos received more than $66,000 ($200,000 in 2003 dollars) from this scam. Throughout the 1970s, union officials collected "Christmas gifts" of $300 (the equivalent of $900 in 2003 dollars) from wholesalers. The money was solicited as a holiday gift "for the boys in the union," but the money went to the Genovese crime family's coffers rather than to rank-and-file members.

Wholesalers paid $1,300 ($4,380 in 2003 dollars) a week to Carmine Romano's Fulton Patrol Association to protect their fish from being stolen. Whether this was a protection service or a protection racket was unclear even to those who paid the premiums. Federal prosecutors charged that the Fulton Patrol Association functioned as a protection racket and collected more than $644,000 (the equivalent of $2,000,000 in 2003 dollars) from wholesalers from 1975 to 1979. At the Romanos' trial on RICO charges, the president of the employers' Wholesale Fish Dealers Association testified that "if the thieves knew that the union was looking out for us . . . they wouldn't bother us . . . [b]ecause the thieves would be afraid of the union."[5] Following the Romanos' convictions, the United Seafood Workers, Smoked Fish and Cannery International Union placed Local 359 under trusteeship and ousted Carmine and Peter Romano from their union positions. Their brother Vincent then became a top official in the union.[6]

AIR CARGO AT JFK AIRPORT

Cosa Nostra's influence in the airfreight industry is well documented. For several decades, the Lucchese crime family controlled IBT Local 295 and IBT Local 851, which represented the drivers who brought cargo to and from JFK airport. Once again, control over labor was parlayed into an employers' association, the Metropolitan Import Truckmen's Association (MITA), which operated a cartel.

IBT Local 295 was one of the paper locals that IBT General President David Beck and Vice-President Jimmy Hoffa gave to Johnny Dioguardi in 1956.[7] In 1970, the Lucchese crime family created IBT Local 851.[8] The intent may have been to provide a safe haven for IBT Local 295 officials who were under investigating. Harry Davidoff, a Hoffa protégé, ran Local 851 and Local 295 from the same office. In 1972, his son Mark succeeded him as head of Local 851.[9] In the 1990s, the position passed to Anthony Razza, another Lucchese associate.[*]

Local 851 represented "lead agents" who assign jobs to truck drivers and other airport workers; some lead agents were also associates of the Lucchese crime family. They used advanced information about valuable cargo shipments to arrange give-ups and hijackings. In a give-up, a truck driver leaves the keys in the ignition of his parked truck so it can be stolen according to a prearranged plan. In a hijacking, a Lucchese crew would intercept the truck just outside the airport grounds and wrest it from the driver. Valuables could also be stolen from the warehouse. The most infamous such heist occurred in December 1978; thieves stole nearly $6 million (the equivalent of $17 million in 2003 dollars) worth of cash and securities from the Lufthansa Airlines cargo hangar. It is likely that most of the proceeds went to Lucchese capo Paul Vario.[**][10]

Through its control over the IBT locals, the Lucchese family extorted labor-peace payoffs from freight forwarders by threatening strikes, picketing, work stoppages, slowdowns, and misrouting cargo. When such threats materialize, they can impose heavy costs on freight forwarders, whose business depends upon the speedy delivery of air cargo.

---

[*] In 1993, the U.S. attorney for the Eastern District of New York obtained a criminal RICO indictment against seven individuals, including Anthony Razza, secretary-treasurer of Local 851. The indictment charged them with extortion, labor racketeering, and related offenses. The defendants entered guilty pleas. Razza received a twenty-one-month prison sentence and was barred from the IBT for life. See James B. Jacobs et al. *Gotham Unbound*, 50.

[**] Henry Hill revealed the details of the Lufthansa heist in his autobiographical account of life in the mob (Nicholas Pileggi, *Wiseguy* 1987), which was the basis of the popular 1990 movie *Goodfellas*, starring Robert DeNiro, Joe Pesci, and Roy Liotta.

JAVITS CONVENTION CENTER

From the day the Javits Convention Center opened for business in 1986, the Genovese crime family and, to a lesser extent, the Gambinos and Colombos, used their control over three labor unions that represented Javits Center workers to place members, associates, and friends in high-paying jobs. IBT Local 807 represented workers who loaded and un-loaded the delivery trucks and vans with exhibitors' products and sup-plies. Members of Carpenters NYC District Council assembled the booths and electrical stations and, until July 1995, Exhibition Employ-ees Union Local 829 represented general laborers.

IBT LOCAL 807

Members of IBT Local 807 (Trade Show Division) loaded and unloaded vehicles bringing merchandise into and out of the Exhibition Center. Robert Rabbitt Sr. and his two sons controlled that local. Robert Sr. was convicted of second degree manslaughter in 1985 for fatally stabbing a shop manager. Upon release from prison five years later, he returned to his union position. In 1992, a New York State grand jury indicted him for conspiracy, receiving bribes, larceny, falsifying business records, and possessing stolen property. He pleaded guilty to falsifying payroll records and served one year in prison. In 1994, the Independent Review Board (the court-imposed monitor in the IBT international case) charged Rabbitt with accepting bribes in return for allowing an employer to use nonunion truck drivers and laborers. Rabbitt avoided an IRB sanction by agreeing to a five-year suspension from the union; his son Michael took over his union office.[11] In 1995, the Independent Review Board (IRB) found that Michael had negotiated an agreement with Javits Cen-ter employers that made the job of general foreman a nonunion posi-tion, thereby allowing his father, despite his felony record, to do the same job he did before as a union official. Finding that the Rabbitts gave lucrative center jobs to people connected to organized crime, the IRB recommended that Michael be removed from his position.[12] When he did relinquish it, Michael was guaranteed $236,000 severance pay.

Although the Rabbitts' connection to organized crime has not been proved, there is strong reason to believe that Cosa Nostra called the shots with respect to IBT interests at the Javits Center. Through its hiring hall, Local 807 assigned lucrative Javits Center work from a pool of forty-seven privileged members. One-third of the individuals on that list had documented ties to organized crime; some had not even belonged to the IBT before landing a center job.[13]

CARPENTERS' DISTRICT COUNCIL

In the mid-1980s, the United Brotherhood of Carpenters and Joiners New York City District Council represented approximately thirty thousand workers in twenty-two local unions. (The district council makes major policy decisions for the locals and negotiates the collective bargaining contracts). From the early 1970s, the Genovese crime family controlled the district council through its capo, Vincent DiNapoli.[14] The FBI believed that Teddy Maritas, district council president from 1977 to 1981, was a Genovese crime family associate.[15] In the early 1980s, a RICO prosecution of Maritas, DiNapoli, and others ended in a mistrial. Maritas disappeared the evening before the scheduled retrial, presumably murdered.[16] DiNapoli pled guilty.

The Carpenter's International Union placed the New York City district council under a temporary trusteeship, but that did not purge the union of organized crime's influence. The trustee chose Local 608 president Paschal McGuiness, a Genovese crime family associate,[17] to be district council president.[18] McGuinness put John O'Connor in charge of the district council's daily operations. The Department of Justice charged O'Connor with 127 counts of racketeering, including bribery, extortion, and taking unlawful gifts from contractors.[19] In 1990, he pleaded guilty to five counts and was sentenced to one to three years incarceration and fined $25,000.[20] McGuinness also hired and quickly promoted Ralph Coppola to district council representative at the Javits Center; the Genovese crime family is alleged to have inducted him as a "made member" and soon promoted him to capo.[21]

The racketeers who controlled the Carpenters' district council assigned LCN members, relatives, and friends to jobs with "decorator" companies. (Show managers hire decorating companies to prepare the center for exhibits; the companies employ workers, who are Carpenters' members, to assemble and dismantle the exhibitions.) The Carpenters' job-referral rules dictated that, with limited exceptions, jobs must be assigned to members according to length of time out of work, but the Genovese crime family's interests trumped the rules. Typically, a Genovese family associate gave union officials a preferential hiring list, from which the union officials chose thirty to forty people to work with the decorator companies. Many of these preferred workers had links to the Genovese family. Some were awarded Javits Center jobs as a reward for loyalty and service to the crime family. Others needed legitimate employment as a cover for their criminal careers and to satisfy probation and parole authorities. Employers and employees treated some of these positions as "no-show jobs."

EXPOS LOCAL 829

Workers who set up trade shows at the Javits Center were represented by the Exhibition Employees Union (Expos) Local 829. The Expos chief shop steward, much like the Teamsters general foreman, supervised Expos members and enforced their collective bargaining agreements. Steven Dellacava and Paul Coscia, reputedly associates of the Genovese crime family, were the Expos' chief shop stewards at the Javits Center until mid-1995. (Coscia also served as the vice-president of Local 829.) They determined who could work, where and when.

Although Local 829 apparently did not maintain a pool list for preferential hiring at the Javits Center, it did use selective criteria. Undercover police investigations revealed that to obtain a lucrative center job—up to $100,000 annual salary—an ordinary Expos worker had to buy a membership book.* Individuals with organized crime connections purchased books at lower cost and enjoyed priority in obtaining center assignments.

Expos union officials generated revenue for the Genovese family by other illegal schemes. They padded employers' payrolls with six ghost employees for small shows and up to twenty ghosts for larger shows. Ghost employees shared their "salaries" with shop stewards and the Genovese crime family. Another money-making scheme was the filing of fraudulent workers' compensation claims against the center; injuries sustained outside of work were alleged to have been sustained at the center.[22]

---

* It is not uncommon or illegal for unions to charge new members a fee when they join the union. This "pays back" the union and current members for previous expenditures from which the new members benefit.

WASTE-HAULING INDUSTRY

Circa 1980, commercial-waste hauling in New York City's five boroughs was carried out by approximately three hundred small firms (one to twenty trucks) that together constituted a $1.5 billion-per-year industry. The carting companies were members of borough-based trade associations. LCN controlled both the union and the trade associations. The Association of Trade Waste Removers of Greater New York dominated the industry. For more than thirty years, James Failla, a capo in the Gambino crime family, was its president. The other Cosa Nostra–linked waste-hauler trade associations were the Kings County Trade Waste Association (Genovese), the Greater New York Waste Paper Association (Genovese), and the Queens County Trade Waste Association (Gambino).[23]

Approximately four thousand carting industry truck drivers were members of IBT Local 813, run by Bernard Adelstein. His reign over the union began in 1951 when Carlo Gambino, who later became boss of the Gambino crime family, placed him in Local 813.[24] The McClellan Committee focused on the ties between Adelstein and Vincent Squillante, a high-ranking official of the New York City Cartmen's Association and a prominent organized crime figure. It branded Adelstein the "abject tool" of organized crime. According to the committee, "[F]ar from fighting Squillante . . . [Adelstein] provided vital cooperation as [Squillante] moved . . . to ruthless czardom of the garbage industry."[25]

The situation did not change in later decades. In 1989, Salvatore (Sammy) Gravano, the Gambino crime family underboss who became the most famous and productive government cooperating witness of all time, testified that Adelstein took orders from Gambino capo James Failla; Failla exercised de facto control over IBT Local 813 while simultaneously serving as president of the employers' association. A former IBT Local 813 employee testified that Adelstein and Failla worked together in "controlling and manipulating the [waste hauling] industry in the New York City metropolitan area."[26]

Rick Cowan, an undercover police officer, spent several years implementing a sting operation by posing as a carting company executive. In *Takedown: The Fall of the Last Mafia Empire,* he and Douglas Century provide a fascinating picture of the connection among the carting companies, IBT Local 813, and the mob.[27] In one instance, Failla prevented an IBT Local 813 strike by calling a meeting of waste haulers (employers, *not* union members) and ordering them to "keep the trucks rolling."[28] According to Cowan and Century, "[E]ven though this was a meeting of management, a lot of the company owners in attendance also belonged to IBT Local 813. So if they went on strike, they'd only be striking against themselves."[*29]

Under the Gambino, Genovese, and Lucchese crime families' influence, the commercial-waste-hauling firms operated a "property-rights" system that bound every commercial customer to one carter. No other carter was allowed to solicit or accept a customer's business. IBT Local 813, under Adelstein's control, served as the cartel's enforcement arm. Local 813 drivers would refuse to work for a company that had fallen out of favor with Cosa Nostra; likewise, if a carter tried to hire nonunion drivers it would be struck and/or sabotaged. In 1989, Robert Kubecka, a "rebel" waste hauler on Long Island, had his trucks' tires slashed and windshields broken. A Gambino crime family associate offered to solve his union problems for a $20,000 payoff. (Kubecka was murdered later that year for cooperating with a law enforcement investigation.) Jerry Kubecka, Robert's father, and himself the owner of a rebel carting company, charged that IBT Local 813 threatened his customers with labor problems and violence unless they submitted to being serviced by their assigned waste hauler.[30]

CONSTRUCTION

Approximately one hundred building trades unions represent New York City construction workers.[31] The mob's influence and control over many of these unions provides a constant stream of bribes in exchange for labor peace and/or relief from labor contract provisions. Once Cosa Nostra established a power base in the construction unions, it was a small step to organizing and policing employer cartels in the construction niches corresponding to each union's jurisdiction. For example, control over the union local whose members pour ready-mix concrete led to the establishment of a mob-controlled cartel in that crucial con-

* Frank Giovinco, nephew of Genovese associate Joe Giovinco, controlled LIUNA Local 958. Carting companies, whose employees were Local 958 members, made cash payments to the boss of the Genovese crime family, Vincent "Chin" Gigante, in exchange for labor peace. (Cowan and Century, *Takedown: The Fall of the Last Mafia Empire*, 94–95, 247–48.)

struction niche. There were also well-established cartels among drywall, window-replacement, and painting contractors.

Labor peace extortion was commonplace. For example, Attilio Bitondo and Gene Hanley, business agents for Carpenters Local 257, were indicted in 1987 on multiple counts of extortion over a ten-year period.[32] Among other things, they threatened to sabotage contractors by assigning them only unqualified and incompetent workers.[33] In the 1970s, Carpenters Union officials received payoffs to permit two carpentry firms to hire nonunion workers, who were paid by the number of drywall sheets installed (that is, piecework) rather than by the hour, thereby avoiding paying overtime and fringe benefits.[34] In December 2001, the U.S. Attorney for the Southern District of New York indicted a new generation of Carpenters officials for the same scheme.[35] The defendants included 73 members of the Parrello crew of the Genovese crime family, who were indicted on 98 counts, including extortion, labor racketeering, loan-sharking, illegal gambling operations, selling counterfeit money, and gun trafficking. The indictment charged 9 defendants with labor racketeering involving Locals 11 and 964, which together made up the Suburban New York Regional Council of Carpenters. These defendants were alleged to have arranged for nonunion workers to complete carpentry jobs, which allowed the defendants them to embezzle more than $1 million that should have been paid into the Suburban Council of Carpenter's pension funds.[36]

The construction unions' pension and welfare funds have been persistently defrauded. One common scheme is for contractors to bribe union officials to allow the contractors to employ nonunion workers for whom pension and welfare payments do not have to be made. Union members who complained were blacklisted, threatened, or assaulted. Corrupt pension and welfare trustees could embezzle funds by withdrawing money in their own or in fictitious names, by making "loans" that would not be repaid; by paying for nonexistent goods and services; and by taking kickbacks from contractors and service providers.[37] Dissident union members who challenged the leadership of mob-dominated unions were the most vulnerable; they might be blacklisted or beaten. Uncooperative employers faced sabotage. Because of the presence of so many known organized crime figures, actual violence was rarely necessary. A threat, even implicit, sufficed.

A comprehensive audit of labor racketeering in the huge New York City construction sector is impossible, but the New York State Organized Crime Task Force and subsequent investigators have identified organized crime's influence or control over the following construction unions:[38]

International Brotherhood of Teamsters

- Joint Council 16: Joseph Trerotola, president of the Joint Council, became a vice-president of the International IBT with Cosa Nostra's approval. Patsy Crapanzano, the council's vice-president, was tied to the Genovese crime family. Gerald Corallo, president of Teamster's Local 239 and son of former Lucchese crime family boss Antonio Corallo, was listed as a member of the council's advisory board.
- Local 282: John O'Rourke, president from 1931 to 1965, was closely associated with Lucchese family members Johnny Dioguardi and Anthony Corallo. John Cody, president from 1976 to 1984, was an important Gambino crime family associate.
- Local 580 (Ironworkers Union): Peter Savino, an influential member of the local, was a Genovese crime family associate.[39] In 1984, control of the union passed to Joseph Marion of the Lucchese crime family;[40] Lucchese family associate John Morrissey was also an important figure in the local.[41]

Laborers Union

- Blasters and Drill Runners Local 29: President Louis Sanzo regarded Lucchese family soldier Samuel Cavalieri as his boss. Cavalieri's son was the administrator of the local's pension fund.
- Cement and Concrete Workers Local 6A: Ralph Scopo, president of the District Council, was a soldier in the Colombo crime family. His sons, Joseph and Ralph, were affiliated with both the District Council and Local 6A, Joseph serving as president of Local 6A.
- Cement and Concrete Workers Local 20: Vice-Presidents Luigi Foceri and Frank Bellino were members of the Lucchese crime family.
- Cement and Concrete Workers Local 18A: Genovese family capo Vincent DiNapoli controlled the local.
- Housewreckers Union Local 95: Vincent Gigante, boss of the Genovese crime family, controlled the local.
- Local 66: Vice-President Peter Vario was a member of the Lucchese crime family.
- Mason Tenders Local 13: Mike Copolla, a capo in the Genovese

family, controlled the union. Basil Cervone used his power over the local and the District Council on behalf of Genovese crime family.

- Mason Tenders Local 23: President Louis Giardina was a soldier in the Gambino family.
- Mason Tenders Local 46: Peter A. Vario, nephew of Paul Vario, a Lucchese crime family capo, was business manager of the local.
- Mason Tenders Local 59: Patsy D. Pagano, secretary-treasurer until 1974, was part of the Pagano faction of the Genovese family. Daniel Pagano, who later ran the local as its business manager, was a Genovese family member. His cousin, a Genovese soldier, controlled the union in the 1980s.

United Brotherhood of Carpenters

- District Council: Teddy Maritas, president from 1977 to 1981, had a close relationship with Genovese capo Vincent DiNapoli; the FBI considered Maritas as a Genovese family associate. The next president, Paschal McGuiness, was also a Genovese associate. In 2000, President Michael Forde was indicted for labor bribery. His codefendants included a number of Lucchese family members, including acting boss Steven Crea.[42] Crea pleaded guilty. Forde was convicted in 2004.[43]
- Local 17: In 1987, the Genovese family consigliere awarded Liborio Bellomo control of the local, the largest in the District Council. In 1989, Genovese associate Enrico Ruotolo was elected business manager.
- Local 608: President Paschal McGuinness (who also became president of the District Council) was a Genovese crime family associate. A later president, Michael Forde, and business agent Martin Deveraux were convicted in 2004 for accepting bribes from contractors in a case involving the Lucchese family.[44]

Other Construction Industry Unions

- Builders and Allied Craftsmen, Local 1: President Santo Lanzafame was charged with accepting bribes in exchange for allowing job stewards to file fraudulent union documents to cover up violations orchestrated by Lucchese crime family members.[45] The judge dismissed the indictment on legal-insufficiency grounds and also under the state's Organized Crime Control Act's interest-of-justice provision.

- International Union of Operating Engineers, Locals 14 and 15: Locals 14 and 15 represented workers at major building sites including the Museum of Modern Art and the federal courthouse in Brooklyn.[46] In 2003, alleged Genovese soldier Louis Moscatiello; Colombo capo Vincent Ricciardo; acting Colombo boss Joel Cacace and son Joel Jr.; and alleged Colombo underboss John DeRoss and son Jamie; and dozens of union officials were indicted in both the Southern District of New York and Eastern District of New York for running no-show job schemes at construction sites across New York City. The SDNY case focuses on Genovese control over these locals; the EDNY targets the Colombos. Joel Cacace, the acting boss of the Colombo family, admitted to the murder of Assistant U.S. Attorney Bill Aronwald's father. Several top officials of Locals 14 and 15 pled guilty to racketeering and receiving unlawful labor payments.
- International Union of Operating Engineers, Waterproofers Local 66: John Morrissey, an associate of the Lucchese crime family, collected labor peace payoffs.[47]
- Painters Union, District Council 9: Martin Rarback, secretary-treasurer until 1967, was an associate of, or at least closely associated with, Cosa Nostra. The Lucchese crime family controlled Jimmy Bishop, secretary-treasurer from 1973 to 1990.[48]
- Plasterers Local 530: Genovese Family capo Vincent DiNapoli created the union, which Louis Moscatiello, a Genovese crime family associate, ran as business manager.
- Plumbers Union, Steamfitters Local 638: George Daly, the union's business agent, was an associate of Gambino family boss Paul Castellano and Gambino soldier Thomas Bilotti.

SEABORNE CARGO IN THE PORT OF NEW YORK

Through its power base in the International Longshoremen's Association, Cosa Nostra has been a presence in New York City's waterfront throughout the twentieth century. There is documented mob control of at least six ILA locals.[49] In 1990, the government filed a civil RICO suit against these six unions; their executive boards and officers; the Genovese and Gambino crime families; the Westies, an Irish organized

crime group allied with the Gambino family; and five shipping companies. The Gambino crime family controlled Local 1814 in Brooklyn and
Locals 824, 1809, and 1909 in Manhattan; the Genovese crime family
controlled Locals 1804 and 1588 in New Jersey.[50]

The leaders of Brooklyn Local 1814, at one time the largest ILA local
in the country, had decades-long ties to the Gambino crime family. Capo
Anthony Anastasio, brother of the Gambino family boss Albert Anastasia (the brothers spelled their names differently), ran the union in
the 1940s and 1950s. In 1963, his son-in-law Anthony Scotto succeeded
him in both the union and organized crime. Scotto served as both president of Local 1814 and as a vice-president of the International. He
was banned from union office after a 1980 RICO conviction, but he remained affiliated with the union through 1990.[51] Anthony Pimpinella, a
Gambino soldier, and Anthony Ciccone, a Gambino family capo,[52] both
held positions in the local and International in the 1980s.[53] Ciccone, who
was prohibited from participating in union activities after 1991, maintained his influence into the 2000s through his connection to Local
1814's president.[54]

The Gambino family, in collaboration with the Westies, controlled
ILA Locals 824, 1809, and 1909, collectively known as the West Side (of
Manhattan) locals.[55] Gambino boss John Gotti was named with John
Bowers (president of three locals, as well as of the International) in a
1990 federal lawsuit alleging corruption in the West Side locals (as well
as in Locals 1814, 1804, and 1588).[56] The lawsuit resulted in a consent
decree, in which the government sought to eradicate the influence of
organized crime in local unions affiliated with the ILA on the New
York/New Jersey Waterfront.[57]

Genovese family capo Michael Clemente ran dock operations in
New Jersey for Cosa Nostra as early as the 1960s, when he was banned
from union office for extortion. Twenty years later, he was still involved.[58] Tino Fiumara, a member of the Genovese crime family, represented Clemente in dealing with ILA Local 1804, of Bergen, New Jersey,
and ILA Local 1588 of Bayonne, New Jersey.[59] Thomas Buzzanca, president of Local 1804 in the early 1980s, was also a member of the Genovese family.[60] According to federal prosecutors, as recently as 2002, at
least six officials of Local 1588, including President John Timpanaro,
were Genovese crime family associates.[61] Joseph Lore, another Genovese associate, stole hundreds of thousands of dollars from Local 1588

during the 1990s; he held no position in the union, but his girlfriend served as its office manager, and other mob-connected officials helped him divert funds from union officers' and members' salaries.[62]

Though only the six unions noted in the preceding paragraph were named in the 1990 civil RICO suit against the New York/New Jersey ILA,[63] later evidence pointed to mob influence in other ILA locals. In 1998, the Waterfront Commission accused Louis A. Saccenti, who ran New York Local 1235, of being a Gambino crime family associate.[64] Salvatore Gravano, underboss of the Gambino family, appointed his former bodyguard to be the delegate of Local 1 of Newark, New Jersey, to the Atlantic Coast District of the ILA in the early 1990s.[65] The U.S. Department of Justice believes that Anthony Ciccone attempted to control the management of Local 1 as recently as 2001.[66]

Cosa Nostra used its influence in the ILA to exploit the locals, the shipping industry, and the longshoremen. It determined who worked on the docks and, most importantly, which ships were unloaded and when, and in what order waiting trucks were loaded. Shippers had to make payoffs to ensure that their ships were loaded and unloaded expeditiously and to avoid labor unrest. The cost of delay gave the union representing longshoremen leverage over shippers. Furthermore, Cosa Nostra orchestrated thefts from the shipping companies. Labor racketeers bribed port employees to facilitate cargo theft, solicit illegal labor payoffs, and extort stevedores (companies that load and unload seaborne cargo).[67] The labor racketeers victimized the ILA's members through embezzlement, benefit-fund fraud, and through intimidation and violence.

CONCLUSIONS

The unions discussed in this chapter are not the only New York City unions influenced by LCN. There is evidence of an organized crime presence in the moving and storage industry, linen services, restaurants and nightclubs, and other businesses and industries.[68] Daniel Castelman, chief of investigations for the Manhattan district attorney, has said that "[e]very industry I've ever seen the mob take control of started with its influence in the union."[69]

Jonathan Kwitny's book *Vicious Circles* describes Mafia involvement in the meat industry in the 1960s.[70] He writes that Local 174 of the

Amalgamated Meat Cutters' Union, which represented butchers, "was merely a branch office" of the mob. Frank Kissel, the secretary-treasurer of the local, was a close friend of mobster Lorenzo Brescia[71] and also worked with the Lucchese family's Johnny Dioguardi. Money flowed to the union and the mob from the Meat Trade Institute, an employers' association.[72]

An investigation of the Newspaper and Mail Deliverers Union of New York and Vicinity led to the indictment of several union officials and an alleged member of the Bonanno crime family, James Galante, in April 1996. Members of the union distribute papers for the *New York Times, Daily News, New York Post, El Diario,* and the *Metropolitan News Company.* Union officials were accused of several illegal schemes, including placing fictitious workers on payrolls, stealing newspapers, promoting certain employees in violation of seniority procedures, and assaulting union members who complained about illegal activities.[73]

Several dozen clear cases easily support the proposition that labor racketeering in New York City has been extensive and long lived. It is likely that some unions that have been infiltrated, even controlled, by organized crime have so far not been identified. Of course, the majority of New York City unions have not been and are not influenced by organized crime.

5

Organized Labor's Response to Organized Crime

Is the government going to be here in the year 2050? The year 3000? I
don't know, but I think it's something that we should be talking about
because of the tremendous burden on our membership. . . . They've
eliminated certain pockets of corruption in the union, and I think it's
time for us to move on.

> —James P. Hoffa, following his election victory as general
> president of the International Brotherhood of
> Teamsters (Dec. 7, 1998)

I have had more obloquy and more scorn from the labor movement for
representing [Jock] Yablonski and [Ed] Sadlowski [reformers who ran
in the 1970s against corrupt and dictatorial presidents of the United
Mine Workers and United Steelworkers respectively] and helping reformers in the Laborers and other unions than I ever got from representing people under attack during the McCarthy period in the 1950s.
The problems we went through in the McCarthy period were nothing
compared to labor's recriminations against those who have become
spokesmen for union democracy.

> —Joseph Rauh (famous civil rights lawyer)

Other than the brief flurry of antiracketeering activity in the 1950s,
occasioned by the unification of the AFL and CIO and then by the
McClellan Committee hearings, the mainstream American labor movement has mostly denied or minimized organized crime's influence over
labor. While the AFL-CIO has steadfastly maintained that it is the government's responsibility to investigate and prosecute crime, it has opposed practically every government initiative aimed at fighting labor
racketeering.

Organized labor's refusal to ally with the government against organized criminal elements in the labor movement is incomprehensible
to law enforcement officials who view themselves as labor's liberators.
However, the labor movement's suspicion and distrust of local, state,
and federal governments has a long history. During labor's formative years, the government, acting through law enforcement agencies,
often helped employers break strikes and punish strikers. In the late
nineteenth and early twentieth centuries, labor activists were often arrested and prosecuted, frequently for conspiracy. Distrust was exacerbated in the 1920s and 1930s when the government ruthlessly suppressed leftist elements in the labor movement. Labor's suspicion of
government was confirmed by the Taft-Hartley Act (1947), which,
among other things, prohibited jurisdictional strikes (interunion disputes over which union has jurisdiction over a particular kind of work)
and secondary boycotts (boycott of one company to force another company to recognize a union); outlawed the closed shop; permitted the
union shop only on a vote of a majority of the employees; and removed
all protections of wildcat strikes (unauthorized work stoppage when
labor agreement is still in effect). A decade later, organized labor's
distrust of the government was reaffirmed with the passing of the
Landrum-Griffin Act (1959), which labor leaders regarded as under-
mining their ability to maintain discipline in their organizations. When
President Ronald Reagan fired striking air traffic controllers in 1981,
many labor officials saw another manifestation of a century-long government hostility toward organized labor. Likewise, they regarded
DOJ's civil RICO suits against racketeer-ridden unions as more of
the same.

SAMUEL GOMPERS (1886–1924)

Samuel Gompers and others founded the American Federation of
Labor in 1886.[*] Gompers served as president from 1886 to 1924. In the
name of a strong labor movement, he turned a blind eye to labor's re-
liance on gangsters to battle against strike-breaking thugs recruited by

---

[*] The American labor movement, of course, began much earlier in the nineteenth century.
Indeed, it has roots in the eighteenth century. See, e.g., Howard Zinn, *A People's History of
the United States* (New York: Harper & Row, 1980).

antilabor employers.[1] He was unwilling to criticize the gangsters' infiltration of numerous unions.[2]

Gompers was friendly with "Umbrella" Mike Boyle,[3] boss of Local 134 of the International Brotherhood of Electrical Workers in Chicago. Boyle's nickname referred to the umbrella he hung on a bar counter into which contractors seeking favors (that is, to avoid being held to the terms of their union agreements) could deposit payoffs.[4] Boyle, like many early labor leaders, was also an employer. He held a financial interest in an electrical manufacturing company, which sought to dominate the Chicago market. Gompers promised that Chicago union members would not install electrical switchboards made outside Chicago. In return, Boyle helped Gompers fight off legislation that would prohibit the "closed shop," a union-favored contract clause that commits an employer to hiring only union workers.[5] In 1917, Boyle was convicted of a federal antitrust violation, fined $5,000, and sentenced to a year's imprisonment. Gompers successfully lobbied President Woodrow Wilson to commute the sentence.[6]

In order to counter the influence of the Central Federated Union, an AFL competitor, Gompers wanted to build up an AFL-affiliated New York City Building Trades Council.[7] Toward this end, he reached out to the notorious Robert Brindell, czar of the New York building trades, and gave him an AFL charter for a Dock and Pier Carpenters Union. Brindell forced the Board of Business Agents into the AFL-affiliated Building Trades Council;[8] the business agents obediently elected him president for life and made him the highest paid labor official in the United States.[9]

In 1922, the New York State legislature appointed the Lockwood Committee to investigate graft and racketeering in the building trades. When the committee announced that it would focus on Brindell, Gompers denounced the committee as "another part of the employers' effort to discredit the labor movement and shackle the unions with government control."[10] He insisted that the labor movement itself could take care of corrupt labor officials: "I think that the Legislature should not interfere in the matter at all, regrettable and bad as the condition may be."[11] Then he famously declared, "God save Labor from the courts."[12] Ultimately, Robert Brindell was sentenced to prison for a term of five to ten years for extorting labor peace payoffs from employers.[13]

During his long reign as AFL president, Gompers did little to prevent, investigate, or punish labor racketeering.[14] He was a realist. If the

AFL were to expel racketeer-ridden unions, it would lose substantial dues revenue and weaken its position vis-à-vis employers and competing labor federations.[15] In addition, Gompers may have feared that an attack on labor racketeers would fail and result in his being deposed from the AFL presidency or worse.[16]

WILLIAM GREEN (1924–1952)

When Gompers died, William Green became AFL president, immediately promising to combat corruption and racketeering. At the 1930 AFL Convention, he stated, "If there is brought to my attention the racketeer moving under the garb of trade unionism and I can place my hands on him with convincing evidence, I will drive him from this movement, *if I can* (emphasis added)."[17] That situation seems never to have arisen; Green regularly asserted that he could do no more than exhort union officials to purge racketeers from their respective unions.[18] For example, in 1932 the AFL's Executive Council forwarded to P. J. Morrin, president of the International Iron Workers' Union (IIWU), an accusation that the IIWU's New Jersey representative, Thomas Brandle, had accepted a $10,000 ($135,000 in 2003 dollars) bribe from an employer association.[19] Green asked Morrin to take action "to safeguard the integrity, the good name and standing of your own International Union, as well as the organized labor movement."[20] When Morrin did not act, Green reemphasized that "you have the power to deal with this case of Brother Brandle to which I am calling your attention, and neither the [AFL] Executive Council nor any other International Union has any authority to do so."[21] Nevertheless, Morrin actually ordered Local 45 not to oust Brandle. The AFL took no action for more than a year. Finally, Morrin did expel Brandle from the union.[22]

In 1935, when Special Prosecutor Thomas E. Dewey began his investigation of racketeering in New York City, Green appointed a committee to "assist" Dewey.[23] But the chief function of the committee as described by Green was "to explain to Mr. Dewey that these [labor racketeering] charges were actuated by spite."[24]

David Dubinsky, president of the International Ladies' Garment Workers' Union (ILGWU) (1932 to 1966), went to the 1940 AFL convention intent on strengthening the AFL's authority to deal with racketeering in its affiliated unions. Dubinsky proposed giving the AFL's Executive Council summary power to order a union affiliate to expel any officer or officers convicted of an offense involving moral turpitude or of using an official position for personal gain. Moreover, the resolution called for national and international unions to adopt rules and procedures to punish corrupt officers.[25]

The AFL's Resolutions Committee opposed Dubinsky's proposal on the ground that the AFL "is a federation of self-governing national and international unions who have been guaranteed their right to self-government, which includes their election and selection of officers and control over their conduct." Green challenged the ILGWU leaders and other critics to "show any racketeering in the American Federation of Labor."[26] He declared:

> Our national and international unions are autonomous bodies, chartered by the American Federation of Labor, governed by their own laws and administered by the officers of said organizations. . . . We have never assumed and never will assume dictatorial policies toward national and international unions affiliated with the American Federation of Labor, but with all the power we possess we appeal to the membership of every International Union affiliated with the American Federation of Labor to keep the American labor movement clean, maintain it on a high plane, and if there is any attempt on the part of wrongdoers to seek to secure control of their movement, to deal with them vigorously at once.[27]

The AFL convention passed a watered-down resolution authorizing its Executive Council, when it believed that an international union was not fulfilling its responsibility, to act against corrupt officers, and to "apply all of its influence to secure such action as will correct the situation."[28]

In 1942, the Executive Council had an excellent opportunity to act. Three hundred members of Painters Local 102 complained to President Green that the International Painters Union had refused to remove a business agent who was a convicted bribe taker connected to organized crime. Green urged Painters Union President Lawrence P. Lindelhoff to take action.[29] When Lindelhoff failed to act, the Executive Council assigned AFL Vice-President Matthew Woll to investigate. Despite the guilty jury verdict, Woll reported that he was unable to determine whether the business agent was guilty. Moreover, he emphasized that the AFL did not have authority to intervene in internal union affairs:

"The Federation has no compulsory or disciplinary power. The power delegated to it is that of the use of its influence." Therefore, he suggested that the aggrieved painters take their charges to the Painters' international convention. The AFL Executive Council left final consideration of the matter to Green, who took no further action.[30]

CONGRESS OF INDUSTRIAL ORGANIZATIONS (1938–1955)

In 1938, five international unions broke away from the AFL to found the Congress of Industrial Organizations (CIO), a rival labor federation dedicated to aggressively organizing unskilled workers in the mass-production industries. The CIO was led by John L. Lewis, head of the United Mine Workers of America (UMWA); Sidney Hillman, leader of the Amalgamated Clothing Workers; David Dubinsky of the International Ladies' Garment Workers' Union; and leaders of the Textile Workers and the Typographers unions. The CIO grew rapidly and had almost 2.5 million members by 1940.

Because members of CIO unions worked in factories and mines, they were less vulnerable to intimidation than the geographically scattered craft unionists, who worked in small groups. Furthermore, the companies organized by CIO unions were much larger than the characteristically small AFL employers and far more difficult to intimidate. These gigantic corporations could also control or temper competition (by explicit or implicit agreements with one another) without the need for organized crime bosses to set up and police cartels. CIO trade unionism was more ideological (left wing) than the AFL's business unionism.* Indeed, the AFL sometimes excoriated the CIO for being a tool of the Communist Party.[31] In return, the CIO branded the AFL racketeer ridden.

John L. Lewis, longtime president of the United Mine Workers, was the first president of the CIO. He had immense power and prestige, as did his successor, Walter Reuther of the United Auto Workers. Among early and midcentury labor leaders, Reuther stands out for his vigorous stand against corruption and racketeering. For example, in 1954, when

---

* Business unionism is the trade-union philosophy and activity that concentrates on the improvement of wages, hours, working conditions, and so on, rather than on reform of the capitalist system.

the New York Insurance Board disclosed welfare fund irregularities among some local affiliates of the Retail, Wholesale and Department Store Union (RWDSU), Reuther wrote to Max Greenberg, the president of the RWDSU, that he expected those involved to be disciplined. Greenberg later reported that three locals had been placed under trusteeship, and one had been expelled.[32] At the 1954 CIO convention, Reuther announced, "The CIO does not recognize any autonomous right of crooks and racketeers to use the good name of the CIO as a cloak for their corruption."[33] The convention approved the creation of the CIO Standing Committee on Ethical Practices to investigate cases of corruption and to recommend corrective action when necessary.

GEORGE MEANY (AFL PRESIDENT 1952–1955; AFL-CIO PRESIDENT 1955–1979)

When George Meany became AFL president in 1952, he hoped for a merger with the CIO. However, the CIO's critical attitude toward organized crime's influence in AFL-affiliated unions was a serious obstacle. Meany seized upon racketeering scandals in the International Longshoremen's Association (ILA) to demonstrate that the AFL was ready to act decisively against labor racketeering.[*][34] He wrote, "The Executive Council has the power now to apply all of its influence in order to correct a situation such as the press reports indicate exists in the New York waterfront." While insisting that the AFL is not a "police force," Meany affirmed the labor federation's responsibility "to see that unions protect their members and, if they do not, that the AFL ought to tell the corrupted union that it is not protecting its members and [that] we would like to have them let us know within a reasonable time what they have done about it." The Executive Council appointed three vice-presidents to study the problem. The result was a February 3, 1953, Executive Council letter to the ILA stating, "No affiliate of the American Fed-

---

[*] Under the leadership of Harry Bridges (1901–1990), the West Coast ILA had broken away from the international union in 1940 and become the International Longshoremen's and Warehousemen's Union (ILWU), a militant and progressive union affiliated with the CIO. A book-length biography of Bridges has yet to appear, but there is much information about him in encyclopedias and general labor histories. See also the Harry Bridges Center for Labor Studies at http://depts.washington.edu/pcls/complaborhist.htm.

eration of Labor has any right to expect to remain an affiliate, on the grounds of organizational autonomy, if its conduct is such as to bring the entire movement into disrepute."[35] The AFL urged the ILA to remove any person with a criminal record from office; reform "shape-up" hiring (in which union officials choose the day's workers from among casual laborers who turned up at the piers); restore democratic processes within the union; and remove officers tainted by corruption.[36]

When he failed to receive a satisfactory reply, Meany advised the ILA that the Executive Council would recommend the union's suspension from the AFL. Indeed, the AFL's 1953 convention voted 79,079 to 736 to expel the ILA and chartered a competing union, the International Brotherhood of Longshoremen (IBL). However, in a blow to reformers, the longshoremen voted to continue being represented by the ILA.[37] The defeat demonstrates what has been proved time and again in efforts to clean up racketeer-ridden unions: labor racketeers have enormous staying power, and even when put to the test, usually win elections on account of intimidation, election fraud, and charisma.

THE MERGED AFL-CIO AND THE ETHICAL PRACTICES CODES

When talks about a merger between the AFL and CIO began, AFL officials complained about communist influence in CIO affiliates; CIO officials expressed concern about racketeer influence in AFL affiliates. The merger moved forward when both sets of leaders agreed that there would be no place for either communists or racketeers in the house of labor. In 1955, AFL President George Meany became the merged AFL-CIO's first president, a position he would hold until 1979.

The AFL-CIO constitution[38] authorized an Executive Council to appoint a committee to investigate charges that a union affiliate was dominated by corrupt influences and, if confirmed, to make recommendations for remediating the situation. The AFL-CIO's first convention (1955) vested a Committee on Ethical Practices "with the duty and responsibility to assist the Executive Council in carrying out the constitutional determination of the Federation to keep the Federation free from any taint of corruption . . . in accordance with the provisions of the constitution."[39] In June 1956, the Executive Council authorized the Ethical Practices Committee to conduct hearings into corrupt practices and to formulate a set of principles to keep the federation and its affiliates free from corruption and racketeering.[40] The promulgation of these ethical practice codes was the high-water mark of the American labor movement's response to corruption and racketeering.

The Ethical Practices Committee formulated six ethical practice codes. Code #1 stated, "A charter should never be issued to persons who are known to traffic in local union charters for illicit or improper purposes." Code #2 prohibited any salaried union official from receiving additional remuneration from health, welfare, or retirement funds. It also mandated regular auditing of union financial records. The union had a responsibility to remove a fund administrator who received an unethical payment. Code #3 stated, "No person should hold or retain office . . . who has been convicted of any crime involving moral turpitude offensive to trade union morality." Code #4 prohibited union officials from maintaining investments or business interest that posed a conflict of interest. Code #5 called for proper financial practices. Code #6 required democratic elections and the protection of union members' rights.[41] While remaining on the books, by the early 1960s these codes were defunct.

GEORGE MEANY AND THE MCCLELLAN COMMITTEE

The 1957–1959 McClellan Committee's hearings exposed serious corruption in five unions: the Bakery and Confectionery Workers, the Allied Trades Union, the International Union of Operating Engineers, the United Textile Workers Union, and most importantly, the International Brotherhood of Teamsters.[42] Dozens of labor officials, most notably IBT President Dave Beck, refused to answer questions.* IBT Vice-President (and soon thereafter president) Jimmy Hoffa refused to answer some questions and was evasive and combative in his answers to others. The senators insisted that the AFL-CIO had a responsibility to act.[43]

---

* Beck became IBT general president in 1952. Called before the McClellan Committee in March 1957, he took the Fifth Amendment sixty-five times when questioned about an interest free loan of between $300,000 and $400,000 (or, according to the committee chair, a misappropriation of more $320,000 of union funds). State and federal officials indicted Beck on corruption and tax charges. He did not seek reelection. Jimmy Hoffa succeeded Beck as general president in 1957.

Early in 1957, the Executive Council proposed as a formal policy that "all officials of the AFL-CIO and its affiliates should freely and without reservation answer all relevant questions asked by proper law enforcement agencies, legislative committees and other public bodies seeking fairly and objectively to keep the labor movement free from corruption."[44] IBT President Beck criticized this statement for infringing on member unions' autonomy. Meany replied, "If the AFL-CIO follows the proposal of your organization and equivocates on this question, we will get legislation that will hurt every one of our members and hurt every one of our unions. . . . We will be under Government control."[45] The proposed statement passed with only Beck dissenting.

Meany told the McClellan Committee that only "very, very small portions of the trade union movement are burdened by corruption." Hoping to stave off federal legislation, he promised to take action.[46] "I don't think that we should be a law enforcement agency, but I think that we have a right and a duty and an obligation to our people to try to run unions just as clean as they can be run. And run them for the benefit of members and not for the benefit of George Meany or anybody else."[47] Meany put action behind his words by removing Beck from the AFL-CIO Executive Council on account of Beck's refusal to answer both the McClellan Committee's questions and the Executive Committee's questions.[48]

ENFORCEMENT OF THE ETHICAL PRACTICES CODE: UNITED TEXTILE WORKERS

Even before the McClellan Committee hearings commenced, Meany had begun an investigation of the United Textile Workers of America (UTWA). When the UTWA sought an AFL-CIO loan, Meany asked to see the union's financial records. He received what appeared to be falsified documents. In response to AFL-CIO queries, the UTWA Executive Board promptly cleared its officials of wrongdoing. Meany explained to the McClellan Committee:

> [I]t disturbed me a great deal—maybe I was naive—because I thought all that was necessary was to acquaint the ruling [International Union] body [with the fact] that money was being used in a loose fashion. . . . Apparently, I was too optimistic about that.[49]

The AFL-CIO Committee on Ethical Practices held its own hearing, found that UTWA officers had altered financial reports to cover up mis- use of funds, and ordered the UTWA to eliminate various abuses and to dismiss three union officers.[50]

On December 4, 1957, the AFL-CIO Executive Council suspended the UTWA from the labor federation. That action caused the UTWA Executive Board to agree to the AFL-CIO's original terms. At a special convention in March 1958, it elected a new president and passed several reforms. Still not satisfied, Meany demanded the removal of a vice-pres- ident and the continuation of the union's probationary status. The union complied and remained on AFL-CIO probation until February 16, 1960.[51]

BAKERY AND CONFECTIONERY WORKERS UNION

The AFL-CIO Ethical Practices Committee also took action against the Bakery and Confectionery Workers Union (Bakers). Treasurer Curtis Sims brought charges against President James G. Cross and Vice-Presi- dent George Stuart for the misuse of union funds. After clearing the two men of charges, the Bakers' Executive Board brought charges against Sims for injuring the union's reputation and suspended Sims from of- fice. The McClellan Committee and the AFL-CIO Ethical Practices Com- mittee both decided to investigate.[52]

The Ethical Practices Committee, finding that the Bakers were not in compliance with the AFL-CIO's constitutional standards, ordered the union to correct the abuses and to remove the guilty parties from office. The Bakers refused to expel Cross or to reinstate Sims. On November 5, 1957, Meany announced that the AFL-CIO had suspended the Bakers from membership.[53]

A month later, the Appeals Committee of the AFL-CIO convention recommended that the Bakers be expelled unless the union fully com- plied with the AFL-CIO's requirements. When the union failed to com- ply, it was expelled and a new union chartered. In January 1961, Cross resigned in exchange for $250,000 severance pay and the union's com- mitment to pay his future litigation expenses. Later, Cross, Jack Olson, and four vice-presidents of the old union were convicted of embezzling union funds. With Cross out of the picture, the old and new unions ne- gotiated a merger.[54]

DISTILLERY WORKERS

In June 1956, the AFL-CIO Ethical Practices Committee turned its attention to the Distillery Workers Union (Distillery Workers). Sol Cilento, executive vice-president in charge of New York City Local 2 had been indicted on bribery and conspiracy charges related to the union's welfare fund. His codefendants were former Building Service Employees president and mob-associate George Scalise and his LCN-sponsor, Anthony Pisano, once a member of Al Capone's organization.[55] The government alleged that the three men had received kickbacks on fund loans totaling more than $300,000 (about $2 million in 2003 dollars) over a two-year period. The three were acquitted, but a fourth codefendant was sentenced to prison.[56] When the Distillery Workers refused to cooperate with the Senate Subcommittee on Welfare and Pension Funds' investigation, the Executive Council directed the union to show cause why it should not be suspended from the federation.[57] The union denied the need for reform. The Executive Council decided to suspend the union unless it accepted one year's probationary status and the appointment of a monitor to supervise its affairs. Its back against the wall, the Distillery Workers accepted probation and a monitor. In January 1961, the AFL-CIO dissolved its monitorship and terminated the probationary status.[58]

UAW-AFL JOHN DIOGUARDI

John Dioguardi, a capo in the Lucchese crime family and notorious labor racketeer, was appointed president of the United Auto Workers Union (UAW-AFL) Local 102 in New York at the 1951 convention despite never having been employed in industries whose workers were represented by that union.* A year later, the New York City Crime Commission and Manhattan District Attorney Frank Hogan accused Locals 102 and 227 of various wrongdoings. (Dioguardi was associated with both locals, though he held office in only Local 102.) In February 1953,

---

* The UAW-AFL should not be confused with the United Automobile Workers (of Walter and Victor Reuther), which descends from the AUW-CIO. When the AFL and CIO merged in 1957, the UAW-CIO took the name UAW; the UAW-AFL was renamed the Allied Industrial Workers (AIW).

the AFL Executive Council ordered the international union to revoke Local 102's charter or face suspension. The UAW-AFL complied by dissolving Local 102.[59]

The Manhattan District Attorney's office convicted Dioguardi on state tax evasion charges, but he returned to union politics over UAW-AFL President Lester Washburn's opposition. In April 1954, Washburn expelled Dioguardi from the union and lifted the charters of six Dioguardi-dominated locals. Incredibly, the UAW-AFL's Executive Board overruled Washburn, cleared Dioguardi of wrongdoing,[60] and reinstated him. Washburn resigned in protest.

Eventually Dioguardi also resigned, but that did not end the union's troubles. In 1955, a Senate subcommittee investigated Chicago UAW-AFL Local 286, which was dominated by Angelo Incisco, a notorious organized crime figure. The UAW-AFL revoked the local's charter on February 1, 1956, but rescinded its action the following day. The board then allowed Incisco to disaffiliate the local from the union (that is, to turn the local into an "independent union"), and taking one-fifth of the entire international union's assets.[61]

On August 27, 1956, the AFL-CIO Committee on Ethical Practices declared that the Allied Industrial Workers of America ("AIW," the UAW-AFL's new name) "may be dominated, controlled, or substantially influenced in the conduct of its affairs by corrupt influences in violation of the Constitution of the AFL-CIO."[62] The Executive Council gave the AIW the choice of accepting a monitorship and eliminating "corrupt influences" within ninety days or be expelled. The union complied, tossing four New York locals out of the union. A special convention replaced the international president. In October of 1957, the Executive Council lifted the AIW's probationary status and the monitorship ended a few months later.*[63]

INTERNATIONAL BROTHERHOOD OF TEAMSTERS

David Beck's conduct at the McClellan Committee hearings prompted the AFL-CIO Executive Council to suspend Beck from the Council and to order an investigation of the IBT.[64] The AFL-CIO Ethical Practices

---

* In 1993, the AIW merged with the UPIU (United Paperworkers International Union).

Committee reported to President Meany that Beck and Vice-Presidents Brewster and Hoffa had misused union resources and union pension funds for personal purposes; used their official positions for personal profit and advantage; engaged in improper activities relating to health and welfare funds; engaged in extortion and bribery; failed to abide by the AFL-CIO policy against refusing to cooperate with congressional committees; failed to ensure that racketeers were not granted union charters; and that Hoffa had associated with known racketeers, including Johnny Dioguardi.[65] The AFL-CIO Executive Council ordered the IBT to report on its effort to eliminate corrupt elements by October 25, 1957.[66]

The Teamsters showed no interest in complying. Facing federal and state criminal charges, Beck chose not to seek reelection at the 1957 Teamsters convention. Jimmy Hoffa, with the support of Johnny Dioguardi and other organized crime figures, became the new general president. The AFL-CIO Executive Council suspended the IBT on October 24. The Appeals Committee rejected the IBT's appeal and recommended expulsion.[67] The 1957 AFL-CIO convention voted four to one to expel the IBT. However, the Executive Council held the door open for the Teamsters readmission if someone other than Hoffa became president. Removed from the AFL-CIO, the IBT no longer had to abide by the federation's no-raiding pact; it was free to compete with AFL-CIO affiliated unions. In the next two decades, the IBT formed locals to represent teachers, security guards, police officers, and many other workers. Consequently, the IBT became by far the largest and strongest private-sector union in the United States, with approximately two million members in 1960.

THE LANDRUM-GRIFFIN ACT

The revelations of labor racketeering brought out by the McClellan Committee's hearings made some form of federal legislation a foregone conclusion. Meany told a Congressional committee that "[u]nless certain safeguards are established, both through self-policing and legislation, the inducements and opportunities for illicit gain or improper practices will persist and there will be those who will yield to them."[68] The AFL-CIO opposed a union members' bill of rights and some other

proposals but eventually supported a union financial disclosure requirement as long as the U.S. Department of Labor (DOL) would be the
responsible federal agency.

John L. Lewis, president of the United Mine Workers of America
(UMW) opposed *any* remedial legislation: "We find ourselves opposed
to the plan for Congress to enact regulatory or punitive legislation af-
fecting welfare funds . . . there is ample legislation on the statute
books."[69] He explained that the UMW opposed any governmental en-
croachment into the affairs of labor organizations and sharply criticized
Meany: "I am completely impatient with the attitude of the present
leaders of American labor who are, in effect, at the present time saying
to the Federal Congress, 'Please, gentlemen of the Congress, hurry up
and enact a statute that will compel leaders to be honest and stop us
from thieving from our membership.'"[70]

The Senate ultimately passed the Kennedy-Ives bill, requiring registration of pension and welfare plans with the secretary of labor; detailed reporting of receipts and expenditures; and public disclosure. In
addition, the bill provided criminal penalties for failure to file, false filing, and embezzlement.[71] The bill passed the Senate, but failed in the
House of Representatives. The AFL-CIO announced that the "failure of
Congress to pass the Kennedy-Ives bill can be laid squarely on the
doorstep of those who sought not an anti-corruption bill, but an antilabor bill."[72]

In 1958, the Democrats won majorities in both houses. There
seemed at that point no possibility that Congress would pass a bill less
favorable to labor than the Kennedy-Ives Bill.[73] The AFL-CIO reiterated
that "[w]e are determined that there be legislation which will eliminate
the opportunities for corruption and at the same time preserve the traditional and legitimate functions of trade unions. In our opinion . . .
S.505 (now Kennedy-Ervin Bill) meets this test."[74] During the debate,
Senator McClellan introduced a "bill of rights for union members." The
AFL-CIO opposed it, arguing that it would weaken responsible unions
and generate nuisance litigation. Nevertheless, Congress passed this
bill of rights by a one-vote margin.[75] President Dwight D. Eisenhower
signed it into law.

The Landrum-Griffin Act (formally the Labor-Management Reporting and Disclosure Act, LMRDA) required unions to file with the
DOL reports on income, expenditures, and salaries; it required bonding
of officers and staff members; it forbade officers from having certain

conflicts of interest; and it prohibited union loans of more than $2,000 to officers or members. It empowered the secretary of labor to seek judicial relief if union members' rights were denied or their benefit funds misused. The law made embezzling union funds a federal offense.[76]

The AFL-CIO denounced passage of the Landrum-Griffin Act, which provided the legal foundation for union democracy, with the following formal statement: "This measure was designed to destroy organized labor, but we will not be destroyed.... Our cause is just and we continue to move forwards...."[77] A year later, the AFL-CIO excoriated the law as "the worst legislative blow suffered by the labor movement since enactment of the Taft-Hartley Act in 1947."[78]

POST–LANDRUM-GRIFFIN DEVELOPMENTS

In 1959, the ILA appealed to the AFL-CIO for readmission. The AFL-CIO agreed on condition that the ILA submit to any order issued by President Meany, provide whatever reports the federation might require, and permit Meany to attend ILA Executive Council meetings. The ILA also agreed that the AFL-CIO could impose any discipline it deemed appropriate.[79]

In 1960, a New York–New Jersey Waterfront Commission report concluded that the elimination of the "criminal domination and control (on the waterfront) . . . has not been fully accomplished."[80] The commission proposed that (1) former convicts, already barred from holding union office, be made ineligible to hold any position in a union pension and welfare fund; (2) additional misdemeanors be added to the list of offenses that bar individuals from working on the docks; (3) required registration of longshoremen with the Waterfront Commission and prohibition from interfering "with the duties of licensed or registered personnel without justification in law."[81] The ILA, strongly opposing all these proposals, unsuccessfully sought an AFL-CIO resolution condemning the Waterfront Commission and urging Congress to repeal the act. However, the AFL-CIO's 1963 convention did give the ILA part of what it wanted by opposing pending federal legislation that would have *expanded* the Waterfront Commission's powers. In the end, Congress did not expand the commission's powers.[82]

Following the passage of the Landrum-Griffin Act, President Meany took no further initiatives against labor racketeering. By the early 1960s, the Ethical Practices Committee was dormant. The AFL-CIO ignored several questionable situations. For example, in 1963, Maurice Hutcheson, president of the powerful Carpenters Union, was convicted of bribing an Indiana official to obtain advance information on highway routes.[83] Although the conviction was later reversed on appeal, Hutcheson was convicted of contempt of Congress and sentenced to six months in jail for refusing to answer committee questions. President Meany called Hutcheson a "man of character . . . an able, devoted and conscientious representative of the American trade union movement."[84]

A more disturbing example of Meany's indifference to labor corruption surrounded the power struggle in the United Mine Workers in the late 1960s. In 1969, Jock Yablonski, leader of an insurgent movement, sought to unseat President Tony Boyle (1963–1972). Although there was no organized crime labor racketeering in the UMW, Boyle ruled the union like a ruthless dictator.[85] The election campaign was marked by threats and violence. When Boyle won the election, Yablonski charged election fraud and sought to have the result overturned. Shortly thereafter, he, his wife, and daughter were murdered. Yablonski's campaign manager asked Meany to allow Yablonski's followers to state their complaints about Boyle to the AFL-CIO Executive Council so that labor might "clean its own house without Senate or Administrative inference."[86] Meany rejected the request on the ground that "the AFL-CIO traditionally refrains from intervening in the internal affairs of its own affiliates, let alone outside organizations. Incredibly, Meany asserted that government or AFL-CIO initiatives to attack labor corruption or racketeering would violate a union's "democratic structure."[87] In 1974, Boyle was convicted of first degree murder for having hired Yablonski's assassins.

LANE KIRKLAND (1979–1995)

If Meany's approach to combating labor corruption was passive, that of his successor, Lane Kirkland, was virtually nonexistent. In 1979, at the height of LCN's influence in the IBT, the AFL-CIO invited the Teamsters back into the labor federation. Kirkland argued that the Landrum-Griffin Act, by assigning the job of policing the unions to the federal government and its agencies, relieved the AFL-CIO of responsibility for addressing corruption and racketeering in its member unions.[88] Said Kirkland, "All sinners belong in the church. All citizens owe fealty to their country, and all true unions belong in the AFL-CIO."[89]

In the late 1980s, the Department of Justice was rumored to be preparing an unprecedented civil RICO suit against the Teamsters general president, general executive board, and the heads of several Cosa Nostra crime families. The Teamsters wanted to rejoin the AFL-CIO. Reconciliation promised benefits for both sides. The Teamsters would increase the AFL-CIO's membership by 15 percent, thereby enhancing the federation's finances and political clout. Moreover, as an AFL-CIO affiliate, the IBT would be bound by the federation's noncompete rule, that is, not competing to decertify other AFL-CIO unions.[90] The IBT hoped that, with AFL-CIO support, it could derail the DOJ's civil RICO lawsuit, perhaps with federal legislation outlawing court-imposed RICO trusteeships.[91]

During the 1980s, the federal government again conducted hearings into labor racketeering and considered Landrum-Griffin reforms.* In 1981, Senator Sam Nunn (D.-Ga.), chairman of the Senate Permanent Subcommittee on Investigations when the Democrats controlled the Senate, introduced legislation: (1) providing for the automatic suspension of union officers found guilty of wrongdoing (instead of waiting for the resolution of a final appeal), and (2) making it a felony for an employer to pay a bribe of $1,000 or more to a union representative.[92] The AFL-CIO supported this proposed legislation except for the automatic ten-year suspension period. Kirkland explained, "Both reason and human feeling support the view that there are situations in which a 10 year disqualification is too severe."[93] Kirkland argued that corruption is an individual, not an institutional, problem and insisted that the AFL-CIO lacked power and authority to attack racketeering in its affiliated unions. "As spokesman for organized labor the AFL-CIO asks for that [federal governmental] protection, emphasizes that the trade union movement sees such protection as a benefit, and pledges its cooperation in a joint endeavor with the Federal Government to maintain the hard-earned honor of our institutions."[94]

Kirkland told the senators that the AFL-CIO's codes of ethics were

---

* According to Eleanor Hill, chief counsel for the Democrats on the Permanent Subcommittee on Investigations, mainstream labor was not supportive of Senator Nunn's hearings. Personal interview by author.

not being actively enforced because the Landrum-Griffin Act usurped the federation's ability to act against racketeering and that conflicts would arise if two investigative/enforcement procedures (one by the AFL and one by federal agencies) operated simultaneously. Since the government had superior fact-finding tools, it should bear the responsibility for rooting out wrongdoing. Moreover, the AFL-CIO had only the drastic power of expulsion to use in corruption and racketeering cases. "It is as though you only had capital punishment as a punishment for every rank of crime."[95] Apparently, Kirkland was not aware of or rejected the probation and monitoring that the AFL-CIO had used in the mid 1950s and did not consider use of fines.

Senator Warren Rudman (R.-N.H.) expressed the frustration caused by union officers' repeated invocations of the Fifth Amendment at congressional hearings. He asked whether the AFL-CIO's policy of disciplining members who refused to answer questions put by congressional committees still applied. Kirkland called it "an intricate question," backing away from the AFL-CIO's McClellan Committee–era position. It seemed clear that the AFL-CIO would no longer punish union officials who refused to testify at congressional hearings.[96]

The AFL-CIO supported a 1984 amendment to the Landrum-Griffin Act, which required union officers to relinquish their offices immediately upon conviction rather than months or years later when appeals had been exhausted. However, the IBT opposed even that law on the ground that while it barred convicted union officials from all union offices, it did not prohibit a convicted corporate official from holding a corporate position in a unit other than labor relations.[97]

A 1985 book by labor lawyers David Elbaor and Laurence Gold denied the existence of any organized crime problem in the labor movement.

> Today's anti-labor campaign, the intent of which is to associate unions with organized crime, corruption, and unsavory practices, is the lineal descendant of earlier efforts to tar the labor movement with simplistic yet sensational identifications between union action and Bolshevism, Communism, and other "un-American" thoughts.[98]

Elbaor and Gold criticized the Department of Labor for departing from its historic mission to protect workers and for participating in criminal investigations against union officials. According to the authors: (1) nearly all union-related crimes are isolated offenses by individuals; (2) DOJ only prosecutes theft of such small sums when the defendant is a union officer; (3) federal prosecutors seek to establish new theories of labor crimes by criminalizing traditional union activities; and (4) the government has abandoned civil and criminal enforcement of managements' reporting and disclosure requirements.[99] They concluded that "[t]he government's campaign, by perpetuating the myth of union corruption with stepped-up and highly publicized prosecutions, maligns labor's reputation and thereby threatens its future."[100]

AFL-CIO'S OPPOSITION TO RICO TRUSTEESHIPS

In 1987, the AFL-CIO Executive Council issued a statement opposing the rumored DOJ civil RICO suit against the IBT. "If the Justice Department brings suit seeking supervision over an international union, the AFL-CIO will do whatever is useful and productive in the legal circumstances to prevent such supervision."[101] However, the Executive Council added: "We support full and vigorous law enforcement aimed at the racketeers and the sharpsters who seek to prey on our movement; the government has an obligation to trade unions and their members to provide such enforcement."[102]

In order to mobilize support against the civil RICO suit, the AFL-CIO established an organization called Americans against Government Control of Unions (AAGCU). The AAGCU launched a public relations campaign that called the rumored suit a Reagan administration conspiracy to crush organized labor. One of its promotional statements equated "the possible [DOJ] lawsuit to the suppression of free trade unions in Poland, the Soviet Union and Nazi Germany."[103] According to the AAGCU, "the Justice Department's proposal for a government takeover of any union in this country conflicts with the basic American concept of free trade unionism and violates the 1st Amendment guarantees of free speech and association."[104]

President Kirkland publicly stated that there was "no justification whatsoever" for the Justice Department to seek to have the Teamsters put under a court-ordered trusteeship "simply because the leadership is influenced by organized crime." He said, "organized crime influence is not a "problem of any significance at this time,"[105] and that a trusteeship is not "the proper relationship between a government and a private institution in a free society."[106]

Calling court-imposed union trusteeships contrary to the spirit of free trade unionism,[107] Kirkland warned that a civil RICO suit against the Teamsters would be a "clear abuse of the government's prosecutorial power." He insisted that the Department of Justice should prosecute those who violate the law, but not seek sanctions against unions themselves. The AFL-CIO issued a statement declaring, "In a democratic society, labor unions must be controlled by their members, not by the government."[108] With AFL-CIO and IBT prodding, 246 House and Senate members delivered a letter to the DOJ urging that no civil RICO suit be brought against the IBT.[109]

The AFL-CIO criticism of and lobbying against the DOJ suit continued even after the lawsuit was filed and settled. Kirkland described Judge David Edelstein's decisions enforcing the settlement, as "the latest in a string of orders directed at maximizing the government's control over the Teamsters" and reasserted that "this kind of judicial interference with the right of union members to self-government and with the right of unions to their autonomy is excessive and unreasonable."[110]

In 1989, President Kirkland testified before the Senate Permanent Subcommittee on Investigations that the use of trusteeships violated union members' constitutional right of association: "Government control of a private association is thus fundamentally illegitimate in that the officials who exercise control are not drawn from, are not selected by, and are not responsible to the association members."[111] In Kirkland's opinion, corruption is an attribute of individuals, not organizations, and is properly dealt with by prosecuting racketeers rather than imposing expensive trusteeships that deny the membership control of its union.[112] Kirkland stated that civil RICO suits should be brought against unions only if, despite successful criminal prosecutions, there is a clear and present danger of ongoing criminality. In addition, even if RICO suits are necessary, trusteeships are not; DOL and DOJ, according to Kirkland, could deal with union members suspected of having ties to organized crime without resorting to unions trusteeships.[113] Likewise, labor lawyer Laurence Gold pointed out, there are other less intrusive equitable remedies, such as government oversight of elections, government scrutiny of expenditures, and injunctive relief against individual wrongdoers.[114]

The IBT and the AFL-CIO proposed amending RICO to (1) preclude the "wholesale removal of a union's elected officers and their replacement, for an indefinite period, by a court appointed trustee"; (2) to make it clear "that such a trusteeship, in any form, not be imposed unless and until there has been a full and final evidentiary hearing and the government has demonstrated, by clear and convincing evidence, that the interests of union members cannot be protected by any less intrusive means"; and (3) "that RICO be clarified so that no union is precluded from using its resources to hire legal counsel to defend itself or its officers."[115]

The Senate Permanent Subcommittee on Investigations took the AFL-CIO's criticisms seriously. Its 1990 report recommended that RICO trusteeships in labor cases "only [be imposed] in the most extreme circumstances" and called on the Justice Department to seek alternative remedies. Noting the AFL-CIO's opposition to RICO trusteeships, the subcommittee report called on the attorney general to issue guidelines limiting the circumstances under which DOJ would seek to have RICO trusteeships imposed on labor unions. The report recommended that a liaison be established between law enforcement agencies and the AFL-CIO to enhance cooperation.[116] These proposals were not implemented, although it has become DOJ policy to allow unions an opportunity to see and comment on RICO complaints before they are filed.

In 1996, the AFL-CIO opposed the plan of the House of Representatives Subcommittee on Human Resources and Intergovernmental Relations to hold hearings on the DOL's response to labor racketeering cases. The AFL-CIO's legislative director stated, "All they've dragged up are old news reports. They will look foolish if they try to have hearings."[117] When the hearings were officially announced in July, the AFL-CIO charged the Republican leadership with using the hearings as "an organized smear campaign against union leaders" to divert attention away from the Republicans' own agenda.[118] AFL-CIO President John Sweeney (1995–) charged that the hearings were being held to retaliate for the federation's $34 million ad campaign against Republican legislative initiatives.[119]

The AFL-CIO attacked the House Judiciary Subcommittee on Crime's 1996 hearings on the 1994 consent agreement settling DOJ's civil RICO suit against LIUNA[120] as a waste of taxpayer money and an abuse of congressional power.[121] Its press release defended LIUNA president, Arthur E. Coia, calling him a leader in "cleaning up corruption wherever he could find it. Coia and the Laborers union should be applauded for their bold actions to crack down on the last vestiges of mob control in their union—not witch-hunted because of past problems and their current opposition to [House Speaker Rep. Newt] Gingrich's attacks on working families."[122] (Subsequently, the former prosecutors hired to reform LIUNA charged Coia with having ties to organized crime; Coia was forced out of office after being convicted of corruption in federal court in Rhode Island.)

AFL-CIO officials continue to reject government antilabor racketeering initiatives as a figment of the prosecutorial imagination or a sinister plot to destroy the labor movement. The AFL-CIO's general counsel, Jon Hiatt, pointed out that the government seeks to impose RICO trusteeships on labor unions, but not on corporations, despite rampant corruption in the latter.[123] Laurence Gold expressed a similar position: "I question whether comparable cases are being brought against people in other walks of life."[124] On December 6, 2001, an AFL-CIO resolution demanded termination of the Independent Review Board, established to enforce the settlement in the IBT international case.[125]

> The goals of the Teamsters consent decree have now been secured. No legitimate reason remains to justify continued government intervention in that organization. It is time for the consent decree to end and the Teamsters Union returned to the full democratic control of its members.[126]

In early 2002, the AFL-CIO criticized the proposed fiscal year 2003 DOL budget for providing a $3.9 million increase for the Office of Labor-Management Standards (OLMS), which had requested $3.4 million and forty additional staff positions for "enhanced enforcement and outreach assistance activities to ensure compliance" with the LMRDA.[127] The OMLS's ambition was to audit at least 1 percent of labor organizations each year and to increase the transparency of union finances by, among other things, requiring that LMRDA reports be made available to the public. The AFL-CIO questioned the increase in the OLMS budget for investigations into unions while cutting programs "that directly enforce workers' job-based rights and protections." It also criticized as unnecessary the proposed 9 percent budget increase and twenty-five new employees for the DOL's Office of Inspector General.[128]

CONCLUSION

Over the course of the twentieth century, with a few significant exceptions, the leaders of the U.S. labor movement have accommodated rather than opposed labor racketeers. To be sure, a few labor leaders, like David Dubinsky, Walter Reuther, Harry Bridges, and George Meany, denounced organized crime's presence and influence in the labor movement as a serious problem. However, except in the 1950s, most labor leaders accepted organized crime as a fact of life and/or believed that an all-out effort to purge racketeers from the labor movement would be disastrous for labor. And some AFL-CIO positions, like denunciation of Landrum-Griffin and DOJ's civil RICO suit against the IBT, were hostile to anti–labor racketeering efforts.

In truth, there was probably not much that honest labor leaders on their own could do about organized crime. Entrenched labor racketeers backed by LCN are formidable. The AFL's failed effort in replacing the ILA with a new, honest longshoremen's union demonstrates the sagacity of Gompers's and Green's judgment that the AFL had limited options for dealing with corruption and racketeering in its constituent unions. An AFL-CIO crusade against labor racketeers might well have weakened the labor movement, certainly in the short run. But a middle position might have achieved some success. Denunciation of labor racketeers, cooperation with government enforcement agencies, and creative use of sanctions like probation and monitoring did achieve some success in the late 1950s in cases involving the Distillery Workers, the Bakery and Confectionary Workers, and perhaps one or two other unions.

6

Labor Racketeering and the Rank and File

But if the 1980s were difficult for most unions, for the Teamsters they were tragic. A combination of politicians, mafia-connected union officials, and trucking employers came to dominate the highest levels of the Teamsters. Under the control of these outsiders, during the worst years of the employers' attacks on the unions in the 1980s, the Teamsters negotiated a series of sweetheart contracts. These contracts sold out the interests of union members and weakened the labor movement as a whole.

—Dan La Botz, "The Fight at UPS: The Teamsters' Victory
and the Future of the New Labor Movement,"
Solidarity pamphlet (1997), 9

It is beyond belief that 10,000 members would sit by and watch these things done and never utter a peep, unless a substantial number of the membership were fearful for their lives or their jobs.

—U.S. Second Circuit Court of Appeals, in
affirming Judge Ackerman's decision in
the IBT Local 560 case, 780 F.2d at 278

Rank-and-file union members are labor racketeers' primary victims. In racketeer-ridden unions, workers suffer financially when the terms of their collective bargaining contracts are not enforced, when their pension and welfare funds are defrauded, and when their dues are used to reimburse corrupt officers' personal expenses. Their personal safety is put at risk when corrupt officers refuse to press their safety-related grievances with employers, or worse, when officers turn a blind eye to unsafe conditions in exchange for bribes. The potential effectiveness of unions in negotiating contracts, enforcing contract provisions, handling grievances, organizing, running hiring halls, and handling finances is undermined when union officials are appointed on the basis of their loyalty to organized crime. The union movement is weaker to the extent that union officials are racketeers rather than committed organizers; individual unions are weaker to the extent that union official have few administrative skills and little interest in furthering the interests of the membership. The members of racketeer-ridden unions suffer on account of the wholesale violation of their rights of free speech, participation in union elections, and fair representation in grievance proceedings.

Why does the rank and file tolerate such "leadership?" The most obvious answer is that the uncoordinated many are at the mercy of the highly organized few. In the case of nation-states, repressed populations rarely are able to overthrow totalitarian dictatorships that rely on carrots and sticks, including extreme violence, to maintain their power and privilege. So too, rank-and-file union members have almost no chance of overthrowing organized crime–backed racketeers. To be sure, some union members have testified at congressional hearings, provided information to investigative journalists, campaigned as independents for union office, lodged complaints with the Department of Labor, brought lawsuits to redress their grievances, and even begun reform organizations. Tragically, scores of such individuals have ended up losing their jobs, their physical security, and even their lives. Until the federal government cleared the way by launching a war on organized crime generally and on labor racketeers specifically, rank-and-file dissidents and reformers had little hope of liberating their unions from the grip of organized crime. Even with the government's assistance, successes have been few and hard won.

THE WEAKNESS OF THE RANK AND FILE

We have already seen (Chapter 2) that it was relatively easy for a small group of organized criminals to infiltrate and take over a union comprising hundreds and thousands of members. This should not be surprising. History is replete with examples of small, tightly knit groups specializing in violence, terrorizing, and dominating disorganized collectivities.[1] Labor racketeers only need to intimidate or otherwise neutralize a small number of union officials and active members, not the vast majority of the rank and file that is only weakly involved in union affairs. Not only are Cosa Nostra organized crime families closely knit groups that can draw on their expertise in intimidation and violence, they have been able to count on the cooperation of corrupt employers, the passivity of the AFL-CIO, and the cooptation of politicians.

It would be a mistake to imagine labor racketeers pitted in stark opposition to the membership. The racketeers typically enjoy some support and popularity at the early stages of their infiltration, and they attract new supporters as their hold on the union tightens. Labor racketeers are adept at establishing patronage systems. This is easiest to accomplish when the union operates a hiring hall (as in the construction industry) that can be used to reward cooperation and loyalty. Those in charge of the hiring hall can dispense the choicest (best-paid; best-conditions) work assignments to their friends, allies, and supporters. The racketeers can appoint their supporters as shop stewards and business agents. In a short time, the infiltrated union's entire administrative cadre will consist of individuals loyal to the racketeers. Contrariwise, dissidents and others who oppose the dominant clique will be frozen out of lucrative work assignments and union offices. If irritating enough, they will be blacklisted and thereby driven out of the industry and out of the union. Even where there is no hiring hall (that is, where employers do all their own hiring), the racketeers can easily make a "troublesome" union member unemployable by indicating to employers that continued employment of the individual might lead to labor problems.

The threat and actual use of violence is a massive inhibitor to anyone considering running for office against the incumbent regime. The history of many unions includes beatings and murders of dissidents who challenged the dominant clique. The collective memory of many unions' rank-and-file holds stories of dissidents murdered for challenging those in power.

Even if a union member is courageous enough to run for office against a mob-connected incumbent, it is almost impossible for him/her to win. Incumbent labor racketeers have complete control over the union's communications with the rank and file. Their newsletters provide a steady diet of proincumbent propaganda. Thus, while incumbents enjoy widespread name recognition, insurgents will likely be known only to a small circle. Incumbents cannot legally use union personnel and resources for their campaigns,[2] but in practice they can count on the active support of the union's whole administrative infrastructure. When racketeers have anticipated insurgent opposition, they have passed rules outlawing campaign donations by nonunion members, further limiting the insurgents' chances.[3] They have consistently turned to red-baiting, that is, branding critics as communists or radicals.*

The rank-and-file electorate is difficult for insurgents to reach, much less mobilize. Only a small percentage of union members are highly interested and involved in union affairs; the great majority are apathetic. Most members look to their unions to negotiate collective bargaining agreements, provide grievance representation, and pay their pensions, but they do not keep up with union politics or governance.[4] Typically, less than 5 percent of eligible members turn out at regular union meetings; less than 25 percent vote in union elections. Many union members do not know who runs their union or whether those in charge are doing a good job; many may have no idea that certain officers are organized crime members, associates, or puppets. They may chafe at mediocre contracts, favoritism, and lack of accountability to the membership, but accept this reality as inevitable.

The historian David Witwer documents an unsuccessful effort by reformers in LIUNA (NYC) Local 282 to wrest control of their five thousand–member union away from an organized crime–connected clique led from the early 1970s by labor racketeer John Cody.** In 1975, a few members formed a group called FORE (Fear of Reprisal Ends). They received nationwide attention when the TV news show *60 Minutes*

---

* Labor journalist Dan La Botz provides this example from a mid-1980s union insurgency in a Teamster local in Long Island City, New York: "'They did something that was very unfair, calling me, branding me as a Communist,' says [Nick] Montalvo. They went to warehouses where he wasn't known, and told workers who had never met him that Montalvo was a Communist. 'That was the only type of campaign they could put up against me—and they used it, to no avail, but they used it.'" Dan La Botz, *Rank-and-File Rebellion: Teamsters for a Democratic Union* (New York: Routledge, 1990), 138.

** David Witwer points out that although the rank-and-file members did not know about all of the ways that the incumbents were exploiting the members and looting the union, they did recognize that their collective bargaining agreements were being selectively enforced and that their grievances were being ignored. "The Landrum-Griffin Act: A Case Study in the Possibilities of and Problems in Anti-Union Corruption Law," 27 *Criminal Justice Review* 301 (2002) at 312.

presented a segment on them. They ran candidates against the Cody group in three elections before dissolving. Witwer explains:

> The FORE members cited several reasons for their successive defeats at the polls. . . . Members had come to doubt that rank-and-filers were competent to run the union effectively. Also a sense of apathy and defeatism pervaded the membership. As one FORE member put it, "they feel there is no way you can beat the incumbents and everybody is afraid. . . ." The incumbents also benefited from a sort of insiders' coalition within the local. Many members held appointed positions that brought more overtime and increased seniority . . . ; other members were notified about lucrative long-term job assignments. Both groups could be counted on to bring in their friends and relatives to vote for the incumbents. One FORE member estimated that through this kind of patronage network the incumbents could count on . . . the votes . . . of a quarter to a fifth of the total membership . . . in addition to these factors, there remained the key issue of intimidation. . . . Too many acts of intimidation occurred to be covered in the present article.

Not only do incumbent labor racketeers have practically insurmountable advantages over insurgents in union elections, they also control the election machinery. They decide where elections will be held and the method of voting; they count the ballots and report the results. There is a long and sordid history of fraud in union elections. Moreover, under the Landrum-Griffin Act, only the Department of Labor can go to court to challenge the results of a union election and the DOL may not initiate action until its investigation confirms that election fraud "probably made a difference" in the election's outcome.

Even if an insurgent somehow wins a union election, he may be foiled by lower-level union officials who remain loyal to the racketeers. At every juncture, the reformer will face overt and covert opposition and sabotage. Furthermore, a local union reformer can be thwarted by an organized crime–controlled district council or international union. There are many examples of international unions manufacturing charges of malfeasance against local union reformers, accusing them of violating the union's constitution or bylaws and punishing them with expulsion from office or from the union altogether. A racketeer-influenced international union can lodge trumped-up charges against and replace local or district council officers with a trustee who is loyal to the ruling faction. Under the Landrum-Griffin law, trusteeships imposed on locals by the international union are presumptively valid for eighteen months.[5] In reality, given the time it takes to launch a legal challenge against such a trusteeship along with the challenger's high burden of persuasion, it is practically impossible for a trusteed local or district council to overcome the eighteen-month presumption.

INDIVIDUAL DISSIDENTS: ACTS OF DEFIANCE

"Dissident" is an unfortunate term, conjuring an image of a curmudgeon who cannot get along with anybody. Nevertheless, it is an appellation that union reformers routinely and proudly use in referring to themselves and one that others have long used to describe union insurgents. If I were writing on a fresh canvas, I would prefer the term *union reformer or insurgent*, but I will defer to the prevailing nomenclature.

However they are labeled, people willing to fight hopeless battles against massively stronger opponents frequently seem obsessed by systemic injustice to which the society appears oblivious. After months and years of futilely seeking the support of international union officials, the Department of Labor, journalists, and prosecutors, many union dissidents appear defensive and even paranoid. They believe the world is against them; of course, to a substantial extent, this is true.

It takes enormous courage for union members openly to criticize labor racketeers. Twentieth-century history is full of examples of critics being intimidated, threatened, beaten, and killed. Consider this statement provided by LIUNA reformer Chris White for the government's 1990s civil RICO suit against the Laborers International Union:

> I have been a member of the Laborers' International Union of North America (LIUNA) for over twenty years and a member of Local 942 of LIUNA in Fairbanks Alaska for about the past eighteen years. For more than fifteen years, I have attempted to work within the union to make it more democratic and responsive to the needs of the rank and file. My efforts, and those of my fellow union members who participated with me in those efforts, were met with vicious suppression, including economic reprisals, violence, and threats of violence. My home has been vandalized, my friends have been beaten, shot at, assaulted with knives and guns. Over the years, I have observed a clear

pattern within LIUNA of chilling the rights of LIUNA members and preventing democratic participation in the union's affairs. Meaningful democracy is dead within LIUNA.*

Table 6-1 lists just some of the murders that can be attributed to labor racketeers. These murders were identified by means of a limited review of court cases, newspaper stories, articles, and books. Undoubtedly there are many (perhaps even more than those listed here) that I have failed to discover. Moreover, we should also keep in mind that for every murder there probably have been a score of beatings. Some of these, like the attack with sulphuric acid that blinded crusading *Daily Mirror* columnist Victor Riesel, were very serious indeed.** There are myriad documented incidents of dissidents being attacked at national conventions and local union meetings when they asked to be recognized in order to voice a criticism or make an unwelcome nomination.

While all of these murder victims listed in Table 6-1 were individuals who had a conflict with the incumbent union power structure, not all of these victims had unblemished records. Jimmy Hoffa, for example, had a career-long history of alliances with organized crime groups, but after Hoffa went to prison, organized crime preferred Hoffa's successor, Frank Fitzsimmons, as Teamsters general president.[6] Although Hoffa was hardly a dissident or reformer, his murder sent shock waves through the rank and file. We can imagine an ordinary Teamster thinking, "If LCN would murder Jimmy Hoffa for challenging its authority, what would happen to me if I started complaining?" A few of the notorious murders listed in Table 6-1 (e.g., Jock Yablonski) had nothing to do with Cosa Nostra. Nevertheless, I include Yablonski and a few others because, arguably, every high-visibility murder of a union dissident sends shock waves through the whole labor movement.

---

* The government offered Chris White's declaration as part of its draft civil RICO complaint against LIUNA, U.S. v. LIUNA (N.D. Ill.). The case was settled before the complaint was filed. Years later, White was actually elected to a minor post in the local. It appears that the government's intervention has had a significant effect on LIUNA's governance and political culture.
** Johnny Dioguardi was charged with having ordered this vicious attack. When the two key witnesses against him were murdered, all charges were dropped.

Table 6-1

Murders Associated with Labor Racketeering

Victim	Year Murdered	Circumstances Surrounding the Murder
Steve Kelliher	1923	Organized crime figure and labor leader; shot dead at the behest of Tommy Maloy.
Jacob Kaufman*	1931	Popular union organizer who for years had tried to persuade the courts to kick Tommy Maloy out of the unions. Killed after filing suit against Maloy and announcing that he would run against Maloy in an open election.
Dennis Ziegler*	1933	Dissident in Operating Engineers Local 569 in Chicago. Murdered.
Harry Koenig	1936	HEREIU Local 16 (New York) official. Murdered at the HEREIU national convention.
Norman Redwood	1937	Head of Laborers Local 102 in New York City. Killed by an assassin who hid in the bushes outside his home.
Peter Panto*	1939	Leader of an insurgent group in the ILA local in Brooklyn's Red Hook district; led a revolt against the corrupt union leadership of Joseph Ryan and mob boss Albert Anastasia. Lured from his home late at night and never seen again.
William Lurye*	1949	Union organizer stabbed to death in a telephone booth on West 35th Street in New York City. Two organized crime figures were arrested, but the witnesses could not make a positive ID. One witness stated he had been approached by a racketeer union official and given $100 to forget the defendants' identification.
Ed Murta*	1950s	Leader in the Carpenter's Union on Long Island; murdered.
John Acropolis*	1950s	President of Teamsters Local 456 in Westchester County, New York; murdered.
Anthony Castellito	1961	IBT Local 560 official. Murdered by Local 560 boss and LCN capo Tony Provenzano.
Walter Glockner*	1963	Local 560 member murdered the day after an argument with one of the Provenzano brothers.
Robert "Lonnie" DeGeorge*	1964–67	Union dissident in IBT Local 107 in Philadelphia. Murdered outside the local's headquarters. Francis Sheeran was charged with the murder, but the case was eventually thrown out.
Dow Wilson*	1966	Reformer in the International Painters Union in San Francisco. Murdered after criticizing and challenging International Union officers and policies. Ben Rasnick, a West Coast Painters Union leader, was convicted of ordering the murder.
Lloyd Green*	1966	Leader of the Painters Local 1178 and close ally of Dow Wilson. Murdered two weeks after Wilson.
Jock Yablonski*	1969	Murdered, along with his wife and daughter, at the end of his unsuccessful campaign to replace Tony Boyle as president of the United Mine Workers. Boyle was eventually convicted of ordering the murder.
Joe Caleb*	1972	Popular dissident in LIUNA Local 478 in Miami. Murdered after asking questions about the administration of the multimillion-dollar LIUNA trust fund controlled by District Council President Bernard Rubin, a reputed ally of the Chicago mob.
Frank Murray*	1973	Charismatic leader of ILA Local 1247 in Jersey City. Disappeared and presumed murdered after leaving an ILA meeting in midtown Manhattan.

(continued)

Table 6-1 (continued)

Victim	Year Murdered	Circumstances Surrounding the Murder
John Cammilleri	1974	A union member, allegedly tied to organized crime. Murdered after supporting an opposition candidate for union office in Buffalo Local 210.
Jimmy Hoffa	1975	Former IBT general president disappeared and presumed murdered by LCN because of his campaign to regain the Teamsters general presidency.
Danny Evangelista*	1976	Reformer opposed Theodore Maritas's candidacy for New York District Council of Carpenters presidency. Shot to death while sitting at his desk in Local 385 headquarters.
Al Bramlett*	1977	HEREIU officer murdered in Las Vegas after opposing the move of HEREIU Local 226 health and welfare funds to Illinois.
Danny Green	1977	Teamster official and racketeer associated with the Cleveland LCN. Murdered.
Willie Nordstrom*	1978	President of Carpenters Local 488 in the Bronx who criticized the union leadership; shot to death.
Robert Flotte*	1979	Put together a caucus of white, black, and Mexican workers in Longshoremen's Local 6 in San Francisco. Murdered outside the union hall.
John McCullough*	1980	President of the Philadelphia Roofers Local 30. Shot to death at his home by Willard Moran, reputedly due to unwillingness to accede to mob-dominated Local 54's determination to organize the bartenders in Atlantic City.
Nicholas Altieri	1981	An official in ILA Local 10. Murdered because LCN feared he might become a government cooperating witness.
Gene Viernes and Silme Domingo*	1981	Leaders of an insurgent caucus who pledged to oust racketeers in Seattle. Assassinated soon after winning ILA Local 36 election.
Ben Medina*	1982	After announcing his reform candidacy for a top job in LIUNA Local 332 in Philadelphia, five masked men broke into his home, bound and gagged his wife, and beat him to death.
Bobby Love*	1982	The business manager of LIUNA Local 194 in Baltimore intended to run for president on a reform ticket. Murdered two days after Medina.
Teddy Maritas	1983	Genovese crime family associate and District Council president of New York City Carpenters Union, 1977–1981. Murdered by the mob to prevent possible cooperation with federal prosecutors.
Danielle Forgione, Jr.	1984	Business manager of LIUNA Local 948 in Florida. Murdered while under investigation for looting the pension fund.
Harry Serio*	1989	Secretary-treasurer of IBT Local 478. Ambushed and shot to death as he entered the union offices on Route 22 in Union, New Jersey. Serio had earlier announced his intention to challenge the incumbent president and expose "sweetheart" deals with Lucchese-related air freight companies.
Robert Kubecka	1989	A waste hauler in Long Island who challenged Cosa Nostra control over IBT Local 813. Murdered for cooperating with a law enforcement investigation.
Jimmy Bishop	1990	A labor racketeer allied with LCN, Bishop was murdered as part of an intragang war over which LCN faction would control Painters District Council 9.
Anthony Cuozzo	1992	Former vice-president of IBT Local 295 in Jamaica (Queens), New York. Murdered.

* Victim was a union dissenter/reformer.

FRANK SCHONFELD STORY

One of the very few examples of rank-and-file union reformers succeeding in defeating a mob-dominated union occurred in the 1960s when Frank Schonfeld, a courageous member of the twelve-thousand-member New York City Painters Union District Council 9, challenged the entrenched mob-supported regime.* The mob-controlled leaders had signed lackluster collective bargaining agreements, been convicted for rigging bids on various projects, and provoked the scorn of many New York area painters. According to Herman Benson, who was personally familiar with Painters District Council 9 at the time, "The union continued to crumble: it ceased to exist on the job sites as a protector of working conditions. The contract was not enforced. Between 1953 and 1967 there was not a single general membership meeting of DC 9 painters."[7]

In 1961, Schonfeld ran for secretary treasurer (the District Council's top office). The District Council immediately brought charges against some of his allies. Despite Landrum-Griffin's guarantee that candidates for union office be given membership lists so they can contact the electorate, Schonfeld was provided only a partial list of members. Moreover, the incumbent regime's ballot counting was highly suspicious. Schonfeld was defeated, 3,700 votes to 1,700, but won a majority in locals where he had access to accurate membership lists.

After the election, the incumbent regime brought disciplinary charges against Schonfeld and suspended him from the union, but a federal judge nullified that maneuver. According to Benson, for the next six years Schonfeld and other insurgents continued to hold meetings, run candidates, and publish a newsletter, but they faced relentless opposition: "Schonfeld and his supporters were being starved out, blacklisted, denied the right to work." In 1967, the Manhattan district attorney brought a conspiracy case against the District Council 9's top official, along with various painting contractors and city officials, charging them with operating a bid-rigging cartel on New York City painting contracts. The secretary-treasurer had to resign and the Painters International placed the District Council under a trusteeship that organized crime continued to dominate.

* In *Rank and File Rebellion,* La Botz recounts a rank and file rebellion in IBT Local 138 in Long Island City, New York, that removed an entrenched labor racketeer probably (according to La Botz) connected to the Colombo crime family.

The Schonfeld group went to court to have the International Union's trusteeship dissolved. The Department of Labor weighed in (as usual) on the union's side. However, a federal judge found for the insurgents. "The history of D.C. 9 elections extending into the period of the trusteeship has been marred by fraud and other irregularities. [The International Union's officers] witnessed, with apparent indifference, the repeated silencing of the opposition's views at meetings, and blatant improprieties in local balloting."[8] Schonfeld was able to resume his campaign. The judge ordered that the election be overseen by the American Arbitration Association. In September 1967, Schonfeld won a stunning victory.

Schonfeld now held the district council's top office, but the old regime held on to most other district council offices and opposed Schonfeld at every turn. Mob-backed factions of the Carpenters and Teamsters unions now raided the district council, splitting away certain locals. At Schonfeld's instigation, the rank and file voted by referendum to revamp the makeup of the district council in order to better reflect the size of the local unions composing the district council. However, the Painters International Union vetoed the change, thereby continuing to stymie Schonfeld's reform efforts. Once again the International charged him with union disciplinary violations and removed him from office; once again, a federal judge reinstated him. However, in 1973, after just two three-year terms, Schonfeld was defeated by Jimmy Bishop, a candidate allied with the Lucchese organized crime family and supported by the International Union and the members of the clique that had controlled the district council for decades. The reform was over. (In 1990, Jimmy Bishop was murdered by another organized crime faction.)

RANK-AND-FILE REFORM MOVEMENTS

A few racketeer-ridden unions have spawned national or at least regional dissident "movements." It is difficult to calculate the size of these movements or to gauge their strength because the Internet permits a single individual to post a Web site, service email subscribers, and so on.

The best-known and most effective of the rank-and-file reformist organizations is Teamsters for a Democratic Union (TDU). TDU was founded in 1976.* In 1980, it merged, under the same name, with the Professional Drivers Council, a (Ralph) Naderite public interest organization that lobbies for improved safety conditions in the trucking industry.[9] TDU surveyed workers; organized special committees to analyze safety and other problems in the industries in which Teamsters were employed; and came up with proposed rank-and-file contract demands. During its formative years, TDU focused primarily on improving Teamster contracts, but it gradually turned its attention to reforming the union's governance. Its goal was to organize a sizeable militant Teamster minority.[10] By the mid-1980s, TDU published a regular newsletter, *Convoy Dispatch,* and claimed to have ten thousand members. A flavor of what TDU stands for can be gleaned from its Rank and File Bill of Rights, which can be found on its Web site.** Among the rights sought by TDU are a fair grievance procedure, direct election of officers, equality among Teamsters, and an end to discrimination. TDU sometimes backs candidates in union elections. It campaigned hard for Ron Carey in the 1991 trustee-supervised election and helped make Carey's victory possible. However, TDU often criticized Carey's administration.

Carey (again backed by TDU) won the 1996 election against a strong challenge by James P. Hoffa (Jimmy Hoffa's son). The election was marred by charges that the Carey campaign had used union funds on behalf of its candidate. Ultimately, the court-appointed elections officer voided the election, disqualified Carey from the rerun election, and the IRB expelled him from the union. In the 1998 rerun election, TDU supported Tom Leedham, a prominent reformer. Leedham won 39 percent of the vote, but lost to James P. Hoffa (55 percent). In 2001, Hoffa defeated him again, this time by nearly a two-to-one margin (Hoffa, 200,168; Leedham, 108,389).

There is no other dissident rank-and-file labor movement with the organizational coherence and strength of TDU. Nevertheless, there are always dissident voices, more so now with the advent of the Internet.

---

* A predecessor rank-and-file organization called TURF (Teamsters United Rank and File) was set up in 1971 in the aftermath of a national wildcat strike that challenged Frank Fitzsimmons's leadership of the IBT. In a few years, TURF fell apart because of internal dissension. In 1975, a group of Teamster activists formed a coalition called Teamsters for a Decent Contract and a parallel organization, UPSurge, to organize UPS workers to fight for a better UPS contract.
** TDU's Rank and File Bill of Rights can be found on the Web at http://solidarity.igc.org/teamster/tdu/htm.

And these voices have been encouraged by the federal government's campaign against labor racketeering. Recently, for example, a group of mostly African-American longshoremen in Charleston, Virginia, "the Charleston Five," were jailed for peacefully picketing a shipping company. The "Workers Coalition," which consists largely of officers from the Charleston Five's local union, criticized ILA International President John Bowers for waiting over a year before making a public statement supporting them.[11] The dispute has broadened into a more general challenge to the International's leadership.

THE ASSOCIATION FOR UNION DEMOCRACY

The Association for Union Democracy (AUD),[12] founded by Herman Benson and a small number of other labor radicals and idealists, is the only independent nongovernmental organization that advocates and litigates on behalf of rank-and-file union members. AUD has always been a hand-to-mouth organization with a small office in Brooklyn, a few paid staffers, and a tiny budget. Still, AUD published a regular newsletter, "Union Democracy Review," which exposes egregious assaults on union democracy as well as the occasional legal and electoral victories of rank-and-file reformers. It also holds conferences and organizes training courses and educational programs. Dissidents from any union can contact AUD for advice, including sometimes legal assistance from a very small number of volunteer lawyers.

CONCLUSION

Rank-and-file union members fit into our story mostly as victims. Labor racketeers are in the business of stealing from rank-and-file union members and selling out their rights and interests. The lack of much rank-and-file rebellion against labor racketeers does not indicate appreciation, respect, or satisfaction. Rank-and-file union member rebellion, like other rebellions against authoritarian regimes capable and willing to use violence, is extremely difficult. The collective action problem explains a great deal. It is immensely costly for any individual union member to protest against or try to organize opposition to incumbent labor racketeers. For the most part, reformers have been tragically unsuccessful, the victims of blacklisting, disciplinary actions, beatings, and murder. In their struggles to win basic civil rights within their unions, "dissidents" have not been able to count on the mainstream labor movement, the government, law enforcement agencies, intellectuals or even the civil liberties community for support. It has been a very lonely struggle.

The federal government's post-1980 campaign against Cosa Nostra has opened up space for insurgents to play a more active role. Even so, reform does not just spring to life naturally, and fear of the labor racketeers' return to power is a major inhibitor. Moreover, there is no guarantee that the first wave of non–Mafia connected reformers will have the competence and integrity to establish well-functioning democratic unions. Still, it must be emphasized that no meaningful reform of historically racketeer-ridden unions can be achieved without the mobilization of rank-and-file union members.

7

Attacking Labor Racketeering
Prior to Civil RICO (1982)

This is a preliminary report on the organized crime influence in the labor unions today in the United States. The picture that it presents is thoroughly frightening. At least four international unions are completely dominated by men who either have strong ties to or are members of the organized crime syndicate. A majority of the locals in most major cities of the United States in the International Brotherhood of Teamsters (IBT), Hotel and Restaurant Employees Union (HERE), Laborers International Union of North America (Laborers), and International Longshoreman's Association (ILA) unions are completely dominated by organized crime. The officials of these unions are firmly entrenched; there is little hope of removing them by a free election process. Convictions for misconduct have been sparse and when one corrupt official is removed another soon takes his place. The result has been a complete domination of certain industries by hoodlums. Management personnel in the companies who must deal with these hoodlums have despaired of getting help from law enforcement authorities. They pay the price of labor peace so that they may survive. The cost is passed on to the consumer.
—Peter Vaira and Douglas Roller, *Report on Organized Crime and the Labor Unions* (1978), 1

From the early 1930s until the mid-1970s, Congress was much more active than local, state, and federal law enforcement in calling attention to organized crime generally and to labor racketeering specifically. The Copeland Committee in the 1930s, the Kefauver and McClellan Committee hearings in the 1950s, and the Senate Permanent Subcommittee

on Investigations in the 1970s and 1980s publicized the problem, proposed new laws and increased sentences. By contrast, the federal enforcement agencies—the Federal Bureau of Investigation (FBI), the Department of Justice (DOJ), and the Department of Labor (DOL)—for
different reasons, did not make organized crime or labor racketeering
a high priority. Occasionally, an LCN member was convicted, usually of
a nonlabor racketeering offense like income tax evasion or murder.
Local police and prosecutors mostly ignored organized crime. The federal law enforcement campaign against the Cosa Nostra has roots in the
1950s and 1960s, but came of age after FBI Director Hoover's death in
1972 and in the wake of Jimmy Hoffa's assassination in 1975. Since then,
the FBI and DOJ have mounted and sustained a huge organized crime
control program.

CONGRESS ADDRESSES LABOR RACKETEERING:
THE HOBBS ACT

In 1933, the U.S. Senate Committee on Commerce (called the "Copeland
Committee" (after its chairman, New York's Democratic senator, Roy
Copeland) held hearings on "racketeering," including the role of mobsters within national and local labor organizations.[1] Witnesses from the
AFL Building Trade Unions' Anti-Racketeering Subcommittee complained to the Senate Committee that "most of the unions in New York
were saturated with rackets."[2] Employer-witnesses complained that
labor racketeers extorted payoffs by threatening business-destroying
labor problems.

The Copeland Committee's hearings led to passage of a federal extortion statute, the Anti-Racketeering Act of 1934.[3] Labor leaders opposed the draft bill on the grounds that it could be used to prosecute
bona fide strikes and job actions. To alleviate that concern, the final bill
exempted from the definition of extortion union conduct aimed at "the
payment of wages by a bona-fide employer to a bona-fide employee."
The act also included a union-friendly proviso:

> that no court of the United States shall construe or apply any of the
> provisions of this Act in such a manner as to impair, diminish or in any
> manner affect the rights of bona fide labor organizations in lawfully

carrying out the legitimate objectives thereof, as such rights are expressed in existing statutes of the United States.

A few years after passage of the Anti-Racketeering Act, federal prosecutors used the law to prosecute several Teamsters who prevented out-of-town trucking companies from driving trucks into New York City unless the companies paid the Teamster defendants for their assistance in guiding the trucks into the city. The Supreme Court reversed the convictions, holding that the Anti-Racketeering Act exempted from prosecution bona fide union demands, even if unreasonable.[4] The decision, in effect, destroyed the act's potential to punish and deter labor racketeering; the racketeers could avoid criminal liability by disguising extortions as legal, albeit unreasonable, demands for unnecessary and undesired goods or services.

Congress quickly sought to pass a new extortion statute that would definitely cover conduct like that of the defendants in the Teamsters case. The new Hobbs Act (1946) eliminated the Anti-Racketeering Act's exemption for payment of wages by bona fide employers to bona fide employees, but its sponsors assured labor and its supporters that the law could not be used to prosecute strikers.[5] In the decades that followed, the Hobbs Act was used against individuals who hijacked trucks, against corrupt state and local politicians, and occasionally against labor racketeers. In 1956, another labor racketeering prosecution reached the U.S. Supreme Court. The defendant union officials had attempted to extort money (for their own pockets) by forcing an employer to pay for both fictitious and superfluous services; the Court upheld the conviction against a challenge that the law was unconstitutional.[6] The decision was a green light for federal prosecutors to go after labor racketeers. They convicted a number of union officials who extorted payoffs from employers.[7] However, in 1973, the Supreme Court reversed a Hobbs Act conviction against strikers who had used high-powered rifles and explosives on the grounds that the Hobbs Act could not be used to punish individuals for pursuing a lawful union goal, even via criminal means.[8]

The Hobbs Act played an extremely important role in the civil RICO litigation brought against racketeer-ridden unions in the 1980s and 1990s. Prosecutors alleged and courts upheld the applicability of the Hobbs Act to LCN members and union officials who extorted union members' Landrum-Griffin rights (that is, intangible property). These Hobbs Act violations constituted "predicate offenses" that satisfied RICO's requirement of proof of "a pattern of racketeering activity."[*]

THE TAFT-HARTLEY ACT

In 1947, over organized labor's strenuous opposition, Congress passed the Taft-Hartley Act, which, according to its sponsors, sought to restore "a more balanced relationship" between labor and management.[9] President Harry Truman vetoed the act, but Congress overrode the veto. Taft-Hartley gave employees the right to refrain from participating in union activities, added certain union conduct to the National Labor Relations Act's list of unfair labor practices, and banned Communists from serving as union officers. It also made it a federal crime for an employer to give or lend money or anything of value to a union, union official, or union welfare fund and for a labor official to demand or accept anything of value from an employer. These criminal provisions have frequently been used to punish labor racketeers for taking employer bribes in exchange for sweetheart deals.

In 1956, the United States Supreme Court upheld the conviction of ILA President Joseph Ryan for taking payoffs from a stevedoring company in violation of the Taft-Hartley Act.[10] The president of a stevedoring company had given Ryan $1,000 each year from 1946 to 1951 in violation of Taft-Hartley. The district court found Ryan guilty, but the court of appeals reversed, holding that the president and principal negotiator of an international union was not a "union representative" for purposes of the Hobbs Act. The Supreme Court reinstated the conviction, ruling that Ryan violated Taft-Hartley by accepting money from an employer.[11] In other cases in the years that followed, Taft Hartley proved useful in persuading employers who had bribed union officials to become cooperating witnesses.[12]

---

[*] In *Bellomo v. United States*, 297 F.Supp.2d 494 (E.D.N.Y., 2003), for the first time a federal court held that denial of union democracy rights does not violate the Hobbs Act. If that decision prevails, a key government tool in the remediation of labor racketeering would have been lost.

THE DOUGLAS COMMITTEE AND RACKETEERING
IN THE PENSION FUNDS

After World War II, unions began to negotiate in earnest for employer-funded pension and welfare funds. (Such benefits are attractive to both management and labor because they are not taxable to employees while being tax deductible for employers.) Essentially, employers agreed to contribute a certain amount of money on behalf of their workers to funds to be used for union members' pensions, medical and dental care, and legal services. The funds (sometimes called Taft-Hartley plans) are controlled by an equal number of labor- and management-appointed trustees and administered by a fund administrator. Soon, such funds accumulated hundreds of millions, even billions, of dollars. Not surprisingly, labor racketeers immediately saw them as attractive targets for exploitation by embezzlements, fraudulent loans, kickbacks, and other manipulations.[13]

In the mid-1950s, the Senate Committee on Labor appointed a subcommittee, with Senator Paul Douglas (D.-Ill.) as chairman, to investigate corruption in union pension and welfare funds. The subcommittee illuminated widespread corruption, fraud, and abuse, especially in the Teamsters' Central States Pension and Welfare Fund. In 1959, in response to the abuses uncovered by the Douglas Committee, Congress passed the Welfare and Pension Plan Disclosure Act (WPPDA), which required pension and welfare plans to report certain fund information to the DOL. Congress intended the disclosure requirement to provide employees with enough information to monitor their plans effectively. This proved to be wishful thinking and abuses continued. In 1962, Congress strengthened the WPPDA by adding criminal provisions to punish fund administrators and trustees who took kickbacks from vendors of goods and services; the law assigned enforcement authority to the DOL.[14]

Continuing mob exploitation of union benefit funds was one factor leading Congress to pass ERISA (Employee Retirement Income Security Act) in 1974.[15] ERISA's criminal provisions dealt with (1) theft or embezzlement from employee benefit plans; (2) false statements or concealment of facts in relation to documents required by ERISA; and (3) offers, acceptances, or solicitations to influence operations of employee benefit funds.[16] Thus, federal prosecutors were armed with criminal laws to attack labor racketeers.

MCCLELLAN COMMITTEE HEARINGS (1957–1959)
AND THE LANDRUM-GRIFFIN LAW (1959)

The McClellan Committee's hearings (1957–1959), including some very sharp exchanges between Robert Kennedy and Jimmy Hoffa, were widely covered by newspapers, magazines, and television. They generated inexorable momentum for Congressional action. In 1959, Congress passed the Labor-Management Reporting Act of 1959 (LMRDA), popularly known as the Landrum-Griffin Act. The law bans persons with criminal records from holding union office. It also guarantees to union members basic democratic rights (speech, candidacy, voting) within their labor organizations. It declares that union officers stand in the role of fiduciaries vis-à-vis the rank and file membership.* It also seeks to achieve accountability to their memberships by requiring unions to file various financial and organizational reports with the U.S. Department of Labor.[17] For the most part, Landrum-Griffin's enforcement tools are civil rather than criminal. Congress assigned enforcement authority to the DOL, which delegated that authority to its Office of Labor-Management Standards (OLMS). OLMS can investigate and take enforcement actions on its own. In addition, aggrieved union members can bring their complaints to OLMS or, in some cases, to the National Labor Relations Board or directly to a federal court. Unfortunately, there have never been more than a handful of public interest lawyers available to help union members vindicate their Landrum-Griffin rights. OLMS enforcement has been lackluster, at best.[18]

Landrum-Griffin contains a few criminal provisions, including a wide-ranging prohibition on the use of violence to deny or interfere

---

* SEC. 501 (a) The officers, agents, shop stewards, and other representatives of a labor organization occupy positions of trust in relation to such organization and its members as a group. It is, therefore, the duty of each such person, taking into account the special problems and functions of a labor organization, to hold its money and property solely for the benefit of the organization and its members and to manage, invest, and expend the same in accordance with its constitution and bylaws and any resolutions of the governing bodies adopted thereunder, to refrain from dealing with such organization as an adverse party or in behalf of an adverse party in any matter connected with his duties and from holding or acquiring any pecuniary or personal interest which conflicts with the interests of such organization, and to account to the organization for any profit received by him in whatever capacity in connection with transactions conducted by him or under his direction on behalf of the organization.

with the democratic rights the law guarantees.* Another provision makes it a federal crime to embezzle funds from a labor union.** Still other provisions prohibit unions from making loans to or paying fines for union officers and filing false reports with the DOL. Over the years, the Department of Justice has used these provisions to obtain a number of convictions. For example, in *U.S. v. Bertucci* (1964), defendants were convicted for beating union members with pipes and baseball bats when those members[19] attempted to enter the union hall to vote on a collective bargaining agreement. The court explained that "[t]he LMRDA gives to the individual union members certain rights which when interfered with by a union, its officials or its agents can be redressed civilly against them. In addition, there are criminal sanctions imposed against a person who interferes with those rights."[20]

In 1961, Attorney General Robert F. Kennedy urged Congress to pass the Interstate and Foreign Travel in Aid of Racketeering Act, popularly known as the Travel Act.[21] Its sought to make federal law enforcement assistance available to attack organized crime that crosses state borders.[22] In his submission letter to the Senate Judiciary Committee, Kennedy stated, "Over the years an ever-increasing portion of our national resources have been diverted into illicit channels. Because many rackets are conducted by highly organized syndicates whose influence extends over state and national borders, the Federal Government should come to the aid of local law enforcement authorities in an effort to stem such activity."[23] Therefore, the Travel Act provided federal law enforcement with jurisdiction over use of interstate facilities to promote a number of illegal activities typically associated with organized crime.[24] The Travel Act was an early step toward establishing a legal basis for a federal war on organized crime.

---

* 29 U.S.C. 530. It shall be unlawful for any person through the use of force or violence, or threat of the use of force or violence, to restrain, coerce, or intimidate, or attempt to restrain, coerce, or intimidate any member of a labor organization for the purpose of interfering with or preventing the exercise of any right to which he is entitled under the provisions of this Act. Any person who willfully violates this section shall be fined not more than $1,000 or imprisoned for not more than one year, or both.
** 29 U.S.C. 501(c). Any person who embezzles, steals, or unlawfully and willfully abstracts or converts to his own use, or the use of another, any of the moneys, funds, securities, property, or other assets of a labor organization of which he is an officer, or by which he is employed, directly or indirectly, shall be fined not more than $10,000 or imprisoned for not more than five years, or both.

RICO (1970)

The 1967 report of the President's Commission on Crime and the Administration of Justice presented, among other things, a frightening (and exaggerated) picture of Cosa Nostra as a well-coordinated nationwide conspiracy.[25] Subsequent congressional hearings focused on LCN's infiltration of the legitimate economy, especially labor unions and businesses. For example, on March 11, 1969, Senator McClellan (D.-Ark.) told fellow senators:

> Closely paralleling its take-over of legitimate business, organized crime has moved into legitimate unions. Control of labor supply through control of unions can prevent the unionization of some industries or can guarantee sweetheart contracts in others. It provides the opportunity for theft from union funds, extortion through threat of economic pressure, and the profit to be gained from the manipulation of welfare and pension funds and insurance contracts. Trucking, construction and waterfront entrepreneurs have been persuaded for labor peace to countenance gambling, loan-sharking and pilferage. All of this, of course, makes a mockery of much of the promise of the social legislation of the last half-century.[26]

McClellan, Senator Roman Hruska (R.-Neb.), and others argued that the federal law enforcement agencies and courts did not have adequate powers to defeat organized crime. After hearings, Congress passed the Racketeer Influenced and Corrupt Organizations Act (RICO), which made it a federal crime to use "dirty" money (proceeds of racketeering activity or collection of an unlawful debt) to acquire an interest in, or to seize an interest in, or to conduct the affairs of an "enterprise," including labor unions, by means of a pattern of racketeering activity (defined as commission of at least two of a long list of crimes within a ten-year period).[27] RICO crime is punishable by up to a twenty-year prison sentence, plus an additional twenty years for a conspiracy to violate RICO. In addition, a defendant can also be convicted and sentenced for the predicate offenses that establish the "pattern of racketeering activity" (for example, a Hobbs Act offense, labor bribery, murder, fraud). Because it was new and complex, RICO was not used much for about a decade but by the late 1970s it had become the statute of choice in organized crime prosecutions.[28] It provided federal prosecutors the advantages of draconian punishment provisions, mandatory criminal forfeiture, liberal rules on joinder of defendants and offenses, and a means of prosecuting criminal conduct that theretofore had not been reachable under federal law.

RICO also contains two civil remedies. One empowers RICO victims to sue their victimizers for treble damages. For obvious reasons, victims have not chosen to sue LCN members. The other civil RICO remedial provision authorizes the U.S. attorney general to seek and the federal courts to grant injunctions and other equitable relief to prevent defendants from committing future RICO violations. Beginning in the early 1980s, this remedy became the preferred weapon for attacking labor racketeering because it enabled the Department of Justice to obtain injunctions and consent decrees providing for court monitoring and reform of racketeer-ridden unions.

FEDERAL ENFORCEMENT AGENCIES AND LABOR RACKETEERING

Although Congress showed strong interest in labor racketeering, investigated the problem, publicized it, and passed substantive criminal legislation that featured severe punishments, the laws were not much used until the late 1970s. For the FBI, this "hands-off" policy reflected Director J. Edgar Hoover's unwillingness to devote FBI personnel or resources to organized crime investigations. Hoover's view was that organized crime was a local phenomenon and, in any event, of far less importance than other problems, especially the threat of communist subversion.

Absent FBI investigations, federal prosecutors could do little to combat organized crime generally and labor racketeering specifically. Except for a small number of DOJ personnel at central headquarters in Washington, D.C., federal prosecutors work for the 93 U.S. attorneys (one for each federal judicial district) who, as presidential appointees, operate with a good deal of autonomy from their boss, the U.S. attorney general. In theory, the U.S. attorneys can develop their own priorities depending upon the particular crime problems in their jurisdictions; in reality, they depend on the FBI and other federal enforcement agents to bring cases to them. Even though the FBI is also a part of the U.S. Department of Justice, it has substantial autonomy. (J. Edgar Hoover, of course, had almost complete autonomy. After his death, Congress limited future FBI directors to a single ten-year term.) Hence, it would have been impossible for DOJ attorneys themselves to launch a successful attack on organized crime or labor racketeering without the FBI director's support.

Congress gave the Department of Labor authority to enforce the Landrum-Griffin Act and an array of pension and welfare laws. But the DOL is a cabinet-level department whose main mission is to look after the concerns of organized labor, not to punish abuses by organized labor. Over the years some Senators and Congressmen have used hearings to criticize the DOL for failing to investigate and prepare cases against labor racketeers.

Despite these structural, bureaucratic, and political obstacles to the enforcement of the anti–labor racketeering laws, there were occasional prosecutions in the 1950s. Things accelerated dramatically in 1961 when Robert F. Kennedy became U.S. attorney general. Kennedy immediately turned the office's attention to organized crime. He made prosecution of IBT President Jimmy Hoffa his top priority.[29] He expanded OCRS and sent prosecutors around the country to investigate and prosecute organized crime.[30]

President John F. Kennedy was assassinated in November 1963. His brother resigned as attorney general in early 1964. Later that year, Hoffa was convicted, first of jury tampering and then of pension fund fraud. In 1967, when his appeals were exhausted, he began serving a lengthy prison term. Reacting to the 1967 President's Crime Commission's report and to Senator McClellan's and other congressmen's lobbying, Congress provided federal law enforcement with electronic eavesdropping authority (1968), the Witness Security Program (1970), and RICO (1970).

J. Edgar Hoover died suddenly in 1972. The FBI passed into new hands. There were no interest groups pressing for a federal war on organized crime. Pressure came from DOJ prosecutors and FBI agents themselves. A modern-day law enforcement agency was affronted by the machinations of a notorious crime syndicate. The FBI found the Cosa Nostra crime families an enemy worthy of the attention of a first class law enforcement agency. Perhaps the post-Hoover FBI judged itself by the power and status of the criminals who it successfully investigated.

Following up on the 1967 President's Crime Commission's understanding of the organized crime problem, FBI agents and federal prosecutors launched their campaign to control organized crime by focusing on gambling, believing it to be LCN's chief moneymaking activity. But federal judges were critical of prosecuting bookmakers and gamblers in federal courts. They were not convinced that gambling was a serious national problem, and several made it clear to U.S. attorneys that they did not think that these gambling cases belonged in federal court. When the gamblers were convicted, they often drew light sentences. The organized crime campaign floundered.

President Richard Nixon pardoned Jimmy Hoffa in December 1971[31] in order to obtain the endorsement of the Teamsters of his reelection. Hoffa remained popular with rank-and-file Teamsters, but his former protégé, Frank Fitzsimmons, then serving as IBT general president, wanted to keep the position. Thus, he persuaded the Nixon administration to condition Hoffa's pardon on Hoffa's abstention from union affairs for ten years. Hoffa agreed but immediately went to court to challenge the condition and began campaigning to reclaim the Teamsters presidency.[32]

The Cosa Nostra crime families had even more influence in the IBT under the compliant Fitzsimmons than with the feisty Hoffa. On July 30, 1975, Hoffa disappeared; a mob "hit" was immediately presumed (and is now believed to have been orchestrated by Anthony Giacalone, a leader of the Detroit Cosa Nostra family, and Tony Provenzano, president of IBT Local 560 and a capo in the Genovese crime family).[33]

A revitalized OCRS established federal organized crime strike forces in thirteen cities. The strike forces comprised personnel from DOJ, IRS, DOL, and other federal and local agencies and reported directly to OCRS in Washington rather than to the U.S. attorneys.[34]

After Hoffa's assassination, the OCRS and the FBI switched their organized crime control focus from gambling to labor racketeering. The promotion of labor racketeering as an enforcement target was motivated by the goal of eradicating LCN, not by a commitment to cleaning up unions or guaranteeing union democracy. The revitalized post-Hoover FBI launched several ambitious labor racketeering investigations, including, in the late 1970s, the massive UNIRAC (Union Involved Racketeering) investigation of the International Longshoremen's Association. UNIRAC began as a Miami Strike Force project that

expanded to New York City and then to all major east coast ports. It resulted in the conviction of 130 businessmen, union officials, and Cosa
Nostra members, including Anthony Scotto, an ILA vice-president and
a capo in the Gambino crime family.[*][35]

Another FBI investigation, PENDORF (Penetration Dorfman), fo-
cused on Cosa Nostra control over the IBT Central States Pension Fund
(CSPF) and resulted in the convictions of IBT General President Roy
Williams, Joe Lombardo (member of the Chicago Outfit), and Allen
Dorfman (Chicago Outfit associate who represented the mob's interest
in the CSPF) for attempting to bribe U.S. Senator Howard Cannon (D.-
Nev.) to oppose trucking deregulation. Cosa Nostra later assassinated
Dorfman because of concern that he might become a cooperating gov-
ernment witness.[36]

The FBI's STRAWMAN investigation focused on a conspiracy by
four Cosa Nostra families to use the CSPF to obtain interests in Las
Vegas casinos and to skim profits from those casinos; it resulted in convictions of Joey Aiuppa (boss of the Chicago Outfit); Jackie Cerone (underboss of the Outfit); Angelo La Pietra and Joe Lombardo (Oufit capos);
Frank Balistrieri (boss of the Milwaukee LCN family); and Thomas and
Milton Rockman (associates of the Cleveland crime family).

The FBI's LILREX (Long Island Labor Racketeering and Extortion)
investigation targeted racketeering in New York City and Long Island's
construction industry. The investigation probed the relationship between organized crime and the industry, leading to the prosecution of
Theodore Maritas, president of the New York City–area District Council of Carpenters. Prosecutors charged Maritas with taking $125,000 in
payoffs in return for allowing contractors to use nonunion labor on

---

[*] *Time* magazine reported Scotto's conviction this way: "As a vice president of the International Longshoremen's Association and head of its Local 1814 in Brooklyn, Anthony
Scotto, 45, has long been laden with two very different reputations. A personable and ar-
ticulate man who favors $500 pinstripe suits and expensive Manhattan restaurants, Scotto
has lectured at Harvard University on labor relations, serves as a trustee of the Brooklyn
Academy of Music and counts some of New York's most prominent politicians among his
friends. But because of his occupational affiliation with the city's notoriously corrupt
waterfront and his 1957 marriage to the niece of mobster Albert Anastasia, police consider
Scotto to be a criminal. In 1959, the FBI went so far as to identify him as a *capodecina*,
or lieutenant, in the Mafia family of Carlo Gambino, an allegation that the union leader
vehemently denied." "Scotto: Out of the Dock," *Time*, November 26, 1979, 61.

Manhattan and Queens construction projects and with unsuccessfully attempting to extort $100,000 more. Maritas was murdered on the eve of the trial. His five codefendants, including Lucchese crime family capo Vincent DiNapoli, were convicted. Jack McCarthy, a labor consultant with a string of labor racketeering convictions, pleaded guilty to a conspiracy count.[37]

The LIUNA investigation focused on Cosa Nostra racketeering in the Laborers International Union of North America (LIUNA). The investigation resulted in several convictions, but notable acquittals for retired Outfit boss Tony Accardo and LIUNA president Angelo Fosco. Tampa organized crime boss Santo Trafficante avoided trial on account of poor health.[38]

A joint DOL and DOJ investigation of the CSPF began in the fall of 1975. The fund, more than 70 percent invested in real estate and casinos (mostly Las Vegas), was notorious for lending money to organized crime figures and their associates. The IRS sought to revoke the fund's tax-exempt status, leading to a settlement in which twelve of the fund's sixteen trustees resigned. The CSPF agreed to hire an independent fiduciary (Equitable Life Insurance Society) to handle investments.[39] The trustees retained authority to purchase goods and services, to administer pension benefits, and to handle money from the time it was paid into the fund each month to the time (approximately thirty days later) it was deposited with the institutional fiduciary. Corruption and racketeering continued.

In 1981, the DOL filed a lawsuit against all current and former trustees of the CSPF, alleging violations of their fiduciary obligation. The lawsuit resulted in a consent decree that prohibited the fund from employing or doing business with any person who had been convicted of a felony or misdemeanor involving a breach of fiduciary responsibility and required the appointment of an independent special counsel to monitor the fund's operations.[40] The agreement and oversight subsequently were extended until September 22, 2002, and then to September 22, 2007.

Slowly, the DOL began paying increased attention to labor racketeering. In 1978, Congress established a system of independent inspectors general, accountable to Congress, in all cabinet-level federal agencies.[41] An inspector general's mission was to combat fraud, waste, and abuse. Congress specifically charged the DOL's inspector general with responsibility for investigating labor racketeering. This job was assigned to the new Office of Labor Racketeering (OLR), which would play an important role in many future investigations. OLR's agents (many recruited from other federal law enforcement agencies) were the most law enforcement–oriented personnel in DOL history, and they participated fully in the federal organized crime strike forces.*

In 1986, the President's Commission on Organized Crime reported that the labor racketeering problem, exposed by the McClellan Committee almost thirty years earlier, had worsened. But, despite the PCOC's criticism, the government had begun an unprecedented attack on LCN. The first civil RICO suit against labor racketeers (IBT Local 560) produced a wide-ranging court decree, including a court-monitored trusteeship. More such suits, following up on criminal cases of the 1970s and 1980s, were in the works.

The DOJ's and the FBI's campaign against Cosa Nostra was most vigorous and most successful in New York City, where, of course, there were the most organized crime families, members, and associates. The FBI organized separate units to focus on each family. Eventually, based upon extensive electronic surveillance and some important LCN defectors, the federal prosecutors brought RICO criminal cases against each of the Cosa Nostra crime families, charging key members with participating in the affairs of the enterprise (the crime family itself) through a pattern of racketeering activity (any number of predicate racketeering offenses).

After the successful completion of the family RICO cases, Rudy Giuliani, then U.S. attorney for the Southern District of New York (Manhattan and the Bronx) brought the most ambitious criminal RICO case in U.S. law enforcement history. In the 1985 so-called "commission case," Giuliani's office brought together in a single trial as defendants the bosses and several other leaders of the five Cosa Nostra crime families in the city, charging them with participating in the affairs of a Cosa Nostra "commission" through a pattern of racketeering activity. According to the indictment, the commission had been established by LCN bosses in 1931 to resolve disputes and regulate relations between the families. Perhaps it originally included LCN bosses from around the country, but the commission of the 1980s consisted only of the five NYC bosses. The indictment charged the defendants both with operating the

---

* For information and some history of the OLR, see http://www.oig.dol.gov/public/programs/oi/main.htm.

commission through a pattern of racketeering activity and with con-spiring to operate it as a racketeering enterprise. The indictment alleged that through the enterprise, the defendants engaged in or aided and abetted murders, narcotics trafficking, loansharking, and labor racket-eering.[42]

Much of the prosecution's case centered on the defendants' domi-nation of the New York City LIUNA Local 6A. The prosecution sought to prove that, using its control over this Concrete and Cement Workers Union, the commission enforced a concrete cartel, which permitted only a handful of contractors to bid on concrete contracts in excess of $2 million. In exchange for this lucrative opportunity, the cartel mem-bers agreed to kick back to the commission 2 percent of the contract prices. After six days of deliberation, the jury found the defendants guilty of seventeen racketeering acts and twenty related charges of ex-tortion, labor payoffs, and loan sharking. Giuliani announced that "[t]he verdict reached today has resulted in dismantling the ruling council of La Cosa Nostra."[43] The commission case was the highest profile and most important organized crime prosecution in U.S. his-tory. It demonstrated, even to the skeptics, that the federal govern-ment, when aroused to action, had the ability to defeat the nation's most powerful crime syndicate. During the 1980s, prosecutors sent the boss of every Cosa Nostra crime family, and sometimes their succes-sors, to prison.

STATE/LOCAL EFFORTS

Most law enforcement in the United States is local. Police departments are organized at the town and city level; prosecutors, at the county level. This decentralized, small-unit law enforcement is not suited to complex organized crime investigations and prosecutions. Moreover, for much of the twentieth century, police departments in many large cities were severely compromised and/or corrupted in the investiga-tion of organized crime.[44] Consequently, with a few notable exceptions, local law enforcement did not seriously oppose organized crime gener-ally or labor racketeering specifically.[45]

The most notable exception was Thomas E. Dewey who served as Special New York City anti-racketeering prosecutor from 1935 to 1937 and then as Manhattan district attorney from 1937 to 1941.[46] In 1936,

using New York State law, Dewey launched an investigation and prosecution of racketeering in the city's restaurant sector, where Dutch
Schultz had taken control of the labor union and the employers' association. Although Schultz was murdered (by the mob for plotting to assassinate Dewey), Dewey's team indicted fourteen defendants on embezzlement and extortion charges. The prosecution's closing argument
told the jurors: "This is the first time that a full industrial racket has
been presented in a single case. If there is anything that is important to
the community today, it is a warning that rackets can be prosecuted and
broken."[47]

When Dewey moved on to the governorship, he was succeeded as
district attorney by Frank Hogan, whose thirty-two-year tenure in office earned him the nickname "Mr. District Attorney." Hogan's office
convicted the occasional organized crime figure, including the labor
racketeer Joseph Fay.[48] As vice-president of the International Union
of Operating Engineers, Fay extorted contractors working construction sites along the eastern seaboard.* In February 1945, Hogan's office
charged Fay and an associate with conspiracy to extort $703,000 from
contractors on the Delaware aqueduct water-supply project. Some labor
leaders sharply criticized the indictment. In a kind of response, Hogan
told the jury: "Labor is not on trial here. . . . These men are business partners in crime, and the business of the partnership is extortion. . . . They
are shakedown artists—ruthless, grasping thieves who have lined their
pockets at the expense of the laboring man they represent."[49] Fay was
convicted and sentenced to seven and a half to fifteen years in prison.
Nine years later, in 1954, Hogan convicted Johnny Dioguardi for failure
to pay state income taxes.

Despite Hogan's early success, labor racketeering continued to
flourish. In April 1985, in the wake of media allegations of rampant
corruption and racketeering in the New York City construction industry, Mayor Edward Koch urged Governor Mario Cuomo to appoint
a special prosecutor. Instead, the governor requested the New York
State Organized Crime Task Force (OCTF), a standing state agency,

---

* According to labor historian Harold Seidman, Fay "shined as a good fellow. In the de-
pression years he had been perhaps the most conspicuous spender Atlantic City has had.
In one night he is reputed to have lost as much as $50,000 in various Atlantic City gam-
bling resorts. His luxurious ten-room house in the exclusive Forest Hills section of
Newark was purchased in 1930." Harold Seidman, *Labor Czars* (New York: Liveright,
1938).

undertake "an intensive and comprehensive investigation."[*] The OCTF initiated an unprecedented multidisciplinary investigation of the almost century-long problem. In addition to utilizing standard law enforcement techniques and investigative strategies, it engaged economists, political scientists, labor relations specialists, and construction industry experts. Its 1988 report on the problem and its recommendations for reform are a major contribution to our understanding of labor racketeering. Among other things, the report found that the city's five Cosa Nostra crime families controlled more than a dozen construction unions and several construction companies.

While the OCTF investigation was under way, Governor Cuomo established the Construction Industry Strike Force (CISF), comprising prosecutors, investigators, analysts, accountants, and support staff from OCTF and the Manhattan District Attorney's office. The CISF obtained or significantly contributed to the convictions of officials in a number of construction unions, including the laborers, carpenters, teamsters, bricklayers, and mason tenders unions. The work of the ad hoc CISF led the Manhattan DA to establish a permanent labor racketeering unit.[50]

CRIME COMMISSIONS

Systemic organized crime racketeering and the corrupt relationship between urban political regimes and organized crime led to the establishment of crime commissions in several major U.S. cities.[51] Some of the commissions were arms of the legislature; others were citizen groups (often businessmen) formed without government funds or authority. For example, the famous Chicago Crime Commission was founded in 1919 by thirty-five members of the Chicago business community. Eventually, it came to comprise more than two hundred businesses and professional leaders. Over the years it has issued many important reports on the state of organized crime in Chicago. Another prominent organization, the Pennsylvania Crime Commission, was established as an in-

---

[*] The New York State Organized Crime Task Force (OCTF) under the leadership of Ronald Goldstock launched some of the most innovative organized crime prosecutions in the country, including successfully planting a recording device in the car of Lucchese family crime boss Anthony Corallo.

vestigative agency of state government. For decades it exposed organized crime's activities, including gambling, drug trafficking, and labor racketeering.[52]

The crime commissions do not have prosecutorial authority. In fact, some have very limited investigative authority, but they provide a forum to which people can bring complaints and information. In effect, the crime commissions call attention to the problem of organized crime at the state and local levels much in the way that Congress does at the national level.

CONCLUSION

Until the late 1970s and early 1980s, neither the federal nor state and local governments had a plan or program to attack organized crime, much less labor racketeering. In part, this was due to corruption. In many cities organized crime figures were influential in labor, business, and politics. Their influence often reached into the police departments, where they were able to choose, or at least veto, commissioners, chiefs, and heads of departments. Even where such corruption did not occur, city police departments did not have the legal, financial, or technical expertise to mount a meaningful campaign against organized crime.

To be sure, there were sporadic eruptions of law enforcement activity. From time to time, federal prosecutors did convict LCN members, some of whom were labor racketeers. For example, in 1931 U.S. Treasury Department agents used income tax evasion charges to convict Al Capone (1899–1947), the most powerful Chicago organized crime figure and labor racketeer. Joseph "Socks" Lanza (1904–1968), who organized the United Seafood Workers Union and used his labor power to dominate the New York City's Fulton Fish market, the largest wholesale fish market in the country, was sent to prison in 1932 for federal antitrust crimes; in 1943, the city's prosecutors successfully prosecuted him for extortion. In 1966, federal prosecutors obtained a labor racketeering extortion conviction against Anthony Provenzano, who served as an IBT vice-president as well as president of IBT Local 560; in 1979, federal prosecutors convicted Provenzano of murdering a union dissident. In 1973, federal prosecutors obtained a stock fraud conviction against John Dioguardi (1915–1979), one of the most powerful and prolific labor racketeers in American history. Over the course of his career he wielded power in the Teamsters, Auto Workers, and several other unions. In 1979, Anthony Scotto, vice-president of ILA and a NYC Gambino crime family capo, was convicted of violating RICO. Labor racketeering was finally on federal law enforcement's radar screen, but decades of inaction had allowed the problem to become deeply entrenched.

Even when labor racketeers were successfully prosecuted and sent to prison, there was little if any impact on racketeer-ridden unions because another organized crime figure would fill the shoes of the imprisoned racketeer.[53] Thus, at a Senate hearing in 1978, then Assistant U.S. Attorney General Benjamin Civiletti testified that more than three hundred union locals remained controlled or heavily influenced by organized crime.[54] According to DOJ attorneys Peter Vaira and Douglas Roller's report, *Organized Crime and the Labor Unions* (1978), organized crime's influence in the labor unions "presents a thoroughly frightening picture. At least four international unions are completely dominated by men who either have strong ties to or are members of the organized crime syndicate."[55] In 1980, the Senate Permanent Subcommittee on Investigations' hearings on the IBT, ILA, LIUNA, and HEREIU revealed widespread looting of pension and welfare funds.[56]

Once the FBI committed itself to a war on organized crime the tide began to turn. By the mid-1980s, the agency was involved in a full-scale attack on LCN. There were several hundred agents working on organized crime cases in New York City alone. Separate squads mapped each of the five families' tables of organization and money-making activities, then designed strategies to dismantle them. Faced with a realistic prospect of being imprisoned for life, numerous Cosa Nostra members, even capos, consigliere, and bosses, began to serve as cooperating government witnesses. The family RICO cases and the commission case brought the full resources of the federal government down on organized crime. It is against that background that we can understand and assess the extraordinary post-1980 campaign to eliminate labor racketeering.

Appendix
Congressional Labor Racketeering Hearings (1950–2000)

1950–1954

Strikes and Racketeering in the Kansas City Area, House Committee on Education and Labor Special Subcommittee on Strikes and Racketeering, 1953

Investigation of Welfare Funds and Racketeering, House Committee on Education and Labor Subcommittee on Union Welfare Funds and Racketeering, 1953.

Investigation of Racketeering, House Committee on Government Operations & House Committee on Education and Labor Special Subcommittee on Strikes and Racketeering, 1953.

Investigation of Racketeering in the Washington, DC Area, House Committee on Government Operations Special Committee on Antiracketeering, 1954.

Investigation of Racketeering in the Pittsburgh PA Area, House Committee on Government Operations Subcommittee on Public Accounts, 1954.

Investigation of Racketeering in the Minneapolis, MN Area, House Committee on Government Operations Subcommittee on Public Accounts, 1954

Investigation of Racketeering in the Cleveland Ohio Area, Parts 1–2, House Committee on Government Operations Subcommittee on Anti-Racketeering, 1954.

1955–1959

Laundry Workers International Union Welfare Fund, Vols. 1–5, Senate Committee on Labor and Public Welfare, 1955.

Violation or Non-Enforcement of Government Laws and Regulations in the Labor Union Field, Parts 1–2, Senate Committee on Government Operations Permanent Subcommittee on Investigations, 1957.

Published and Unpublished Hearings Conducted by the Senate Select Committee on Improper Activities in Labor or Management, a.k.a. the "McClellan Committee"

Investigation of Improper Activities in Labor or Management: Parts 1–58, 1957–1958 (counted as 58 separate hearings)

Chattanooga, Tennessee, Numbers Rackets and Judicial Corruption, 1957.

Election Fraud, Local 1843, United Steelworkers of America, Pittsburgh, Pa., 1957.

Investigation of Improper Activities in Labor or Management Field-New York Area, 1957.

Statement of Anthony Valente, President of the United Textile Workers of America, 1957.

Statement of Lloyd Klenert, Secretary-Treasurer of the United Textile Workers of America, Vol. 1, 1957.

Teamsters Union Activities in the Detroit Area, 1957.

Teamsters Union Activities in the Tennessee Area, 1957.

Testimony of John L. Cowling, 1957.

Testimony of Nunzio Squillante, 1957.

Testimony of Paul Dorfman, 1957.

Amalgamated Meat Cutters Union in New York City Area, 1957.

Consolidated Edison Corporation, Vol. 1 & 2, 1958.

Interview of Irvin Paul Miller, 1958.

James R. Hoffa, 1958.

Juke Box Industry Union Problems, Detroit Area, 1958.

Kohler Case, 1958.

Staff Interrogation, 1958.

Labor Unions Illegal Activities Investigation, Vols. 1–3, 1958. (3 separate hearings)

Perfect Circle Co. Strike Investigation, 1958.

Staff Interrogation of Robert P. Whitman, 1958.

Staff Interrogation of Joseph P. Pizzo, 1958.

Statement Prepared by Emil Mazy, Secretary-Treasurer, United Auto Workers, 1958.

Teamsters Union Activities in Gary, Indiana, 1958.

Teamsters Union Activities in the Philadelphia Area, 1958.

Teamsters Union, Vol. 1, Vol. 2, 1958.

Testimony of Maxwell Raddock and Morris Horn, 1958.

Testimony of Melvin L. Bishop, 1958.

Amalgamated Meat Cutters and Butcher Workmen, 1958.

Amalgamated Meat Cutters and Butcher Workmen of North America, 1958.

Carpenters Union Investigation, 1958.

Carpenters Union Publishing Activities, 1958.

Juke Box Industry Union Problems, Detroit Area, 1958.

Coin Operated Machines, 1958.

Acid-Throwing Violence Against Truck Drivers in the Tampa, Florida, Area, 1959.

Coin Operated Machines, 1959.

Deposition of Randall Gray, 1959.

Milwaukee News Conference of the Chief Counsel, 1959.

New York Newspaper Distribution, 1959.

Proposed Hearings on the United Automobile Workers Union, 1959.

Publication of Illinois Teamsters News, 1959.

Teamsters Union Activities in Michigan, 1959.

Teamsters Union Activities in Michigan, 1959.

Teamsters Union Activities in New York, 1959.

Testimony of Charles Johnson, Skill Games Rental, Inc.

Testimony of Frank J. Smith, 1959.

Testimony of George F. Fitzgerald and James R. Hoffa, 1959.

Testimony of Sylvia S. Hart, 1959.

Testimony of Walter Schuler, 1959.

Testimony of Randolph Gray and Mrs. Gertrude Gray, 1959.

United Association of Journeymen and Apprentices of the Plumbing and Pipefitting Industry, 1959.

United Automobile Workers Union Hearings Problems, 1959.

Staff Interview, 1959.

Published and Unpublished Hearings Conducted by Various House and Senate Committees

Violation or Nonenforcement of Government Laws and Regulations in the Labor Union Field, Senate Committee on Governmental Operations Permanent Subcommittee on Investigations, 1957.

1960–1964

Local 706, Plumbers and Steamfitters Union, El Dorado, Ark., Senate Select Committee on Improper Activities in the Labor or Management Field, 1960.

Attorney General's Program to Curb Organized Crime and Racketeering, Senate Committee on the Judiciary, 1961.

James R. Hoffa and Continued Underworld Control of New York Teamster Local 239, Senate Committee on Government Operations Permanent Subcommittee on Investigations, 1961.

Relationship Between Teamsters Union and Mine, Mill and Smelter Workers, Part 1, Senate Committee on the Judiciary Subcommittee to Investigate the Administration of the Internal Security Act, 1962.

Relationship Between Teamsters Union and Mine, Mill and Smelter Workers. Abuse of Tax Exemptions by Subversive Labor Organizations, Part 2, Senate Committee on the Judiciary Subcommittee to Investigate the Administration of the Internal Security Act, 1962–63.

1965–1969

Diversion of Union Welfare—Pension Funds of Allied Trades Council and Teamsters Local 815, Senate Committee on Governmental Operations Permanent Subcommittee on Investigations, 1965.

Labor Racketeering Activities of Jack McCarthy and the National Consultants Associated, Ltd., Senate Committee on Governmental Operations Permanent Subcommittee on Investigations, 1967.

1970–1974

1975–1979

Teamsters' Union Central Pension Fund, Senate Committee on Labor and Human Resources Subcommittee on Labor, 1976.

Teamsters' Union Central Pension Fund, Senate Committee on Governmental Affairs Permanent Subcommittee on Investigations, 1977.

Teamsters' Central States Pension Fund and General ERISA Enforcement, Parts 1 & 2, House Committee on Ways and Means Subcommittee on Oversight, 1977.

Racketeering in the Sale of and Distribution of Cigarettes, Senate Committee on the Judiciary Subcommittee on Laws and Procedures, 1977.

Labor Union Insurance Parts 1–2, Senate Committee on Governmental Affairs Permanent Subcommittee on Investigations, 1977.

Teamsters Central States Pension Fund, Senate Committee on Governmental Affairs Permanent Subcommittee on Investigations, 1977.

Central States Teamsters Fund, House Committee on Ways and Means Subcommittee on Oversight, 1978.

Labor Management Racketeering, Senate Committee on Governmental Affairs Permanent Subcommittee on Investigations, 1978.

Fraud and Racketeering in Medicare and Medicaid, House Select Committee on Aging, 1978.

1980–1984

Labor Union Insurance, Part 3, Senate Committee on Governmental Affairs Permanent Subcommittee on Investigations, 1980.

Review of Progress on Teamsters' Central States Pension Fund Reform, House Committee on
Ways and Means Subcommittee on Oversight, 1980.

Oversight of Labor Department's Investigation of Teamsters Central States Pension Fund, Senate
Committee on Governmental Affairs Permanent Subcommittee on Investigations,
1980.

Government's Ability to Combat Labor Management Racketeering, Senate Committee on Governmental Affairs Permanent Subcommittee on Investigations, 1981.

Fraud and Abuse in Pensions and Related Employee Benefit Plans, House Select Committee on
Aging, 1981.

Teamsters Central States Pension Fund Reform and ERISA Enforcement Remedies, House Committee on Ways and Means Subcommittee on Oversight, 1982.

Labor Management Racketeering Act of 1981, Senate Committee on Labor and Human Resources Subcommittee on Labor, 1982.

Oversight of Teamsters' Union, Senate Committee on Labor and Human Resources, 1983.

Labor Management Racketeering Act of 1983, Senate Committee on Labor and Human Resources, 1983.

Hotel Employees and Restaurant Employees International Union, Parts 1–5, Senate Committee
on Governmental Affairs Permanent Subcommittee on Investigations, 1982–1983.

1985–1989

*Waste, Fraud and Abuse at Federally Funded Wastewater Treatment Construction Projects: The
Potential Effects of Organized Crime Infiltration and Labor Racketeering in the New York Con-
struction Industry,* House Committee on Government Operations Subcommittee on
Environment, Energy and Natural Resources, 1988.

1990–1994

1995–2000

Oversight of the Department of Labor's Efforts Against Labor Racketeering, House Committee
on Government Reform Subcommittee on Human Resources and Intergovernmental
Relations, 1996.

Hearings on the Invalidated 1996 Teamster Election, House Committee on Education and the
Workforce Subcommittee on Oversight and Investigations, 1997.

Oversight of the Department of Labor's Efforts Against Labor Racketeering, House Committee
on Government Reform, 1998.

Who Pays for the Rerun Teamsters' Election, House Committee on Education and the Workforce Subcommittee on Oversight and Investigations, 1998.

Financial Affairs of International Brotherhood of Teamsters, House Committee on Education
and the Workforce, 1998.

Hearings on Invalidated 1996 Teamster Election, House Committee on Education and the
Workforce Subcommittee on Oversight and Investigations, 1998.

International Brotherhood of Teamsters Re-Run Election, House Committee on Education and
the Workforce Subcommittee on Oversight and Investigations, 1999.

Teamsters Investigation, House Committee on Education and the Workforce Subcommittee on Oversight and Investigations, 1999.

International Brotherhood of Teamsters Financial Reporting and Pension Disclosures, House Committee on Education and the Workforce Subcommittee on Oversight and Investigations, 1998.

International Brotherhood of Teamsters Rerun Election, House Committee on Education and the Workforce, 1999.

Union Democracy, Part VII: Government Supervision of the Hotel Employees and Restaurant Employees International Union, House Committee on Education and the Workforce Subcommittee on Oversight and Investigations, 1999.

International Brotherhood of Teamsters One Year After the Election of James P. Hoffa, House Committee on Education and the Workforce, 2000.

First published in James B. Jacobs and Elizabeth Mullin, "Congress' Role in the Defeat of Organized Crime," *Criminal Law Bulletin* 39:3 (2003).

8

Civil RICO Suits and Trusteeships

As Monitor I had the power to investigate and audit all aspects of the HEREIU, request assistance from any agency of the United States, retain investigators and auditors, attend all meetings of the HEREIU's General Executive Board (GEB), and finally, perform all such functions necessary to fulfill my duties. In addition, I had the power to discipline officials and members, discipline ranging from a fine to permanent removal.

> —Statement of Kurt W. Muellenberg, Esq., former monitor of the HEREIU at the Subcommittee on Employer-Employee Relations, Hearing on the Hotel Employees and Restaurant Employees International Union, July 21, 1999

A trusteeship has the advantage of providing an instant tangible structure that promptly functions in making changes and doing things. It also has the advantage of being separated from the court, thus giving the illusion of independence and opportunity. In a case where financial problems are the chief source of trouble in a Union, or where entrenched incompetence in leadership temporarily undermines the rights of the membership, a trusteeship may be the best choice. That is not the case here, where the court is confronted by a Union that has existed for many, many years as a criminal-dominated organization. The shortcoming of a trusteeship, however, is clearly the distasteful and unworkable act of forcing an authority figure on the existing Union leadership and membership, who they are required to be loyal to, and indeed, expected to like.

> —Louis C. Bechtle, United States District Judge, *U.S. v. Local 30, United Slate, Tile and Composition Roofers, Damp and Waterproof Workers Association*, 686 F. Supp. 1139 (1988)

Note: Part of this chapter is adapted from Jacobs, Cunningham, and Friday, "The RICO Trusteeship After 20 Years: A Progress Report," 19 *Labor Lawyer* 419 (2004).

It took a decade for prosecutors to grasp RICO's potential as a power-ful anti–organized crime weapon.* After 1982, the year federal prosecu-tors filed the IBT New Jersey Local 560 case, the government's most di-rect attack on labor racketeering utilized the RICO civil provision (1964a and 1964b) that authorizes the U.S. attorney general or her/his desig-nee to seek injunctive and other equitable relief to restrain further violations of RICO. Section 1964(a) states:

> The district courts of the United States shall have jurisdiction to pre-vent and restrain violations of section 1962 of this chapter by issuing appropriate orders, including, but not limited to: ordering any person to divest himself of any interest, direct or indirect, in any enterprise; imposing reasonable restrictions on the future activities or invest-ments of any person, including, but not limited to, prohibiting any person from engaging in the same type of endeavor as the enterprise engaged in, the activities of which affect interstate or foreign com-merce; or ordering dissolution or reorganization of any enterprise, making due provision for the rights of innocent persons.

Civil RICO is well suited to systemic organizational criminality that cannot be eradicated by one-shot or even a series of criminal prosecu-tions. The injunctive remedy allows the government and the federal court to implement and enforce a long-term strategy of organizational reform against a racketeer-ridden union.

ELEMENTS OF A CIVIL RICO SUIT

A civil RICO labor racketeering complaint essentially requires the same proof as a criminal RICO case. The government must prove that the de-fendants are likely to continue violating RICO by (1) purchasing an in-terest in an enterprise (the union in this context) with funds obtained

---

* I think the best explanation is that there is a certain institutional inertia in prosecutorial organizations, as in all organizations. Federal prosecutors were accustomed to using con-spiracy statutes, extortion and other substantive crimes, to prosecute organized crime cases. RICO seemed complex and strange. Professor G. Robert Blakey, who drafted the law, spent several years proselytizing for its use. A few prosecutors started experiment-ing with it. As word of success spread, use of the statute became more popular.

through a pattern of racketeering activity (sec. 1962a); or (2) acquiring an interest in an enterprise (the union) through a pattern of racketeering activity (sec. 1962b); or (3) conducting the affairs of an enterprise (the union) through a pattern of racketeering activity (sec. 1962c). In less technical terms, the government must prove that the civil RICO defendants used dirty money to buy their way into a union; took control of a union through extortion, fraud or some other criminal means; or conducted the affairs of a union through criminal activity, such as violence and extortion. Almost all of the civil RICO complaints have been based upon both 1962b and 1962c.

Criminal and civil RICO complaints require proof of a "pattern of racketeering activity," defined as at least two of a long list of federal felonies and their state law equivalents.* The two "predicate offenses" must be related to one another in some way to constitute a pattern; in practice, practically any two qualifying predicate offenses will satisfy the pattern requirement. If the defendants have been previously convicted of two or more RICO predicate offenses, the government lawyers need do no more than enter proof of those convictions to satisfy the "pattern of racketeering activity" requirement. Because civil RICO requires only proof by a preponderance of the evidence while criminal RICO requires proof beyond a reasonable doubt, a civil suit can succeed against certain defendants merely by entering proof of a previous criminal RICO conviction. Alternatively, the RICO predicate offenses can be

---

* In a number of civil RICO complaints, the DOJ lawyers have alleged that the defendants acquired an interest in the union through Hobbs Act extortion. The Hobbs Act, one of the workhorses of federal criminal law, makes extortion that affects interstate commerce a federal crime. Extortion is the taking of property by threatening future harm to person or property. In the civil RICO labor racketeering cases, the government alleged that the defendants extorted "intangible property," the union members' Landrum-Griffin rights. Until recently, the courts acquiesced in this extension of the Hobbs Act to intangible property. However, the Supreme Court's decision in *Scheidler v. National Organization for Women* 537 U.S. 393 (2003) called this theory into question. At least one federal district court has held that, in light of *Scheidler*, the Hobbs Act cannot be used to prosecute the deprivation of intangible Landrum-Griffin rights; in other words, Hobbs Act extortion of intangible union democracy rights cannot be used as a predicate offense to prove "pattern of racketeering activity" to satisfy the requirements of either criminal or civil RICO. (*Bellomo v. U.S.*, 263 F.Supp.2d 561, 575 (E.D.N.Y. 2003). But see *U.S. v. Muscarella*, 175 L.R.R.M 3280, 23–25 (S.D.N.Y. 2004). Even if the *Bellomo* view prevails, there are other RICO predicate offenses that might be proven in labor racketeering cases.

proven at the civil RICO trial itself. Then, all that remains is for the government to persuade the court that aggressive equitable relief (for example, an injunction, a trustee, and so on) is necessary to prevent the defendants from future violations of RICO.

The government's civil RICO complaints typically ask the federal district court judge to enjoin the organized crime defendants from playing any role in the union's administration or affairs. Unless the organized crime defendant is also a union official, there is no legitimate reason for the defendant (who may be in prison anyway) to play any role in the union. Therefore, an organized crime defendant will likely not spend time or money defending himself against a civil RICO labor racketeering lawsuit but instead settle the case by agreeing to have nothing to do with the union. The challenge for the government, the federal judge, and the trustee, if one is appointed, will be to ensure that the organized crime defendant does not continue to exert influence over the union surreptitiously. If the defendant does, the U.S. attorney in charge of the case can petition the judge to hold the noncomplying organized crime defendant in contempt. The judge may also remove from office and perhaps from the union any official who has continued knowingly to associate with an organized crime member.

In their civil RICO labor racketeering suits, DOJ attorneys always name union officials as defendants. Unlike the organized crime defendants, these union defendants have not previously been convicted of RICO predicate offenses; if they had been, they would not be lawfully permitted to hold union office. Thus, government attorneys need to prove that the union defendants themselves violated RICO (1962b) by aiding and abetting the organized crime defendants in their acquisition of an interest in the union or that they violated RICO (1962c) by conducting or aiding and abetting others in conducting the un-ion's affairs through a pattern of racketeering activity, including such RICO predicate offenses as extortion of employers or union members, murder, assaulting or threatening union dissidents, or defrauding the union's benefit funds. It is also possible to obtain judgment against certain (union) defendants whose passive tolerance of LCN labor racketeering might not have been sufficient to support a criminal prosecution for aiding and abetting or for conspiracy. Unlike their organized crime codefendants, the union defendants may have an incentive to defend themselves, especially if the union pays their legal fees.[*]

To recapitulate, in a civil RICO suit, the U.S. attorney names both union defendants and organized crime defendants, and sometimes designates the union or its benefit fund as a "nominal" defendant. Defendants are charged with having violated RICO by (1) acquiring or aiding and abetting the acquiring of an interest in the union through a pattern of racketeering activity, typically by means of violence and intimidation against union members but also by means of taking bribes from employers, election fraud, and theft from union benefit funds, and (2) conducting the union's affairs through a pattern of racketeering activity, usually extortion, theft, and fraud. As a remedy, the U.S. attorney asks the judge to remove the union defendants from their official positions, order organized crime defendants to sever all contacts with the union, enjoin defendants from knowingly associating with organized crime members and associates. The judge is also asked to appoint a trustee empowered to initiate disciplinary charges against union officers and members who violate the decree, union constitution, or bylaws; administer the union's affairs; design and implement a fair election, and monitor a new regime for conformity with the decree, the union's constitution, and federal laws.

The specifics of the civil RICO decrees in labor racketeering cases differ. However, almost always there is a provision that empowers the trustee to act as investigator/prosecutor in initiating disciplinary charges. The judge (or perhaps another trustee) decides whether the facts establish the targeted official's "guilt" and what sanction is appropriate. For example, in the IBT International case, the investigations officer functioned as prosecutor and the administrative officer functioned as trier of fact and sentencing authority. The decree usually provides that union members and officials found guilty of disciplinary violations (for example, knowingly associating with LCN figures) have a right to appeal to the district court judge; if still dissatisfied, they may appeal to the relevant federal circuit court of appeals.

---

[*] Whether the union will be permitted to pay for a union official's legal representation in defending a civil RICO suit is a thorny legal question. Under LMRDA (29 USC 501a), only expenditures for the benefit of the union are legitimate. As things stand today, the union normally pays its officials' legal fees if the official is vindicated, but if the official loses, the union is not permitted to reimburse legal expenses.

Remarkably, the DOJ lawyers have never lost a civil RICO labor racketeering case and only two of the government's 20 civil RICO suits (IBT Local 560 and Philadelphia Roofers Local 30) necessitated trials; all the rest were resolved by negotiated consent decrees that included appointment of a trustee or monitor. The decree itself usually specifies whether the trustee should have full-time and/or part-time assistants, and the amount of the trustee's compensation. See Table 8-1 below for a list of all the civil RICO suits as of February 2005.

"Winning" a civil RICO labor racketeering case by achieving a favorable decree does not necessarily ensure that the racketeer-ridden union will be successfully reformed. These cases are won or lost in the remedial phase. The prosecutors and judges know what they want to accomplish: the eradication of organized crime elements from the union and the establishment of healthy union governance capable of resisting future intrusions by criminal elements. How to achieve these goals is less clear. The first step is to seek appointment of a trustee in whom the Department of Justice and the federal judge have confidence. This requires a person who understands organized crime and who enjoys the confidence of the FBI and DOL investigators (assuming they are still at work on the case). Almost by definition, such a person has to be a former federal prosecutor.

Table 8-1
Civil RICO Suits as of February 2005

Name of Civil RICO Suit	Date Filed, District	Published Opinions Discussing Various Aspects of the Case
1. *United States v. Local 560, International Brotherhood of Teamsters*, No. 82-689	March 9, 1982, D.N.J.	*United States v. Local 560, International Brotherhood of Teamsters*, 581 F.Supp. 279, 115 L.R.R.M. (BNA) 2829 (D.N.J. 1984), *aff'd* 780 F.2d 267, 121 L.R.R.M. (BNA) 2121 (3d Cir. 1985).
2. *United States v. Local 6A, Cement and Concrete Workers*, No. 86 Civ. 4819	June 19, 1986, S.D.N.Y.	*United States v. Local 6A, Cement and Concrete Workers*, 663 F.Supp. 192, 127 L.R.R.M. (BNA) 2540 (S.D.N.Y. 1986).
3. *United States v. The Bonanno Organized Crime Family of La Cosa Nostra, Philip Rastelli, et al.*, No. 87-2974 (IBT Local 814).	August 25, 1987, E.D.N.Y.	*United States v. The Bonanno Organized Crime Family of La Cosa Nostra*, 683 F.Supp. 1411 (E.D.N.Y. 1988); 695 F.Supp. 1426 (E.D.N.Y. 1988), *aff'd* 879 F.2d 20 (2d Cir. 1989).
4. *United States v. Local 359, United Seafood Workers, et al.*, No. 87 Civ. 7351*	October 15, 1987, S.D.N.Y.	*United States v. Local 359, United Seafood Workers*, 705 F.Supp 894, 130 L.R.R.M. (BNA) 2533 (S.D.N.Y. 1989), *aff'd* 889 F.2d 1232, 132 L.R.R.M. (BNA) 2978 (2d Cir. 1989); 55 F.3d 64 (2d Cir. 1995).

(continued)

Table 8-1 *(continued)*

Name of Civil RICO Suit	Date Filed, District	Published Opinions Discussing Various Aspects of the Case
5. *United States v. Local 30, United Slate, Tile, and Composition Roofers, et al.,* No. 87-7718	December 2, 1987, E.D.Pa.	*United States v. Local 30,* 686 F.Supp. 1139, 128 L.R.R.M. (BNA) 2580 (E.D.Pa. 1988), *aff'd* 871 F.2d 401, 130 L.R.R.M. (BNA) 3058 (3d Cir. 1989).
6. *United States v. John F. Long, John S. Mahoney, et al.,* No. 5588 Cr. 943 (IBT Locals 804 and 808)	May 1988, S.D.N.Y.	*United States v. Long* 697 F.Supp. 651 (S.D.N.Y. 1988); 917 F.2d 691, 135 L.R.R.M. (BNA) 2812 (2d Cir. 1990).
7. *United States v. International Brotherhood of Teamsters,* No. 88 Civ. 4486 ("IBT International Case")	June 28, 1988, S.D.N.Y.	*United States v. International Brotherhood of Teamsters,* 708 F.Supp. 1388, 131 L.R.R.M. (BNA) 2161 (S.D.N.Y. 1989); 723 F.Supp. 203, 134 L.R.R.M. (BNA) 2707 (S.D.N.Y. 1989); 725 F.Supp. 162, 134 L.R.R.M. (BNA) 2801 (S.D.N.Y. 1989); 728 F.Supp. 1032, 134 L.R.R.M. (BNA) 2801 (S.D.N.Y. 1989); 728 F.Supp. 1032, 134 L.R.R.M. (BNA) 2281 (S.D.N.Y. 1989); 899 F.2nd 143, 133 L.R.R.M. (BNA) 2827 (2nd Cir. 1990); 905 F.2d 610, 134 L.R.R.M. (BNA) 3161 (2d Cir. 1990); 907 F.2d 277, 134 L.R.R.M. (BNA) 3172 (2d Cir. 1990); 931 F.2d 177, 137 L.R.R.M. (BNA) 2022 (2d Cir. 1991); 941 F.2d 1292, 138 L.R.R.M. (BNA) 2219 (2d Cir. 1991); 964 F.2d 180, 140 L.R.R.M. (BNA) 2022 (2nd Cir. 1992).
8. *United States v. Locals 1804-1, 824, 1809, 1909, 1588, and 1814, International Longshoremen's Association, et al.,* No. 90 Civ. 0963	February 14, 1990, S.D.N.Y.	*United States v. Local 1804-1, International Longshoremen's Association,* 745 F.Supp. 184 (S.D.N.Y. 1990); 812 F.Supp. 1303, 142 L.R.R.M. (BNA) 2533 (S.D.N.Y. 1993); 44 F.3d 1091, 148 L.R.R.M. (BNA) 2217 (2d Cir. 1995); *United States v. Carson,* 52 F.3d 1173, 149 L.R.R.M. (BNA) 2001 (2d Cir. 1995).
9. *United States v. Local 295, International Brotherhood of Teamsters,* No. 90-CV-0970	March 20, 1990, E.D.N.Y.	*United States v. Local 295, International Brotherhood of Teamsters,* 1991 WL 35497 (E.D.N.Y. 1991); 1991 WL 340575 (E.D.N.Y. 1991); 784 F.Supp. 15, 141 L.R.R.M. (BNA) 2625 (E.D.N.Y. 1992).
10. *United States v. District Council of New York City and Vicinity of the United Brotherhood of Carpenters and Joiners of America, et al.,* No. 90 Civ. 5772	September 6, 1990, S.D.N.Y.	*United States v. District Council of New York City and Vicinity of the United Brotherhood of Carpenters and Joiners of America,* 778 F.Supp. 738 (S.D.N.Y. 1991); 941 F.Supp. 349, 154 L.R.R.M. (BNA) 2281 (S.D.N.Y.)
11. *United States v. Edward T. Hanley, et al.,* No. 90-5017 (HEREIU Local 54)	December 19, 1990, D.N.J.	*United States v. Hanley,* 1992 WL 684356 (D.N.J. 1992).
12. *United States v. ILA Local 1558,* No. Civ. 0963	1992, S.D.N.Y.	*United States v. Local 1804-1, International Longshoremen's Association,* 2003 U.S. Dist. LEXIS 1105 (S.D.N.Y., Jan. 29, 2003); *United States v. Local 1804-1, International Longshoremen's Association,* 2003 U.S. Dist. LEXIS 1229 (S.D.N.Y., Jan. 30, 2003); *United States v. ILA Local 1558,* 77 Fed. Appx. 542, 2003.
13. *United States v. Anthony R. Amodeo, Sr., et al.,* No. 92 Civ. 7744 (HEREIU Local 100)	October 23, 1992, S.D.N.Y.	*United States v. Amodeo,* 44 F.3rd 141, 148 L.R.R.M. (BNA) 2226 2nd Cir. 1995).

Table 8-1 *(continued)*

Name of Civil RICO Suit	Date Filed, District	Published Opinions Discussing Various Aspects of the Case
14. *United States v. Local 282 of the International Brotherhood of Teamsters,* No. 94-2919	June 21, 1994, E.D.N.Y.	*United States v. Local 282 of the International Brotherhood of Teamsters,* 13 F.Supp.2nd (E.D.N.Y. 1995).
15. *United States v. Mason Tenders District Council of Greater New York,* No. 94 Civ. 6487	September 7, 1994, S.D.N.Y.	*United States v. Mason Tenders District Council of Greater New York,* 1994 WL 742637 (S.D.N.Y. 1994); 909 F.Supp. 882 (S.D.N.Y. 1995); 909 F.Supp. 891 (S.D.N.Y. 1995)
16. *United States v. LIUNA* (International Union "voluntarily" instituted reforms in exchange for government's not filing signed consent agreement.)	Never filed	*Serpico v. Laborers' International Union of North America,* 97 F.3rd 995, 153 L.R.R.M. (BNA) 2577 (7th Cir. 1996).
17. *United States v. Edward T. Hanley, Hotel Employees Restaurant Employees International Union, and Hotel Employees and Restaurant Employees International Union General Executive Board,* Civ. No. 95-4596	September 5, 1995, D.N.J.	*United States v. Hotel Employees and Restaurant Employees International and Union,* 974 F.Supp. 411 (D.N.J. 1997); *Agathos v. Muellenberg,* 932 F.Supp. 636, 155 L.R.R.M. (BNA) 2509 (D.N.J. 1996).
18. *United States & Laborers' International Union of North America v. Construction & General Laborers' District Council of Chicago & Vicinity,* No. 99C 5229	August 8, 1999, N.D.Ill.	*Laborers' International Union of North America v. Caruso,* 1999 WL 14496 (N.D.Ill. 1999), aff'd, F.3rd 1195, 163 L.R.R.M. (BNA) 2204 (7th Cir. 1999).
19. *United States v. Laborers' International Union of North America Local 210,* No. 99 CV-0915A	November 18, 1999, W.D.N.Y.	*Panczykowski v. Laborers' International Union of North America,* 2000 WL 387602, 166 L.R.R.M. (BNA) 2110 (W.D.N.Y. 2000); *Caci v. Laborers' International Union of North America,* 2000 WL 387599, 166 L.R.R.M. (BAN) 2232 (W.D.N.Y. 2000).
20. *United States v. Hotel Employees and Restaurant Employees International Union Local 69*	April 17, 2002, N.D.N.Y.	
21. *United States v. International Longshoremen's Association et al.,* CV-05-3212	July 2005, E.D.N.Y.	[While this book was in press, the DOJ filed a civil RICO suit against the ILA and served Cosa Nostra figures.]

* This litigation involved the Fulton Fish Market, in which the union was a major player. The case was settled with the appointment of a "market administrator," not actually a union trustee.

SELECTING THE TRUSTEE

In the majority of cases, formal selection of the trustee has been left up to the presiding federal district court judge, with both the government and the union invited to make recommendations. In the HEREIU International case, both the government and the HEREIU sent the judge three names. The judge selected one of the government's nominees, Kurt Muellenberg, a former head of the DOJ's Organized Crime and Racketeering Section. In almost all cases one of the government's nominees has been chosen;* no trustee has been appointed over the government's objection.

In some cases the identity of the trustee has been included in the consent agreement itself. For example, the New York City District Council of Carpenters' consent decree named a trustee (designated as the Investigations and Review Officer (IRO)) and the members of an Independent Hearing Committee (IHC).[1] Under this trusteeship, the IRO would prepare disciplinary cases and the IHC would adjudicate disciplinary charges.

One of the most arresting facts about the government's twenty-year anti–labor racketeering campaign is that the trustees are almost all former federal prosecutors with experience investigating and prosecuting organized crime. Edwin Stier, trustee for a decade over IBT Local 560 was a former state and federal prosecutor. Thomas Puccio, trustee in the IBT Local 295 case, was previously head of the Federal Organized Crime Strike Force in Brooklyn.[2] Of the three members of the Independent Review Board in the IBT International case, William H. Webster was a former FBI director, Charles Carberry was a former assistant U.S. attorney, and Michael Holland was one of just a few labor lawyer trustees.[3] Holland's authority was limited to running the IBT's national election.[4] Table 8-2 provides background on the trustees appointed in the civil RICO labor cases.

---

* In the Chicago Laborers' District Council case, for example, Robert Bloch, formally nominated by LIUNA International, had the DOJ's strong support and approval. See National Legal and Policy Center, *Union Corruption Update*, September 10, 2001. Similarly, in the LIUNA Local 210 case, the international union appointed Gabriel Rosetti to be the trustee; the DOJ then consented to have Rosetti serve as RICO trustee as well. (Stephanie Mencimer, "Ex-FBI Official Pulls at Union's Infamous Roots; Laborers Fight Corruption From the Inside Out," *Washington Post*, June 7, 1998, at A1). In the Philadelphia Roofers Local 30/30B case, however, Judge Bechtle chose Robert Welsh, a former law clerk with an impressive record as a federal prosecutor. Telephone Interview with Robert Welsh, Special Master, Roofers Local 30/30B, in Philadelphia (November 25, 2003).

Table 8-2
Trustees' Backgrounds

Trustee	Union	Background
Eugene R. Anderson (Trustee)	LIUNA Local 6A (New York)	Assistant U.S. attorney and partner in New York City law firm.
Robert E. Bloch (Trustee)	Chicago Laborers' District Council (CLDC)	Labor lawyer, Dowd, Bloch & Bennett.
John A. Boardman (Deputy Monitor)	HEREIU Local 69	HEREIU vice-president and temporary trustee of Local 69 (appointed by President Wilhelm when Wilhelm put the local under trusteeship in March 2002). Formerly president of a HEREIU local in Washington.
Charles Carberry (Investigations Officer)	IBT International	Assistant U.S. attorney, S.D.N.Y., 1979–1985; deputy chief, Criminal Division, 1985–1986; chief, Securities and Commodities Frauds Unit, 1986–1987.
Michael Chertoff (Investigations Officer)	Mason Tenders District Council (MTDC)	Assistant U.S. attorney, Southern District of New York, 1983–1987; first assistant U.S. attorney for District of New Jersey, 1987–1990; U.S. attorney for District of New Jersey, 1990–1994; U.S. Senate special counsel for Whitewater Committee, 1994–1996; partner, Latham & Watkins, 1994–2001; assistant attorney general, Criminal Division, 2001–2003; U.S. 3rd Circuit Court of Appeals, 2003.
Kenneth Conboy (Investigation and Review Officer)	New York District Council of Carpenters	U.S. district judge for the Southern District of New York. Former national appeals master for the Teamsters International nationwide election; New York City commissioner of investigation; counsel to commissioner of New York City Police Department.
Ronald E. DePetris (Independent Supervisor)	IBT Local 851	Chief assistant U.S. attorney, Eastern District of New York, 1982–1986. Assistant U.S. attorney, chief of Fraud Section, and chief of Criminal Division, Eastern District of New York, 1971–1977.
W. Neil Eggleston (Appellate Officer)	LIUNA International	Chief of appeals, U.S. Attorney's Office in Southern District of New York; former Clinton White House attorney.
James Flanagan III	HEREIU Local 54	Deputy director, New Jersey Division of Gaming Enforcement.
Robert Gaffey	ILA Local 1588	Assistant U.S. attorney, Southern District of New York, 1985–1988. Chief counsel to the investigations officer in the IBT International trusteeship.
James Gill	ILA Local 1804-; Local 1909	Five years as an assistant district attorney in Manhattan.
Stephen B. Goldberg (Election Officer)	LIUNA International	Professor of law at Northwestern University; expert in alternative dispute resolutions; served as an attorney for the National Labor Relations Board, 1961–1965.
W. Douglas Gow (Inspector General)	LIUNA International	FBI associate deputy director, Investigations.

(continued)

Table 8-2 (continued)

Trustee	Union	Background
Steve Hammond (LIUNA trustee)	MTDC	Started in LIUNA in 1970 as a member of Local 295, Salt Lake City; elected business manager of Local 295 in 1975; appointed assistant business manager of the Oregon/Southern Idaho/ Wyoming/Utah District Council in 1987. Came to LIUNA International Headquarters in 1989 to serve as assistant director of the Construction and Jurisdiction Department. Appointed director of the department in 1994. (After trusteeship) was assigned as special assistant to the general president (Coia) in 1997. Served as co-chairman and trustee on the New York State Laborers'-Employers' Cooperation and Education Trust (LECET) until August 2003. Was elected by the LIUNA GEB as international vice-president-at-large in August 2000.
Michael Holland (Elections Officer)	IBT International	General counsel, International Union, United Mine Workers of America, 1982–1989. Chairman and trustee, UMWA Health and Retirement Funds, 1993–. Chairman and trustee, National Organizers Alliance Retirement Pension Plan, 1997–.
Joseph Jaffe (Trustee)	ILA Local 1814	Assistant U.S. attorney, Southern District of New York
Frederick Lacey (Independent Administrator)	IBT International	U.S. attorney in New Jersey, 1969–1971; Federal District Court judge, 1971–1986; chairman, U.S. Supreme Court Advisory Committee on Criminal Rules, 1984–1986; judge, Temporary Emergency Court of Appeals, 1980–1986; judge, U.S. Foreign Intelligence Surveillance Court, 1979–1985.
Mary Shannon Little (Court Officer)	HEREIU Local 100	Assistant U.S. attorney, Southern District of New York.
Robert D. Luskin (GEB Attorney)	LIUNA International	Special counsel to the DOJ Organized Crime and Racketeering Section.
Jack McDonald	LIUNA Local 210	Former FBI agent.
Robert McGuire (Trustee)	ILA Local 1588	Commissioner, New York City Police Department, 1978–1983.
Steven A. Miller (Court-Appointed Monitor)	CLDC	Chief, Special Prosecutions Section, U.S. Attorney's Office, Northern District of Illinois, 1991–1995; chief, Bank and Financial Institution Fraud Unit, 1988–1991.
Michael Moroney (Deputy Trustee)	IBT Local 295	Former federal labor investigator.
Kurt Muellenberg (Trustee)	HEREIU International and HEREIU Local 69	Former chief of the DOJ's Organized Crime and Racketeering Section.
Howard O'Leary (Investigations Officer)	HEREIU International	Assistant U.S. attorney, Detroit; partner in the Washington office of Dykema Gossett.
Lawrence Pedowitz (Court-Appointed Monitor)	MTDC	Assistant U.S. attorney, Southern District of New York, 1974–1978; chief of appeals, 1976–1977; and chief, Criminal Division, 1982–1984.

Table 8-2 (continued)

Trustee	Union	Background
Thomas Puccio (Trustee)	IBT Local 295	Office of the U.S. Attorney, Eastern District of New York, 1969–1976 (chief, Criminal Division, 1973–1975; executive assistant U.S. attorney, 1975–1976); chief, U.S. Department of Justice Strike Force, 1976–1982.
Barbara Quindell (Elections Officer)	IBT International	Labor lawyer.
Gabriel Rosetti, Jr. (Trustee)	LIUNA Local 210 (Buffalo)	Thirty-one-year union member.
Robert Stewart (Deputy Trustee)	ILA Local 1588	Career federal prosecutor; head of the Newark Federal Organized Crime Strike Force.
Edwin H. Stier (Trustee)	IBT Local 560	Former assistant U.S. attorney in charge of the Criminal Division, Newark. Former director of the New Jersey State Division of Criminal Justice.
Daniel F. Sullivan (Chief Investigator)	HEREIU International	Supervisor, FBI Baltimore office.
Henry Tamarin (Trustee)	HEREIU Local 100	HEREIU International vice-president; also worked on HEREIU Local 54 trusteeship.
Michael Tobin (Deputy Trustee)	IBT Local 295	Former investigator for Thomas Puccio; no labor background.
Peter F. Vaira (Hearing Officer)	LIUNA International	Executive director of President's Commission on Organized Crime; former chief of DOJ's Organized Crime Strike Force in Chicago; and former U.S. attorney for Eastern District of Pennsylvania.
Robert E. Welsh, Jr. (Special Master)	Roofers Local 30/30B	Assistant U.S. attorney, 1980–1986; and chief of Major Crimes Section, 1984–1986, Philadelphia.

THE DURATION OF THE TRUSTEESHIP

The DOJ favors RICO trusteeships of indefinite duration.[5] The advantage of a trusteeship with no fixed duration is that neither the criminal element nor the rank and file will have cause to anticipate that the trusteeship will soon end with union affairs reverting to the status quo ante. The government wants the rank and file to believe that the trusteeship will remain in place until corruption and racketeering have been thoroughly eliminated. However, a trusteeship without a fixed termination date may cause the trustee (and provide an economic incentive) to operate without hurry, thereby draining the union treasury and unduly delaying the union's return to self-governance. Furthermore, without a fixed or at least presumptive termination date, it may be difficult to bring the trusteeship to an end. The union defendant will always prefer a trusteeship of limited duration, if for no other reason than that the shorter the trusteeship, the less financial drain on the union.

In the majority of labor racketeering cases, the consent decree provided for a fixed-term trusteeship, ranging from as short as eighteen months (e.g., HEREIU International and HEREIU Local 100) to as long as six years (e.g., HEREIU Local 54) (see Table 8-3). Most of the decrees or consent agreements have included an option to extend the trusteeship's duration for a further fixed period.[6]

Table 8-3
Duration of Trusteeships

Union	Date Trusteeship Established	Proposed Duration of Trusteeship	Terms for Extensions	Termination Date
IBT Local 560	June 23, 1986	Indeterminate	Not applicable	Feb. 25, 1999
LIUNA Local 6A (Cement and Concrete Workers, New York)	March 18, 1987	Until elections held in 1990	Extend twice, each time for twelve months.	September 1993
Local 359 (Seafood Workers)	Unknown	Unknown	Several extensions.	July 1994
Philadelphia Roofers Local 30/30B	June 2, 1988	Indeterminate	Not applicable	September 28, 1999
IBT International	1989	Indeterminate	Not applicable	Ongoing
IBT Local 295	April 29, 1992	Indeterminate	As of 2002, the trustee in charge recommend that although the local was ready for court-supervised elections, his trusteeship should continue, in modified form, for at least seven more years.	July 29, 2004, but chief investigator has ongoing duties until after fall 2006 election. Court may reinstate Independent Supervisor for good cause.
United Brotherhood of Carpenters and Joiners of America, New York District Council and Constituent Locals	March 4, 1994	Thirty months	The decree provided: "The Internal Review Officer [to] apply to the Court for an extension or to reduce the length of the term by six months or less, in order to complete work in progress, upon a showing of good cause and upon reasonable notice to the government and counsel for the District Council." (1994 Consent Decree, section 9(a))	June 1999

Table 8-3 *(continued)*

Union	Date Trusteeship Established	Proposed Duration of Trusteeship	Terms for Extensions	Termination Date
HEREIU Local 54	April 12, 1991	Six years	No extensions. (Interview with James Flanagan, July 2002).	March 3, 1997
HEREIU Local 100	October 23, 1992	Eighteen months	Seems that there were terms; details unknown.	Fall 1994
IBT Local 282	June 1, 1994	Four years	Yes, for four years, until May 2003; see amended consent judgment in 13 F.Supp.2d 401	Ongoing
IBT Local 851	August 1994	Unknown	A court order issued October 20, 2000, extended the trusteeship until thirty days after the second set of elections following the trusteeship.	Same as for IBT Local 295
MTDC	December 27, 1994	Four years	Not extended; however, a "Supplemental" consent decree was entered into in January 1999 that provided that the trustee, Lawrence Pedowitz, would act as a "Review Monitor" for another thirty-six months, with power to apply to the Court for restoration of his trustee powers if he concluded the union was being run corruptly.	January 1999
LIUNA International	February 15, 1995	February 11, 1998 (three years)	First one-year extension, February 1998–January 1999, did not alter the agreement. Second one-year extension was announced January 8, 1999, and weakened agreement a bit—DOJ will allow LIUNA to curtail its efforts to accommodate "budgetary constraints," and DOJ can impose consent decree only if a failure to do so would "substantially interfere" with the purposes of the agreement, instead of at its discretion. Second extension was set to expire on January 31, 2000; on January 20, 2000, a new agreement, good till 2006, was reached. This agreement removes the takeover threat. DOJ now can "veto" major changes only in LIUNA's reform effort but cannot implement the previously signed consent decree. (National Legal and Policy Center, *Union Corruption Update,* January 31, 2000)	Set to terminate in 2006

(continued)

Table 8-3 *(continued)*

Union	Date Trusteeship Established	Proposed Duration of Trusteeship	Terms for Extensions	Termination Date
HEREIU International	September 5, 1995	Eighteen months	Muellenberg requested a one-year extension in February 1997; court granted extension, with trusteeship ending March 5, 1998. After termination of trusteeship, Muellenberg continued as one member of a three-person oversight committee with limited authority. (Kurt Muellenberg, Federal Monitor's Final Report as Monitor, 2000)	March 8, 1998; consent decree was not technically lifted until December 1, 2000, when all the disciplinary proceedings ended.
Chicago Laborers' District Council	LIUNA trusteeship began February 1998; court-ordered trusteeship began August 12, 1999	At least two years	It does not appear that there were any explicit terms; there was not an extension.	August 30, 2001
LIUNA Local 210 (Buffalo)	December 1999 (prior LIUNA internal trusteeship from February 1996 to December 1999)	LIUNA appointed internal trustee for two-year term	In 1998, LIUNA extended the trustee's term indefinitely. (Stephanie Mencimer, "Ex-FBI Official Pulls at Union's Infamous Roots; Laborers Fight Corruption from the Inside Out," *Washington Post*, June 7, 1998)	August 2001
HEREIU Local 69	April 17, 2002	Four years	Not applicable	Terminates April 17, 2006, unless extended for cause shown.
ILA Local 1588	January 29, 2003	Eighteen months and possible eighteen months of postelection oversight	Not applicable	Ongoing

THE TERMS OF THE TRUSTEE'S EMPLOYMENT

At first blush, it would seem desirable to have a full-time trustee devoted to reforming a racketeer-ridden union. After all, trustees imposed by international unions on bankrupt and maladministered locals typically serve as full-time officials. However, it would be very difficult to recruit a full-time RICO remedial trustee from the ranks of private-sector law firm attorneys with prior federal prosecutorial or organized crime control experience. To serve full-time, the attorney would have to take an extended or indefinite leave from his or her law firm and perhaps a cut in pay; even so, the salary might be prohibitive for a local union. Furthermore, a union trusteeship is not a step along a career path. Years later, when the trusteeship is terminated, the lawyer/trustee would have to reconnect with his old firm or find a new one. There would be no business and no clients to bring to the firm. He certainly could not count on more union trusteeships because there are so few. Realistically, if the RICO suits required full-time trustees, they would have to be drawn from another pool, perhaps retired prosecutors, or more likely career union officials. Thus, the trustees mostly serve on a part-time basis, compensated at an hourly rate. Their weekly hours might vary from thirty or more at the beginning of the trusteeship to ten or fewer later on, according to the trustee's judgment of what is necessary. The disadvantage of a part-time trustee is that he or she will not take ownership of the task. While operating a law office and/or devoting time to other jobs, the part-time trustee may not have the time and energy necessary to reform, reconstitute, and reconstruct a union that has been operated as a mob fiefdom for decades. However, choosing someone who is not a former prosecutor carries serious disadvantages. It is crucial that government investigators completely trust the trustee and feel comfortable sharing sensitive investigative information with him or her. A union official would be very unlikely to enjoy this kind of trust.

Compensation is an important issue. Attorneys at big law firms bill their time at $300–$500 an hour, rates that union members find staggering. Some trustees have earned more than $100,000 a year for their part-time work.[7] The trustee in the Local 295 case was paid $250,000 a year for his part-time services, and his full-time deputy trustee received $150,000. Ironically, such compensation exceeds the remuneration of mob-connected union officials whose salaries and emoluments prosecutors condemned as bloated, unjustified, and exploitive. On occasion, the trustee's wages have drawn criticism from those who oppose the trusteeship on other grounds and, in some cases, may have undermined the trustee's legitimacy in the eyes of the union's members. For example, the IBT went to court to challenge (unsuccessfully) the $350 hourly rate billed by Frederick Lacey as "Administrator" (one of the three trustees) in the IBT case.[8]

A trusteeship over an international union's central office requires more time, personnel, and resources than a trusteeship over a local union. After the 1991 election, the IBT three-person (plus staff) trusteeship was replaced by a three-person Independent Review Board (IRB). The IRB hired the original investigations officer (Carberry) and authorized a staff of two full-time lawyers and eight full-time investigators. According to Teamsters General President James P. Hoffa, the IRB costs the IBT approximately $8–9 million a year.[9] LIUNA estimates that it spends $5 million a year on the remediation effort led by former federal prosecutor Robert Luskin.[10] By contrast, the HEREIU International trusteeship was a much smaller and cheaper operation.[11]

Covering the costs of a RICO trusteeship over a previously exploited union often presents a major problem. The union's coffers have been plundered by racketeers and depleted by litigation costs. Funding the trusteeship could bankrupt the union or require dues increases that might cause the rank and file to abandon it. In a few cases, the international union, a much deeper pocket, has contributed financial assistance.[12] For example, the IBT Local 851 decree states that the local will set up a fund from which the trustee can draw and that the International IBT will supplement that fund. However, some trusteeships have floundered due to inadequate funding.

THE TRUSTEE'S POWERS

The trustee's powers emanate from the decree. Some trustees have been given all the powers and authority of the union's GEB, in effect empowering the trustee to administer the union, negotiate contracts, handle grievances, and initiate strikes.[13] Such a trusteeship resembles the type of trusteeship that an international union sometimes imposes on an affiliated local.

The RICO trustee who is charged with the responsibility for running the union has to devote a substantial portion of time and energy to day-to-day union administration rather than to organizational reform.[14] In the LIUNA Local 6A trusteeship, Trustee Eugene Anderson and his assistant claim to have been so preoccupied supervising the daily administration of the union that they were unable to interact with the rank and file. On the other hand, the trustee who runs the union is in a position to earn the rank and file's confidence by assisting the membership to achieve its goals rather than functioning solely as a policeman. If the budget permits, trustees who find themselves in this position (e.g., IBT Local 560) usually hire a seasoned union official to handle day-to-day union affairs while they themselves concentrate on investigations, discipline, elections, and communications with the rank and file.

Trustees typically have the authority to examine the union's books and records, and to compel sworn statements by officers, agents, representatives, employees, and members. In many cases (e.g., Roofers Local 30/30B) the trustees have been given authority to review collective bargaining contracts and to veto improper expenditures. Officers of the corrupt regime may have signed various contracts for goods and services with cronies before the trustee assumed his position, in effect providing golden handshakes to members of the heretofore dominant clique. The trustee must also scrutinize the payroll for no-show workers, improper reimbursements, and other fraudulent expenditures.

In some cases the power to bring suit on behalf of the union has enabled trustees to obtain reimbursement from the union's exploiters. For example, in the Mason Tenders District Council case, Monitor Lawrence Pedowitz filed lawsuits against former officers and trus-tees, recovering $12 million of $15 million lost because of their malfeasance. Ronald DePetris, trustee over IBT Local 851, filed two civil RICO claims against freight-forwarding companies and Local 851's former secretary-treasurer, ultimately recovering more than $3 million for the financially strapped union. Such successes obviously contribute to the trustee's credibility and popularity.

THE TRUSTEE'S DISCIPLINARY AUTHORITY

In most, but not all, RICO union cases, the decree prohibits union members, and certainly union officials, from knowingly associating with organized crime members or associates.[*] For example, the consent decree

---

[*] Courts have uniformly rejected challenges based on freedom of association grounds. See *U.S. v. Int'l Bhd of Teamsters*, 745 F. Supp. 908 (S.D.N.Y. 1990), 138 L.R.R.M. (BNA) 2219 (2d Cir. 1991). Courts have found either that the union constitution or the consent agreement provides ample authority to make no-knowing-contact-with-organized-criminals a condition of holding union office.

in the IBT International case gave the independent administrator the IBT general president's disciplinary authority.[15] The independent administrator, Frederick Lacey, held that this authority was sufficient to expel union members, not just officers, for bringing "dishonor and disrepute" to the Teamsters on account of LCN ties. District Court Judge David Edelstein agreed and the Second Circuit Court of Appeals affirmed.[16] The trustees in the LIUNA Local 6A and HERE Local 54 cases had authority to bar candidates who knowingly associate with organized crime figures from union elections, but not the authority to expel such individuals from the union. Under those conditions, the taint of labor racketeering and atmosphere of intimidation continue to prevail.

The union trustees have usually had the power to hire members of the union staff, including business agents who negotiate labor contracts, administer grievances, file unfair labor charges, and make decisions regarding strikes and other job actions. To be successful, the trustee must demonstrate that a new regime has permanently displaced the old one. New leaders must be encouraged to come forward. However, there is a danger that, in making snap hiring decisions, the trustee will appoint people who are incompetent, unpopular, or otherwise not likely to be effective leaders. Moreover, the rank and file may resent having their officers chosen by "the government," failing or refusing to distinguish between the courts/trustee and "the government."

THE TRUSTEE'S ELECTION AUTHORITY

RICO trustees are almost always empowered to implement and monitor elections. Mounting a fair and competitive election is a major step in the union's rehabilitation. Typically, mobbed-up unions have not experienced a fair election in the memory of any living union member. As Judge David Edelstein explained in one of his many opinions in the IBT international case:

> [E]lection rules must not be viewed in a vacuum, but instead placed in their proper context. This Court has reiterated that the [IBT] Consent Decree is a unique attempt to cleanse this union. These election rules are the linchpin in that effort. This Court will only approve election rules that will guarantee honest, fair, and free elections completely

secure from harassment, intimidation, coercion, hooliganism, threats, or any variant of these, no matter under what guise.[17]

The Trustee's Preparation

Ideally, a new trustee should have general knowledge about organized crime, labor unions, labor racketeering, and the history of previous efforts to reform mobbed-up unions. She/he should also know the specific facts of the case at hand, the history and politics of the targeted union, who the racketeers are and how they have exploited the union and its pension and welfare funds, and the local union's relationship to its international union and to the employers for whom its members work.

There is no manual on how to organize and implement a RICO-spawned trusteeship. Remarkably, there has never been a conference or meeting to debrief the trustees or to memorialize their experiences. Their reports have not been assembled in any retrievable way and are usually difficult to obtain. Indeed, in some cases the reports have been purposefully sanitized because the judge or trustee feared their being made public. There has been little contact among the trustees, sometimes as a matter of policy. For example, Judge Bechtle in the Philadelphia Roofers' Local 30/30B case instructed his trustee ("liaison officer") not to contact trustees in other cases lest their mistakes infect the Roofers' remediation.[18]

Typically the newly appointed trustee is briefed by the federal prosecutors who drafted the civil RICO complaint. However, the "briefing" may be no more than one or two informal discussions over lunch. Of course, the newly appointed trustee can read the civil RICO complaint, the settlement agreement, and other legal documents, including past indictments. However, because practically all of these RICO suits have been settled quickly, there are no trial transcripts or even depositions. At best, the new trustee will know the prosecutors' perception of the problem or, more accurately, of the problem's symptoms—e.g., mob influence, bloated salaries, ghost employees, and the sorry state of the union's treasury and benefit funds. Prosecutors cannot convey information about what they themselves do not know, such as the union's politics, culture, and organizational environment, as well as the nature of the business or industry environment in which the union's members work.

In the few cases where civil RICO suits against unions have gone to trial, the judge has had significant influence over the trusteeship. After a yearlong trial in the IBT Local 560 case, Judge Harold Ackerman, appalled by the union's history of corruption and racketeering (in his words "a shameful horror story"), became strongly committed to the trusteeship's success. Without a trial, the judge may not be well versed in the union's problems. Where the judge is only tangentially involved in the case, she or he may leave the structure and powers of the trusteeship to be negotiated by the parties. Judge David Edelstein is a striking exception; even without a trial, he became strongly committed to reforming the IBT and handed down one decision after another supporting the government's trustees' positions.

The trustee, for good reason, is likely to be suspicious of existing union officers. They were probably complicit with and certainly tolerant of the labor racketeers who had exploited the union for many years. The integrity of the international union's officers will also be uncertain. Years, even decades, of organized crime domination of a local or district council could not have gone on without the knowledge, acquiescence, and complicity of some international union officers. The trustee must be wary of appearing friendly to or allied with the incumbent international union officials lest the rank and file conclude that the trusteeship is just for show.

In a few cases the new union trustee has been approached by rank-and-file members, usually "dissidents," who may previously have been bold enough to criticize the ruling clique. Some dissidents provide useful information; others' allegations are distorted by a paranoid worldview, not surprising in light of years of struggle and defeats. Too close an association with these dissidents may undermine the trustee's credibility with rank-and-file union members.[19] However, there are also costs in disappointing or alienating the dissidents.

If the trustee is going to learn more about the union, the information will probably have to come from DOL and FBI investigators, who might or might not continue, after the negotiated agreement, to work on the case, thereby supporting the trusteeship. On one hand, the investigators may be strongly invested in eliminating corruption and racketeering, root and branch. On the other hand, once there is a signed settlement, there may be departmental pressures to move on to new cases.

The Operation of the Trusteeships

What does a trustee in a civil RICO union case actually do to achieve the goals of the consent agreement? There is no "to do" list. Every trustee has had to invent the job, at least to the extent of identifying and prioritizing tasks and allocating time and resources among investigations, disciplinary actions, and union-democracy-building. Because no two situations are the same, it is inevitable and desirable that each trustee attempt to address the exigencies of the case at hand. Moreover, a successful trustee changes priorities and reallocates resources as weeks, months, and years pass. A RICO union trustee has to allocate time both to responding to problems ("problem solver") and to pressing forward with a reform agenda ("organizational reformer"). Some trustees initially confronted so many union administrative problems that they were never able to move into the organizational reform mode.

Trustees have presided over regularly scheduled and special union meetings where, among other things, they have sought to explain the trusteeship to the rank and file and solicited their support. Trustees have contributed regular columns to union magazines and newsletters and published open letters to the membership explaining the civil RICO case, the charges against incumbent officials, and the trustee's role. In some cases, trustees have sought to educate the rank and file about their Landrum-Griffin rights to speak freely, run for office, vote, inspect contracts, and so on. Some trustees have maintained an open door or have met on an appointment-only basis with union members who wanted to convey their concerns or assuage their anxieties. Sorting out bona fide complaints from malicious rumors and politically motivated accusations is a constant challenge.

Trustees have had to pore over books and records to identify legitimate and illegitimate expenditures. In the HERE International case, Trustee Kurt Muellenberg found a shocking lack of bureaucratic rationality in the union's organization.[20] There was no table of organization, no job descriptions, no administrative procedures. Muellenberg's main contribution was probably his recommendations for transforming the union's administration into a modern bureaucracy.

The trustees, at varying levels of intensity, have investigated wrongdoing and wrongdoers. A minority of trustees has had an investigator working specially for the trusteeship.[21] The majority has had to depend on FBI and DOL agents, which means persuading them of their own reliability and integrity.

Trustees have replaced business agents and other union personnel. They have spent time setting up fair election procedures, approving individual candidates, and supervising balloting and counting ballots. Some trustees (e.g., Edwin Stier in the IBT Local 560 case) or their assistants have negotiated collective bargaining agreements, processed workplace grievances, and led job actions.

CONCLUSION

Civil RICO has proved to be a very potent weapon for DOJ lawyers seeking to eliminate LCN's power base in certain unions. The DOJ lawyers have never lost a civil RICO union case, but that hardly means that they have achieved 100 percent of their goals. It has proved easier to draft the civil RICO complaints and to obtain favorable consent decrees than to establish successful union trusteeships. It has come as a surprise and major disappointment to government litigators and reformers that many union members have not greeted the court-appointed trustee as a liberator.

The trustees appointed in civil RICO union cases have been differently empowered, financed, and tenured. Some have exercised the same powers as the union's officers; others have been restricted to a monitoring and reporting role. Some have plugged away at their mission for more than a decade; others have completed their work in just eighteen months. Some have expelled dozens of union officers; others have expelled nobody. Some trustees, as we will see in Chapters 9, 10, and 11, appear to have succeeded in purging labor racketeers and bringing forth a new leadership cadre independent of the faction that corruptly dominated the union for decades; others have failed to free the union from the labor racketeers. Even where liberation has been achieved, there has been very little success in establishing union democracy.

9

The Liberation of IBT Local 560

It is not a pretty story . . . [it] is a harrowing tale of how evil men sponsored by and part of organized crime elements, infiltrated and ultimately captured Local 560.

—Judge Harold A. Ackerman, *United States v. Local 560,*
581 F. Supp. 279, 282 (D.N.J. 1984)

Members were intimidated from expressing their opinions and disagreements. They were intimidated, sometimes it was subtle and sometimes it was not so subtle. The Union was a burden the members suffered. It did not negotiate good contracts, good wages or good benefits. It existed for the benefit of organized crime members who controlled the union, not for the members.

—Peter Brown, Local 560 president, testimony before a
congressional committee in 1999

[T]he goal [of the Trusteeship] has been to transform the culture of the Union from one in which racketeering was acceptable behavior to one in which exploitation of the membership by organized crime, or any other form of corruption, will not be tolerated. I believe we have achieved that goal.

—Local 560 Trustee Edwin Stier, Report and Recommendations of
the Court Appointed Trustee for Teamsters Local 560,
January 1999

INTRODUCTION

In 1982, the 10,000-member IBT Local 560 was one of the largest Teamsters union locals in the country. Its members were employed by 425

Note: This chapter is a substantial revision of James B. Jacobs and David N. Santore, "The Liberation of IBT Local 560," *Criminal Law Bulletin,* March–April 2000.

companies,[1] ranging from large national trucking firms to small cartage companies with as few as three or four drivers. IBT Local 560 members drove trucks, worked in warehouses, on road construction sites, and in laundries.

The Executive Board, which managed the union's daily affairs, consisted of seven elected officers, including president, vice-president, secretary-treasurer, recording secretary, and three trustees. The Executive Board appointed business agents, shop stewards, and benefit plan trustees.[2] The business agents negotiated collective bargaining agreements and handled workers' grievances.[3] Shop stewards enforced the collective bargaining agreements at work sites.[4] Benefit trustees oversaw the administration and operation of pension and welfare funds.

LABOR RACKETEERING IN IBT LOCAL 560

Anthony "Tony Pro" Provenzano, and his two brothers, Nunzio and Salvatore, dominated Local 560 for decades. Tony joined the union in the late 1940s and served as a business agent from 1948 until 1958 when he became president.[5] His rise in Local 560 paralleled his rise in the Genovese crime family, which inducted him as a "made member."[6]

In 1961, Tony enlisted Harold Konigsberg, Salvatore Briguglio, and others to kill Anthony Castellito, Local 560's secretary-treasurer.[7] Tony believed that Castellito had informed authorities about Tony's extortion of a trucking company.[8] Law enforcement authorities also suspected that Tony had ordered the 1963 murder of Walter Glockner, another Local 560 dissident. In 1966, Tony was sent to prison for extorting labor-peace payoffs from a trucking company.[9] While he was doing time, his brother Salvatore ran the union. Tony was incarcerated in the same federal prison as Jimmy Hoffa. The two had a falling out, perhaps accounting for Tony's suspected role in Hoffa's murder.[10] In 1975, federal prosecutors indicted Tony for conspiracy to violate the federal anti-kickback statute.[11] The charge related to a loan from the New York State Teamsters Conference Employee Welfare and Pension Benefit Plan.[12] Tony acted as a broker between the benefit plan's trustee and the borrowers, who had close organized crime ties. The trustee demanded a substantial kickback for putting the loan through. The borrowers balked because other parties to the transaction also demanded payoffs. For his role in smoothing the waters and brokering the deal, Tony was convicted in 1978 and sentenced to a four-year prison term.[13]

In 1978, Tony was sentenced to life imprisonment for his part in the murder of Local 560 dissident Anthony Castellito seventeen years earlier. The Local 560 leadership quickly voted to pay Tony a lucrative pension for the rest of his life[14] and selected his daughter, Josephine, as secretary treasurer. In 1979, at a federal trial, Tony and his henchmen Stephen Andretta, Thomas Andretta, and Gabriel Briguglio were found guilty of violating RICO based upon their labor-peace extortions of two trucking companies. Tony and Thomas Andretta were sentenced to twenty-year prison terms while Briguglio and Stephen Andretta received ten- and seven-year sentences, respectively.[15]

In 1980, Tony's two brothers, Nunzio and Salvatore, along with Michael Sciarra and Irving Cotler were indicted for a nine-year (1971–1980) extortion conspiracy to extort money from four trucking companies. Nunzio Provenzano and Cotler were sentenced to ten years and seven years, respectively; Salvatore Provenzano and Sciarra were acquitted.[16] Tony designated Sciarra to succeed him as Local 560's top official. Gabriel Briguglio himself was murdered while awaiting trial for the Castellito murder. Tony died in federal prison in 1988.[17]

THE CIVIL RICO SUIT

In March 1982, the New Jersey U.S. Attorney's Office, the Newark Federal Organized Crime Strike Force, and the Department of Justice filed a civil RICO[18] complaint against twelve individual defendants, Local 560 and its pension and welfare funds and severance pay plan. As remedies, the government sought (1) to prohibit Tony Provenzano, Nunzio Provenzano, Stephen and Thomas Andretta, and Gabriel Briguglio (the "Provenzano Group") from having contact with any officer or employee of Local 560 or any other labor organization or union employee benefit plan; (2) to remove the Executive Board, which comprised Salvatore Provenzano, Joseph Sheridan, Josephine Provenzano, J. W. Dildine, Stanley Jaronko, Thomas Reynolds, Sr. (Nunzio's brother-in-law), and Michael Sciarra; and (3) the appointment of a trustee to run and monitor Local 560 until free elections could be conducted.[19]

The complaint alleged that Local 560 satisfied the definition of a RICO "enterprise" (any individual, partnership, corporations, association, or other legal entity, and any union or group of individuals associated in fact although not legal entity"). It then alleged two distinct RICO violations: (1) that the individual "Provenzano Group" defendants, associated under the leadership of Tony Provenzano and aided and abetted by past and present IBT Local 560 Executive Board members, violated RICO (1962b) by illegally acquiring and maintaining control of Local 560 through a pattern of racketeering activity; and (2) that the Provenzano Group violated RICO (1962c) by conducting Local 560's affairs through a pattern of racketeering activity.

The first RICO charge alleged that the Provenzano Group and the Executive Board had violated the Hobbs Act by using "actual and threatened force, violence and fear of physical and economic injury in order to create . . . a climate of intimidation which induced members . . . to consent to the surrender of certain valuable property in the form of their union rights."[20] The complaint cited the union defendants' extensive associations with Genovese crime family members; twenty-eight specific crimes (including the murders of Anthony Castellito and Walter Glockner); defendants' failure to take any action to reduce members' fears and perceptions. According to the government, these crimes created and sustained a climate of intimidation that deprived the union members of their Landrum-Griffin rights.[21]

The second RICO charge accused the defendants of conducting the affairs of the RICO enterprise (i.e., Local 560) through a pattern of racketeering activity consisting of at least five predicate racketeering offenses: (1) the extortion of $17,100 from Dorn Transport Company in return for labor peace; (2) the wrongful conversion of $223,785 of Local 560 funds by Anthony Provenzano, who was aided and abetted by past and present members of the Executive Board; (3) the Provenzano Group's wrongful receipt of payments from Interocean Service and Di-Jub Leasing in return for labor peace; (4) the unlawful receipt by Anthony Provenzano of Florida real estate from Thomas Romano in return for making loans available to Romano from Local 560's benefit funds; and (5) Nunzio Provenzano's wrongful receipt of labor peace payoffs from Pacific Intermountain Express Company, Mason and Dixon Lines, Inc., T.I.M.E., Inc., and Helms Express. The government also charged the Provenzano Group with conspiracy to violate RICO.[22]

THE JUDGMENT

Prior to trial, the government entered into consent agreements with several of the organized crime defendants, including Tony Provenzano, Nunzio Provenzano, and Thomas Andretta, all of whom were in prison at the time. These defendants agreed that never again would they serve as union officials nor associate with any enterprise that seeks to control or influence the affairs of a labor organization.[23] The bench trial against the nonsettling defendants consumed fifty-one days spread over the period from January 25, 1983, to May 17, 1983. Some of the most persuasive testimony came from cooperating witness Salvatore Sinno, a former Provenzano Group member and accomplice in the Castellito murder. He explained Tony's role in the Genovese crime family and detailed how Tony gained and maintained control of IBT Local 560.[24] Federal District Court Judge Harold Ackerman (a former labor lawyer) wrote in his opinion: "As described by Salvatore Sinno, the Provenzano Group began its activities as a wholly illicit and criminal enterprise in which each associate accepted orders and assignments from [Tony] Provenzano and each was prepared to collaborate with other associates in carrying out particular assignments."[25]

In his lengthy opinion, Judge Ackerman reviewed the history of corruption in Local 560, emphasizing the Executive Board's failure to take any action against egregious racketeering. Ackerman found that the Provenzano Group violated the membership's Landrum-Griffin rights while the Executive Board had "done nothing to devise or implement measures reasonably calculated to prevent and detect potential 'labor peace' abuses."[26] Furthermore, Judge Ackerman found

> that a significant number of Local 560 members are in fear of the Provenzano Group, that they fear for their jobs and their physical safety, and that through this fear the members were induced by the Provenzano Group to part with their LMRDA-created union democracy rights.[27]

Judge Ackerman determined as well that Local 560 members and the local trucking industry would continue to suffer as long as Local 560 remained a "captive union" and that more criminal prosecutions would not break the Provenzano Group's hold on the union. Therefore, he enjoined imprisoned Provenzano Group members Stephen Andretta and Gabriel Briguglio from any future dealings with Local 560 and Ackerman decided to remove the Executive Board members from office because they had been indifferent to, if not complicit with, the Provenzano Group's racketeering. In justifying this drastic intrusion into the local's governance, the judge systematically reviewed the actions and inactions of each Executive Board member. For example, in commenting on Executive Board member Joseph Sheridan, Judge Ackerman stated:

> Joseph Sheridan must be removed from office for the following reasons:
> - Like J. W. Dildine, Joseph Sheridan professes to earnestly believe that Local 560's problems are the product of a government vendetta.
> - Joseph Sheridan believes that both Anthony and Nunzio Provenzano were convicted of various crimes because of their names.
> - Joseph Sheridan does not believe in the truth of the allegations which resulted in Nunzio Provenzano's conviction in the Braun case.
> - Joseph Sheridan is unable or unwilling to institute controls or safeguards to ensure that Local 560 is not victimized in the future by criminal conduct such as that which occurred in the Seatrain and City-man cases.
> - Joseph Sheridan does not consider Anthony or Nunzio Provenzano to be anything but good labor leaders.
> - If Nunzio Provenzano were eligible to serve on the Executive Board tomorrow, Joseph Sheridan, as a trustee and vice-president of Local 560, would welcome him back with "open arms."
> - Joseph Sheridan's mindset, after all that has occurred over the past thirty years, would make it impossible for him to formulate and promote policies which would be reasonably calculated to prevent or discourage further racketeering activity within Local 560 and ameliorate the current climate of intimidation. As previously noted, his loyalty has been purchased.[28]

THE TRUSTEESHIP

Judge Ackerman reasoned that only "through the imposition of a trusteeship for a curative period of sufficient length can the pattern of abuse be broken and future violations prevented." He held that the trusteeship would last until the union conducted a democratic election. The IBT Local 560 trusteeship started its work in June 1986, after the defendants' appeals had been exhausted.* Judge Ackerman appointed Joel R. Jacobson as trustee, describing him as a "distinguished trade unionist and public official."[29] Jacobson had been an organizer for the International Ladies' Garment Workers Union, and had served as president of the New Jersey CIO and as community relations director of the United Automobile Workers.

Trustee Jacobson identified three major impediments to Local 560's operation as a proper union. Incredibly, LCN domination was not one of them. Rather, Jacobson's diagnosis of the problem focused on (1) lack of rank-and-file solidarity; (2) the disarray of pension and welfare funds and severance pay plan records; and (3) lack of training programs for union officials. Jacobson promised to reform the union by addressing these deficiencies and by impressing the membership with competent and professional administration.[30] In his one year on the job, Jacobson increased union membership by 25 percent and negotiated contracts resulting in wage increases above the national average.[31] However, he did not address the Provenzano Group's continued control over the local. Indeed, he retained most of the shop stewards who had been appointed by the Provenzano Group because he believed (1) that they were needed to carry out collective bargaining and contract administration duties; and (2) that removing elected union officials would not be consistent with the goal of restoring democracy. Jacobson did, though (albeit after considerable delay), replace the business agents

---

* All the defendants, except Stephen Andretta and Gabriel Briguglio, filed notices of appeal. The Third Circuit affirmed Judge Ackerman's remedy and agreed that extorting the membership's LMRDA rights violated the Hobbs Act and constituted RICO predicate acts. *United States v. Local 560, Int'l Bhd of Teamsters*, 780 F.2d 267 (3d Cir. 1985). On May 27, 1986, the Supreme Court denied certiorari. *United States v. Local 560, Int'l Bhd of Teamsters*, 476 U.S. 1140 (1986). After the district court's decision, Sciarra and Sheridan remained in office due to Judge Ackerman's stay pending appeal. On October 19, 1984, Sciarra succeeded Salvatore Provenzano (who in the meantime had been convicted of defrauding the dental benefit fund and of receiving kickbacks) as president of Local 560. He remained in office until superseded by the trustee. Sheridan remained vice-president of Local 560 until removed by the trustee. Joel Jacobson, the first trustee, permitted him to serve as a business agent until February 1987. See *United States v. Local 560, Int'l Bhd of Teamsters*, 694 F. Supp. 1185, 1160 (D.N.J. 1988), aff'd 865 F.2d 253 (3d Cir. 1988), cert. denied, 109 S. Ct. 1345 (1989).

with individuals who had not held leadership positions during the Provenzanos' reign.

Unhappy about the trustee's inability or unwillingness to attack the Provenzano Group's influence, Judge Ackerman replaced Jacobson with Edwin Stier, a former federal prosecutor, New Jersey deputy attorney general, and director of the New Jersey Division of Criminal Justice. As associate trustee, Judge Ackerman chose Frank Jackiewicz, an IBT member for forty-six years who had served as shop steward, vice-president, and secretary-treasurer of IBT Local 843.* Ackerman charged Stier and Jackiewicz to "create and foster conditions under which union democracy will be restored and racketeer influence will be eliminated."[32] To achieve the court's objective, the trustee would possess the authority previously exercised by the union's Executive Board. The trustee would

- Possess the same powers accorded to the Executive Board as stipulated by the Local 560's by-laws and constitution (including participation in the affairs of all bodies related to Local 560);
- Negotiate contracts, pursue grievances, conduct organizing campaigns and participate in all lawful activities granted to a labor organization;
- Initiate, settle, and defend litigation on behalf of the local;
- Hire and fire Local 560 employees and set their wages and terms of employment;
- Appoint and remove business agents and shop stewards, subject only to the limitations established in the local's by-laws and constitution; and
- Retain or terminate any outside legal, accounting or consulting professionals.[33]

Prior to the 1998 union election, Stier was compensated $1,467 a week for essentially full-time work. Following the 1998 election, he was paid $150 per hour. Local 560, through outside counsel representing the Executive Board, argued that the postelection rate was excessive and

---

* Jacobson blasted his dismissal and Stier's appointment, stating, "[Judge Ackerman] wanted a whistle blower and that's what he has now. . . . [Ackerman is encouraging] union busting. I want no part of it." Rod Leith, "Ex-Teamster Trustee: Judge Sought Whistle Blower," 8, *Record*, October 1987, at A46.

beyond the union's ability to pay. Judge Ackerman disagreed, ruling that if anything "the trustee's . . . hourly rates have been seriously undervalued." He noted that Stier worked many more hours than he actually billed. Moreover, he held that Local 560 had failed to show that it could not pay the fees.[34]

When Stier and Jackiewicz took over, they found that the Provenzanos' influence was still pervasive. Tony's portrait still hung on the wall at Local 560's headquarters. Union members still regarded the Provenzano Group's handpicked successor, Michael Sciarra, as the man in charge.[35] Stier believed that to eradicate corruption and racketeering from Local 560, it would be necessary (albeit not sufficient) to transform Local 560 into a democratic union.[36] He announced that the trusteeship would operate according to the following principles:

- Union officers and business agents should understand that in performing their duties they must place the interests of the membership as a whole ahead of any other individual, group, or entity;
- Union leadership should recognize that any compromise with individuals associated with organized crime creates a risk that they will gain a foothold in the union;
- Local 560 members should be cognizant that they have the right to hold their officials accountable; and
- An atmosphere should exist at union functions and on the job site in which members are free to question their leadership's performance and voice dissenting perspectives.[37]

Stier pursued three reform strategies. First, with Jackiewicz's assistance, he sought to provide the membership effective representation. Second, he endeavored to expose past and present exploitation of the union and its pension and welfare funds. Third, he encouraged Local 560 members to participate in the union's affairs.

Stier adopted procedures and initiated programs that would demonstrate the advantages of an honest union. For example, he established contract-negotiating committees with rank-and-file members. To encourage the flow of information upward from the job sites, Stier maintained an open-door policy, urging members to bring complaints directly to him. He started a union newspaper, *The 560 Free Press*, and hired a professional journalist as editor.[38] Stier retained most of the business agents appointed by Jacobson, some of whom by then had received training at the IBT Leadership Academy. Still, after decades of racketeer control and with many members of the Provenzano clique still active in Local 560, few union members stepped forward to participate in union affairs.

After two years of union administration by the trustees, Stier scheduled an election.[39] Toward this end, he convened craft-specific meetings by dividing members into groups based on occupation. Placing members in smaller groups afforded potential candidates opportunities to meet the rank and file. He organized training sessions on the rights and obligations of union members and union officers, the IBT constitution, and Local 560's by-laws. Stier issued fair election procedures, convened a nominations meeting, and launched a voter registration drive.[40]

The Provenzano Group fought to retain its grip on Local 560.[41] It organized Teamsters for Liberty (TFL), a self-proclaimed civil liberties organization dedicated to "the termination of the Trusteeship and to the prevention of '[the] government['s] takeover of our union.'"[42] The TFL circulated petitions demanding an end to the trusteeship. It wrote to and met with government officials; invited public officials, labor leaders, and celebrities to its rallies; published its own newspaper, *We the People*; and retained attorneys to attack the trusteeship on an array of issues.[43] The TFL dominated membership meetings. It selected former Local 560 president Michael Sciarra, the Provenzanos' handpicked successor, as its candidate for president and Joseph Sheridan for vice-president.[44]

Stier and Robert Stewart, chief of the Newark federal Organized Crime Strike Force, went back to court to prevent Sciarra and Sheridan from running for Local 560 office.[45] The government charged that Sciarra was the designated representative of Matthew Iannello, a capo in the Genovese crime family.[46] It played recordings of intercepted conversations between Ianniello and various members of the pre-trusteeship Executive Board. These conversations illuminated Iannello's position within the Genovese crime family and his intention to retain control of Local 560. In one conversation, Iannello told Stanley Jaronko (a union officer whom Judge Ackerman had found to have aided and abetted the Provenzano Group) that he had to "run the shop, or do something with the shop" and then "let Mike [Sciarra] run the show."[47]

Judge Ackerman requested that another federal judge, Dickinson R. Debevoise, hear the government's motion to bar Sciarra and Sheridan from the upcoming election. The federal prosecutors sought to prove that Sheridan had been responsible for negotiating a sweetheart contract between Local 560 and Walsh Trucking and Consolidating Company in 1978 and that, thereafter, Sciarra and Sheridan arranged sweetheart contracts with Walsh Trucking.* Furthermore, the government presented evidence on Sciarra's mishandling of members' grievances against New England Motor Freight (NEMF) in support of Local 560's sweetheart contract with NEMF.[48] Finally, Stewart sought to show that Sciarra and Sheridan assisted a New Jersey attorney in setting up a fraudulent prepaid legal services scheme for Local 560 members.

According to Judge Debevoise, the government would "unquestionably be irreparably injured if preliminary injunctive relief [were] not granted. . . . All [the government's work] will have been expended for no purpose if an election returns Local 560 to the Genovese family and its minions."[49] Consequently, in September 1988, Judge Debevoise issued a preliminary injunction barring Sciarra and Sheridan from running for union office.[50]

Still the Provenzano Group did not give up. It chose Daniel Sciarra, Michael Sciarra's brother, and Mark Sheridan, Joseph Sheridan's nephew, to carry the banner for the Provenzano Group.[51] In a heavy blow to the court and the trusteeship, Sciarra and Sheridan prevailed by a two-to-one margin.[52] It appeared that Local 560 members preferred to be represented by individuals backed by the old regime than by reformers supported by the government and the court-appointed trustee.**

* The government alleged that beginning in late 1977 and continuing for a decade, Iannello, acting on behalf of the Genovese crime family, conspired with Anthony Provenzano and other Local 560 officials and with New Jersey trucking magnate Francis J. Walsh, Jr., to engage in a payoff scheme that enriched the conspirators at the expense of Walsh's employees.

** Extensive interviews with rank-and-file Local 560 members conducted by Harvard Professor Linda Kaboolian following the election revealed that union members resented the government's interference with their right to run their union as they chose. While some union members blamed Provenzano for some of Local 560's problems, that blame did not carry over to Daniel Sciarra and Mark Sheridan.

DISQUALIFYING MICHAEL SCIARRA

Daniel Sciarra appointed Michael Sciarra and Joseph Sheridan as Local 560 business agents.* Stewart went to court to block the appointments, but Judge Debevoise decided not to prohibit Sciarra and Sheridan from serving as business agents, reasoning that the election had severed the link with the old regime, thereby entitling the Executive Board to a presumption that it would act lawfully and in the best interest of the membership.

The naiveté of Judge Debevoise's presumption was soon apparent. Michael Sciarra exercised de facto control of the union. By the third postelection union meeting, there were no longer any dissenting voices. Sciarra's supporters, strategically positioned throughout the meeting hall, intimidated would-be critics.[53] Indeed, they loudly heckled Stier. Sciarra himself physically threatened a Department of Labor agent at the union hall.[54]

In February 1990, Robert Stewart again asked Judge Debevoise to oust Sciarra and Sheridan from their positions as business agents.[55] Sheridan agreed to resign his office. Judge Debevoise granted the motion to oust Sciarra, concluding that "[a]s long as Michael Sciarra holds any position within Local 560 he will be able through his forceful and dominating personality, through his hold on a large and vocal segment of the membership and by virtue of the inexperience and subservience of the present officers and Board members to dominate and control the Local."[56]

Two months after Judge Debevoise removed Sciarra from his business agent position, the government sought to enjoin Sciarra permanently from any participation in Local 560 affairs.[57] After a two-day trial illuminating Sciarra's relationship with the Genovese crime family, Debevoise permanently enjoined Sciarra from "holding any office or

* In January 1989, the government obtained an order that required Michael Sciarra and Joseph Sheridan to show cause why they should be permitted to serve as business agents. The court initially concluded that there was not sufficient evidence to prohibit Sciarra and Sheridan from serving as business agents. The court reasoned that the election had severed the link in the chain of criminality and that the newly elected Executive Board was entitled to a presumption that it would discharge its duties lawfully and in the best interest of the local. New predicate acts of misconduct were necessary to prohibit Sciarra and Sheridan from assuming such positions. See *United States v. Local 560, Int'l Bhd of Teamsters*, 974 F.2d at 324.

position of trust within or otherwise endeavoring to influence the affairs of Local 560."[58] Nevertheless, Sciarra continued to exert influence.

In early 1991, the government sought to expand the permanent injunction against Sciarra.[59] This time Judge Debevoise permanently barred Sciarra from holding any position in Local 560, participating in any Local 560 functions, visiting the union hall, or attempting to influence the union's affairs.[60] This was the most drastic court-imposed sanction any court had ever applied to a union member who had not been convicted of a crime.

Still, Sciarra exercised de facto power. The day after Judge Debevoise barred him from participating in union affairs, Sciarra met with Executive Board members Daniel Sciarra, Robert Marra, Peter Granello, and Alfred Vallee to settle a dispute between Vallee and the others. The Executive Board still looked upon Sciarra as its leader.[61] Jobs were still awarded according to a member's loyalty to the Provenzano/Sciarra clique.[62] During a December 1990 membership meeting to nominate delegates to the IBT International convention, TFL supporters physically assaulted a Sciarra critic.[63]

In September 1991, the Local 560 Executive Board went to court seeking termination of the trusteeship.[64] Stewart counterattacked, requesting court-ordered procedures for allocating construction jobs* and enhancement of the trustee's investigative powers.[65] After a hearing,** but prior to the judge's decision, the Executive Board and the government entered into a settlement agreement, pursuant to which (1) the Executive Board would comprise six members;[66] (2) Daniel Sciarra would resign as president;[67] and (3) the local's secretary-treasurer, Robert Marra, recording secretary, Alfred Vallee, and trustee Peter Granello would retain their positions. Marra, Vallee, and Granello were to select one individual from among the remaining two trustees (James Bartolomeo and Nicholas Juliano) and the vice-president (Mark Sheridan) to serve as a trustee.[68] They selected Bartolomeo.[69] The court authorized

---

* Construction jobs performed by Local 560 members generally related to road and highway construction.

** The evidentiary hearing focused on the discriminatory allocation of construction jobs and an attempt to defraud the welfare fund in favor of a Sciarra relative. The evidence showed that a business agent coerced two employers to file false employment records on behalf of Daniel and Michael Sciarra's niece's husband who recently died of a drug overdose, thus enabling the widow fraudulently to receive life insurance proceeds. See *United States v. Local 560, Int'l Bhd of Teamsters,* and Mezzina and Conlon, Complaint, at 22–29.

Stier to fill two empty trustee positions with any Local 560 member in good standing.[70]

The settlement sought to eliminate corruption in the construction unit by authorizing Stier to appoint a new business agent and by ordering the Executive Board to create a fair job referral plan for road construction jobs.[71] Eventually, the board designed a complex formula for ranking members' eligibility for job assignments.[72]

In September 1992, after becoming aware that Michael Sciarra was continuing to associate with Executive Board member Robert Marra and had attempted to defraud the benefit funds, Stier and Stewart obtained yet another court order, this one providing that the Local 560 Executive Board would be expanded to seven members headed by the president.[73] Robert Marra was forced to resign.[74] The board appointed Alfred Vallee as president[75] and Peter Granello as secretary-treasurer. Vallee and Granello had exhibited autonomy from the Sciarra group during their careers with Local 560. For the first time in living memory, the board was composed of a majority of officers independent of the Provenzano Group. In 1994, in an act of telling independence, the board removed three of its own members for failure to fulfill their fiduciary duties to the membership.[76] By 1995, six of the seven Executive Board members had no previous ties to the Provenzano Group.

With the Executive Board's consent, the court gave Stier new powers to investigate violations of Local 560's constitution and by-laws and authority to render binding decisions against union members.* Between 1995 and 1998, four Local 560 members were expelled because of contact with Michael Sciarra and/or defrauding the union; a fifth member resigned in anticipation of formal charges. All told, during Trustee Stier's tenure, eighteen individuals charged with misconduct were expelled or resigned from the union.[77]

---

* These procedures allowed Stier to investigate any member's conduct. If he uncovered actionable wrongdoing, he would serve the member with specific charges. The member could present a defense to the Executive Board and Stier. Thereafter, Stier would forward his decision and proposed remedial action to the Executive Board for consideration. After reviewing the board's comments, Stier would finalize his decision and present it to the member, who, if dissatisfied, could appeal to the district court judge. See Consent Order at 3–12 (Feb. 22, 1995), *United States v. Local 560, Int'l Bhd of Teamsters*, 581 F. Supp. 279 (D.N.J. 1984) (82–689), Report and Recommendations, at 13–14.

THE 1998 ELECTION

In 1998, three conditions convinced Stier to proceed with another election for Local 560 officers. First, union members were able to secure job referrals from the union without having to cater to Sciarra loyalists. This was most important in the construction unit, which Stier used as a barometer for the union as a whole. The job referral system now operated according to objective criteria, not loyalty to the Provenzano Group. Second, most of the organized crime–connected Local 560 members had been ousted from the union. Third, a new group of leaders now held union offices. Stier observed that membership meetings were "drastically different from those that were held during the era when the Sciarra group dominated . . ." and that "Local 560 members now viewed the Executive Board as the membership's representatives and not as an arm of the government."[78]

The incumbent Executive Board ran as one slate, led by Peter Brown, whom the board had appointed as acting president in 1997. Brown had been a member of Local 560 since 1978 and was an early supporter of the trusteeship. In 1990, Brown was fired from his trucking company job, in his view due to Michael Sciarra's influence. Brown's fortunes turned with those of the trusteeship. He was appointed as a business agent (1993) and then as a trustee (1995).[79] Brown's slate faced two competing slates. A different Daniel Sciarra, this one Michael and Daniel's nephew, led one of the slates. Alfred Laurie, a former office manager during Sciarra's administration, led the other.[80] The Sciarra and Laurie slates branded Brown and his running mates "government men."

Stier decided that mail balloting would maximize participation and minimize intimidation. He required candidates to keep detailed records on campaign donations and expenditures. Forty-six percent of the 4,400 eligible Local 560 members voted in the election.[81] Brown received 1,049 votes (55 percent) and Daniel Sciarra, 376 (20 percent).[82] The power and prestige of the Provenzano Group had finally been broken. Peter Brown was sworn in as president of Local 560 on March 19, 1999, by IBT president James P. Hoffa, whose father had been murdered by a group of LCN figures, probably including Tony Provenzano. When Brown died in 2004, he was succeeded by Thomas McGinley who has carried on in the same style of reformist leadership.

TERMINATION OF THE TRUSTEESHIP

On February 25, 1999, Trustee Stier, the DOJ, and the DOL recommended that the court end its supervision of IBT Local 560.[83] The DOJ lawyers told Judge Ackerman that the union was now democratically governed. Judge Ackerman terminated Stier's monitoring and investigative roles, but required the Executive Board to name Stier as a trustee of the local's pension and welfare funds.[84] Furthermore, Ackerman approved a four-year consent decree between the Justice Department and the union that allowed Ackerman to put Local 560 back under trusteeship if systemic corruption or Cosa Nostra influence re-emerged.[85] As with the previous consent decree, union members could be expelled for knowingly associating with Cosa Nostra members or expelled union members.[86] No such problems occurred over the course of the next four years.

FACTORS THAT LED TO THE PURGING OF COSA NOSTRA FROM LOCAL 560

Although court-appointed trustees have monitored, supervised, or managed other "mobbed-up" union locals and even internationals, one scholar recently commented that "only Local 560 has seen a real transformation."[87] This is particularly impressive because no union local was more thoroughly dominated by organized crime than IBT Local 560. What accounts for the successful transformation of Local 560? Undoubtedly, there was a confluence of favorable forces, but the most important was the structure and continuity of the trusteeship, the judges' support of the trustee, and the trustee's stamina and skill.

THE FRAMING OF THE TRUSTEESHIP

The persistence into the 1980s of labor racketeering in Local 560 provides strong support for the conclusion that criminal prosecutions alone cannot eliminate entrenched labor racketeering. The Provenzano Group proved very resilient. When Tony Provenzano, his brothers and henchmen went to prison, they chose loyal subordinates to fill their vacated positions. Civil RICO permitted a comprehensive attack on the whole corrupt regime. But the preconditions for a comprehensive remedy were the relentless persistence of the DOJ attorney, the willingness of two district court judges to act decisively, and a trustee's commitment to seeing the job through to a successful completion.

IMPORTANCE OF THE TRIAL

A lengthy trial enabled Judge Ackerman to learn firsthand the depth of the corruption and racketeering in Local 560, which he branded a "multifaceted orgy of criminal activity."[88] Over the course of the fifty-one-day bench trial, witnesses detailed organized crime's entrenchment in IBT Local 560. Ackerman heard Genovese capo (and the government's star witness) Salvatore Sinno testify about the link between the union and Genovese crime family.[89] He listened to Executive Board members express admiration for Tony Provenzano, a convicted murderer, labor racketeer, and organized crime member. Such testimony persuaded Ackerman to impose a heretofore unprecedented remedy, a court-appointed trustee empowered with all the authority of the union's Executive Board.[90] It should not be forgotten that Ackerman himself had been a union lawyer before being appointed to the bench and was thus almost uniquely qualified to understand the "situation on the ground" that needed to be changed. Furthermore, Ackerman had had considerable experience in a prior institutional reform case involving the Essex County jail.

Most all civil RICO actions against mobbed-up unions have been resolved by negotiated consent decrees. In such cases, the judge who approves the decree may not fully grasp the magnitude of the corruption and not have become personally committed to ending it. Without a trial, the government may have negotiated a settlement with Local 560 that was not as far-reaching as Judge Ackerman's order. Furthermore, because of the trial, Ackerman was in a position to deal confidently with subsequent DOJ motions. At every step of the way, Stier benefited from the strong support of the federal Organized Crime Strike Force, especially Assistant U.S. Attorney Robert Stewart, who stayed with the case from beginning to end. Judge Ackerman's and Judge Debevoise's determination were also critical.

WIDE-RANGING TRUSTEESHIP

Judge Ackerman defined the trustee's goal in broad and ambitious terms. He empowered the trustee "to act as he may, in good judgment, to administer the affairs of Local 560 and to create and foster conditions under which union democracy will be restored and racketeer influence will be eliminated."[91] The remedial decree authorized the trustee to implement whatever policies he deemed necessary and in the best interest of the local. Unlike trustees in other civil RICO consent decrees, Stier was not burdened with the time-consuming process of repeatedly having to petition the court for approval prior to instituting reforms.

TRANSFORMING THE ROLE OF THE TRUSTEE FROM UNION MANAGER TO CORRUPTION FIGHTER

Although Ackerman applauded the efforts of his first trustee, Joel Jacobson, he knew that a different approach was needed to "insure that the documented egregious pattern of racketeering activity does not re-emerge. . . ."[92] Jacobson had extensive experience in union governance, but not in combating organized crime. Clearly, investigative and prosecutorial expertise was needed. When Ackerman appointed Edwin Stier and Frank Jackiewicz, he wrote that the two men "bring to the task at hand unique talents which in combination are essential for this new phase of the trusteeship."[93] With Stier's appointment, Ackerman in effect redefined the trustee's primary job as purging organized crime.

Stier's prosecutorial background turned out to be critically important. He worked easily and effectively with FBI and DOL investigators and with federal prosecutors. Still, it may also have been important that Stier did not fully delegate his union administrative powers to Jackiewicz, believing it necessary to participate personally in Local 560's affairs, including collective bargaining, strikes, and picketing, in order to understand the organization and culture of the local and to establish credibility with the rank-and-file membership. It is certainly important that Stier was able to devote practically all his time to the trusteeship for several years. At the time he took the job, he operated like a full-time consultant rather than like a big-law-firm partner whose duties as a trustee may be just one of many professional responsibilities.

DEVELOPMENT OF NEW UNION LEADERS

To succeed in reforming IBT Local 560, Trustee Stier needed to recruit and develop a new cadre of union leaders. It was a major challenge because, for decades, the only members with leadership experience were either members or supporters of the Provenzano Group.

From the outset, Stier sought to create an atmosphere conducive to the emergence of new leaders. He appointed several members to the contract-negotiating committees, a role once reserved for Tony Provenzano's henchmen. As new people began to assume official responsibilities, Stier steadily delegated more administrative responsibilities. He did not offer training programs for emerging leaders because he feared that the membership would view participants as government pawns.[94] In distancing himself from the local's government, Stier helped to legitimize the board as an independent body.

Union members who had not held office before gained experience as shop stewards and Executive Board members. As time passed, these leaders gained the respect of the general membership. The 1998 election of Peter Brown illustrated this shift. Brown, who had been vilified for his protrustee stance in the 1980s, soundly defeated his opponents in the 1998 election and was easily reelected in 2001 and 2004.

PURGING ORGANIZED CRIME

Stier's dogged effort to purge organized crime's influence from Local 560 was essential to the reform project. Stier had to excise every vestige of the Provenzano/Sciarra regime. If union members thought there was any chance of organized crime regaining control of the union, they would not support the reform effort. Stier realized the paramount importance of eliminating the Genovese crime family's handpicked successor, Michael Sciarra, and his successor, Daniel Sciarra, from Local 560.

DOJ's assistance was essential for Stier's success. When Stier sought judicial intervention, he was steadfastly supported by Assistant

U.S. Attorney Robert Stewart, who had drafted the RICO complaint and tried the case against the Local 560 officers. Stewart drafted virtually all of the government's motions relating to Local 560. Few government attorneys involved in union RICO cases have had Stewart's longevity. His knowledge of the multiple challenges faced by the trusteeship allowed him to respond effectively to Stier's concerns. Stewart and Stier acquired enough evidence to prove that the Genovese crime family had designated Michael Sciarra as boss of the local. Judge Debevoise enjoined Michael Sciarra and Joseph Sheridan from running for office. Later, Sciarra was expelled from the union.

Two federal judges played critical roles in eradicating organized crime from the union. Judge Harold Ackerman realized the extent of organized crime's entrenchment in the union and resisted the temptation to bow to the local's initial desire for self-regulation. He did not back off in the face of the TFL's rallies or characterization of the civil RICO as antiunion.

Judge Debevoise's decision to grant an injunction to forbid Michael Sciarra from running for Local 560 office came at a crucial moment. Although Michael Sciarra still exerted influence after his brother Daniel was elected president, had Michael been elected by the membership, the Provenzano Group's power would have been legitimated.

STIER'S LONGEVITY AND CREATIVITY

Civil RICO provided a means for achieving reforms, but successfully reforming a racketeer-ridden union like Local 560 requires significant time. By serving for *ten years*, Trustee Stier provided constant pressure for reform. No other trustee in any labor racketeering case has served that long. The trustee's longevity symbolized to the rank and file the court's determination to reform the union; it also provided the trustee with invaluable knowledge and experience. Prosecutors and judges may wish for a quick fix in such cases, but the history of the IBT Local 560 case indicates that the trustee's own determination is an important factor. As time passed, Local 560's membership changed. Through the natural process of relocation and retirement, many Local 560 members who had lived under the Provenzano Group's reign were succeeded by workers who had not experienced Cosa Nostra's domination and had never met or seen the Provenzanos.[95]

REFORMING THE PENSION AND WELFARE FUNDS

Stier assigned high priority to the protection of the pension and welfare funds.* One of his first acts as trustee was to appoint himself the funds' sole trustee. He ordered a background check on all companies and individuals that provided services to the funds. Stier made Local 560's funds the first in the country to be invested solely in index funds, so that an active fund manager was not required. To further insure the integrity of the funds, Stier hired Deloitte & Touche to perform regular audits, which were made available to the membership. Stier also hired a full-time controller to serve as chief financial officer. The pension and welfare funds' performance improved markedly, producing increased member benefits. This achievement boosted Stier's credibility and popularity.[96]

CONCLUSION

Although, prior to the government's 1982 civil RICO suit, sporadic criminal prosecutions sent Tony Provenzano, his brothers, and several associates to prison, the prosecutions did not loosen the racketeers' grip on the union. Remarkably, the indictments and convictions did not break, or perhaps even weaken, the Provenzanos' control over Local 560.

The failure of past criminal prosecutions led the Newark federal Organized Crime Strike Force to initiate the first-ever civil RICO action against a labor organization. Replacing the Executive Board with a court-appointed trustee paved the way for purging LCN and ultimately returning the local to its members. Judge Ackerman and Trustee Stier

---

* Between early 1974 and late 1977, members of the Provenzano clique looted one of the local's benefit funds of more than half of its assets. In 1974, Thomas Romano, a real estate developer, met with then Local 560 president Salvatore Provenzano (whom Tony had installed while he himself was in prison) to discuss a loan for a condominium project in Florida. The fund trustees, including Salvatore Bruguglio and Stephen Andretta, lent Romano $4.6 million. After the loan was granted, Tony purchased a Florida home from Romano at a sharply discounted price. A year later, even though the Florida real estate market was in a downturn, Romano secured an additional $1.8 million loan for the project. In 1977, Romano sold Tony Pro another property at a below-market price. *United States v. Local 560, Int'l Bhd of Teamsters*, 780 F.2d, 294.

succeeded because of a confluence of factors, some well planned and executed, others merely fortuitous. Judge Ackerman's novel decree focused not only on the need to run the union honestly but also on the need to purge LCN's influence. His wide-ranging decree paved the way for Stier to reform the local. Stier's skill in developing a new cadre of union leaders eventually led to the reconstruction of the union and to significant numbers of members recognizing that the new union was far better than the old. From an *ex ante* perspective, one could not have anticipated the determination and perseverance of Judge Ackerman, Trustee Stier, and Assistant U.S. Attorney Stewart. Yet, *ex post* it seems likely that the trusteeship would not have been successful without their sustained commitment. Ultimately, Stier succeeded because of two interrelated strategies. He and Stewart kept continuous pressure on the Provenzano Group, purging its members from the union. Stier identified, encouraged, and supported future leaders from the local's rank and file.

The successful use of civil RICO against IBT Local 560 demonstrated a new and powerful weapon against labor racketeering. After *United States v. Local 560*, the Justice Department brought similar suits against many other racketeer-ridden unions. However, victory at the trial and the imposition of a trusteeship are only necessary preconditions for success; they do not guarantee success.

10

The New York City District Council of Carpenters

Most of the people whom the Carpenters union refers to jobs at the Javits Center are either members and associates of the Genovese family, or friends and relatives of Genovese family members and associates.

> —Testimony of former Colombo crime family capo
> Salvatore Miciotta as quoted in Kenneth Conboy,
> *Second Interim Report of the Investigations and
> Review Officer*, March 13, 1995

The IRO [Investigations and Review Officer] has justified his more intrusive role by arguing the following: The District Council does not have a strong tradition of democratic leadership, and has never held an election wherein the rank-and-file membership directly elected the leadership. The complaint in the civil RICO action alleged various acts of corruption, fraud, and violence, and the IRO contends that his staff's own observations of last summer's local union elections confirmed the view that incumbents often use their positions to "manipulate the system" and that the opposition is targeted for intimidation and economic reprisal.

> —Judge Charles S. Haight, Jr., *U.S. v. NYC Dist. Council of
> Carpenters*, 880 F. Supp. 1051, 1067 (S.D.N.Y. 1995)

The New York City District Council of Carpenters, located in Manhattan, is one of the city's largest unions, representing approximately thirty

---

Note: This chapter is based on James B. Jacobs and Kristin Stohner, "Ten Years of Court-Supervised Reform: A Chronicle and Assessment," 6 *California Law Review* 3 (2004).

thousand members.* At the time the U.S. attorney's office brought the 1990 civil RICO suit, the district council negotiated, implemented, and enforced collective bargaining agreements, and handled disputes, grievances, and arbitrations on behalf of twenty-two local Carpenters unions. The collective bargaining agreements require employers to make contributions on behalf of their employees to union pension and welfare funds. Although the funds are governed by an equal number of employer-appointed and union-appointed trustees, in reality, the union-appointed trustees control the funds.

Before the 1990 civil RICO settlement, district council officers also served as officers in their home locals and thereby drew two salaries, one from the local and one from the district council. For example, Frederick Devine, president of the district council (1991–1996), also served as Local 1456's president. John Abbatemarco, the district council's first vice-president, also served as Local 257's vice-president.[1]

In the 1970s and 1980s, the Genovese crime family controlled the district council through Vincent DiNapoli, a capo in the crime family who had also become a powerful figure in the drywall industry. According to the FBI, Teddy Maritas, district council president from 1977 to 1981, was a Genovese crime family associate.[2] Eventually, Maritas disappeared, presumed murdered because the boss of the Genovese family suspected him of cooperating with federal prosecutors. Thereafter, the mob continued its control over the district council through presidents Paschal McGuinness (1982 to 1991) and Fred Devine (1991 to 1996).

The Genovese crime family maintained its grip on the district council by intimidation and violence and by controlling access to jobs. Like most construction workers who go from project to project working for different employers, carpenters often depend upon their union for jobs. Collective bargaining agreements require contractors to call the union's

---

* The United Brotherhood of Carpenters (UBC) International Union, headquartered in Washington, D.C., has approximately 520,000 members in the United States and Canada. Available at http://www.carpenters.org/home.html. Its constitution requires a regional ("district") council whenever two or more locals exist in the same locality. (Constitution of the United Brotherhood of Carpenters and Joiners of America, § 26(B)). Each district council has its own by-laws, officers, treasury, and jurisdiction over contracts, grievances, and benefit funds. The affiliated local unions elect delegates to the district council in proportion to the size of their memberships. *United States v. Dist. Council*, 778 F. Supp. 738, 743 (S.D.N.Y 1991).

hiring hall when they have a construction contract to perform. Thus the union can blackball "troublemakers" and reward loyal supporters by withholding or assigning work.[3]

For many years, the Genovese crime family used the district council to create and maintain a drywall cartel.[4] The cartel rigged bids, allocated contracts, and fixed prices. Some Genovese crime family members, like DiNapoli, held ownership interests in drywall companies. The union could prevent drywall contractors who were not members of the cartel from performing their contracts by assigning them incompetent or purposefully destructive workers, or by disrupting the whole construction project by calling strikes and slowdowns.

In the early 1980s, a federal RICO prosecution of Maritas, DiNapoli, and others based on the drywall cartel resulted in a mistrial.[5] On the evening before the retrial in March 1982, Maritas disappeared, never to be seen or heard from again.[6] DiNapoli pleaded guilty. While DiNapoli served a five year prison term, his brother, Louis, allegedly represented the Genovese crime family's interest in the district council. Soon after DiNapoli's release from prison, he was prosecuted in the Genovese "family RICO" case, which brought to trial a number of the top figures in the Genovese family, charging them, among other things, with operating a poured-concrete cartel in the city's construction industry. DiNapoli was convicted and sentenced to another long prison term.[7]

The Carpenters International Union placed the New York City district council under trusteeship.[8] The trustee merged four locals to create Local 17, thereby purposefully or inadvertently consolidating the Genovese crime family's influence over carpenters' jobs in upper Manhattan and the Bronx.[9] The trustee also chose Local 608 president, Paschal McGuinness, a Genovese crime family associate, to be the new district council president.[10] McGuinness put John O'Connor in charge of the district council's daily operations. In 1990, O'Connor pled guilty to receiving a bribe from an employer and was sentenced to one to three years in prison, and fined $25,000. McGuinness was acquitted.[11]

Violence and corruption flourished under McGuinness's presidency. McGuinness gave preference to Genovese family associates for high-paying and desirable jobs at the Jacob Javits Exhibition Center.[12] Six of the ten violent acts cited as predicate offenses in the government's 1990 civil RICO suit against the district council occurred during McGuinness's presidency, including an assault with an iron pipe against a dissident member at a job site and the nonfatal shooting of John

O'Connor.[*] Further, the government alleged that McGuinness himself committed seven of the racketeering acts listed in the civil RICO complaint; all involved accepting bribes in exchange for not enforcing terms of the union's collective bargaining agreement. In a deposition, Marcello Svedese, a district council officer from 1981 to 1989 and a cooperating government witness, explained McGuinness's ties with organized crime:

> I have known Paschal McGuinness to associate with various organized crime figures in connection with the district council. I was present at a meeting between McGuinness and Louis DiNapoli, a made member of the Genovese Family, and I have discussed organized crime and the district council with McGuiness on many occasions.[13]

THE 1990 CIVIL RICO SUIT AND SETTLEMENT

In September 1990, the U.S. attorney for the SDNY filed a civil RICO complaint against the New York City District Council of Carpenters' former and current officers and six LCN figures.[14] The complaint named the district council, its constituent local unions, and its benefit funds as the RICO enterprise. It alleged two separate RICO violations: (1) that the LCN defendants, aided and abetted by past and present district council officers, violated RICO (1962b) by acquiring an interest in and control over the union through a pattern of racketeering activity, and (2) that (in violation of 1962c) the defendants conducted the district council's affairs through a pattern of racketeering activity.

The first RICO count alleged that "the defendants . . . unlawfully . . . affect[ed] commerce . . . by extortion [i.e., violated the Hobbs Act] . . . in that they obtained and attempted to obtain property" by violence and intimidation.[15] The "property" that the defendants allegedly extorted was the union members' Landrum-Griffin rights.[16] The RICO complaint alleged a pattern of racketeering activity based upon fifty-four predicate acts including murders: assaults with firebombs, iron pipes, knives, and guns; appointments to union leadership positions of inexperienced, incompetent, and corrupt individuals; union officials' associa-

---

[*] According to government investigators, John Gotti, boss of the Gambino crime family, ordered the assault on O'Connor because O'Connor (probably unwittingly) was responsible for trashing a restaurant in which Gotti held an interest. At Gotti's trial, O'Connor testified *for the defense.*

tions with known organized crime members; the defendant union officers' failure to take action to rid the union of corruption; and abuse of their union office. The government also charged the defendants with conspiracy to violate RICO.[17]

The second RICO count was based upon § 1962(c) (participating in the affairs of an enterprise through a pattern of racketeering activity); it also cited fifty-four predicate racketeering acts including extortion, receipt of illegal payoffs, mail fraud, and operating a benefit fund unlawfully.[18] The government sought preliminary and permanent injunctions (1) to prohibit the organized crime defendants and those in active concert with them from having contact with the district council or any other labor organization; (2) to prohibit current, former, and future officers of the district council from committing racketeering acts and from associating with any member or associate of LCN; (3) to appoint a court liaison officer with the authority necessary to prevent racketeering activity and to ensure union democracy; (4) to enjoin union members and officers from interfering with the court liaison officer's execution of her or his duties; and (5) to grant the government further preliminary relief if necessary. The government also requested a court-supervised election of district council officers.

THE SETTLEMENT

The parties settled the case in March 1994.[19] The U.S. attorney agreed to drop the civil RICO complaint in exchange for significant district council reforms designed to purge the union of organized crime and promote union democracy. The consent decree's stated purpose was to ensure a democratic union. Toward that end, the parties agreed that there should not be any criminal element or LCN corruption in the district council and its constituent locals. All union officers agreed to be permanently enjoined from (a) committing any act of racketeering activity; (b) knowingly associating with any member or associate of any LCN crime family or other criminal group, or with any person prohibited from participating in union affairs; and (c) obstructing or otherwise improperly interfering with the court-appointed officer's efforts to enforce the consent decree.

The consent decree named former Federal District Court Judge Kenneth Conboy as the court-appointed Investigations and Review

Officer (IRO). The district council would pay $65,000 each month to cover the compensation and expenses of the IRO and the Independent Hearing Committee (IHC). If the IRO's expenses exceeded $65,000, the United States Brotherhood of Carpenters and Joiners of America (UBC) International would contribute up to an additional $15,000. Any disciplinary charges brought by IRO Conboy against union officers or members would be tried before a five-person IHC.

The IRO's powers included investigating district council operations and individuals; bringing disciplinary charges against union officers and members;* exercising veto authority over union officers' decisions; recommending organizational reforms; formulating and implementing new job referral rules; and organizing and supervising the district council's 1995 elections.[20] Conboy's decision would be final unless, on appeal, the district court found it to be arbitrary and capricious. His term of office was set at thirty months, renewable for up to an additional six months upon a showing of good cause. His supervisory authority over elections would terminate after certification of the 1995 election results.

In order to "eliminate the corruption, favoritism and cronyism that existed under the old system," the consent decree provided that each local union in the NYC district council would have thirty days to implement new job referral rules, which had to include nondiscriminatory and nonexclusive job referrals ("nonexclusive" means that an employer does not have to hire employees exclusively through the hiring hall); registering members' eligibility for job referral; a procedure that refers jobs to members who have been on the waiting list the longest; effective dissemination of the job referral rules; maintenance of accurate job referral records; and access by union members to job referral information.[21]

The consent decree ended the longtime practice of union officials drawing multiple salaries. It also required that for seven years the district council would give prior written notice to the government and to the IRO of proposed changes to any rules or procedures covered by the consent decree.

---

* The IRO could initiate a disciplinary action against a union officer or member by serving that person with a specific written charge. Within a week after service of the charge, a panel composed of three IHC members would be selected. The IRO would choose one panel member, the charged party would choose another, and the two members would choose the third member. A hearing would be conducted within thirty to sixty days according to the rules and procedures applicable to labor arbitration hearings.

District council officers had always been chosen by delegates hand-picked by the local unions' leaders. The consent decree instructed the IRO to implement and supervise the first rank-and-file election in the district council's history.[22] Toward that end, IRO Conboy drafted rules for conducting a secret-ballot election, including guidelines for "nominating candidates, disseminating information about nominated candidates to the membership at union expense, and conducting a secret ballot election."[23] Additionally, the consent decree empowered the IRO to hire or designate other persons or entities to assist in carrying out the rules, to resolve all election disputes, and to certify the election results.[24]

To summarize, the consent decree empowered the IRO to

- initiate and serve disciplinary charges against any member of the district council and its constituent locals for any matter constituting an offense under any applicable law, the union's constitution or its by-laws, working rules or obligations;
- take such reasonable steps as are lawful and necessary to be fully informed as to the district council's activities;
- study and recommend reforms of the district council's and its locals' operations (including but not limited to procedures for investigating and disciplining misconduct and procedures for filling vacancies in union offices);
- supervise the adoption, implementation, and operation of the job referral rules;
- supervise all phases of a secret ballot election of the district council executive board scheduled for June 1995 and any special elections that might occur before then; and
- employ or engage the services of any personnel necessary to assist in the proper discharge of the IRO's duties.

IMPLEMENTING THE CONSENT DECREE

Recognizing the importance of obtaining rank-and-file support, IRO Conboy published an open letter to the membership in the union's newsletter, *The Carpenter*, explaining his responsibilities. He announced three basic objectives for the trusteeship: (1) to cleanse the union of corrupt individuals; (2) to reform the job referral system; and (3) to conduct a direct rank-and-file election for union officers. "I hope to have your support and cooperation as I oversee the enactment of these important reforms over the coming months. I would also encourage any member to contact me . . . on an entirely confidential basis, with any suggestions or information that would enable me to perform my duties more effectively."[25] The district council's officers went to court to stop Conboy from publishing IRO reports in *The Carpenter*. They argued that such reports improperly cast the union's officers in a bad light. Judge Charles Haight ruled in Conboy's favor.[26]

Conboy's new job referral rules required that union members be referred to jobs according to the length of their unemployment. Five months after the rules were implemented, Conboy found that complaints about job referrals had decreased dramatically.[27] "The rules are generally being followed most of the time." However, he also reported that some locals, especially Local 17, continued to operate an "informal system" that reserved the best jobs for a pool of favored members.

THE LOCAL 17 TRUSTEESHIP

Local 17, the largest local in the district council, was created in 1981 by the merger of four local unions. Ironically, although the merger's declared purpose was to prevent corruption and racketeering, its effect was to consolidate the Genovese crime family's control over jobs and influence within the district council.[28] A jurisdictional dispute between two Genovese crime family crews resulted in the Genovese crime family consigliere's "awarding" Local 17 to Barney Bellomo's crew.[29] The June 1989 election generated a slate of candidates consisting of Genovese crime family associates. Enrico Ruotolo was elected business manager; three years later he was selected as Local 17's delegate to the district council.[30]

Conboy filed disciplinary charges against Ruotolo, alleging that he lied on a deposition, referred union members to a nonunion contractor, referred ineligible union members to jobs, and routinely associated with LCN members.[31] Moreover, Conboy's investigation of Local 17 illuminated a dire financial situation, numerous job rule violations, and links to organized crime.[32] Thus, Conboy requested that the Carpenters (UBC) International union impose a trusteeship over Local 17. In April 1995, the general president complied, appointing a trustee whom Conboy found cooperative and helpful.[33]

THE JACOB JAVITS EXHIBITION CENTER INVESTIGATION

In July 1994, Conboy began investigating Cosa Nostra's control over carpenters' jobs at the Javits Center, which is owned and operated by a public corporation (New York Convention Center Operating Corporation).[34] The district council's two representatives at the Javits Center were Anthony Fiorino and Leonard Simon. Fiorino was Genovese crime family acting boss Barney Bellomo's brother-in-law, and Simon was Genovese capo[35] Ralph Coppola's brother-in-law.[36] President Fred Devine, who himself had been linked to the Colombo family,[*] appointed Fiorino and Simon to their positions.[**] Conboy found that Fiorino and Simon filled all carpenter jobs from a "pool list" of one hundred carpenters,[37] many of whom had criminal records, ties to organized crime, or both.[38]

In September 1994, Conboy attempted to implement a nondiscriminatory job referral system for coveted Javits Center jobs.[39] Fiorino and Simon, with Devine's support, opposed Conboy's plan, proposing instead that the collective bargaining agreement be amended to insulate their Javits Center pool list from the job referral rules. Devine refused Conboy's demand that Fiorino and Simon be replaced. In October 1994, Simon resigned his position as the Carpenters union's top official at the Javits Center, but he remained at the center as a highly paid shop steward. Conboy brought a disciplinary action against Simon, charging that

---

[*] Marcello Svedese testified to Devine's relationship with the Colombo crime family: "A number of times, Freddie Devine told me that he had connections in the Colombo Organized Crime Family. On one occasion, I saw Vincent 'Jimmy' Angellino meeting with Freddie Devine in Devine's District Council office. . . . Angellino . . . was a Capo in the Colombo Organized Crime Family." Salvatore Gravano knew of another connection: "I am aware that Fred Devine is associated with Thomas Petrizzo, a capo in the Colombo Organized Crime Family." Salvatore Gravano Decl. at 4, *United States v. Dist. Council,* 1994 WL 704811 (S.D.N.Y. Dec. 16, 1994) (No. 90 Civ. 5722 (CSH)) (Feb. 10, 1993).

[**] Devine asserted that he had removed Ralph Coppola as the Carpenters chief steward at the Javits Center because of his ties to organized crime. Letter from Frederick Devine to Ralph Coppola of Aug. 6, 1991. But Coppola continued to supervise Genovese operations at the center even though he technically no longer worked there. Alphonse D'Arco Decl. at 7, *United States v. Dist. Council,* 1994 WL 704811 (S.D.N.Y. Dec. 16, 1994) (No. 90 Civ. 5722 (CSH)) (May 24, 1994). Devine denied having known about Fiorino's association with organized crime when he appointed him to oversee job referrals at the center. Frederick Devine Dep. at 140–42, *United States v. Dist. Council,* 1994 WL 704811 (S.D.N.Y. Dec. 16, 1994) (No. 90 Civ. 5722 (CSH)) (Sept. 1, 1994).

he brought discredit to the union by using a pool list, allowing non-union members to work at the center, submitting a false application to the international union, and receiving compensation from an employer in violation of the Taft-Hartley Act. These charges led Simon to resign from the union.[40]

In December 1994, Conboy filed disciplinary charges against Fiorino, alleging eight violations of the UBC's Standards of Conduct, including knowingly associating with members of organized crime; discriminating against rank-and-file members; threatening a union member with physical harm; acting on behalf of a contractor seeking to hire non-union members; participating in a labor bribery scheme; allowing men suspended from the union to continue working at the Javits Center; falsely representing his own qualifications as a carpenter when he applied for union membership; and violating the district council bylaw against invoking the Fifth Amendment before a committee of investigation. The IHC panel found most of the charges proved and expelled Fiorino from the union for life.[41] Judge Haight affirmed.[42] On the charge that Fiorino knowingly associated with organized crime members, he wrote:

> To the extent that Fiorino's contacts with Bellomo and Capolla antedate the execution of the Consent Decree in March 1994, they cannot be said to violate the decree. But a union member's knowing association with members of organized crime may be regarded as conduct "discreditable" to the union, and thus violative of the district council's by-laws and the local's constitution. . . . [T]here is clearly substantial evidence of [Fiorino's] knowing association with Bellomo; and particularly considering Bellomo's prominence in the Genovese crime family, as described by cooperating witnesses, that association is sufficient in itself to sustain Charge One against Fiorino.[43]

In light of the district council's and Devine's unwillingness to reform job referrals at the Javits Center, Conboy petitioned Judge Haight to (1) invalidate portions of the collective bargaining agreement governing district council job referrals in the trade show industry and the manner of compensating the district council's representatives at the center; (2) require the district council to refer trade show jobs in accordance with the consent decree; and (3) authorize the IRO to oversee district council activities in the trade show industry.[44] Judge Haight again ruled in Conboy's favor.

The media closely covered Fiorino's disciplinary hearing, thereby generating political momentum to eliminate organized crime's influence at the Javits Center. The Governor's Office announced a plan whereby the center would hire a permanent workforce, eliminating dependence on the union's hiring hall. In July 1995, current employees were forced to resign and reapply for their jobs if they desired. The center also accepted job applications from nonincumbents.[45] Applicants were screened for criminal records and ties to LCN. The center hired five hundred workers, half of whom had not previously worked there. The new "exhibit workers" were represented by the Carpenters union, but as state employees, they were covered by a new collective bargaining agreement.[46] A short time later, the New York State comptroller found that the Javits Center had experienced a "complete turnaround" with respect to corruption, operations, and exhibitors' satisfaction.[47]

THE 1995 DISTRICT COUNCIL ELECTION

The district council attacked the IRO's Final Election Rules (FERs), complaining that the IRO's power under the consent decree was limited to supervising the election and did not extend to running the election. Judge Haight held that Conboy had acted properly.[48]

The district council charged that Conboy had in a number of ways "exceeded his authority and abused his discretion."[49] The district council objected to the FERs because they lacked exceptions for candidates running unopposed; providing candidates with access to union membership lists, including addresses; expense of required mailings; lack of restrictions on the content of campaign literature; complexity of the rules; method of listing candidates' names on the ballots; confidentiality of nominating petitions; prohibition on local unions' endorsements of candidates; inclusion of the position of second vice-president; and in-person voting. Judge Haight ruled against each of these objections.[50] With respect to Local 608's request that the election be delayed, Judge Haight wrote,

> I think there is some urgency to holding the election as soon as possible. . . . The 1995 election will ideally not only be a fair and democratic one, but will also reveal a variety of information about the current state of the union and its practices. The sooner the election can be held

and the results studied, the better the sense the IRO will have of the proper focus of the remainder of his tenure.[51]

In order to keep corrupt candidates off the ballot, Conboy required each candidate to have been in good standing as a union member for twelve consecutive months prior to nomination; a UBC member for two consecutive years immediately prior to nomination; never convicted of a crime making him or her ineligible under federal law to hold union office.[52] Once having satisfied the eligibility requirements, a prospective candidate had to submit a nominating petition signed by at least 125 members in good standing. If the IRO certified his or her candidacy, the candidate would have the right to make speeches at membership meetings and to obtain a mailing list of eligible rank-and-file voters. Each candidate had the right, at his or her expense, to hire an observer to witness the distribution of campaign literature and to observe conduct at the polling site. The rules provided candidates equal opportunity to place campaign material in *The Carpenter.* Conboy limited campaign contributions to $250 per member and required disclosure of campaign contributions and expenditures. The rules called for in-person voting by machine ballot except that a member living seventy-five miles or more from headquarters could use a mail ballot. Each candidate could name one member in good standing to the election committee, which would monitor the balloting and count the votes. The committee's decision would be subject to review by the election officer (an assistant appointed by the IRO) or the IRO. The rules defined election misconduct (including but not limited to voting fraud, ballot tampering, and forgery) for which the IRO could bring disciplinary charges.

The IRO rejected only two of nineteen nominating petitions. Fifteen of the seventeen candidates who formally accepted nomination were affiliated with one of four slates. The Unity and Experience slate, led by incumbents Fred Devine and Robert Cavanaugh, put forward candidates for all five executive committee positions (president, first vice-president, second vice-president, secretary-treasurer, and chairman of the trustees). The Membership's Choice slate also contested all five positions. Conboy believed that its presidential nominee, Local 608 President Patrick Harvey, was the only candidate with enough support to seriously challenge Devine. But Harvey was not obviously a reform candidate having invoked the Fifth Amendment during the 1990 RICO case and being closely associated with Paschal McGuinness.[53]

Conboy's most important and time-consuming election task was compiling a master list of eligible voters.[54] In 1994, the district council provided him with a list of 40,000 eligible voters. Conboy found that less than half (16,719) were eligible to vote. He hired a temporary staff to assist in the election, which was conducted primarily by means of voting machines. No individuals other than the temporary staff and two election observers from each slate were allowed into the voting room.

About 46 percent of eligible voters (7,684 union members) cast ballots. All candidates on the Unity and Experience slate, which received 58.7 percent of the total vote, were victorious, *thereby returning to office incumbents and others associated with the clique that had long dominated the union.*[55] Much the same thing had happened in the Local 560 case: Michael Sciarra and his brother Daniel dominated the first fair election in that union's history.

These election victories demonstrate just how deeply labor racketeers are entrenched in certain unions. They maintain power by manipulating both sticks and carrots. Decades of domination may have convinced rank-and-file members that opposition will be futile and dangerous. Likewise, the labor racketeers operate a pervasive patronage system that provides many benefits to loyalists, who then have a vested interest in perpetuating the regime. In addition, many labor racketeers are charismatic personalities to whom rank and filers are attracted. Finally, most union members are apathetic, paying little attention to union governance and policies.[56]

OTHER INVESTIGATIONS

Conboy's investigations continued. In 1996, his office charged five local union officers with violating district council bylaws by invoking the Fifth Amendment when questioned during the civil RICO suit. In 1997, four of them (including 1995 presidential candidate Patrick Harvey) resigned rather than go through the disciplinary hearing process.[57] (The fifth officer ultimately signed a settlement agreement barring him from union office for life.)[58]

After receiving information about a Local 257 member who was extorting payments from a contractor, Conboy and the Manhattan district attorney persuaded the contractor to cooperate. The union member was arrested in October 1996 for taking a subsequent payoff.[59] He was later convicted of a misdemeanor and settled the IRO's charges by agreeing to be barred from union office.[60] Conboy also brought charges against a former delegate and trustee of Local 348 for refusing to submit to a deposition concerning his association with a Colombo family capo.[61]

In 1997, the IRO charged the president of Local 531 with interfering with the IRO's work and with using union funds to purchase a vehicle. The official agreed to be barred from union office for life.[62] In 1998, a former Local 257 officer paid a fine to settle charges that he knowingly accepted shop steward referrals for which he was ineligible.[63] The former president of Local 257 was investigated for receiving illegal payments from contractors, violating district council rules, and for putting himself on the out-of-work list although he was employed.[64]

INTERNATIONAL UNION'S TRUSTEESHIP OVER
THE DISTRICT COUNCIL

Because the victors in the 1995 election were allied with the same faction that had controlled the district council for many years, Conboy urged Carpenters International President Douglas McCarron to impose a trusteeship on the district council, thereby replacing the incumbent officers. According to Conboy, "In light of such entrenched corruption, it was clear to us that the only realistic hope of returning the district council to its membership required the intervention of the International."[65] He stressed the importance of replacing the district council's incumbent officers with "strong and independent outside leadership."[66] McCarron complied on June 25, 1996, appointing Carpenters Vice-President Douglas Banes to take over the administration of the district council.

The district council appealed McCarron's actions to the International union's general executive board. More than one hundred people testified, including Banes and Conboy.[67] Conboy testified that Fred Devine took cash payoffs, appointed Fiorino, refused to dismiss Fiorino, made corrupt job referrals, and mishandled the district council's benefit funds.[68] The hearing committee concluded that Devine and the other officers mismanaged the district council's cash reserve so that its net worth dropped from $6.45 million in 1991 to $224,060 in 1996. Devine spent $389,000 on private jets in a period of thirty months. Devine supplied the staff with luxury cars and paid twice what legitimate automobile dealers would charge. Devine's $25,000 car allowance did not include gas, oil, maintenance, or insurance. The union paid Devine's girlfriend $60,000 as a "consultant"; Devine's chauffeur was paid $60,000 a year out of trust fund money; and Devine used trust fund money to employ Genovese crime family associates. The hearing committee concluded that the International union's trusteeship had been properly imposed and extended its duration.[69]

The Banes trusteeship seemed to make some significant reforms aimed at remedying the financial crisis and combating corruption. A few of Devine's protégés, including his son and Bernard Cohen, the district council's general counsel, were terminated.[70] Subsequently, the Manhattan district attorney charged Cohen with stealing more than $150,000 from the district council by overbilling and by inflating the expenses of a lobbyist who worked for him. Ultimately, he pleaded guilty to falsifying records.[71] Devine was convicted on six felony grand larceny counts.[72]

Banes moved to put the district council back on sound financial footing by reducing unjustifiable salaries, cutting costs, and rationalizing operations.[73] In May 1997, the International reorganized the New York City district council into a more centralized "full service district council" whose officers would be accountable to and elected by the rank and file. Moreover, the job referral system would be run by business agents employed by and subject to removal by the district council. Some local unions would be merged.[74] In announcing the plan, President McCarron said, "Despite the [IRO's] supervision, the consent decree and federal investigations, corruption continues in many local unions throughout the district council. Only a fundamental structural change . . . can eradicate the problem and return the Union to its members' control."[75] McCarron declared that the "membership has been poorly served by the present structure," and noted that the district council had lost approximately five thousand union members in five years, depleted its $6 million treasury, and incurred upward of $5 million in debt. He predicted that centralization of authority in the district council would provide the solution.[*]

[*] Lawsuits by local unions and individual carpenters significantly delayed the restructuring plan's implementation. Ultimately, the court held that the plan did not violate the consent decree (*Local Unions v. United Bhd of Carpenters*, 1997 WL 630179 (S.D.N.Y. Oct. 9, 1997)) and that prior court approval of the restructuring plan was not required (*United States v. Dist. Council*, 972 F. Supp. 756, 759 (S.D.N.Y. 1997)).

TERMINATING THE IRO AND THE UBC TRUSTEESHIP

In October 1996, the court approved another six-month extension for IRO Conboy. Because of the district council's shaky financial status, Conboy consented to a reduction in compensation from $65,000 a month to $45,000 and agreed not to seek further extensions. On March 3, 1997, President McCarron voluntarily extended Conboy's tenure through March 4, 1998, and then to June 5, 1998. On June 4, 1998, the parties agreed to a final twelve-month extension.[76] One year later, Judge Haight wrote

> The district council's refusal to extend the IRO's tenure means that the IRO will not be able to discharge the last vestiges of his previously delineated responsibilities. Accordingly, this is likely the last opportunity that the Court will have to address former Judge Conboy in a formal opinion. I seize the opportunity to thank him for his tireless and invaluable service to the parties and to the Court during the course of an arduous, complex and challenging case. The Court's IRO has been the very model of a modern Court-appointed officer. Ave atque vale.*

In 1999, the Carpenters International Union dissolved its trusteeship over the New York district council. In January 2000, almost ten years after the civil RICO case was filed, Local 608's President Michael Forde** was elected president of the district council.[77] Ominously, two years before Conboy had charged Forde with violating job referral rules in assigning jobs among Local 608 members.[78] In 2000, the Manhattan district attorney charged Forde and several Cosa Nostra codefendants

---

* *United States v. Dist. Council,* 1999 U.S. Dist. LEXIS 8781, at *22 n. 4. Conboy also had his critics. For example, "[T]he IRO's tenure under the consent decree was about to expire at the time the UBC took over our council, the UBC extended his tenure at the time of the take over at the cost of sixty-five thousand a month. Ever since, the IRO has been writing shining reports to the court regarding Mr. McCarron's actions and it seems every time he writes a report he gets another extension of his tenure." *Impediments to Union Democracy Part II* app. F., 101, available at http://edworkforce.house.gov/hearings/105th/eer/ud62598/lebo.htm (statement of William S. Lebo, a member of Local 45 (June 25, 1998). Conboy's Sixth Interim Report charges that some union members who complained about the International trusteeship were Devine supporters with ties to organized crime. Sixth Interim Report, at 11–12.

** Forde's father, who preceded Forde as president of Local 608, had been convicted of Taft-Hartley crimes in the 1980s.

with taking bribes in exchange for ignoring violations of the collective bargaining agreement.

The thirty-eight codefendants included union officers, contractors, and eleven alleged organized crime figures.[79] Steven L. Crea, the Lucchese crime family boss, was the leading organized crime figure among the defendants.[80] According to the district attorney, the Lucchese crime family took money from contractors in exchange for promising protection from labor problems. Forde thus became the fourth consecutive district council president since 1980 to be charged with labor racketeering. (See Table 10-1 below for a list of labor racketeering prosecutions related to the New York City District Council of Carpenters.) Nevertheless, he was elected in 2002 as executive secretary treasurer (the new title for the district council's top officer) with 80 percent of the vote.[81]

Table 10-1
Labor Racketeering Prosecutions Related to the NYC District Council of Carpenters

Case	Result
United States v. Maritas, Cr. No. 81-122 (E.D.N.Y.)	Former District Council President Theodore Maritas and Genovese capo Vincent DiNapoli were indicted for RICO violations.
United States v. Giangrande, 805 F.2d 391 (2d Cir. 1986)	District council officer Artie Giandrande, convicted after trial for conspiracy, mail fraud, and illegal labor payoffs.
People v. Bitondo, Ind. No. 7952/87 (N.Y. Sup. Ct. N.Y. Co.)	Local 257 officers Attilio Bitondo and Gene Hanley were indicted for receiving illegal payoffs and engaging in extortion.
United States v. Cervone, et al., Cr. No. 87-579 (E.D.N.Y)	Henry Walaski, an officer of Local 531 and district council delegate, was convicted for violating RICO and receiving illegal payoffs.
People v. Holden, Ind. No. 9352/87 (N.Y. Sup. Ct. N.Y. Co.)	Local 608 shop steward William Holden was convicted of criminal contempt and perjury in an investigation of the Carpenters Union.
People v. Forde, Ind. No. 7951/87 (N.Y. Sup. Ct. N.Y. Co.)	Martin Forde, an officer of Local 608, was convicted for receiving an illegal labor payoff.
People v. Zeidman, Ind. No. 7950/87 (N.Y. Sup. Ct. N.Y. Co.)	District Council First Vice-President Irving Zeidman was indicted for accepting labor payoffs.
United States v. Waller, Cr. No. 88-466 (E.D.N.Y.)	Local 531 officer Robert Waller, Jr. was convicted of extortion.
People v. Hubelbank, Crim. Complaint No. 9N072405/89 (N.Y. Crim. Ct. N.Y. Co.)	District council trustee and former Local 135 officer Israel Hubelbank was convicted of accepting illegal labor payoffs.
People v. Moscatiello, Ind. No. 8081/89 (N.Y. Sup. Ct.)	Local 17 business manager Benedetto Schepis was indicted for crimes involving Local 135.
People v. Forde, Ind. No. 5544/00 (N.Y. Su. Ct. N.Y. Co.)	District Council President Michael Forde and his business agent Michael Devereaux convicted by a Manhattan jury of accepting $100,000 in cash as part of a $50,000 promised bribe from a defunct construction company.

ASSESSING SUCCESSES AND FAILURES

Successes

According to Conboy, the trusteeship was successful in purging the district council of mob-affiliated and corrupt officials, conducting a free and fair election in 1995, cleaning up the Javits Center, and revamping the job referral system. He filed disciplinary charges against a number of union officials, including Anthony Fiorino, Lenard Simon, and Enrico Ruotolo. IRO Conboy and Trustee Banes removed from union office all of the 1995 incumbents. The 1995 election gave members the right to vote directly for officials, but the election did not produce a break with the regime that had long dominated the union.[*]

The job referral system was substantially reformed. Conboy wrote in March 1996 that "it can safely be said, given the high volume of carpenters referred from the out-of-work lists, and diminishing number of complaints we receive concerning the referral process, that the average rank and file member has greatly benefited from the implementation of the job referral rules."[82] A year later, Conboy reported that complaints had declined to an average of two or three a month, which his office was able to resolve informally.[83]

In July 2001, however, Eugene Clarke, a member of Local 608, filed a complaint with the district council's executive committee alleging that Local 608 was appointing shop stewards in violation of the referral rules. He complained that some employees who supported Michael Forde received job assignments out of turn and that others, like him, did not receive job assignments because they opposed Forde.[84] While not admitting wrongdoing, the district council agreed to change the job referral rules to require more oversight of shop steward appointments[85] and to hire former Assistant U.S. Attorney Walter Mack as Independent Investigator, responsible for investigating allegations of job referral rule violations.[**][86]

It is hard to say whether the centralization of the district council

---

[*] A dissident group, Carpenters for a Democratic Union International (CDUI), demands "one member, one vote" for all union positions, direct membership votes on contracts, and direct election of delegates. See http://www.ranknfile.net/.

[**] In April, 2005, over the government's opposition, the court granted the district council's motion to terminate Mack, but on the condition that a successor acceptable to the court be appointed.

at the expense of the locals qualifies as a success. On the one hand, the district council can be more easily monitored and held accountable for racketeering in its constituent locals. On the other hand, a leading advocate for union democracy commented at a 1988 congressional hearing on union democracy:

> The delegate system is no substitute for direct elections. A membership of thousands armed with the right to vote, cannot be easily manipulated by the officers above. But a delegate body of 150 can be dominated by an officialdom which dispenses favors and perks to only 76 lucky delegates. Direct elections allow the member-voters to control the officers. Election by delegates allows the officers to control the delegate-voters.[87]

Failures

Although the 1995 election was conducted fairly, Fred Devine was reelected president, thereby perpetuating the old regime's control. Fraud, corrupt practices, and racketeering continued. The UBC negated the 1995 election by imposing a trusteeship on the district council, thereby removing Devine. Michael Forde's slate won the 1999 election. Just months later, the Manhattan district attorney charged Forde and several top Cosa Nostra figures with orchestrating a bribery scheme whereby contractors paid off union officials in exchange for their allowing the contractor to use nonunion labor on a hotel renovation project.[88] Even though indicted, Forde won the 2002 district council election.

The goal of the 1994 RICO suit—purging organized crime's influence from the district council—has clearly not been achieved. The alliance between labor racketeers and corrupt union officials has proved resilient. As long as rank-and-file Carpenters Union members see or perceive "business as usual," they will be cynical about prospects for reform and unwilling to stand up against the old regime. Not only have the government, the court, and the court-appointed trustee been unable to end mob influence in the district council, they have been unable to prevent LCN labor racketeers from expanding their influence to Westchester County (just north of New York City). In December 2001, the Department of Justice indicted seventy-three members of the Parrello Crew of the Genovese crime family on ninety-eight counts, including extortion, labor racketeering, loan sharking, illegal gambling operations, selling counterfeit money and gun trafficking.[89] Nine were accused of labor racketeering involving Locals 11 and 964, which together constituted the Suburban New York Regional Council of Carpenters. These defendants were alleged to have arranged for nonunion workers to complete carpentry jobs, allowing the defendants to embezzle more than $1 million that should have been paid into the Suburban Council's pension funds.[90]

Whether the IRO could have done anything more to facilitate a reform movement among the New York City carpenters is an important question. In the IBT Local 560 trusteeship, the trustee reached out to the rank and file, appointed some individuals to steward positions and other offices, and successfully encouraged other members to become involved in union governance and politics, helping eventually to bring a reform slate to power. Stimulating reform in the building trades is undoubtedly more difficult because work is seasonal and insecure; workers move from one job and contractor to another. Because the union determines whether an individual gets work, it is risky for a rank and filer to challenge the incumbent clique. Because the district council comprises some twenty locals spread out across the metropolitan area, it is difficult for an insurgent candidate to achieve the name recognition necessary to defeat an incumbent union officer.

Still, there is some reason for optimism. The relentless governmental and judicial efforts to purge LCN from the district council have clearly succeeded to a significant extent. The old labor racketeering element has been severely weakened. The membership has had a taste of free elections and fairer work assignments. The union's finances are much more transparent and accountable. The pension and welfare funds are more secure. Achieving further reform, however, will require the emergence of a new cadre of union leaders.

11

The Four International Unions

The President's Commission on Organized Crime (PCOC) focused most of its resources on documenting and excoriating corruption and racketeering in the IBT, HERE, LIUNA, and ILA. The PCOC sharply criticized the federal government for not aggressively seeking to purge LCN's influence from these influential international unions. Twenty years have passed. Each of these unions has been the target of extensive civil RICO litigation and remedial efforts. There has been a great deal of progress, but it is still too soon to pronounce any of the four international unions free of labor racketeering.

THE IBT

> Roy it's a bad situation. . . . You can run, but you can't hide. My advice to you is to cooperate or get your family killed. Roy, these are bad people. And they were here a long time before you and me came. And they'll be here a long time after we're gone. They've infiltrated into every big local union, every conference and pension fund—even the AFL-CIO! I'm tied as tight as I can be.
> —Jimmy Hoffa to Roy Williams. Quoted in James Neff,
> *Mobbed Up: Jackie Presser's High Wire Life in the
> Teamsters, the Mafia and the FBI* (1989)

Soon after the PCOC issued *The Edge,* rumors began to circulate that the Department of Justice was considering a civil RICO complaint against the IBT's General Executive Board. To head off such a lawsuit, IBT General President Jackie Presser launched a lobbying and public relations campaign seeking support from politicians and the AFL-CIO.[1] Presser accused the Reagan administration generally and the DOJ particularly of union bashing:* "Takeovers of unions are nothing new—Communists and Fascists have been doing so for decades. However it is a sad day in the history of the United States and the American labor movement when such tactics are employed." Presser must have been pleased by the positive response from the nation's political leaders: 246 members of Congress signed a petition urging the Department of Justice not to file a civil RICO suit against the IBT.[2] According to the petition: "The exercise of such authority . . . would establish a precedent which strikes at the very foundation of our democracy." Senator Orin Hatch (R.-Ut.) said that the DOJ suit against the IBT "flies in the face of democratic principles" and "is a terrible precedent."[3] This unprecedented intervention on behalf of a potential federal racketeering defendant (without any public information about the factual basis for DOJ's rumored complaint) illustrates the enormous political power of the nation's largest private-sector union as well, perhaps, as the cynicism of the politicians in associating the racketeer-ridden IBT with democratic unionism and American democracy.** The AFL-CIO also responded positively to Presser, inviting the Teamsters to return to the house of labor after thirty years in exile.

On June 28, 1988, Rudy Giuliani, U.S. attorney for the Southern District of New York filed one of the most remarkable lawsuits in American history, a civil RICO suit against the International Teamsters Union. The complaint named as defendants the union's leaders and the leaders of the nation's dominant crime syndicate—specifically, the International Brotherhood of Teamsters, the Cosa Nostra "Commission,"*** 26 Cosa Nostra members and associates including Genovese crime family boss

---

* The PCOC questioned whether an investigation of Jackie Presser had been delayed because of Presser's political support for President Ronald Reagan in 1980 and 1984. (Steven Kurkjian, "Panel Says Organized Crime Corrupts Unions," *Boston Globe*, January 15, 1986.)
** The IBT was and is the largest private-sector union in North America. It had approximately 2 million members at its peak in the 1960s and has about 1.4 million members in 2005. The IBT began as a union for horse-drawn vehicles and then trucks, but with the expulsion from the AFL-CIO in the 1950s, it became a kind of conglomerate union, representing all sorts of workers, including those in freight, warehousing, manufacturing, construction, private security, and air transportation.
*** The Commission, established by LCN bosses in 1931 to resolve disputes among organized crime families, originally comprised prominent LCN bosses from around the country, but by the 1980s, it either consisted of the five New York City LCN bosses or perhaps the five families had their own NYC metropolitan-area commission.

Tony Salerno (or perhaps underboss if, as seems likely, the crafty Vincent Gigante actually ruled the family), Lucchese boss Anthony Corallo, Chicago Outfit boss Joey Aiuppa, and Milwaukee crime family boss Frank Balistrieri. The other defendants were the IBT's General Executive Board (GEB), and eighteen present and former GEB members, including President Jackie Presser and General Secretary-Treasurer Weldon Mathis.[4] The complaint charged that the organized crime defendants, aided and abetted by the union defendants, violated RICO (1962b) by acquiring an interest in the IBT through a pattern of racketeering activity, including extortion, violence, fraud, and violation of the IBT members' Landrum-Griffin rights. The complaint further alleged that the defendants violated RICO (1962c) by conducting the affairs of the IBT through a pattern of racketeering activity, including extortion fraud, violence, and other criminal conduct. The complaint cited a litany of violent acts by LCN members and associates against Teamsters members who dared to criticize or question the ruling clique and against employers who refused to accede to the labor racketeers. The government alleged that despite 191 criminal convictions and 22 civil enforcement actions, neither the IBT general president nor any member of the union's GEB had conducted any investigations or disciplinary actions regarding labor racketeering.[*]

Giuliani asked the court to remove the GEB members and to establish a trusteeship to oversee the union's affairs and supervise a national election.[5] In preparing for trial, the government's star witnesses were former General President Roy Williams (1981–1983) and former Cleveland LCN boss Angelo Lonardo, both of whom had become cooperating government witnesses.[6]

Despite a GEB resolution prohibiting defendants from making individual settlements with the government, three vice-presidents, recognizing the personal financial and emotional costs of litigation, quickly broke ranks. For example, Robert Holmes, Sr., a Teamster for fifty-two years, agreed to resign all union positions in full settlement of the complaint against him.

On March 13, 1989, the IBT (as an entity) and the DOJ agreed to a consent decree. The union acknowledged "that there have been

[*] Harold Friedman, head of IBT Joint Council 41 and the IBT Ohio Conference, explained that to have inquired into a fellow IBT officer's indictment or conviction would have been "bad manners."

allegations, sworn testimony and judicial findings of past problems with Cosa Nostra corruption of various elements of the IBT," and agreed that the IBT should be free of any criminal element, and should be governed democratically "for the sole benefit of its membership without unlawful outside influence."[7] The consent decree provided for a permanent injunction barring the organized crime defendants from any future involvement with the IBT; changing the IBT constitution to require democratic elections for International officers; prohibiting IBT members from knowing association with LCN members and with expelled members; and, most important, the appointment of a trusteeship made up of three court-appointed officers—independent administrator, investigations officer, and elections officer—to oversee the union's reform. Judge David Edelstein appointed former federal judge Frederick Lacey as independent administrator, former assistant U.S. attorney Charles Carberry as investigations officer, and labor lawyer Michael Holland as elections officer. If the 1991 election were to be certified as having been conducted in conformity to the new election rules, the three-person trusteeship would be replaced by a three-person Independent Review Board (IRB).

The consent decree gave the Independent Administrator (IA) authority to discipline (by means of expulsion, suspension, or fine) union members and officers, and to impose trusteeships on IBT locals controlled by LCN. It also empowered the IA to veto any IBT decision that would further the interests of labor racketeers. The IBT general president and GEB retained day-to-day administrative authority and the authority to negotiate collective bargaining agreements.

The investigations officer (IO) was charged with responsibility for investigating corruption in Teamsters local, regional, and international unions and for recommending to the IA disciplinary action against individuals found to have violated the IBT constitution. As soon as the consent decree was filed, the IO began investigating and preparing disciplinary charges against many of the civil RICO defendants and other IBT officials. Soon there began to flow a steady stream of disciplinary cases that continues to this day (February 2005).

The consent decree set out rules for future national elections, including direct secret balloting and a prohibition on candidates accepting campaign donations from employers, foundations, trusts, or similar entities. It left other election procedures to be developed by the elections officer (EO), who was empowered to oversee direct 1991 and 1996 rank-and-file secret-ballot elections for the union's international officers.

William McCarthy, with the support of the New England Patriarcha crime family, became general president following Jackie Presser's death in July 1988. After signing the consent decree, General President McCarthy had an immediate change of heart. He described the consent decree as failing to provide "the vindication and exoneration the Teamsters deserve. . . . [T]his suit should never have been filed in the first place." Numerous IBT locals filed lawsuits asserting that they were not bound by the consent decree because they were neither defendants in the civil RICO suit nor signatories to the consent agreement.[8] Judge Edelstein thwarted this strategy, first by combining all IBT/consent decree litigation in his court and then by ruling that the consent decree did bind the IBT locals.[9] He declared:

> The International IBT and all of its subordinate entities are merely structures created to represent and serve its constituent membership. Indeed, the law governing lawsuits against labor unions embodies the underlying philosophy that a union is no more than its membership. Legally, an unincorporated association is a collective substitute for its members individually. Under the IBT Constitution, all members of the Union—officials and rank and file alike—are jointly members of both their individual local and the International IBT.[10]

The IBT refused to reimburse some of the court-appointed officers' expenses and resisted the IA's efforts to inform the rank and file of actions against corrupt IBT officials. At its 1991 convention, the IBT refused to enact constitutional amendments to which the consent decree committed it. As the IBT's opposition mounted, so too did Edelstein's resolve. He ruled time and again against the IBT, persevering until he achieved compliance with his orders.

IA Lacey served as the trier of fact and sentencing authority on charges brought by IO Carberry against Teamsters officials and members. Typical charges included membership in or knowing association with members of Cosa Nostra,[11] failure to investigate corruption within the local, joint council, or international in which the individual held office, refusal to testify at a disciplinary hearing,[12] embezzlement,[13] and assault.[14] Sentences ranged from reprimand to expulsion from the union. On appeal, Edelstein consistently upheld IA Lacey's decisions.

IO Carberry and his staff reviewed old criminal cases and audited locals with a reputation for being influenced by organized crime.[15] The FBI provided a wealth of information. Some IBT members came forward to report wrongdoing. When Carberry found sufficient evidence, he filed disciplinary charges. IBT Vice-Presidents Harold Friedman and Anthony Hughes were his first targets. Because both officials had been convicted of racketeering (but had appeals pending in the Sixth Circuit), it seemed to follow that they should be expelled from the union. However, they argued that Carberry had no authority to charge (and Lacey to discipline) them on the basis of convictions that occurred before the consent decree was signed. Judge Edelstein disagreed:

> [T]he ultimate aim of the consent decree is to guarantee free elections and to rid the IBT of the hideous influence of organized crime . . . the election oversight may imperil unfairly-elected officers, and the prosecution scheme may ultimately suspend corrupt members.

A 2004 study found that since the signing of the consent decree in 1989, 670 charges had been brought against 583 members and officers of the Teamsters.[16] These charges involve members or officers of 128 locals, led by Local 813, with 58 members and officers charged. Eighty-five local union presidents have been charged. The most frequent offense is embezzlement. Many of those charged entered "plea bargains" with the IRB, agreeing to suspension, resignation, fine, restitution, and other sanctions. The most frequent sanction, meted out to 201 Teamsters, was permanent expulsion.[17] Pursuant to IRB investigations and recommendations, the IBT International Union placed thirty-five locals and one joint council under trusteeship.

Elections officer Holland created a three-step process for the election of the IBT general president, general secretary, and GEB members. First, the IBT locals would hold secret-ballot elections for delegates to the IBT convention. Second, the delegates would nominate candidates for national office. Third, all rank-and-file members would vote in a secret-ballot election supervised by independent monitors. The IBT opposed these proposed reforms, arguing that the consent decree empowered Holland only to *monitor* the electoral process for fraud, not to establish new election rules. Judge Edelstein ruled that Holland had not exceeded his authority.[18]

At the 1991 IBT convention, the delegates rejected the constitutional amendments to which the consent decree committed the union. The DOJ lawyers, anticipating the revolt, had asked Edelstein to impose the constitutional changes by court order; the judge issued an injunction to that effect. At the convention itself, the delegates railed against Edelstein, the government, and the consent decree.

The first direct election of international IBT officers took place in 1991. There were three candidates: R. V. Durham, a member of the GEB; Walter Shea, a career Teamster administrator who had essentially run the union during much of the Fitzsimmons administration; and Ron Carey, a self-styled reformer who headed a large New York City IBT local. Judge Lacey ruled ineligible a fourth candidate, James P. Hoffa, a lawyer and son of Jimmy Hoffa, because he had never been a Teamster. Carey enjoyed the support of the Teamsters for a Democratic Union (TDU), the best-developed rank-and-file reform group in the American labor movement.[19] He promised to eradicate mob influence in the Teamsters. To many observers, his election, with 48.5 percent of the vote, was a huge victory for reformers and proof of the trusteeship's success (although only one-third of eligible Teamsters voted).[*] Nevertheless, Carey kept an arm's-length distance from the court-appointed officers, calling the trusteeship improper, unnecessary, and undemocratic. Carey eliminated the practice of top officials drawing multiple salaries, trimmed the IBT budget, sold some of the union's airplanes and other extravagant possessions, created an Ethical Practices Committee, and imposed trusteeships on a number of mob-controlled locals. He led the Teamsters strike against United Parcel Service, the union's largest employer, and achieved a favorable contract.

After certification of the 1991 election, a three-member Independent Review Board (IRB) replaced the three-person court-appointed trusteeship. The U.S. attorney general's appointee to the IRB was Frederick Lacey. The IBT appointed Carey's campaign manager, E. Harold Burke. When Lacey and Burke were unable to agree on the third member, Judge Edelstein appointed former FBI director William Webster.

---

[*] An early 1990s survey found that half of the IBT members surveyed could not name the IBT International general president. See Robert Bruno, *Reforming the Chicago Teamsters: The Story of Local 705* (De Kalb: Northern Illinois University Press, 2003).

The IRB immediately hired Charles Carberry to serve as investigations officer. (Burke was later replaced by Grant Crandall, a distinguished labor lawyer and general counsel of the United Mine Workers Union.)

The 1996 election was vigorously contested. Carey's opponent was James P. Hoffa who, by signing on as an assistant to an IBT local president in Chicago, became eligible to run in the 1996 election. Carey won by a slim majority (52 percent), but the elections officer (Barbara Quindell, who had replaced Michael Holland) refused to certify the result because of campaign finance violations. She found that Carey's campaign illegally funneled $885,000 of IBT funds to political action groups (associated with the national Democratic Party), which arranged donations of the same amount to Carey's campaign.[20] In other words, she found that the Carey campaign had, by means of a crude money laundering scheme, illegally utilized almost $1 million of IBT funds on behalf of Carey's campaign. She ordered that the election be rerun.

In November 1997, yet another elections officer (Kenneth Conboy, the same man who served as trustee (IRO) in the District Council of Carpenters case) barred Carey from the rerun election because of the money laundering scheme; the IRB affirmed and subsequently expelled Carey from the union.[*] James P. Hoffa won the 1998 rerun (of the 1996) election by a wide margin, and, in 2001, his Hoffa Unity Slate of candidates for the General Executive Board overwhelmingly won a five-year term. That same year, a former U.S. attorney for the District of Columbia, Joseph Di Genova, replaced Grant Crandall as the IBT's representative on the IRB, and former U.S. attorney general Benjamin Civiletti replaced Judge Lacey as the government's representative; William Webster continued to serve.[**]

Hoffa campaigned on the promise of doing everything possible to terminate the IRB. After the election, he announced that he was hiring Edwin Stier to head an internal anticorruption unit that would eventually demonstrate to the government and the court that the IBT could police itself. Stier brought enormous credibility to the internal reform effort, called Project RISE (Respect, Integrity, Strength, Ethics) because he had served so successfully as trustee in the IBT Local 560 case.[***]

---

[*] Carey was subsequently prosecuted and acquitted (October 12, 2001).

[**] Judge David Edelstein died in August 2000. The IBT case was then assigned to Judge Loretta A. Preska.

[***] Stier also appointed a ten-member Board of Advisors to monitor Project RISE's progress and to make suggestions where appropriate. I served as a member of that board.

Project RISE had three components: a rank-and-file initiative to draft an ethical practices code and enforcement machinery; a professional investigative initiative to assess the state of corruption and racketeering throughout the union; and an initiative to write an internal history of labor racketeering in the Teamsters. Stier hired a former justice of the New Mexico Supreme Court to chair the ethical practices code committee composed of twenty rank-and-file members from across the United States and Canada. The group met over a period of eighteen months and produced an impressive set of ethical rules, disciplinary procedures, and enforcement machinery. However, the Hoffa administration took the position that it would not implement the code until the IRB's enforcement authority was phased out. As of summer 2005, there is no sign of such a prospect.

The second Project RISE component was an investigation of continued organized crime influence in the IBT. For this job, Stier chose James Kossler, the former organized crime coordinator in the New York City FBI office. Kossler, in turn, hired a number of former FBI agents and DOL investigators from around the country. The Kossler team conducted at least a cursory investigation of every IBT local that had ever been alleged to have been infiltrated or influenced by organized crime. It found no indication of organized crime influence in the vast majority of these previously tainted locals. In several locals where questionable influences still existed, IRB investigations and disciplinary proceedings were under way. Kossler's team also continued to investigate.

Project RISE's third component was a comprehensive history of the connection between organized crime and the IBT. The principal author was Howard Anderson, one of Stier's law partners and a former congressional staffer. The history (*The Teamsters: Perception and Reality*), published by the IBT,[21] seems primarily addressed to the U.S. attorney for the Southern District of New York and to Judge Preska, who presides over the consent decree. Its basic theses are (1) that mob infiltration of the Teamsters was the consequence of a strong organized crime syndicate, a weak governmental organized crime control effort, and an unwillingness of the IBT leadership to confront LCN; and (2) that currently a strong federal organized crime control effort, plus a strong IBT antiracketeering commitment, plus a much-weakened LCN add up to a healthy, independent, and honest Teamsters union.

Unfortunately, Project RISE disintegrated in spring 2004. Stier and Kossler resigned, charging that the Hoffa administration was blocking their investigation of LCN influence in their Chicago-area IBT locals and their joint council. Stier and Kossler had come to believe that they had been overly optimistic in their initial assessment of the state of many IBT locals and that organized crime continues to exercise influence, especially in Chicago. The Teamsters leadership took the position that Project RISE was too expensive and that Stier had overstepped his mandate; Hoffa appointed Edward McDonald, former head of DOJ's Brooklyn Organized Crime Strike Force to investigate Stier's charges. A public version of McDonald's report, released in July 2005, concluded that Stier's and Kossler's accusations of organized crime involvement in the Chicago-area IBT were baseless.

IBT CONCLUSION

In 1986, the PCOC considered reforming the IBT nearly impossibile. However, the FBI and DOJ campaign against organized crime greatly weakened the crime syndicate. The federal civil RICO suit against the IBT international and the court-imposed trusteeship that it produced, backed by Judge Edelstein's steadfast determination to enforce the letter and spirit of the consent decree, triggered major changes in the IBT. None of the defendants in the 1989 DOJ civil RICO suit remain in office. The Independent Administrator and its successor, the Independent Review Board, have expelled hundreds of organized crime figures and associates from the union, placed or been responsible for placing dozens of corrupted locals under international union trusteeships, thereby allowing, in some cases, reformers to take control of their locals,* and produced three fair and competitive international elections.

Separate court-appointed trusteeships over a few of the most corrupt locals (e.g., IBT Local 560) have also shown impressive results. Until 2004, the James P. Hoffa administration, under the auspices of Project RISE, seemed committed to rooting out vestiges of organized crime

---

* Professor Robert Bruno's in-depth case study of IBT Local 705 in Chicago (*Reforming the Chicago Teamsters*, 2003) shows how the consent decree led to the IBT's imposition of a trusteeship over Local 705, opening the door for reformers to compete for union office. He concludes that although the International's trustee did a good job, he was unable to change the rank and file's positive attitude toward the old regime. He attributes real reform to the strenuous efforts of reformist elements in the local.

in order to persuade the government and the court to retire the consent decree and dissolve the Independent Review Board. Where they were once vilified, former FBI agents and federal prosecutors had access to IBT headquarters, President Hoffa, and his top staff. Unfortunately, events in the first half of 2004 cast a dark shadow over the credibility of the IBT's commitment to reform. The collapse of Project RISE means that the IBT's internal reform effort has been, at best, partially success-ful. Labor racketeers quite possibly remain a force to be reckoned with, especially in certain Chicago-area locals. Moreover, the Chicago Outfit has not been as vigorously prosecuted or as significantly weakened as LCN families in other cities.* Of course, the IRB remains in place for the foreseeable future, thereby assuring ongoing investigation and discipli-nary action.

HEREIU

Numerous allegations of possible association with organized crime groups were known over the years, yet no investigations were ever conducted by the HEREIU to ascertain the facts. Mr. [General Presi-dent Edward] Hanley rewarded family and friends, especially from the Chicago, IL area with positions with the International Union without evaluating the needs of the union. All these appointments were approved by the General Executive Board without questions or challenges.

—Kurt Muellenberg, Court-Appointed Monitor of
HEREIU, August 26, 1988.

In 1958, the McClellan Committee found that LCN Chicago Outfit boss Tony Accardo controlled three Chicago-area Hotel and Restaurant Workers locals. Joey Aiuppa, Accardo's lieutenant and later his succes-sor, was secretly the boss of one of these locals. *The Edge* concluded that the Chicago Outfit controlled HEREIU and that General President Ed Hanley, who had been promoted from one of the Chicago-area locals to

---

* In April 2005, the Chicago U.S. attorney's office announced a massive indictment against at least fourteen organized crime figures who were charged with numerous counts of murder, loan sharking, illegal gambling, and tax fraud. *U.S. v. Calabrese et al.,* no. 02 CR 1050 (N.D. Ill. April 25, 2005).

the general presidency, was the Outfit's tool. A 1984 Senate Permanent Subcommittee on Investigations report noted that Hanley had used mergers of locals, international trusteeship of locals, and personnel transfers to solidify the international union's control over local union officers and treasuries. It accused him of hiring a number of LCN members and associates as international union organizers and for other union positions. In addition, according to the Senate Subcommittee, LCN controlled several HEREIU locals in Chicago and other cities.

HEREIU LOCAL 54

The government's effort to reform HEREIU began with HEREIU Local 54 in Atlantic City.* In 1979, the local's longtime president, Ralph Natale, an associate of Philadelphia's Bruno LCN crime family, was sentenced to thirty years' imprisonment for a variety of offenses. To take his place, President Hanley appointed Frank Gerace, an associate of Nicodemo Scarfo, the Philadelphia LCN crime family capo in charge of the family's Atlantic City interests.[22] The U.S. Senate Subcommittee identified Local 54 President Gerace and Local 54's vice-president as pawns of Scarfo and the imprisoned Natale.[23]

In 1981, the New Jersey Casino Control Commission and the Division of Gaming Enforcement, established to prevent organized crime from penetrating Atlantic City casinos, found that LCN, through Gerace, controlled Local 54. It ordered Local 54 to remove Gerace and two others from union office. The commission warned that if the union failed to comply, it would be prohibited (under New Jersey law) from collecting dues from casino employees, which would cause the union's demise. After a protracted battle in the courts, the U.S. Supreme Court affirmed New Jersey's power to impose more stringent antiracketeering regulations than those imposed by federal law.[24] Gerace resigned his union presidency, but Local 54 continued to employ him as a "consultant."[25]

In 1984, the Senate Permanent Subcommittee on Investigations, after a three-year investigation of the Hotel and Restaurant Workers, concluded that the Philadelphia LCN controlled Local 54 and exerted

---

* The local had experienced extraordinary growth when casino gambling in Atlantic City was legalized in 1978. Local 54's membership swelled to 22,000.

"substantial influence" over the HERE International Union. At sub-committee hearings, thirty-four witnesses, including both HEREIU officials and reputed mobsters, refused to answer questions, asserting the Fifth Amendment right against compelled self-incrimination. The subcommittee's report found that the Atlantic City and Las Vegas lo-cals' dental plans served as slush funds for LCN figures.[26] In the wake of the report, federal prosecutors brought criminal ERISA charges against several union officials and filed a civil suit against Local 54's dental plan and the plan's administrators and service providers. The union and certain providers settled these lawsuits in 1988, agreeing to pay the benefit plan $3.85 million.

In December 1990, the U.S. attorney for the Northern District of New Jersey filed a civil RICO suit against Local 54, General President Edward Hanley, nine former and current Local 54 officers, and ten LCN members and associates, alleging a twenty-year pattern of racketeering. Those named in the suit included Nicodemo Scarfo (Bruno's successor as boss of the Philadelphia LCN family); Philip Leonetti (former Phil-adelphia LCN underboss); Anthony Piccolo (acting boss of the Philadel-phia LCN family); and, nominally, Local 54's affiliated benefit plans and severance fund.[27] The suit charged that Ralph Natale and other organ-ized crime figures had prevented democratic elections within Local 54 by threatening to kill union members who opposed or ran against mob-backed candidates. The consent decree removed eight Local 54 officers and employees from their union positions and permanently enjoined Frank Gerace from participating in HEREIU affairs.[28] Two defendants were enjoined from holding office in Local 54 for ten years, and two others for seven years. The LCN defendants were permanently en-joined from participating in Local 54's affairs. President Hanley agreed not to interfere with the remedial effort or to make any changes in Local 54's organization without a court-appointed monitor's approval.

U.S. District Court Judge Garrett E. Brown appointed the U.S. at-torney's nominee, James F. Flanagan (former deputy director of the New Jersey Division of Gaming Enforcement), as "monitor" of Local 54's affairs. Flanagan's authority extended to investigating, auditing, and reviewing all aspects of Local 54's and its affiliated benefit plans' operations. The court also empowered Flanagan to serve as trustee of HERE International Welfare and Pension Funds. Monitor Flanagan would exercise full powers of a trustee, but with respect to union affairs, he would have only the authority to petition the court to protect Local

54 members' rights. The consent decree postponed Local 54's 1991 election until Flanagan could implement democratic election procedures.[29] The judge provided that the "monitorship" would last at least two full election cycles.

When Flanagan assumed his duties, he found the local's finances and operations in shambles. There was no representation available for members who wished to file grievances against their employers. Pursuant to the consent agreement, the union's officers (including business agents) were fired or resigned. Flanagan held quarterly membership meetings, provided education and training to union members, and revitalized grievance handling.[30] He severed questionable contracts with service providers linked to organized crime. President Hanley, with Flanagan's agreement, assigned two experienced HEREIU officials to assist him. Flanagan also hired Michael Holland (the first elections officer in the IBT case) to consult on elections and an accounting firm to conduct annual audits.

Holding a democratic election was the top priority. Flanagan used the local's newsletter to encourage members to vote. He formulated new election procedures, including a grievance procedure to resolve election disputes. Candidates had to pass both FBI and DOL background checks.

In the first election, held in 1993, three of four candidate slates were controlled or influenced by LCN. These slates put forward candidates backed by competing organized crime groups, one headed by the imprisoned Natale and the other by John Stanfa, who, with Genovese crime family support, had attempted to take over the Bruno/Scarfo family after Scarfo was convicted on RICO charges in 1990.[31] Using tapes of Natale's intercepted phone conversations from prison, DOL agents exposed Natale's plan and Flanagan disqualified Natale's candidates.[32] All told, Flanagan disqualified eight candidates because of their organized crime associations. Judge Brown upheld these disqualifications.

Only 22 percent of eligible voters cast ballots in the 1993 secret ballot elections for Local 54 officers. The victors were all individuals who had never held union office before and had no connection with the old regime. In the August 1996 election, more than ninety candidates competed for union office, including four candidates for president. There were no allegations of organized crime involvement. Thirty-three percent of the union membership voted.[33] All the incumbent officers were ousted. Local 54, one of the most racketeer-ridden union locals in the country, had been liberated and even transformed into a union with truly competitive politics. The monitorship was proclaimed a success by all parties and dissolved in February 1997.[34]

HEREIU LOCAL 100

In 1992, the U.S. attorney for the Southern District of New York filed a civil RICO suit against HERE Local 100.[35] The complaint charged that President Anthony Amodeo and Vice-Presidents Anthony Amodeo Jr. and Jack DeRoss were running Local 100 on behalf of the Gambino and Colombo LCN crime families. It also charged that the defendant union officers employed organized crime members and associates in union jobs and committed or tolerated bribery, extortion, and violence. The case was settled by a consent decree that barred the Amodeos from the union and installed former Assistant U.S. Attorney Mary Shannon Little as trustee. The trusteeship lasted eighteen months and ended with the election of new union leadership.

CIVIL RICO SUIT AGAINST HEREIU

In September 1995, DOJ filed a civil RICO complaint against the 250,000-member Hotel and Restaurant Employees International Union (HEREIU), alleging that since the 1970s its General Executive Board (GEB) members had conspired with organized crime figures to obtain illegal payments from employers, embezzle union assets, and violate union members' Landrum-Griffin rights. Simultaneously, HEREIU and DOJ filed a consent decree[36] whose stated purpose was to free "HEREIU and all its locals from the direct or indirect influence of organized crime, now and in the future."[37] The defendants agreed not to commit crimes; associate with organized crime members and associates; allow barred individuals from exercising control or influence over HEREIU's affairs; and not to obstruct implementation of the consent decree. The consent decree also required that HEREIU, at its next national convention, adopt an ethical practices code and establish a public review board to implement and enforce it.

Federal District Court Judge Garrett E. Brown (who had presided over the HERE Local 54 case) appointed Kurt Muellenberg, a retired career federal prosecutor, who had served as head of DOJ's Organized Crime and Racketeering Section, as monitor for a term of eighteen months. The consent decree empowered Muellenberg to remove HEREIU local, regional, and international officials for violating any provision of the settlement, committing any crime involving the union or its employee benefit plans, or furthering the influence of any organized crime group. Muellenberg had authority to appoint and discharge union employees and candidates for union office and to disapprove collective bargaining agreements. The court ordered that at its 1996 convention HEREIU adopt an ethical practices code that would define prohibited conflicts of interest by union officers. Muellenberg appointed former FBI agent Daniel F. Sullivan as chief investigator and former Assistant U.S. Attorney Howard E. O'Leary as investigations officer. The consent decree provided for an eighteen-month monitorship with the possibility of an extension. When the term expired, the monitorship was extended for an additional twelve months.

Muellenberg found that many HEREIU locals had a history of organized crime infiltration; did not follow their bylaws; gave inadequate notice of membership meetings; failed to document expenses; failed to submit officers' bonuses and raises to the membership for approval; failed to train officers, business agents, and organizers; and failed to promulgate or maintain standards for personnel, pay scales, job descriptions, and performance.[38] The international union reimbursed business expenses without submission of receipts or explanations. According to Muellenberg, it "suffered from a management deficit and did not subscribe to generally accepted business practices."[39] He described the international union as an agglomeration of employees and officers without any clear rules or procedures. "There is no budget, no organizational chart, no job descriptions for employees, and no manual."[40] He charged that President Hanley hired friends and family members to union positions and as consultants, remunerated them generously, and ran the union like a personal fiefdom.

Muellenberg dissolved eleven improper trusteeships, which the international had imposed to provide jobs to cronies, including organized crime figures and associates. He placed five other locals under trusteeship because federal prosecutors had charged officers of those locals with embezzlement and/or filing false reports to the Department of Labor.[41] In addition, he permanently barred twenty-three individuals from participating in union affairs because of organized crime associations or failure to cooperate with the monitor. He barred two individuals from participation in union affairs for thirteen years, and two others from holding a position of trust in the union for three years.[42]

Muellenberg devoted much time to investigating President Hanley, who, according to the PCOC, had been put in power and kept there by the Chicago Outfit. Ultimately, Muellenberg charged Hanley with using union automobiles and the union airplane for personal purposes, receiving unearned salary and pension contributions, associating with organized crime members, and setting up a paper local near his Wisconsin vacation home so an individual whom Hanley appointed as that local's president could serve as factotum for Hanley and his friends. On February 19, 1998, Hanley agreed to retire and pay HEREIU $13,944 relating to his purchase of HEREIU-leased automobiles. He also assumed payment of the premiums on a life insurance policy that the union had purchased for him.[43] In return, Muellenberg agreed to cease investigating Hanley's actions during his tenure as general president. Hanley's retirement package included a $350,000 annual salary for life. Hanley's son, Thomas W., agreed to resign for one year and to reimburse HEREIU $25,000 in order to end an investigation into his abuse of union expense accounts.[44]

Muellenberg loaded his August 25, 1998, final report with recommendations for rationalizing the union's administration. On September 1, 1998, HEREIU's GEB voted to implement all of Muellenberg's recommendations on structure, governance, and operations of the international and locals.[45] Just before the monitorship was terminated in 1999, Muellenberg expelled John Agathos and John Agathos Jr. from their positions as Local 69 (Secaucus, N.J.) president and health and pension fund administrator, respectively, because of their links to organized crime.

The monitorship was superseded by a three-person (later expanded to five) Public Review Board (PRB); Muellenberg, Archbishop James P. Keleher of Kansas City, and former Illinois governor James R. Thompson were appointed to the board, which is responsible for overseeing implementation of the ethical practices code. It has authority to review member complaints and to conduct hearings to insure ethical standards in the union's operations, and power to suspend or expel members found to have violated the code. Hanley was replaced as general president by John W. Wilhelm, a well-respected HEREIU official who had never been accused of associating with nor influenced by organized crime. But neither has Wilhelm repudiated Hanley and the old regime. He has publicly said that he does not believe that LCN ever exerted significant influence in his union and that the monitorship would be useful because it would be "an independent, expert, well-resourced investigation that [would show] that the national leadership of this International Union is not corrupted, controlled, or influenced by organized crime."[46] In 1999, Wilhelm named the HERE International headquarters building in Washington, D.C., for Edward Hanley.

HEREIU CONCLUSION

In striking contrast to the huge fifteen-plus-year ongoing trusteeship in the IBT case, Muellenberg, with only a small staff to assist him, served as monitor for just thirty-six months. The weight of his efforts was directed at improving the union's administration and accounting. The new administration adopted the monitor's recommendations for improving the union's management. The union added a progressive ethical practices code to its constitution and a public review board to enforce it. Hanley's successor enjoys a progressive reputation and bears no organized crime taint, but he has not repudiated Hanley or acknowledged the union's long history of ties to LCN.

Although some of HEREIU's most notorious members were expelled and Hanley was forced to resign,[*] Muellenberg's investigations and disciplinary actions were not nearly as extensive as those of the independent administrator and IRB in the IBT case. Muellenberg focused surprisingly little attention on identifying or purging organized crime's influence from the union. He also did not make it a top priority to investigate and remedy racketeering in HEREIU locals. No change was made in HEREIU's election procedures.

---

[*] Although some commentators criticized the deal with Hanley as letting a labor racketeer off too easily, it is easier to suspect organizational criminality than to prove it. Corruption by high-level officials is difficult to prove because such individuals have the resources and capacity to cover their tracks and give apparent legitimacy to their exploitative conduct. Furthermore, prosecuting Hanley might have taken years. A further obstacle to punishing wrongdoing is posed by ERISA, which prevents pension forfeiture, even against an official who has stolen money from his union. James B. Jacobs, Coleen Friel, and Edward O'Callaghan, "Pension Forfeiture: A Problematic Sanction for Public Corruption," *American Criminal Law Review* 35: 57–92 (1997).

THE FOUR INTERNATIONAL UNIONS

Whether HEREIU has been purged of LCN influence is an open question.* In April 2002, the New Jersey U.S. Attorney's Office brought a civil RICO suit against HERE Local 69, a local over which Muellenberg had imposed a trusteeship three years before. Dave Freeback, the trustee whom Muellenberg had appointed to reform the local, was himself forced out of office in 2001 after charges of financial mismanagement and dishonesty. The 2002 civil RICO lawsuit charged that, for fifteen years, Genovese crime family members and associates had used extortion and intimidation to influence Local 69's affairs and that the local's officers had failed to investigate or take any action whatsoever to remedy the situation. Indeed, according to the complaint, Local 69's officers colluded with LCN labor racketeers in exploiting the local and its members. The federal prosecutors alleged that the local, among other things, had made $524,000 in "severance payments" to the Agathoses, father and son. The district court appointed Muellenberg to serve as monitor over the local and empowered him to investigate the union, approve and disapprove union expenditures, review and take action on collective bargaining agreements, and otherwise supervise the union's affairs. In 2005, Freeback pled guilty to federal charges of embezzling money from both the union and its benefit fund. Muellenberg's monitorship continues as this book goes to press, but Local 69 is slated to be merged out of existence in 2006.

LIUNA

In summation, Mr. Chairman, we are extremely proud of everything we have accomplished to date to ensure all Laborers the corruption-free, fully-democratic union they deserve. We also recognize that there is much work still to be done and our commitment to democracy and reform remains as deep and unyielding as ever.
—LIUNA General Counsel Michael S. Bearse, Testimony at the
Laborers International Union of North America, House
Subcommittee on Employer/Employee Relations,
May 4, 1998

---

* On July 8, 2004, HERE merged with UNITE (formerly the Union of Needle Trades, Industrial and Textile Employees), forming UNITE HERE.

> The so-called LIUNA "internal reform effort" is a failure and a
> sham. . . . This latest extension is extremely inadequate. It's an out-
> rage. . . . From Connecticut to California, NLPC [National Legal and
> Policy Center] continues to get reports from dissidents of the wide-
> spread corruption that still exists in many LIUNA locals.
> —National Legal and Policy Center President Peter Flaherty,
> January 7, 1999

Historically, LIUNA, at the international and local levels, especially in
Chicago and New York City, was, like HEREIU, closely tied to Cosa
Nostra crime families. Outfit boss Tony Accardo exercised a great deal
of influence in the union for many years.[47] He and his successors controlled LIUNA's general presidents (Peter Fosco and his son Angelo)[*]
and the officers of many locals.

In late 1994, the DOJ presented LIUNA officials with a 212-page
civil RICO complaint, alleging that LCN crime families dominated the
800,000-member union,[48] and alleging 100 predicate racketeering acts.
The complaint named 39 defendants, including General President
Arthur A. Coia, General Secretary-Treasurer Rollin P. "Bud" Vinall, all
10 LIUNA vice-presidents and the union's general counsel. The complaint alleged that the defendants violated the rights of LIUNA members through intimidation, violence, and economic coercion, and that
the union defendants violated their (Landrum-Griffin-imposed) fiduciary duty to the membership by failing to investigate, prevent, or remedy corruption.

As a remedy, the government sought the expulsion of Coia and the
other union leaders, and requested that one or more "court liaison officers" be appointed to carry out the duties of the general president and
the General Executive Board (GEB) and to prevent any GEB action that
would violate union members' rights or perpetuate criminal influence
in the union. The draft complaint requested that the union's constitution be amended to prohibit discriminatory hiring hall practices, and to
provide for direct rank-and-file election of officers. The DOJ lawyers
also included a request for a court-appointed elections officer.

Following its usual procedure in such cases, before filing the com-

---

[*] Angelo named his son Peter. And this Peter, like father and grandfather, was also active
in LIUNA. Robert Luskin and the civil RICO–spawned reform team removed Peter from
office.

plaint, DOJ offered the union an opportunity to respond to the allegations. DOJ offered to meet with LIUNA's representatives, albeit not with LIUNA's longtime general counsel, who was a defendant in the suit. At that point, General President Arthur Coia hired Robert Luskin, a former federal organized crime prosecutor, to represent the union in negotiations with DOJ.

Luskin sought to persuade Coia that it would be a waste of millions of dollars to contest the government's overwhelming case and that, if the case went to trial, the court would almost certainly impose an external monitor like the IRB in the IBT case. Simultaneously, Luskin sought to persuade the DOJ that an *internal union reform effort* could produce more reliable long-term reform then a court-imposed trusteeship, which, based upon IBT Local 560 and the HEREIU experiences, seemed to alienate the rank and file and solidify support for the entrenched regime.

After three months of negotiations, LIUNA and the DOJ announced a unique settlement. The DOJ agreed to forgo filing its civil RICO complaint if LIUNA installed an internal reform team and reform program acceptable to DOJ. According to the settlement, LIUNA would sign a consent decree agreeing to an external court-appointed monitor, but the DOJ would refrain from filing the signed consent decree for ninety days; after that time, the DOJ could file the consent decree at its sole discretion if it was dissatisfied with LIUNA's reform effort. Subsequently, the agreement was extended to 2001 and then, with certain modifications, to 2006.* The signed consent decree has never been filed. Instead, reform has proceeded under the auspices of a LIUNA reform team.

In order to satisfy the DOJ, LIUNA adopted an ethical practices code (drafted by Luskin) and established four new positions: (1) GEB attorney, filled by Robert Luskin, to investigate and prosecute violations of the ethical practices code; (2) inspector general, filled by Douglas Gow, retired high-level FBI official, to investigate violations of the ethical practices code; (3) independent hearing officer, filled by

---

*Although some critics contend that the settlement let LIUNA off too easily, I do not agree. The settlement put DOJ in a "heads I win, tails you lose" position. The DOJ obtained a signed consent agreement that included everything it asked for in the civil RICO complaint. The DOJ could make this remedy effective, at its sole discretion, any time after ninety days had passed from the date of the settlement. Moreover, the DOJ itself, rather than a judge or court-appointed trustee, would monitor and judge LIUNA's remedial efforts. It is hard to see how the government could have obtained a better resolution.

Peter Vaira, former chief of the DOJ's Chicago Organized Crime Strike Force and former U.S. attorney in Philadelphia, to serve as judge and arbitrator in disciplinary cases; and (4) appellate officer, filled by Neil Eggleston, a former federal prosecutor assigned to replace John Serpico, a Chicago labor racketeer, who had been in charge of hearing disciplinary appeals from throughout the union. Luskin hired two dozen former FBI agents, two full-time law firm associates, and one full-time person to work on job referral reform. Inspector General Gow hired three full-time staff members. The reform unit also had authority to place corrupted LIUNA locals into trusteeship.

The newly appointed LIUNA officers established a confidential toll-free telephone number and a confidential post office box to solicit complaints from the LIUNA membership. By mid-1996, the reform officers had charged Serpico and Vice-President Robert Cavone with knowingly maintaining organized crime ties and had begun more than 345 investigations; expelled from the union 25 officers and members for violating the ethical practices code; removed all of the officers of LIUNA Local 210 (Buffalo, N.Y.); placed Chicago LIUNA Local 8 under emergency trusteeship; and sent Steve Hammond to work with Trustee Michael Chertoff (former federal prosecutor and later Secretary of Homeland Security) to clean up the racketeer-ridden New York City Mason Tenders District Council.* The reform team also initiated an investigation of General President Coia.[49]

At its convention, LIUNA amended its constitution to require direct rank-and-file secret-ballot election of the general president and general secretary-treasurer. It also expanded its GEB from ten to thirteen members, requiring that nine members be elected regionally so that the board would be more accountable to the membership. As well,

---

* The following illustrates the kind of legal energy required to remove just one union actor from the scene. (There have been scores of similar cases.) The draft civil RICO complaint named Sam Caviano, a vice-president and regional manager for the New York City area (including the Mason Tenders), as a defendant. The government alleged that Caviano was a tool of the Genovese crime family. Luskin charged Caviano with a disciplinary violation, and Vaira suspended him from the union. Caviano then filed suit in federal district court challenging the disciplinary procedure. The judge ruled for the government on summary judgment. Then the government and Caviano signed a settlement agreement, agreeing that he would resign voluntarily. During the interim, he also attempted to continue running the union's benefit funds, changing the trust agreements to perpetuate his power as trustee. Luskin sued in federal court and obtained a preliminary injunction removing Caviano from the benefit funds.

it changed its procedures for selecting convention delegates and eliminated several locals whose primary purpose seemed to be to provide convention votes to organized crime. LIUNA also hired an independent elections officer (Northwestern University Law School Professor Stephen B. Goldberg) and two deputy election officers, jointly selected by the government and union, to monitor union elections at the local, regional, and international levels. The union adopted uniform job referral rules to prevent discriminatory hiring-hall practices. Luskin hired an independent accounting firm to audit LIUNA's finances.[50] Still, in the 1996 international election for general president, the only candidate to challenge Coia was Bruno Caruso who charged that Coia was *too cooperative with the government.* Coia was reelected, once again demonstrating the unwillingness or inability of racketeer-ridden unions to vote labor racketeers out of office.

In November 1997, Luskin filed disciplinary charges alleging that Coia knowingly associated with organized crime members, permitted organized crime to influence union affairs from 1986 to 1993, and accepted illegal payoffs from a LIUNA service provider. The hearing, which lasted from April 14, 1998, until June 23, 1998, included more than five hundred exhibits. Testimony filled thousands of transcript pages. Independent Hearing Officer Vaira "acquitted" Coia of the allegations of organized crime association and influence but found him "guilty" of accepting illegal benefits from a LIUNA service provider. He fined Coia $100,000 but did not remove him from office.[51] The U.S. Attorney's Office in Rhode Island immediately brought criminal tax evasion charges against Coia, based upon benefits Coia had received from the service provider. Before the criminal trial, the parties entered into a plea agreement whereby Coia agreed to relinquish the general presidency and become *general president emeritus for life* at an annual salary of $335,516.[52] The GEB appointed Terrence O'Sullivan, Coia's chief of staff, as his successor.

When Luskin brought disciplinary charges against a mobbed-up local, there was a hearing before Hearing Officer Vaira. If Vaira sustained the charges, the local and its officers could appeal to the federal district court judge presiding over the suit, but Luskin and Vaira were consistently upheld. When the officers of the local union were removed, Luskin appointed replacements. By 2002, 226 officers and members had been expelled from the union, 127 of these because of ties to organized crime. As of early 2004, nearly three dozen LIUNA locals and district councils had been placed under trusteeships or monitoring because of mismanagement, connections to organized crime, or corruption.

In 2001, the DOJ and LIUNA amended and extended their agreement. The government recognized and publicly acknowledged the success of the Luskin-led reform effort and relinquished the so-called contingent consent decree, i.e., the DOJ gave up the option of filing the signed consent decree imposing an external IRB-type monitor. The parties agreed that LIUNA's future obligation would be to maintain the existing reform program. If LIUNA fails to do that, the DOJ could secure an injunction restoring the reform program. This agreement will be in force until the conclusion of LIUNA's 2006 general election. Luskin does not anticipate the completion of his work in the foreseeable future.

LIUNA CONCLUSION

In 1994, the DOJ prepared the first major attack on LIUNA labor racketeering at the national level. The civil RICO complaint led to a creative settlement between the government and the union. LIUNA hired four former federal law enforcement figures to enforce its new code of ethics. This internal reform project has scored many important successes. Hundreds of corrupt and/or organized crime–connected officers and members have been purged. Dozens of locals have been put under trusteeships. The international union suspended John Serpico, labor racketeer and political power broker, from his union positions in 1995.* Many other officers and members were also expelled or suspended.

Nevertheless, there is no sign of union democracy. There is no insurgent rank-and-file movement and very few contested elections. The reformers are regarded as "government men" or "policemen"; a culture of reform has not yet taken hold. New election procedures were not implemented. There remains a great deal of labor racketeering in the locals and in certain regional unions, like the New York City Mason Tenders District Council. Indeed, from 1999 to 2002, corrupt union officials were prosecuted for defrauding LIUNA locals in Chicago (Local 5), Des

---

* Serpico then signed on as a "consultant" for a Chicago local of the International Union of Allied Novelty and Production Workers. He also served for a time as president emeritus of the Central States Joint Board, which provides administrative services to Chicago-area unions. In the summer of 2001, Serpico and two associates were convicted of taking kickbacks in exchange for steering union business to certain companies.

Moines (Local 177), and Niagara Falls (Local 91), and others.[53] In January 2005, the LIUNA General Executive Board imposed a trusteeship over Local 29 (New York City) in order to "eliminate organized crime corruption within the local."[54] Also in January 2005, the LIUNA reform unit charged that there was rampant organized crime–connected corruption in LIUNA Local 734 which operates in southern New Jersey and Pennsylvania.

ILA

[W]orkers of the Port of New York are being exploited in every possible way and . . . they are not receiving the protection which they have every right to expect as trade unionists. . . .

—Letter, Executive Council, AFL, to officers and members of
the ILA, February 3, 1952; quoted in Vernon H. Jensen,
Strife on the Waterfront: The Port of New York since 1945
(Ithaca: Cornell University Press, 1974), 105

When we began this case three years ago, we were shocked at the extent to which the ILA was controlled by organized crime.

—The FBI's top official in New York, according to
New York Times reporter Frank Swoboda,
New York Times, February 15, 1990

Of the four most racketeer-ridden international unions named by the President's Commission on Organized Crime, only the ILA has not (at least as of winter 2005) been subject to a civil RICO suit, although such a suit has been rumored for almost a decade to be in the works. Perhaps the government has refrained from bringing such a suit in order to see whether its omnibus 1990 civil RICO suit against ILA locals in the New York City/New Jersey area produces the necessary reforms.

On February 14, 1990, the U.S. Department of Justice filed a civil RICO suit[55] against six ILA locals representing dock workers in the New York/New Jersey port as well as their executive boards and officers; the Genovese and Gambino crime families; the Westies, an Irish organized crime group allied with the Gambino family; and five waterfront employers.[56] The complaint charged that the waterfront had "been the setting for corruption, violence, and abuse of waterfront labor and business by New York La Cosa Nostra Families" for more than fifty years. It alleged that the Genovese and Gambino organized crime families control and exploit the ILA locals and their members and the shipping industry. According to the government, despite the many criminal convictions that resulted from the FBI's massive UNIRAC (Union Racketeering)* investigation in the late 1970s, the Genovese and Gambino crime families, by means of their influence in the ILA, continued to exert influence in many eastern seaboard ports. The government cited dozens of instances of embezzlement, solicitation and receipt of bribes, benefit fund fraud, extortion of employers, and violation of the rank and file's Landrum-Griffin rights as RICO predicate acts.

To remedy these alleged RICO violations, the Department of Justice asked the court to enjoin the organized crime defendants from participating in ILA affairs, having any dealings with union officers and employees, and committing racketeering acts. The DOJ requested the court to require the defendants to disgorge the proceeds of their RICO violations and to enjoin the defendant union officials from knowingly associating with Cosa Nostra members or associates. The complaint also asked the court to appoint "liaison officers" for each of the ILA locals to "discharge those duties of the Executive Board[s]"; "review the proposed actions of the Executive Board[s]"; implement fair elections; and oversee union reform.

ILA LOCAL 1804-1 (BERGEN, N.J.)

On March 25, 1991, ILA Local 1804-1 and its Executive Board and officers entered into a consent judgment with the DOJ. Local 1804-1's current and future Executive Board and its officers agreed to be enjoined from racketeering activity and from knowingly associating with members or associates of organized crime.[57] The consent judgment provided for a monitor to oversee Local 1804-1's operations until the 1997 election. The monitor would have full access to all union documents and

---

* "Perhaps the modern era in the government's anti–organized crime war dates to the FBI's massive UNIRAC investigation of the International Longshoreman's Association in the late 1970s. The labor racketeering investigation, the subject of special Senate hearings in 1981, resulted in the conviction of 130 businessmen, union officials, and Cosa Nostra members, including Anthony Scotto." (Jacobs et al., *Busting the Mob*, 6.)

information; authority to discipline union officers, agents, employees, and members; power to investigate corruption or abuse of union funds; and supervisory authority over the union's 1994 and 1997 elections. In addition, the monitor had authority to review and veto union expenditures, union contracts, personnel decisions, and proposed changes to the union's constitution and bylaws.

Local 1804-1 agreed to pay the monitor's salary and operating expenses and not to oppose or interfere with the monitor's execution of his duties. The consent judgment provided that Local 1804-1's constitution be amended to include salary caps for officers, election of shop stewards, and a prohibition on union loans to union officers and members. It permitted Local 1804-1's Executive Board to remain in office but required several board members to pay $100,000 to Local 1804-1's treasury. Ten years after the settlement, other than the expulsion of several officers, very little had changed.

ILA LOCAL 824, ILA LOCAL 1809, AND ILA LOCAL 1909 (MANHATTAN WEST SIDE LOCALS)

On March 26, 1991, Locals 824, 1809, and 1909—collectively known as the (Manhattan) West Side Locals—and their Executive Boards and officers signed a consent judgment with the DOJ. Without admitting wrongdoing, the defendant union officials agreed to be enjoined from knowingly associating with any member or associate of organized crime.[58] Executive Board members John Potter and Thomas Ryan resigned, agreeing to be enjoined from holding ILA office in the future. ILA International President John Bowers (also president of the three West Side Locals) and Executive Board member Robert Gleason agreed to resign their memberships in an employer association, the NYSA (New York Shipping Association)-ILA Contract Board. The consent judgment also provided that the Department of Labor would supervise the West Side Locals' 1991 and 1994 elections and that the DOL would have access to union records necessary to carry out this responsibility.

Local 1909 agreed to implement fair job referral rules and procedures; discontinue no-show jobs; discipline those who violate hiring or employment procedures; and accept the court appointment of an employment practices officer whose term would run until certification of the 1994 union election. He or she would be paid by the union, have full access to union records and report to the court at least every six months. The West Side Locals agreed not to obstruct, oppose, or otherwise interfere with the work of the DOL or the employment practices officer. Incredibly, President John Bowers proclaimed the consent judgment "a complete victory," asserting that nothing exceptional had been granted to the government in exchange for the settlement.

The remaining civil RICO defendants went to trial in spring 1991, but only four defendants persisted to judgment; the rest settled. On June 1, 1991, Anthony Scotto, one of the most powerful labor racketeers in U.S. history in light of his high rank in both Cosa Nostra (capo) and in the ILA (international vice-president), agreed to pay $50,000 and to be banned permanently from union office and association with the union, and with employers with whom the union had collective bargaining agreements. When, subsequently, Scotto was sentenced to prison in a separate criminal case, Anthony Ciccone succeeded him in both the Cosa Nostra and union roles.

ILA LOCAL 1814 CONSENT DECREE (BROOKLYN)

ILA Local 1814, its Executive Board and officers entered into a consent decree with the DOJ in December 1991. The individual defendants and officers, without admitting wrongdoing, acknowledged past allegations, testimony, public findings, and criminal prosecutions. They agreed to be enjoined from knowingly associating with organized crime members or associates.[59]

The consent decree provided for a court-appointed monitor to have full access to the union's books, records, and other information; disciplinary authority; and supervisory authority over the 1993 and 1996 elections. The monitor, paid by the union, would hold veto power over union expenditures, contracts, appointments, and proposed constitutional and bylaws amendments. The monitor, Joseph Jaffe (a former assistant U.S. attorney in SDNY), was authorized to hire legal counsel, accountants, consultants, investigators, and any other personnel necessary to assist him in carrying out his duties.

The consent decree required amending Local 1814's constitution to provide for secret-ballot, rank-and-file elections of shop stewards and limitations on officers' compensation. Moreover, two Executive Board members had to resign their Local 1814 positions and agree not to be employed by the ILA in the future. Ciccone had to resign his office but was permitted to remain a union member and receive union benefits.[60] The other members of the Executive Board were also permitted to keep their positions. The "monitorship," which expired after the 1996 election, did not accomplish much change in Local 1814. Although the union is far less influential than it once was because there are few functioning cargo operations left on Brooklyn's docks, the Gambino crime family's influence remains strong, as demonstrated by the June 2002 indictment of Gambino crime family members and union officials for operating ILA Local 1814 as a racketeering enterprise.[61]

The federal indictment alleged, among other things, that the Genovese and Gambino crime families conspired to control selection of ILA officials. Moreover, the government charged that, despite the 1991 consent decree that prohibited Anthony Ciccone from participating in ILA and waterfront affairs, he continued to be in charge of the Gambino family's interests in the ILA (including Local 1814 and Local 1). Among its specific allegations, the government charged that the mob defendants accepted a $400,000 payoff from two brothers who wanted the contract to provide prescription drugs to the ILA's health and welfare program. A jury found all defendants guilty.[62]

The ILA international union reacted to these indictments by placing Local 1814 in trusteeship. ILA International Executive Board member Robert Gleason was named trustee. Eventually Gleason was replaced by an ILA official from outside the New York/New Jersey area. Hoping to prevent a civil RICO suit, the ILA International hired former federal Brooklyn Strike Force head, Andrew Maloney (the same individual later hired by James P. Hoffa as special counsel when Ed Stier and Jim Kossler resigned), to monitor MILA.

LOCAL 1588 (BAYONNE, N.J.)

On January 3, 1992, the last of the six locals named in the 1990 civil RICO suit, Local 1588 and its Executive Board, entered into a consent agreement. ILA Local 1588's secretary-treasurer, Donald Carson, was convicted in 1988 of RICO conspiracy and extortion involving Local 1588.[63] In 1990, Local 1588's president and secretary-treasurer declined to run for re-election. The consent order acknowledged that "the new executive board already has taken steps to return Local 1588 to fiscal soundness and to remove the taint of organized crime corruption."

The consent decree established an "ombudsman," who would function until the 1993 election or longer at the option of the union's Executive Board or membership.[64] The ombudsman's office was to be staffed by two individuals, one appointed by the court and one by the union. The court appointed Robert Gaffey, formerly an assistant U.S. attorney and later chief counsel to the investigations officer in the IBT International case. The ombudsman was charged with enforcing the union's constitution and bylaws. Although the ombudsman had power to file disciplinary charges after consulting with the union's Executive Board, it had few other powers and a paltry budget. The consent agreement provided for election of stewards and constitutional changes to disciplinary procedures, Department of Labor supervision of the local's 1993 election, and an injunction preventing two named individuals from serving as shop stewards or in any other ILA office or position.

Ombudsman Gaffey's main achievement was to generate a slate of reform candidates to oppose Donald Carson's Genovese-controlled slate. The "reform" slate won the 1993 election; the office of ombudsman expired. Unfortunately, the new head of Local 1588 was convicted of stealing union funds and removed from office. The brief trusteeship must be regarded as a complete failure.

In 2003, the government brought a civil contempt proceeding against Local 1588, asserting that the local had violated the 1992 consent judgment. Arguing that an outside trustee was unnecessary, the ILA put Local 1588 in trusteeship. Nevertheless, the judge ruled for the government and appointed former New York City Police Commissioner Robert McGuire as trustee and gave him sweeping powers over all aspects of union operations. MaGuire hired Robert Stewart, formerly chief government counsel in the IBT Local 560 case, as his deputy trustee. In an effort to strengthen the foundations of a democratic union, McGuire and Stewart hired Carl Biers, the former executive director of the Association for Union Democracy. This is a very important experiment that ought to tell us much about the potential of a union democracy specialist to transform a thoroughly corrupted and exploited union into a democratic union.

ILA CONCLUSION

The remedial litigation to reform the ILA achieved, at best, very limited success. In January 2002, the U.S. attorney's office (Brooklyn) announced an indictment against eight leaders and members of the Genovese crime family, including its boss Vincent Gigante, alleging extortion from waterfront employers and businesses in the New York City metropolitan area, northern New Jersey, and Miami.[65] The indictment accused the mob defendants of conspiring to violate the rights of ILA members by defrauding the union's pension and welfare fund. It also charged them with extorting firms that repair cargo containers.

Six months later, in June 2002, a federal grand jury returned a second series of indictments against seventeen members and associates of the Gambino crime family, including the boss (Peter Gotti); two captains (one of whom was Local 1814 boss and LCN capo Sonny Ciccone); four soldiers; and ten associates, including the ILA Local 1814's president and vice-president. Both the January and June 2002 indictments alleged the same type of labor racketeering that has been repeatedly exposed since the 1950s. Despite prosecutions, investigative commissions, civil RICO suits, and trusteeships, LCN continues to exert powerful influence over the ILA locals throughout the New York/New Jersey port. In 2004, the government announced yet another major ILA indictment, this one naming as defendants the incumbent presidents of ILA Local 1804-1, ILA Local 1235 in New Jersey, and seven Miami locals (1922; 1922-1; 2062). The indictment alleged that the three officials functioned as Genovese crime family associates. According to the indictment, the Genovese family created the three locals in the 1960s that would represent workers who repair and service cargo containers and serve the interests of the crime family.[66]

CONCLUSION

It is difficult to appreciate the amount of legal energy that has been poured into the effort to reform the IBT, LIUNA, HERE, and ILA. In terms of number of motions, decisions, orders, opinions, and reports by judges and their trustees, these cases may be unparalleled in the history of American law. One colleague tells me that she counted two hundred signed opinions/orders by Judge David Edelstein in the IBT international case; that does not, of course, include orders of his successor, Judge Preska. The written opinions by the General Executive Board and the appellate officer in the LIUNA case fill more than a dozen volumes. The total number of hours that assistant U.S. attorneys, judges, and trustees have devoted to these cases is staggering. Half a dozen ambitious scholars would be consumed for years by the task of documenting and assessing the impacts of this legal intervention. So far, however, evaluation has attracted little governmental or scholarly interest.

It is striking how different the reform efforts directed against the four racketeer-ridden international unions has been. The ILA has not yet been subject to a civil RICO suit against its central headquarters and General Executive Board. Such a suit has been rumored for several years. The possibility, indeed the threat, of such a suit has itself had consequences. The ILA has hired an outside lawyer to recommend and implement reforms that might prevent a civil RICO suit. Quite possibly the international union operates differently because of the civil RICO threat. Of course, the operation of the several New York/New Jersey locals has been substantially affected, although it does not appear that any of those trusteeships can be called a substantial success. Indeed, Local 1588 is now in a second-round trusteeship and major organized crime prosecutions have exposed extensive LCN involvement in several of the other locals.

The trusteeship in the HEREIU case is by far the least intensive and comprehensive of those imposed on the four international unions. Compared to the others, that trusteeship was brief in duration, scantily staffed, and minimally intrusive. If the kind of massive remedial effort that took place in the IBT and LIUNA cases was necessary, it is hard to believe that the relatively minimalist effort in the HEREIU case could have been sufficient (assuming, of course, some rough parity in the extent of the racketeering). Nevertheless, there are several important achievements. Ed Hanley was removed from office. A small number of mob-associated officers were expelled from the union. A few locals were placed under trusteeships. The new president has better credentials than the presidents of the other three international unions, but even he has not repudiated the old regime. Investigations of labor racketeering in the HEREIU, to my knowledge, have more or less ceased. Although the union is clearly less mob influenced than it was, we do not know whether HEREIU has been substantially liberated. If so, it is crucial to determine how this could have been accomplished with such a comparatively inexpensive and short-term effort.

LIUNA was never placed under a formal trusteeship, but the reform effort that the union agreed to implement is the functional equivalent of a RICO trusteeship, albeit without judicial involvement. The people whom the union hired to carry out the reforms necessary to forestall the civil RICO suit's being filed were drawn from the same pool of former prosecutors and retired law enforcement personnel who served in practically all the civil RICO union cases. One of the rationales for preferring this approach was that the rank and file would be less alienated by an internal effort than an external one, but this is not obviously borne out by events. The reform unit hired by LIUNA and led by Robert Luskin is, in every sense of the term, an "outside" group. These are not home grown union officials working within the system to clean things up. These are former prosecutors and FBI agents carrying out criminal-type investigations and bringing aggressive disciplinary actions to expel mob-tainted union officials and to place mob-tainted locals under trusteeship. While, in theory, the LIUNA reform unit is not as secure as a trusteeship that owes its existence to a judicially enforceable consent decree, in fact it is absolutely secure. LIUNA officials know that if they were to disband the reform unit, a DOJ civil RICO suit would swiftly ensue.

The IBT remedial effort is the most formal, the most resource intensive, and has the longest duration. In striking contrast to the LIUNA remediation, the IRB operates at arm's length from the union, much like a prosecutor's office. The IBT takes no ownership of the IRB and, in fact, is critical and hostile toward it. This encourages the rank and file to see the remediation effort as unreasonably imposed by the government on their "misunderstood and mistreated" union. That being said, there can be no denying or minimizing the enormous impact that the IRB has had on the organization, personnel, and operation of the IBT. With hundreds of officials expelled and dozens of locals in trusteeship, the IBT has been and continues to be subjected to a thorough organizational cleansing. There is much reform to applaud, but it would be a mistake to declare the mission accomplished.

One interesting and important observation is that none of the four unions has been taken over by a reformist regime that condemns and repudiates that union's past association with organized crime and embraces the government as liberators. Even Ron Carey, the most reform oriented of the new wave of officials in these unions, did not go that far. He may have condemned the organized crime element in the IBT, but he did not embrace the government as a liberator. In part, this speaks to the unhappy history of government suppression of unions in the late nineteenth and early twentieth centuries. In part, it may speak to the strength of organized crime's influence in these unions.

POSTSCRIPT

In July 2005, the U.S. Attorney for the Eastern District of New York (Brooklyn) filed the long-awaited and long-rumored civil RICO suit against all 31 members of the International ILA's Executive Council as well as several leaders and members of Cosa Nostra. This suit follows up and builds upon the recent criminal prosecutions of Gambino and Genovese Crime Family members for labor racketeering in Brooklyn and Staten Island(Gambino) and New Jersey and Miami (Genovese).

The RICO complaint charged the defendants with conspiring to dominate the ports by placing organized crime members and associates into high-ranking ILA positions and rigging union elections. The complaint called long-time ILA President John Bowers "a Genovese Crime Family associate" and charged the defendants with conspiring to eventually replace the 80 year old Bowers with General Organizer Harold Daggett whom the complaint also refers to as a "Genovese Family associate." Furthermore, the U.S. Attorney alleged that the Gambino Family agreed to support Daggett as Bowers' successor in exchange for several Gambino members and associates being appointed to top union and benefit fund positions.

One of the most salient racketeering episodes charged in the complaint is that the defendants defrauded the ILA membership by arranging to award a major health fund contract to a company connected to Cosa Nostra.

In terms of relief, the U.S. attorney is asking the federal court to bar Bowers, Daggett, several other top ILA officials as well as alleged mobsters Peter Gotti, Jerome Brancato, and Anthony Ciccone from employment by the union or by any company doing business in the Port of New York. In addition, the government seeks a court-appointed trustee to run and reform the ILA and its associated pension and welfare funds and to hold a fair election for Executive Council positions. Finally, the U.S. attorney is asking the court to order the defendants to disgorge the proceeds of their labor racketeering activity. See *U.S. v. ILA et al.*, case 1:05-cv-03212-ILG-WP (E.D.N.Y., filed July 6, 2005).

The ILA defendants have vowed to fight the suit.

12

Evaluating Civil RICO

Furthermore, it can be argued that the long-term effect of this type of RICO suit may be to decrease the overall level of democracy in the labor movement. A proliferation of RICO trusteeships could foster a siege mentality among members of organized labor...This siege mentality phenomenon underscores the importance of the judiciary clearly articulating the reasons and standards for imposing a trustee. Only by making clear to union members that corruption and not organized labor is the target of the RICO litigation can the government and the courts avoid exacerbating the very problem they seek to correct.

—Professor Clyde Summers, University of Pennsylvania
Law School, at http://www.ipsn.org/court_cases/
union_receiverships_under_rico.htm

Where you can identify individual criminal conduct, it should be investigated and punished severely. But where it has gone on for so many years and it has become so much a part of the fabric of the organization that you are dealing with, civil RICO represents a drastic, but nonetheless often necessary solution.

—Benito Romano, U.S. Attorney, SDNY, Hearings before the
Senate Permanent Subcommittee on Investigations of the
Committee on Governmental Affairs, 101st Cong.,
1st sess., April 4, 1989

Evaluating the success of RICO union trusteeships is essential, but extremely complex. It is incredible that more than twenty years of civil RICO litigation against racketeer-ridden unions has been conducted without any evaluation whatsoever. Not a single conference or workshop has ever been convened. Successes and failures have never been identified, much less documented or analyzed. All U.S. attorneys considering civil RICO union suits have had to begin from scratch or with only vague ideas as to what kind of relief to ask for. They have no record to guide them in anticipating or addressing posttrial or postsettlement problems of organizational reform.

Evaluation questions abound. At what point in the remedial process is an evaluation appropriate? If the life of the trusteeship has been extended, should evaluation similarly be delayed? In the event that the trusteeship was established for an indefinite term, should evaluation await the trusteeship's termination, no matter how long that takes?* Ideally, a trusteeship should be evaluated at several points in time. We would like to know, for example, what progress has been made after the first two years, and then after five years, if the trusteeship lasts that long. (Indeed, this is essential so that midtrusteeship corrections can be made.) We should also like to know what the situation looks like several years after the trusteeship's termination. Did the union revert to its pretrusteeship condition? Is it now a democratic union accountable to the membership?

The conceptual problems are matched by the problems involved in obtaining accurate empirical evidence on which to make an informed judgment about successes and failures. How can an evaluator assess the status of organized crime's influence on union affairs? Dissidents may believe that new union officers are corrupt. They can hardly be blamed for being suspicious, but they may be incorrect. Developing reliable informants is a major challenge for investigators and takes a great deal of time, energy, and resources. If FBI and DOL agents have remained on the case, they may have informants who can provide accurate information about the current relationship between organized crime and the union. Unfortunately, the FBI and DOL agents may have moved on to

---

* Another concern is that it may not be obvious when a trusteeship has ended. In a number of cases, when the original trusteeship ended, the judge maintained the court's jurisdiction and continued monitoring through a new arrangement. For example, in the Mason Tenders District Council case, after the expiration of the trusteeship, a "supplemental" consent decree was entered into in January 1999 that provided that the trustee, Lawrence Pedowitz, would act as a "Review Monitor" for an additional thirty-six months, with power to apply to the Court for restoration of his trustee powers if he concluded the union was being run corruptly. *United States v. Mason Tenders District Council of Greater New York*, 1994 WL 742637 (S.D.N.Y. 1994); interview with Lawrence Pedowitz (Nov. 2002).

other cases or, if still involved, lack accurate information about new officials. Even if the investigators have or think they have accurate information, they are likely to be holding it for future prosecutions and
therefore be unwilling to divulge it to university-based researchers or to
other evaluators. They may not even be willing to share their information with the trustee (which is an argument in favor of drawing trustees
from the ranks of former law enforcement officials).

The very meaning of "success" is debatable. Do we mean whether
the trustee achieved the goals defined by the federal prosecutor in
charge of the case? But what if those goals were under- or overly ambitious? What if the goals were only partially achieved? The anti–
labor racketeering initiatives were launched to purge Cosa Nostra
from the unions; union democracy was a means, not an end. Nevertheless, it now seems clear that without establishing some modicum
of union democracy, at least fair elections, a trusteeship cannot be
successful. Certainly, from the rank and file's perspective, nothing
positive will have been achieved if one set of racketeers is replaced
by another set, even if the new racketeers are affiliated with another
organized crime group or are unaffiliated with any organized crime
group.

It is essential to recognize that we are talking about an *evaluative
process*. We can begin by identifying three basic criteria of success: (1)
the purging of organized crime figures and their allies from the union;
(2) competitive elections; and (3) a complete break with the racketeer-
dominated regime that controlled the union before the civil RICO suit
was filed. Ideally, evaluators would have enough information, including court documents, media accounts, and interviews to assess whether
each trusteeship has met these criteria.

The Department of Justice's Organized Crime and Racketeering
Section[1] and its National Institute of Justice are logical candidates to
evaluate civil RICO union trusteeships.[2] We desperately need an ongoing "Program for the Evaluation of Civil RICO Union Litigation"
that would carry out or contract for case studies, conferences, and
workshops; store and index key documents; and encourage empirical
research. Such a unit could draw on the vast experience of trustees in
other institutional-reform cases involving schools, prisons and jails,
and mental hospitals.[3] It might also prove useful to examine the experiences of democratic reform initiatives in eastern European countries.

THE POTENTIAL AND LIMITS OF CIVIL RICO

Civil RICO appears to be the best available weapon for combating labor racketeering. Without any new investigation, federal prosecutors can bring a civil RICO action following up on previous criminal prosecutions against union officials and organized crime figures who have dominated and exploited a particular union. Indeed, the very preparation of a civil RICO labor racketeering complaint can be an important step toward conceptualizing the problem. Properly drafted, the complaint will identify the roles of and relationship between organized crime figures and union officers in exploiting the union. The litany of past crimes will reveal patterns of intimidation, fraud, extortion, and all manner of corruption.

A comprehensive, fully documented civil RICO complaint is important because, in the absence of a trial, it will serve as the historical and sociological record of labor racketeering in the union. (Unfortunately, these complaints have not been stored in a database nor can they be obtained without considerable effort.) There has been only one full-fledged trial (IBT Local 560) among the twenty civil RICO union cases and one preliminary injunction hearing in which significant testimony was presented (Roofer's Local 30/30B). The rest of the cases were settled. The U.S. attorneys have been extraordinarily successful in obtaining the relief that they asked for, but, in most cases, this relief has not been adequate to remedy the racketeering problem. (My own impressionistic conclusions about the success of all twenty-one civil RICO union trusteeships are presented in Table 12-1.)

For at least two reasons, the settlements in the civil RICO union cases have not been carefully enough thought through. The first reason is that it is a formidable undertaking to analyze thoroughly the labor racketeering problem in a union local, much less a district council or a huge national/international union. Ideally, the U.S. attorney, the judge, and the trustee would want to know a great deal about the industry's economics and labor relations; the history of the racketeer-ridden union; the history of organized crime in the geographic area in which the union operates; the demographics of the union members; the nature of the union members' employment; and the union members' relationships with and attitudes toward their union and employers. In other words, in an ideal world, a U.S. attorney would have a complete case study of the targeted union *before filing the civil RICO suit*.

Table 12-1

Evaluation of Civil RICO Union Trusteeships

Union	Organized Crime Associates Expelled	Elections	Conclusion and Sources
IBT Local 560	The entire Provenzano clique was expunged. The consent decree terminating the trusteeship continued to make knowing association with organized crime members, or with individuals previously expelled from the union, a union-expelled offense.	In December 1998, the Sciarra slate, associated with the Provenzanos, received only 20% of the vote, while a reform slate led by Pete Brown garnered 55%.	Success. Stier, Anderson & Malone, LLC, *The Teamsters Perception and Reality*, 380–83 (2002). Jacobs and Santore, "The Liberation of IBT Local 560," (2001).
LIUNA Local 6A	After the consent decree was signed, 16 of the 25 officers of Local 6A and the District Council resigned their positions, but remained in the union. Nine defendants were allowed to keep their positions.	Neither the 1987 nor 1990 election produced any challengers to the clique that controlled the union.	Failure. The trustee himself did not believe that much was accomplished. Ieromino, "Note, RICO: Is It a Panacea or a Bitter Pill for Labor Unions, Union Democracy and Collective Bargaining?" (1994).
Philadelphia Roofers' Local 30/30B	13 officers removed as a result of a criminal case preceding the civil RICO lawsuit.	Formally fair elections were held, but there was no break with the previous regime. The same clique retained power.	Failure. On March 28, 2003, the Roofers International petitioned the court for a preliminary injunction and imposed its own trustee over the local. *United Union of Roofers v. Composition Roofers Union*, Local 30, 2003 WL 2125062 7 (E.D. Pa. March 28, 2003). Jacobs, Cunningham, and Friday, "The RICO Trusteeships after 20 Years" (2004).
IBT International	Independent Administrator Lacey, and after the 1991 election the Independent Review Board, acted as trier of fact and sentencing authority on almost 500 charges brought by Carberry. There was a massive purge of organized-crime-associated union officers.	The IBT held competitive elections in 1991, 1996, 1998 (re-run) and 2001. None of the old mob-connected clique remains on the GEB.	Provisional success. It is very difficult, however, to assess the situation that exists throughout a million-plus-member union. Jacobs, Panarella and Worthington, *Busting the Mob*, 175–76 (1994). Stier, Anderson & Malone, LLC, *The Teamsters: Perception and Reality* 339–41 (2002).
IBT Local 295	All executive board members except one were expelled from the union. A handpicked successor was also expelled (and subsequently murdered).	No elections.	Probable failure. Still in progress. A 2002 study by the Teamsters International suggests that there is still organized crime influence in the local. Stier, Anderson & Malone, LLC, *The Teamsters: Perception and Reality* 417 (2002).

New York District Council of Carpenters	Several union officials with ties to organized crime were purged from the union.	The 1995 elections resulted in election of members of the clique that had dominated the union for decades. A 1997 international trusteeship removed the District Council's officers. In 1999, Michael Forde was elected president. Subsequently, he was convicted of taking bribes.	Failure. Michael Forde and other officials convicted of taking payoffs from contractors. Jacobs and Stohner, "Ten Years of Court Supervised Reform" (2004).
HEREIU Local 54	Monitor forced eight officers from office, but they remained in the union.	1993 and 1996 elections resulted in a clear break with the old regime.	Success. Jacobs, Cunningham, and Friday, "The RICO Trusteeships after Twenty Years" (2004).
HEREIU Local 100	President and business manager and vice president were enjoined from participating in the affairs of the local. Consent Decree, United States v. Anthony R. Amodeo, Sr., et al. 92 Civ. 7744 (S.D.N.Y. 1992).	The appointed trustee was elected to lead the local, and then re-elected.	Substantially successful. The trustee's last report to the court said that there was no longer "even a hint of organized crime influence." Interview with Mary Shannon Little (Nov. 2002).
IBT Local 282	Three Local 282 stewards removed for committing acts of corruption and for associating with Gambino LCN family members.	Unknown	Unclear. Department of Labor, Office of Inspector General, 1996 Report, available at www.oig.dol.gov/public/reports/sar/sar0996/olr2.htm.
IBT Local 851	As of 2002, 32 members had been disciplined; nine had resigned or been expelled.	Competitive elections held April 2001	Possible success. "Given the deep entrenchment organized crime had for decades in . . . Local 851 . . . the combined actions of law enforcement, . . . Local 851's monitorship and the Teamsters themselves must be viewed as an overall success." Stier, Anderson & Malone, LLC, The Teamsters: Perception and Reality 416 (2002).
Mason Tenders' NYC District Council	More than a score of officials ousted, including several who were alleged soldiers in the Genovese crime family.	The election officer drafted election rules for the 1997 election, recommending that 16 of the approximately 70 candidates for union office be disqualified; the Monitor disqualified 15. United States v. MTDC, 1997 WL 340993 (S.D.N.Y. 1997).	Failure. In September, 2004, the District Council and Local 79 entered into voluntary supervision by LIUNA International. Five top officers resigned; two are facing criminal charges. Hearing on "Impediments to Union Democracy," Before the Subcomm. on Employer-Employee Relations of the House Comm. on Educ. and the Workforce, 105th Cong. (May 4, 1998) (statement of Michael S. Bearse, General Counsel LIUNA).

(continued)

Table 12-1 (continued)

Union	Organized Crime Associates Expelled	Elections	Conclusion and Sources
LIUNA International	More than 300 officials and members have been expelled or forced to resign due to disciplinary changes. LIUNA has imposed more than 40 trusteeships and "supervisions" of various locals and subordinate entities for ties to OC, financial mismanagement or lack of democratic processes. These trusteeships and supervisions have resulted in the removal of approximately 200 officers and the implementation of better financial management and greater democracy.	Election procedures have been reformed. Monitor considered 1996 general elections a limited success. But there has been no decisive change in leadership.	Substantially successful. Very difficult, though, to assess whole International Union. *See, e.g.,* Stephanie Mencimer, "Ex-FBI Official Pulls at Union's Infamous Roots," *Washington Post,* June 7, 1998.
HEREIU International	Muellenberg permanently barred 23 individuals from participating in union affairs because of organized crime associations or failure to cooperate with the monitor. Two individuals were barred for 13 years, and two individuals for three years.	Muellenberg reviewed more than 1064 candidates for election to local union office, approved 64 elections, and postponed or invalidated 3 elections. No decisive change in the International Union's leadership, but current president enjoys an outstanding reputation as a progressive union leader.	Substantially successful. However, it is very difficult to assess whole International Union. National Legal and Policy Center, *Letter to Muellenberg, HERE Public Review Board Member,* Aug. 30, 1999, *at* www.nlpc.org/olap/HERE/990830KM .htm.
Chicago Laborers' District Council	Bloch removed all former CLDC officers, instituted reform policies, and negotiated a new 3-year labor contract for the locals that provided for higher wages, better benefits, and, for the first time, a grievance procedure. The Monitor filed charges against two CLDC officials who are the sons of Chicago LCN figures. Charges were settled so that these two individuals agreed to give up their membership after two more years of union employment.	There was a contested election in 2004. The victorious business manager, president, and secretary treasurer are all unconnected to the old regime.	Unclear. There are still rumors of organized crime influence in some of the locals that comprise the District Council. National Legal and Policy Center, *Union Corruption Update,* September 10, 2001.
LIUNA Local 210 (Buffalo)	30 union members and officials expelled.	One round of competitive elections held. Appears to be a break with several decades of domination by Buffalo organized crime family. Elections did not bring a reform regime to power. Judge re-imposed trusteeship almost a decade after first trusteeship ended.	Unclear. Still in progress.
HEREIU Local 69	No elections have been held. 2002 trusteeship imposed.		Unclear. Still in progress. Administrator appointed by trustee convicted of embezzlement. Local 69 to be merged out of existence.

ILA Local 1588			Failure. The trusteeship imposed in 1991 has to be judged a failure. A second-round trusteeship, imposed in 2003, is on-going. John Timpanaro was installed as ILA Local 1588 president in January 2002. In May 2002 he was indicted on charges of racketeering and extortion. Larry McShane, "On the Waterfront, in the Courtroom; Storied New Jersey Union Local Faces Another Racketeering Trial This Spring," *Washington Post*, Jan. 4, 2004. On January 29, 2003, Federal Judge John S. Martin, Jr. appointed former New York City Police Commissioner Robert McGuire as trustee. McGuire chose Robert Stewart as his deputy. National Legal and Policy Center, *Union Corruption Update*, February 3, 2003.
ILA Local 1814	Several officers had to resign.		Failure. On June 3, 2002, 17 members and associates of the Gambino crime family or officials of ILA Local 1814, including Local 1814 President Frank Scollo, were arrested and indicted for racketeering. The indictment included charges of placing organized crime members in top union jobs and carrying out day-to-day extortion and loan sharking. James Jacobs and Ellen Peters, *Labor Racketeering: The Mafia and the Unions*, 30 Crime and Justice 229, 270 (2003).
ILA Local 1804-1	Some union officers expelled.	Elections did not achieve clear break with past.	Failure.
ILA Locals 824, 1809, 1909 (Manhattan West Side locals)	As part of the consent decree, several officials agreed to resign. Anthony Scotto banned for life. But the locals remained in the hands of the same clique that had dominated for decades.	Elections did not achieve clear break with past.	Failure. A new wave of indictments in 2003 allege the same types of racketeering as in previous decades.

The second reason that settlements have not been adequately thought through is that neither federal enforcement agencies nor federal prosecutorial offices have expertise in carrying out such analyses. Law enforcement agencies and prosecutors are experts in investigations, case preparation, and trial practice. A different set of skills is necessary for succeessful organizational reform. Unfortunately, this expertise has not been incorporated into central DOJ or into the U.S. attorney's offices. Perhaps it is still not too late for the DOJ to establish a unit devoted to union reform or to organizational reform generally. A second-best approach would be for the DOJ to identify a core of consultants (including those FBI and DOL investigators, prosecutors, trustees, and union officials who have performed best in previous cases) to whom U.S. attorneys could turn for assistance as need arises.

To add complications, unless the DOJ can specify the organization and operation of the trusteeship and the identity of the trustee, there is no guarantee that the judge will choose the right trustee and provide the necessary support for the trusteeship. During the remedial phase of civil RICO litigation, the court and court-appointed trustee, not the DOJ, are the chief actors. Frequently, the judge knows very little about the extent of the problem (hence, another reason that the civil RICO complaints should be rich in detail).

In designing trusteeships and choosing trustees, much can be learned from the history of prison and jail litigation and the rich academic literature that it has spawned.[4] The prison and jail litigation has produced a corps of experienced trustees who have developed expertise as, in effect, "turn-around specialists." These individuals go from one case to another; sometimes they supervise several cases in different states at the same time. Federal district court judges presiding over jail and prison conditions of confinement litigation seem amenable to choosing a trustee with a proven track record. So far, this has not been true of the civil RICO union cases.

There is no script for sucessfully performing as a trustee. However, the likelihood that the government, court, and trustee will get it right would be greatly increased if there were a reservoir of information about previous trusteeships. It is incomprehensible, with stakes this high, that the government has not made an effort to evaluate the union trusteeships or even to document the basic facts. We need answers to many questions: Did the DOJ lawyers name the correct defendants? Which consent decree provisions are most important? Did government lawyers seek and obtain key union officers' resignations? What trustee-ship powers are most important? How much money is necessary to support an effective trusteeship? How should the trusteeship be organized? What is the most valuable background for a trustee? How should trustees be compensated? How many hours per week should the trustee devote to the job? Is it essential for the trustee to maintain a presence at union headquarters? When, how often, and under what circumstances should the trustee meet with union members? What kind of investigative and union administrative support services does the trustee require? What should be the trusteeship's duration? What remedial strategies work best? What criteria can the trustee and the court use to determine whether the trusteeship has achieved its goal(s)? When and how should the trusteeship be terminated? To date, these questions remain unanswered and mostly unasked.

Civil RICO complaints seeking to liberate racketeer-ridden labor unions need to produce settlements with provisions that make knowing association with LCN members (or any expelled union members) a union expellable offense. However, a provision by itself is of little value. There must be investigators to ferret out relationships between union officials and organized crime members and associates. There must be disciplinary actions to prove such connections and to press for the imposition of effective penalties. Such ongoing investigative and disciplinary work may alienate union members who are suspicious of government officials and/or easily persuaded by charges leveled against the government reform effort (e.g., represents right-wing Republican agenda; will bankrupt the union). Therefore, "winning hearts and minds" of rank-and-file members should not be ignored. Here again, there may be much to learn from the experiences of court-appointed trustees who have sought to reform schools, jails, prisons and mental hospitals.

Finally, we need to recognize that reforming a union is even harder and more complicated than purging organized crime from a union. We can hardly celebrate the success of a civil RICO lawsuit and trusteeship if Cosa Nostra's influence is replaced by the influence of another group of labor racketeers. Throughout U.S. labor history there have been corrupt union strongmen, independent of organized crime families, who have exploited their unions. One example is Tony Boyle of the United Mine Workers. He was ultimately convicted of ordering the murder of insurgent Jock Yablonski and his family.[5] It is not difficult to find contemporary examples. Recently, for example, the Manhattan District Attorney's Office proved extensive corruption in New York City's District Council 37 of the American Federation of State, County, and Municipal Employees (AFSCME),[6] a union representing 105,000 city employees in 56 locals. Since 1998, there have been more than 30 indictments and more than 20 guilty pleas. According to Manhattan District Attorney Robert Morgenthau, "This is not an anti-labor prosecution. It's a pro-labor prosecution. The victims were the union members."[7]

Admittedly, "independent labor racketeers" can more easily be thrown out by rank-and-file reformers or by government prosecutors than Cosa Nostra labor racketeers. Nevertheless, "independents" can do great harm. Such individuals need to be identified and removed from union affairs before they become so formidable that neither ordinary elections nor ordinary crime control techniques are capable of dislodging them and their cohorts. This threat highlights the need for some kind of institutionalized union corruption and racketeering watchdog, the equivalent of the Security and Exchange Commission (SEC), which, since the 1930s, has monitored, investigated, and brought civil actions against and prosecuted corporate corruption. Enough time has passed to demonstrate clearly that the Department of Labor cannot play this role. It is, and likely must be, too closely associated with labor union officialdom. Perhaps the labor racketeering unit in the main DOJ can fulfill this function, but because administrations change and priorities wax and wane in Washington, D.C., it would be better to institutionalize such a watchdog in a new governmental agency patterned after the SEC.

FAIR ELECTIONS

Elections are a basic and essential method for principals to hold their agents accountable. They provide an opportunity for the electorate to "throw the rascals out" and replace them with agents who represent their interests. But there are real barriers to the union members playing this monitoring role. First, there is a collective action problem. The vast majority of union members are unwilling to invest much time and energy into monitoring their unions. Second, it is difficult to monitor a union, especially a racketeer-ridden union that operates without transparency. The racketeers control practically all information about how the union is being run; they control the union magazine or newsletter and use it as a proincumbent propaganda sheet. A union member who asks to see documents or who publicly questions the officials may cease getting job assignments, lose his or her job, or face physical intimidation and violence. In other words, for rank-and-file union members monitoring costs are extremely high.

Because of the incumbent regime's control over information, union members often do not understand how they are being exploited. They might not realize that their collective bargaining agreements are mediocre or worse. They might be impressed by good paper agreements that, in practice, are not enforced by union officials who take bribes. They may think their pension benefits are excellent only to find when they retire that they face all sorts of hurdles in qualifying for any benefits or that the fund itself has been inexplicably depleted. They might be so used to union business as usual that they cannot conceive of an honestly run union.

Even if union members realize that they have been exploited, they may be unable to vote the incumbents out of office. Many unions have *never* had a competitive election. A competitive election cannot occur without a mobilized opposition, but it is very difficult for opposition to form in the face of intimidation; it is especially difficult when union members are scattered over numerous small work sites throughout a large geographical area. The logistical difficulties of preparing and implementing a fair election should not be minimized. There are experienced organizations capable of providing expert assistance, but it cannot be done "on the cheap."

Federal prosecutors who prepare civil RICO complaints should demand fair elections and the resources, expertise, and monitoring services that can make fair elections possible. The trustee needs to draft election rules carefully, giving attention to nominating procedures, access to membership lists and the union magazine, secret balloting, and honest counting.

One of the toughest and most important decisions for a trustee is when to schedule a new election. On the one hand, the supervising judge and the union members may be impatient to return the union to its membership. On the other hand, an electoral victory for the LCN-backed regime is a major setback to the reform effort. It is essential that

the trustee have the authority to screen candidates and eliminate indi-
vid-uals with ties to the old regime. Nevertheless, experience shows
that labor racketeers do not cede power easily; they have many ingen-
uous strategies for maintaining their control through front men and
proxies. What happens if the LCN-backed faction wins the election? If
the trus-tee accepts the results, the rank and file may conclude that the
trusteeship is a sham. If the trustee rejects the results, the trusteeship's
opponents will condemn the judge and the trustee for being antidemo-
cratic and antilabor. Thus, it is crucial that the trustee prevent such a result from occurring by delaying the election until new union leadership
has emerged. It is also essential that the trustee be empowered to monitor more than one election cycle because the labor racketeers can easily
rebound after a single election defeat.

THE IMPORTANCE OF UNION DEMOCRACY

Ever since the McClellan Committee turned a spotlight on labor racketeering, would-be union reformers have recommended union democracy as medicine. They argue that a union that has significant member
involvement, contested elections, and respect for members' right to be
politically active within the union will be resistant to racketeer takeovers. But these are difficult preconditions to achieve. Practically no
unions have stable "parties" or regularly contested elections. Practically
all unions are controlled and governed by cliques that retain power in-
definitely. Contested elections, which occur very rarely, are almost always the result of a schism within the ruling clique. Perhaps this is a
confirmation of Robert Michels's axiom that all organizations evolve in
the direction of oligarchy.[8] Perhaps it reflects the fact that America's
mainstream labor movement has opposed union democracy? Perhaps
it reflects the fact that because union officials have no career paths beyond their union positions? Whatever the reasons, the lack of democracy (at least competitive elections) is a long-standing reality that civil
RICO union litigation is unlikely to change.

Making union democracy a reality would require a major commitment from the government or perhaps from one of the large private
philanthropic foundations. New legal and other initiatives could build
on the dedicated, but weak, union democracy movement comprising
rank-and-file union activists, intellectuals, and a few not-for-profit or-

ganizations.[*9] Its idealistic proponents champion union democracy not as a means to defeat labor racketeering but as the basis of a healthy labor movement. They believe that only democratic unions fulfill the aspirations of the labor movement and that union democracy will nurture and strengthen democratic values in the larger society. In addition, they argue that democratic unions will have a stronger claim on union members' loyalties, thereby strengthening the union's position in contract negotiations and job actions. The union democracy proponents also believe that union members will find satisfaction and self-actualization through participation in democratic unions.

Union democracy proponents and lawyers have worked tirelessly, and with some limited success, to make union democracy a civil liberties issue. They provide an ear to union members who complain they have been mistreated by corrupt union officials. They file suits with the Department of Labor and with the federal courts, but they are immensely outgunned by the unions that they challenge.[10] The torch has been courageously carried for decades by the minuscule Association for Union Democracy, which operates on a shoestring budget with a handful of staff. The country would be very well served by a governmental or, better yet, a private foundation's serious funding of AUD or some new "Center for Union Democracy."

REGIME CHANGE

A racketeer-ridden union needs an entirely new leadership cadre both to break ties with the past and to shatter the perception that the union is in league with the devil. This is a formidable challenge for federal prosecutors, federal judges, and trustees. Where will new union leadership come from? If for decades the incumbents controlled the union's administration and all its officers, there may be no members who have administrative and governing experience. How will new union leaders be trained? If they are chosen by the government, court, or trustees, the rank and file may regard them as stooges. Ideally, a group of union

---

* Two prominent union democracy NGOs are the Association for Union Democracy (see http://www.uniondemocracy.com) and Labor Notes (see http://www.labornotes.org/index.html). Teamsters for a Democratic Union (TDU) is the most prominent rank-and-file union reform organization (see http://www.tdu.org/TDU_Info/tdu_info.html).

reformers with expertise could move from union to union in trusteeship situations, helping to stimulate regime change. Additionally, their jobs would be easier and more likely to result in success if they could offer members of the liberated union an opportunity to attend a union leadership training program run by organized labor itself. Perhaps the highly regarded labor institutes run by some of the large industrial-type unions could be induced to train a certain number of rank-and-file union members from racketeer-ridden unions currently in trusteeship. Perhaps there is a role for some of the university-based labor programs to provide training. Perhaps wholly new program providers are needed. However it is done, it is clear that identifying, training, and nurturing new union leadership is absolutely essential.

CONCLUSION

The civil RICO union trusteeships have been the best weapon yet devised for attacking labor racketeering. A few have clearly been successful; most have achieved no more than limited successes; many have utterly failed. There is good reason to believe that the civil RICO trusteeship methodology has not yet come close to reaching its full potential. We need a systematic program for collecting data on and evaluating trusteeships. If any doubt remains, it is now time to recognize that reforming racketeer-ridden unions is extremely difficult. There is no magic wand. Naming a former federal prosecutor, now serving as a partner in a prestigious law firm, as trustee and exhorting him to reform the union will not suffice. Effective trusteeships need immense preplanning; comprehensive analysis of the specific labor racketeering problem; careful attention to the civil RICO complaint and settlement; proper empowerment and financing of the trusteeship; shrewd choice of a trustee; a well-thought-through program of reform; an evaluation strategy and patience. We have enough experience to know that success is very hard to achieve.

A successful campaign against labor racketeering requires a sustained attack on organized crime. Both the general anti–organized crime campaign and the more specific anti–labor racketeering initiatives must be supported by adequate resources and conducted with skill and determination. Whether this kind of law enforcement pressure can be maintained in the future is an open question. Al Qaeda's September 11, 2001, attacks on New York City and Washington D.C. led to the reorganization and redeployment of FBI resources. The FBI's top priority now is antiterrorism.[11] For the foreseeable future, the FBI will be judged on how well it carries out its antiterrorism mission. This fact casts a long shadow over future anti–labor racketeering initiatives, especially in the absence of a substantial non-law-enforcement constituency for the anti–organized crime and anti–labor racketeering efforts.

13

Concluding Reflections

I know from experience that some readers will disagree with my assertion that this is a prolabor book, but I do insist upon it. There is nothing anti-American about exposing the horror of U.S. slavery. There is nothing antifamily about exposing the tragedy of family violence. There is nothing antibusiness or anti–capitalist system in analyzing corporate accounting frauds. Indeed, these are all necessary in order to make progress in race relations, family policy and women's rights, and corporate accountability. Likewise, there is nothing antilabor about exposing and explaining organized crime's infiltration and exploitation of the labor movement. Indeed, the heroes of this book are those labor leaders and rank and filers who opposed and struggled against labor racketeering, sometimes at the cost of their lives.

We can learn much about various institutions and organizations by examining how they react to and seek to prevent corruption. This book does not compare labor unions with other institutions and organizations. There is no suggestion that labor unions are more corrupt than, for example, corporations, government, or the legal profession. Indeed, as I complete this book, the United States is experiencing the greatest wave of corporate frauds in our history. Those frauds and corruption in other institutions, organizations, and professions demand their own analyses. To be sure, there will be commonalities, but there will also be significant differences. The most distinctive feature of corruption in the labor movement is the prominent role of the Cosa Nostra organized crime families. This entanglement makes the problem exceptionally difficult to solve.

IS THERE SOMETHING ABOUT UNIONS?

One might well ask whether there is something unique about labor unions that accounts for their attraction and vulnerability to organized

254

crime. In support of that thesis one might call on Robert Michels's "iron law of oligarchy": Organizations evolve toward concentration of power at the top. But Michels meant to posit a rule that would hold true for all organizations, not just or primarily unions. More important, labor racketeering is not just or primarily a story of authoritarian union governance; it is a story of Cosa Nostra infiltration and exploitation.

Unions may well have a distinctive susceptibility to organized crime racketeering. They are attractive targets because they receive a constant flow of dues and pension and welfare contributions that employers automatically deduct from workers' pay. Cosa Nostra has no compunctions about using violence and election fraud; it has expertise in both these methods of seizing organizational control. Once in power, labor racketeers can reinforce control through the many carrots and sticks at their disposal. They also benefit from the absence of competition from other organizations; once a union is recognized as a bargaining unit's exclusive representative, AFL-CIO rules prohibit other unions from challenging that representation.

Perhaps unions are exceptionally difficult for insiders or outsiders to monitor. Very few union members take a strong interest in union governance and, as we have seen, labor racketeers can make the costs of monitoring very high by means of violence, intimidation, and control over information. By contrast, public corporations are more easily monitored by boards of directors, stockholders, the business press, investing institutions, and the Securities and Exchange Commission (SEC). The SEC enjoys an excellent reputation as a well-resourced, independent, competent, and vigorous enforcement agency. Of course, neither it nor the other corporate monitors prevented Enron and the other corporate frauds that looted billions of dollars from corporations, stockholders, and creditors. Nevertheless, these corporate scandals have not been blamed on the SEC or undermined confidence in its regulatory role. If there had been an SEC-like agency responsible for monitoring union violations of Landrum-Griffin, ERISA, and other labor laws, it would certainly have been more difficult for labor racketeers to have taken over and exploited unions. We have seen, however, that with the exception of sporadic congressional investigations and quixotic individual union member protests, labor racketeering was practically unopposed for most of the twentieth century. By the time the FBI and the Department of Justice began to focus on labor racketeering, racketeers were deeply and powerfully entrenched.

A structural explanation may be most useful for explaining why some unions were taken over by organized crime while others were not. For the most part, the racketeering susceptibility of the old CIO industrial unions was low. There was strength in numbers. Union leaders who work alongside hundreds or thousands of other workers in a factory or mine were much harder to intimidate or otherwise displace than union leaders who work for a hotel, trucking company, or construction contractor with a relatively small and/or dispersed workforce marked by high turnover. Likewise, it is much easier for opposition leaders to become known and develop a following when they work in a large site like a factory or a mine. In those industries, employees may work for the same company for many years, even for life. On the other hand, many workers in construction, trucking, hotels and restaurants, and stevedoring work sporadically and for different employers.

There is little or nothing new in labor racketeering. The same organized crime families have engaged in the same type of exploitation for much of the twentieth century. Union officers in racketeer-ridden unions often "inherit" their positions from fathers and grandfathers. The forms of domination that appeared in the 1920s and 1930s still prevail. The cartels, bribes for sweetheart deals, extortion of employers, embezzlements from union treasuries, and frauds on pension and welfare funds all have their roots in the first half of the century.

CONTINGENCIES OF AMERICAN HISTORY

The persistence of labor racketeering is dependent on certain contingencies of American history. Obviously, there would have been no organized crime penetration without the existence of a powerful organized crime syndicate with the expertise and motivation to exploit labor unions, businesses, and industries. Cosa Nostra did not always have to fight its way in the door; it was often invited inside. The bitter opposition of employers to labor unions, including the recruitment of strike breakers and gangsters, created labor's need for a counterforce. Not surprisingly, some organized crime figures who helped to defend labor unions earned the rank and file's gratitude. It was also fortuitous for the labor racketeers that in many nascent unions there was a congenial ethnic base.

It would be naive and factually incorrect to think that labor racketeering developed "under the radar." To the contrary, labor racketeering was consciously permitted, even chosen. Employers would have preferred no unions but, in many cases, they found Cosa Nostra labor racketeers preferable to leftist militant unionists who were ideologically opposed to the capitalist system. We should not forget or discount the willingness of employers to reach out to organized crime figures to obtain sweetheart collective bargaining contracts and the nonenforcement of expensive contractual provisions. Perhaps even more valuable to employers was the role that organized crime figures could play in creating and policing business cartels that fixed prices and limited competition. Such cartels have been commonplace in industries like construction and trucking. Organized crime bosses also functioned as power brokers who could quickly solve jurisdictional disputes between unions and could broker deals with businessmen and politicians.

Throughout most of the twentieth century, especially the first half, the government did not combat organized crime labor racketeers. In the big eastern and midwestern cities where unions and organized crime were strongest, local politicians closely cooperated with the organized crime bosses; frequently there was a symbiotic relationship between the Democratic Party political machines and the organized crime families. The urban political machines could make or break local, state, and national political candidates. Local police and prosecutors, highly politicized in those days, were often influenced, bribed, or intimidated by organized crime groups, or at least unwilling to oppose them. Even if law enforcement was not compromised, it lacked the resources to oppose them. The organized crime bosses were not nearly as influential at the state and federal levels as they were at the local levels, but their influence extended to the highest levels of American politics and government.

For reasons specific to American federalism, there was no federal national police force until the first decade of the twentieth century; even then, the FBI evolved very slowly. Under J. Edgar Hoover's half century of leadership, the FBI was far more concerned with communists, socialists, and other perceived subversives than with city-based organized crime families. Indeed, the FBI, on occasion was willing to form alliances with Cosa Nostra to assure, for example, the security of the ports during World War II and the assassination of Cuban President Fidel Castro in the early 1960s. Remarkably, the FBI posed no significant opposition to organized crime until after Hoover's death in 1972.

Fear and abhorrence of communism and socialism was another

contingency of twentieth-century American history that facilitated labor racketeering. Governments at all levels, but especially the federal and state levels, viewed leftist labor leaders with antipathy and anxiety. They were often willing to use governmental resources to suppress such leaders and their unions even if it meant allying with organized crime figures. American politicians in the first half of the twentieth century were also more comfortable dealing with organized crime bosses than with communists and socialists. New York City mayors William O'Dwyer (1946–1950) and Vincent Impellitteri (1950–1953), for example, were said to have had close relationships with Frank Costello, so-called "prime minister of the underworld" and the top New York City Cosa Nostra figure of his day.

The first alarms about labor racketeering were sounded by social reformers concerned about the plight of oppressed longshoremen. Then investigative journalists found labor racketeering to be a compelling story. *On the Waterfront* contributed greatly to making labor racketeering a public issue. Perhaps the publicity generated by the movie forced the government to respond? But, one need not be a cynic to recognize that it was not the plight of the workers and their lack of rights vis-à-vis their unions that first got Congress involved. Clearly, Senator McClellan and other (especially southern) senators were as much, probably more worried about unions growing too strong than they were about the plight of rank-and-file union members. In the McClellan Committee hearings, concern about the dangers of "big labor" combined with concern about the dangers of "the Mafia," perceived at the time as a foreign-based ethnic threat to the American way of life.

There was never an interest group pressing for the protection of union members' rights against corrupt union leaders. The FBI's post-Hoover initiatives against labor racketeering were the result of the larger war against organized crime. By the mid-1970s, the Department of Justice and the FBI were affronted by the flagrant activities of the Cosa Nostra crime families in the major cities. The war on organized crime began with a campaign against Cosa Nostra's gambling interests, but that strategy encountered serious resistance among federal judges. It was the assassination of Jimmy Hoffa in 1975 that turned federal law enforcement's attention to organized crime's position in the labor unions. From that point on, the anti–labor racketeering campaign was an important part of the war against organized crime.

Congress passed RICO in 1970 to combat organized crime, especially its perceived infiltration of the legitimate economy. Organized crime's threat to unions, as well as legitimate business, was frequently mentioned at the hearings leading up to the bill's passage. However, it was not until 1982 that civil RICO was pressed into service as an anti–labor racketeering tool. The New Jersey federal prosecutors convincingly demonstrated that civil RICO was well suited for use against Cosa Nostra's domination of one of the nation's most racketeer-ridden union locals. Even then, the first lawsuits encountered substantial opposition from the labor movement, many politicians, and members of the public suspicious of the motives of the Reagan-era Department of Justice. By then, however, the Department of Justice and FBI were sufficiently independent that even if political interference had been attempted, it could not have halted the attack on labor racketeering. The FBI and DOJ campaign had taken on unstoppable momentum.

Without civil RICO there could not have been a focused anti–labor racketeering campaign. There is no other nearly as effective way to attack the kind of systemic entrenched organizational criminality in local, regional, and national labor unions. Nevertheless, civil RICO was not initially embraced by FBI agents and federal prosecutors who were much more comfortable with criminal prosecutions. Indeed, the reward system in the FBI was based upon convictions. The use of civil RICO was given a powerful shot in the arm when the FBI leadership decided to count civil RICO cases as equivalent to major convictions.

Although civil RICO has been the most important law enforcement strategy in attacking labor racketeering, it has fallen seriously short of its full potential. The majority of trusteeships have not produced regime change. Many have not produced a single fair, much less competitive, election. The majority have probably not completely purged organized crime's influence from the union. Indeed, the absence of any governmental attempt to evaluate the civil RICO union lawsuits demonstrates the lack of systematic thought about how to utilize civil RICO most effectively.

SIGNIFICANCE OF LABOR RACKETEERING FOR ORGANIZED LABOR AND SOCIETY

Asking the counterfactual question can be an interesting thought experiment that sheds light on the importance and significance of key historical events. What if Japan had not attacked Pearl Harbor? What if the Supreme Court had not declared school segregation unconstitutional in *Brown v. Board of Education?* What if organized crime labor racketeers had not infiltrated and exploited the American labor movement?

If there had been no organized crime and therefore no organized crime penetration of the labor movement, the nascent labor unions would have had more difficulty achieving early victories and ultimate recognition. It is possible that a combination of reactionary employers, politicians, and law enforcement personnel would have crushed unions completely or shaped a completely employer-dominated union movement. It is also possible that corrupt labor czars would have seized power in the very unions that organized crime racketeers eventually controlled.

In light of the fact that labor unions have achieved legitimacy in all Western countries, I think it is more likely that the Wagner Act would have eventually passed and that labor unions would have achieved legitimacy in the United States. The socialists and communists would have been a stronger force in the union movement. With unions in the hands of militant unionists, not labor racketeers, the U.S. labor movement would have been more aggressive in organizing, more appealing to youth and intellectuals and stronger.[*]

A more powerful, socialist-leaning labor movement might have had a significant impact on American politics. The United States is unusual among Western democracies for lack of a labor party. Perhaps, without labor racketeers, the U.S. labor movement would have organized a political party. Alternatively, it might have become an influential "progressive" wing of the Democratic Party, thereby having made the party's long accommodation with southern segregationists less likely. If the United States had had a twentieth-century labor party or a more leftist Democratic Party, our politics might have been completely different.

Even though the foregoing is wild speculation, it does give pause to think seriously about the importance of labor racketeering to the labor movement, U.S. politics, and U.S. society generally. The history of or-

---

[*] The leftist elements in the labor movement were by no means united or comfortable with one another. To the contrary, there were bitter ideological differences among them and these may ultimately have split and weakened the labor movement.

ganized crime and organized labor has been long neglected, even affirmatively denied. I hope this book will stimulate the kind of attention that the topic clearly warrants. One can easily imagine a dozen Ph.D. dissertations documenting how various racketeer-ridden unions actually functioned, how their members fared in comparison to the members of honest unions as well as to nonunionized workers doing the same kind of work. Perhaps, ultimately, we might identify different "types" of labor racketeers, e.g., those who pressed the interests of the workers they represented while skimming money from the union and those who essentially treated the union as an organization to be exploited to the fullest.

WHAT OF THE FUTURE?

This book is not just about days past. Labor racketeering is still occurring. Cosa Nostra still controls local and regional unions and wields influence in several important international unions. Only three of the hard-fought civil RICO union trusteeships can be judged to have been completely successful; for many of the others, it is still too early to say. Some of the trusteeships must be considered complete failures. The Cosa Nostra crime families are much weaker than they were at the height of their power (perhaps in the 1960s or 1970s), but they continue to be a presence in most of the cities where they have existed since the early twentieth century. If, as seems likely, FBI pressure on them wanes, it is possible that they will make a combat.

The effort to reform the American unions controlled by organized crime could be analyzed as an experiment in democratization "from above."[1] As with the American incursion into Iraq, those who are waging the campaign against labor racketeering believe that they can bring democracy to organizations and peoples long dominated by corrupt and autocratic leaders. The law enforcement personnel, DOJ lawyers, federal judges, and court-appointed trustees have had much more time to achieve victory over organized crime in American unions than U.S. military forces have had to achieve victory in Iraq. Nevertheless, as in Iraq, establishing democracy in previously captive labor unions is much more difficult than the "liberators" expected.

DOJ lawyers initially (and with hindsight, naively) believed that their investigators and court-appointed trustees would be welcomed by the rank and file with open arms. Two decades of experience have proved otherwise. There is far more rank-and-file suspicion of the government, the courts, and the trustees than public officials had anticipated or want to admit. The regimes backed by Cosa Nostra continue to exercise influence (even prevail) over many unions that the government and the courts have sought to reform; the Cosa Nostra–backed candidates have won more elections than they have lost.

As in the war to bring democracy to Iraq, the government has much credibility at stake in its anti–labor racketeering campaign. If it loses interest, withdraws, and allows Cosa Nostra to reconsolidate its control, it will be harder in the future to persuade criminals and would-be criminals that U.S. law enforcement has staying power. Likewise, it will be harder to persuade affected citizens to throw in their lot with the government. They will rightly fear that law enforcement will withdraw with the job only half completed.

The American labor movement has much at stake in this twenty-five-year campaign against Cosa Nostra labor racketeering. A victory over Cosa Nostra and labor racketeering could release a great deal of energy within the labor movement if previously cynical union members change their minds about the possibility of reform. It could also release a great deal of pro-union sentiment in the larger society if the labor movement could once again attract the interest and support of idealists and intellectuals. The civil RICO trusteeships should be seen as a positive opportunity for a brighter future rather than as some kind of contemporary version of early-twentieth-century government union busting.

Notes

NOTES TO THE PREFACE

1. New York State Organized Crime Task Force, *Corruption and Racketeering in the New York City Construction Industry: Final Report to Governor Mario M. Cuomo* (New York: New York University Press, 1990), 13–43.

2. Paul Siciliano, "Eyes Wide Shut: Labor Law Textbooks and the Treatment of Organized Crime's Infiltration and Use of Labor Unions," unpublished, NYU School of Law Seminar Paper, 2003. The eight textbooks examined, which span from 1982 to 1996, are Clyde W. Summers et al., *Cases and Materials On Labor Law* (1982); Bernard D. Meltzer and Stanley D. Henderson, *Labor Law: Cases, Materials and Problems* (2d ed. 1985); Douglas L. Leslie, *Cases and Materials on Labor Law: Process and Policy* (2d ed. 1985); Leroy S. Merrifield et al., *Labor Relations Law: Cases and Materials* (8th ed. 1989); Archibald Cox et al., *Cases and Materials on Labor Law* (11th ed. 1991); David P. Twomey, *Labor and Employment Law: Text and Cases* (9th ed. 1994); Walter E. Oberer et al., *Labor Law: Collective Bargaining in a Free Society* (1994); Michael C. Harper and Samuel Estreicher, *Labor Law: Cases, Materials and Problems* (4d ed. 1996).

3. John Landesco, "Organized Crime in Chicago," *The 1929 Illinois Crime Survey* (Chicago: Illinois Association for Criminal Justice, 1929).

4. Ibid., 997.

5. Ibid.

6. G. Robert Blakey, Ronald Goldstock, and Gerard Bradley, "The Investigation and Prosecution of Organized Crime and Labor Racketeering: Labor Racketeering Background Materials," Cornell Institute on Organized Crime, Summer Institute for Federal Investigators and Prosecutors (1979); G. Robert Blakey and Ronald Goldstock, "On the Waterfront: RICO and Labor Racketeering," 17 *Am. Crim. L. Rev.* 341 (1980).

7. Peter Reuter, *Racketeering in Legitimate Industries: A Study in the Economics of Intimidation* (Santa Monica: RAND, 1987).

8. Louis Adamic, *Dynamite: The Story of Class Violence in America* (New York: Chelsea House Publishers, 1958; originally published in 1931).

9. David Witwer, "The Scandal of George Scalise: A Case Study in the Rise of Labor Racketeering in the 1930s," 36 *Journal of Social History* 917 (Summer 2003).

10. Ibid., 924.

11. Ibid., 924–25.

12. Malcolm Johnson, *Crime on the Labor Front* (New York: McGraw-Hill, 1950), 35.

13. Ibid., 54.

14. Ibid., 12.

15. Ibid., 17.

16. Although hiring workers for the stevedoring companies (which loaded and unloaded cargo to and from ships) and public loading companies (which loaded and unloaded cargo to and from trucks at the piers) was technically the employers' job, the hiring bosses were actually members of the ILA.

17. Daniel Bell, "Last of the Business Rackets," *Fortune Magazine*, June 1951; Bell, "The Racket-Ridden Longshoremen," in *The End of Ideology* (New York: Free Press, 1960), 175–209.

18. Philip Taft, *Corruption and Racketeering in the Labor Movement* (Ithaca: New York State School of Industrial and Labor Relations, Cornell University, 1958).

19. Ibid., 33–34.

20. Sidney Lens, *Crisis in American Labor* (New York: Sagamore Press, 1959), 108.

21. Ibid., 112.

22. John Hutchinson, *The Imperfect Union: A History of Corruption in American Trade Unions* (New York: Dutton, 1972).

23. New York State Organized Crime Task Force, *Corruption and Racketeering in the New York City Construction Industry.*

24. Blakey, Goldstock, and Bradley, "The Investigation and Prosecution of Organized Crime and Labor Racketeering."

25. Stephen Fox, *Blood and Power: Organized Crime in Twentieth-Century America* (New York: William Morrow, 1989), 174–220; Virgil W. Peterson, *The Mob: 200 Years of Organized Crime in New York* (Ottawa, Ill.: Green Hill, 1983), 122–34, 277–93.

26. Howard Abadinsky, *Organized Crime,* 7th ed. (Chicago: Nelson Hall, 2002), 245–76.

27. Ibid., 245.

28. Gus Russo, *The Outfit: The Role of Chicago's Underworld in the Shaping of Modern America* (New York: Bloomsbury, 2001).

29. Reuter, *Racketeering in Legitimate Industries.*

30. John Kobler, *Capone: The Life and World of Al Capone* (New York: Putnam, 1971); Mary E. Stolberg, *Fighting Organized Crime: Politics, Justice, and the Legacy of Thomas E. Dewey* (Boston: Northeastern University Press, 1995); Peter Maas, *Underboss: Sammy the Bull Gravano's Story of Life in the Mafia* (New York: Harper-Collins, 1997); James Neff, *Mobbed Up: Jackie Presser's High-Wire Life in the Team-*

sters, the Mafia, and the FBI (New York: Atlantic Monthly Press, 1989); Walter Sheridan, *The Fall and Rise of Jimmy Hoffa* (New York: Saturday Review Press, 1972); Lester Velie, *Desperate Bargain: Why Jimmy Hoffa Had to Die* (New York: Reader's Digest Press, 1977); Arthur Sloane, *Hoffa* (Cambridge: MIT Press, 1991); Dan E. Moldea, *The Hoffa Wars: Teamsters, Rebels, Politicians and the Mob* (New York: Paddington Press, 1978); Thaddeus Russell, *Out of the Jungle: Jimmy Hoffa and the Remaking of the American Working Class* (New York: Alfred A. Knopf, 2001).

31. Stier, Anderson and Malone, LLC, *The Teamsters: Perception and Reality: An Investigative Study of Organized Crime Influence in the Union* (Washington, D.C.: International Brotherhood of Teamsters, 2002); Steven Brill, *The Teamsters* (New York: Simon and Schuster, 1978); Neff, *Mobbed Up.*

32. President's Commission on Organized Crime, *The Edge: Organized Crime, Business, and Labor Unions* (Washington, D.C.: President's Commission on Organized Crime, 1986).

33. Dan La Botz, *Rank and File Rebellion: Teamsters for a Democratic Union* (London: Verso Books, 1990). Critical review by Jonathan Tasini in *Nation*, March 25, 1991, 387–88; Herman Benson, *Rebels, Reformers and Racketeers: How Insurgents Transformed the Labor Movement* (Bloomington, Ind.: AuthorHouse, 2004).

34. Blakey and Goldstock, "On the Waterfront."

35. Ibid., 365.

36. Michael J. Goldberg, "Cleaning Labor's House: Institutional Reform Litigation in the Labor Movement," *Duke L.J.* 903 (1989).

37. James B. Jacobs and Alex Hortis, "New York City as Organized Crime Fighter," 42 *N.Y.L. Sch. L. Rev.* 1069 (1998).

38. James B. Jacobs and Kristin Stohner, "Ten Years of Court-Supervised Reform: A Chronicle and Assessment," 6 *California Law Review* 3 (2004).

39. James B. Jacobs, Eileen Cunningham, and Kimberly Friday, "The RICO Trusteeship After 20 Years: A Progress Report," 19 *Labor Lawyer* 419 (2004).

NOTES TO CHAPTER I

1. See, for example, Alan Block and Sean Patrick Griffin, "The Teamsters, the White House and the Labor Department," 27 *Crime, Law and Social Change* 1 (1997), 1–30.

2. John Landesco, *Organized Crime in Chicago* (Chicago: University of Chicago Press, 1968; originally published in 1929 by the Illinois Association for Criminal Justice); Harold Seidman, *Labor Czars: A History of Labor Racketeering* (New York: Liveright, 1938).

3. Robert F. Kennedy, *The Enemy Within* (New York: Harper and Row, 1960), 239.

4. Victoria C. Hatman, *Labor Visions and State Power: The Origins of Business Unionism in the United States* (Princeton: Princeton University Press, 1993).

5. Ibid.

6. 29 USC § 151.

7. See U.S. Department of Labor, Office of the Assistant Secretary for Policy at http://www.dol.gov/asp.

8. 29 USC § 141–197.

9. Peter Drucker, *The Pension Fund Revolution* (Somerset, N.J.: Transaction Publishers, 1996); originally published as *The Unseen Revolution* (New York: Harper and Row, 1976).

10. Seidman, *Labor Czars.*

11. Howard Kimeldorf, *Reds or Rackets? The Making of Radical and Conservative Unions on the Waterfront* (Berkeley: University of California Press, 1988).

12. See Gus Russo, *The Outfit: The Role of Chicago's Underworld in the Shaping of Modern America* (New York: Bloomsbury, 2001), 159.

13. Malcolm Johnson, *Crime on the Labor Front* (New York: McGraw-Hill, 1950); Sidney Lens, *The Crisis of American Labor* (New York: Sagamore Press, 1959).

14. Landesco, *Organized Crime in Chicago.*

15. Rick Porrello, *The Rise and Fall of the Cleveland Mafia* (Fort Lee, N.J.: Barricade Books, 1995); John Kobler, *Capone: The Life and World of Al Capone* (New York: Putnam, 1971); Robert Cooley and Hillel Levin, *When Corruption Was King: How I Helped the Mob Rule Chicago, Then Brought the Outfit Down* (New York: Carroll and Graf, 2004); Russo, *The Outfit.* This alliance persisted right up to the modern era; see Block and Griffin, "The Teamsters, the White House and the Labor Department."

16. Anthony Summers, *Official and Confidential: The Secret Life of J. Edgar Hoover* (New York: G. P. Putnam's Sons, 1993).

17. Richard Powers, *Secrecy and Power: The Life of J. Edgar Hoover* (New York: Free Press, 1986); Curt Gentry, *J. Edgar Hoover: The Man and His Secrets* (New York: Penguin Books, 1991).

18. Dan La Botz, *The Fight at UPS: The Teamsters' Victory and the Future of the New Labor Movement* (Solidarity Pamphlet, 1997).

19. James B. Jacobs, Christopher Panarella, and Jay Worthington III, *Busting the Mob: United States v. Cosa Nostra* (New York: New York University Press, 1994), especially Part 1.

20. James B. Jacobs and Elizabeth Mullin, "Congress' Role in the Defeat of Organized Crime," 39 (3) *Criminal Law Bulletin* 269–312 (2003).

21. New York State Crime Commission, Final Report of the New York State Crime Commission to the Governor, the Attorney General and the Legislature of the State of New York (Albany: State of New York, 1953).

22. New York Waterfront Commission Act of 1953, 67 Stat. 541, c. 407. The

Waterfront Commission has two commissioners: one appointed by the New Jersey governor, and the other by the New York State governor.

23. John Hutchinson, *The Imperfect Union: A History of Corruption in American Trade Unions* (New York: E. P. Dutton, 1970), 344–46.

24. *De Veau v. Braisted*, 363 U.S. 144, 157 (1960).

25. Kennedy, *The Enemy Within*, 265.

26. 29 USC § 501.

27. Landrum-Griffin Act (Labor Management Reporting and Disclosure Act of 1959), Title 29, U.S.C., Sections 401 et seq.; Clyde Summers, Joseph Rauh, and Herman Benson, *Union Democracy and Landrum-Griffin* (Brooklyn, N.Y.: Association For Union Democracy, 1986).

28. A House of Representatives' Select Committee on the John F. Kennedy Assassination (1979) concluded that the Mafia had the motive and the opportunity to assassinate JFK. ["That organized crime had the motive, opportunity and means to kill the President cannot be questioned."] See U.S. House of Representatives, *Report of the Select Committee on Assassinations,* 95th Cong., 2d sess., House Report No. 95-1828, Part 2, (Washington, D.C.: GPO, 1979), 161. In his autobiography, Bill Bonanno asserts that the Chicago Outfit carried out the assassination and provides details. Scholars and commentators do not seem to have given any credence to that assertion. See Bill Bonanno, *Bound by Honor: A Mafioso's Story* (New York: St. Martin's Press, 1999).

29. Jacobs et al., *Busting the Mob.*

30. G. Robert Blakey and Ronald Goldstock, "On the Waterfront: RICO and Labor Racketeering," 17 *American Criminal Law Review* 341 (1980).

31. Jacobs et al., *Busting the Mob,* 32–33; James B. Jacobs and David N. Santore, "The Liberation of IBT Local 560," *Criminal Law Bulletin* 37(2):125–58 (2001).

32. Jacobs et al., *Busting the Mob,* 183 (Appendix A).

33. Stanley Aronowitz, *From the Ashes of the Old: American Labor and America's Future* (New York: Houghton-Mifflin, 1998). The author, one of the best known liberal scholars of the labor movement, lists a number of reasons for labor's decline but does not mention the impact of actual and perceived racketeering.

34. See, e.g., Robert Bruno, *Reforming the Chicago Teamsters: The Story of Local 705* (De Kalb: Northern Illinois University Press, 2003).

35. Nelson Lichtenstein, *Walter Reuther: The Most Dangerous Man in Detroit* (Champaign: University of Illinois Press, 1995).

NOTES TO CHAPTER 2

1. Harold Seidman, *Labor Czars* (New York: Liveright, 1938); Rich Cohen, *Tough Jews: Fathers, Sons and Gangster Dreams* (New York: Vintage, 1998).

2. Seidman, *Labor Czars,* 45–47.

3. Cohen, *Tough Jews;* Albert Fried, *The Rise and Fall of the Jewish Gangster in America* (New York: Holt, Rinehart and Winston, 1980); Jenna Weissman Joselit, *Our Gang: Jewish Crime and the New York Jewish Community (1900–1940)* (Bloomington: Indiana University Press, 1983).

4. Carl Sifakis, *The Mafia Encyclopedia* (New York: Facts on File, 1987), 185.

5. Gus Russo, *The Outfit: The Role of Chicago's Underworld in the Shaping of Modern America* (New York: Bloomsbury, 2001), 221.

6. James B. Jacobs, Coleen Friel, and Robert Radick, *Gotham Unbound: How New York City Was Liberated from the Grip of Organized Crime* (New York: New York University Press, 1999), 33–47.

7. Seidman, *Labor Czars,* 112–13.

8. Russo, *The Outfit,* 125, 137.

9. Ibid., 141.

10. Ibid., 83.

11. John Kobler, *Capone: The Life and World of Al Capone* (New York: G. P. Putnam's Sons, 1971), 240.

12. Russo, *The Outfit,* 127.

13. Ibid., 148.

14. William F. Roemer, Jr., *Accardo: The Genuine Godfather* (New York: Donald I. Fine, 1996).

15. President's Commission on Organized Crime (PCOC), *The Edge: Organized Crime, Business, and Labor Unions* (Washington, D.C.: President's Commission on Organized Crime, 1986), 146.

16. Ibid., 73–74.

17. Russo, *The Outfit,* 317.

18. PCOC, *The Edge,* 92–93.

19. Rick Porrello, *The Rise and Fall of the Cleveland Mafia* (Fort Lee, N.J.: Barricade Books, 1995), 221; Jim Neff, *Mobbed Up: Jackie Presser's High-Wire Life in the Teamsters, the Mafia, and the FBI* (New York: Atlantic Monthly Press, 1989).

20. Peter Vaira and Douglas P. Roller, *Report on Organized Crime and the Labor Unions.* Prepared for the White House in 1978. Available at http://www.americanmafia.com/crime_and_labor.html.

21. A. D. Hopkins and K. J. Evans, *The First 100: Portraits of the Men and Women Who Shaped Las Vegas* (Las Vegas: Huntington Press, 2000).

22. Ken Prendergast, *Welcome to the Hotel Sterling,* AmericanMafia.Com, January 2003.

23. Neff, *Mobbed Up,* 78–79.

24. William J. Touhy, "Goodbye Tony Ducks," GamblingMagazine.Com, Article 53. Available at http://www.gamblingmagazine.com/articles/53/53-138.htm.

25. Mary E. Stolberg, *Fighting Organized Crime: Politics, Justice, and the Legacy of Thomas Dewey* (Boston: Northeastern University Press, 1995), 171.

26. Sifakis, *The Mafia Encyclopedia*, 76.

27. Joseph Berger, "Raymond Patriarca, 76, Dies; New England Crime Figure," *New York Times*, July 12, 1984, at B7.

28. Seymour M. Lipset, Martin Trow, and James Coleman, *Union Democracy: The Internal Politics of the International Typographical Union* (Glencoe, Ill.: Free Press, 1956).

29. Arthur A. Sloane, *Hoffa* (Cambridge: MIT Press, 1991), 86–87; Walter Sheridan, *The Fall and Rise of Jimmy Hoffa* (New York: Saturday Review Press, 1972), 26–27.

30. *Drywall Tapers and Pointers of Greater New York, Local 1974 of IBTAP v. Local 530 of the Operative Plasterers' and Cement Masons' International Association*, 93 CV 0154 (JG) (EDNY) (January 2005), 6.

31. David Witwer, "The Scandal of George Scalise: A Case Study in the Rise of Labor Racketeering in the 1930s," *Journal of Social History* (Summer 2003), 926.

32. Ibid., 931.

33. Malcolm Johnson, *Crime on the Labor Front* (New York: McGraw-Hill, 1950); Witwer, "The Scandal of George Scalise," 927.

34. Witwer, "The Scandal of George Scalise," 923.

35. James B. Jacobs, Christopher Panarella, and Jay Worthington III, *Busting the Mob: United States v. Cosa Nostra* (New York: New York University Press, 1994), 35.

36. James B. Jacobs and Kristin Stohner, "Ten Years of Court-Supervised Reform: A Chronicle and Assessment," 6 *California Law Review* 3 (2004).

37. John Hutchinson, *The Imperfect Union: A History of Corruption in American Trade Unions* (New York: Dutton, 1972), 364.

38. Peter Drucker, *The Pension Fund Revolution* (Somerset, N.J.: Transaction Publishers, 1996).

39. Peter Reuter, "Racketeers as Cartel Organizers," in H. Alexander and G. Caiden (eds.), *Political and Economic Perspectives on Organized Crime* (Lexington, Mass.: D. C. Heath, 1984), 49–65.

40. Seidman, *Labor Czars*, 80.

41. Stolberg, *Fighting Organized Crime*, 174.

42. Jacobs et al., *Busting the Mob*, 35–40.

43. Peter Maas, *Underboss: Sammy the Bull Gravano's Story of Life in the Mafia* (New York: HarperCollins, 1997), 116.

NOTES TO CHAPTER 3

1. President's Commission on Organized Crime (PCOC), *The Edge: Organized Crime, Business, and Labor Unions* (Washington, D.C.: President's Commission on Organized Crime, 1986), 89–90.

2. Ibid., 92, 114.

3. Ibid., 90–91.

4. Ibid., 89.

5. James Neff, *Mobbed Up: Jackie Presser's High-Wire Life in the Teamsters, the Mafia, and the FBI* (New York: Atlantic Monthly Press, 1989).

6. PCOC, *The Edge*, 123.

7. Ibid., 104.

8. Ibid., 138.

9. Ibid., 120.

10. Ibid., 72.

11. Ibid., 71.

12. Hotel Employees and Restaurant Employees International Union, Parts 1–5, Senate Committee on Governmental Affairs Permanent Subcommittee on Investigations, 1982, 9.

13. Ibid.

14. Ibid.

15. PCOC, *The Edge*, 75.

16. Ibid., 77.

17. *Brown v. HEREIU Local 54*, 468 U.S. 491 (1984).

18. PCOC, *The Edge*, 83.

19. Ibid., 160.

20. Ibid., 146.

21. Ibid., 147.

22. Ibid., 148–49.

23. Ibid., 148.

24. Ibid., 150.

25. Ibid., 153–55.

26. Ibid., 156–57.

27. Ibid., 158–59.

28. Ibid., 162–63.

29. Ibid., 33.

30. Ibid., 37.

31. Ibid., 36.

32. *De Veau v. Braisted*, 363 U.S. 144, 157–58 (1960).

33. PCOC, *The Edge*, 39.

34. Jerry Capeci, "Sonny Pays the Price to Talk," Ganglandnews.com, August 12, 1997. Available at http://www.ganglandnews.com/column40.htm.

35. Senate Permanent Subcommittee on Investigations of the Committee on Governmental Affairs, *Waterfront Corruption*, 1984.

36. PCOC, *The Edge*, 65.

37. Ibid., 172.

38. Ibid., 178.

39. Ibid., 179.

40. Ibid., 201.

41. Ibid., 307.

42. Judith R. Hope and Samuel K. Skinner, "The Crime Commission's Value," *New York Times,* April 21, 1986, at A19.

43. Kenneth B. Noble, "Kirkland Faults Justice Dept. on Union Crime," *New York Times,* March 8, 1986, at 1, 9.

NOTES TO CHAPTER 4

1. Howard Abadinsky, *Organized Crime,* 4th ed. (Chicago: Nelson Hall, 1994); Stephen Fox, *Blood and Power: Organized Crime in Twentieth-Century America* (New York: Morrow, 1989); Virgil W. Peterson, *The Mob: 200 Years of Organized Crime in New York* (Ottawa, Ill.: Green Hill, 1983).

2. James B. Jacobs, Coleen Friel, and Robert Radick, *Gotham Unbound* (New York: New York University Press, 1999), 24. See Allen Richardson, Tony DeStefano, and Thomas Moran, "Trucking Local 102: Who Sat in the Driver's Seat?" *Women's Wear Daily,* August 29, 1977, 1.

3. John S. Martin, Sentencing Memorandum, January 4, 1981, following *United States v. Romano,* 81 Cr. 514 (S.D.N.Y. 1981).

4. *United States v. Romano,* 684 F.2d 1057, 1060 (2d Cir. 1982).

5. Ibid., at 1061.

6. Jacobs et al., *Gotham Unbound,* 41.

7. Stier, Anderson and Malone, *The Teamsters: Perception and Reality: An Investigative Study of Organized Crime Influence in the Union* (Washington, D.C.: Stier, Anderson and Malone, LLC, 2002), 269; and Jacobs et al., *Gotham Unbound,* 54–55.

8. Jacobs et al., *Gotham Unbound,* 55.

9. Stier, Anderson and Malone, *The Teamsters,* 270–71.

10. Jacobs et al., *Gotham Unbound,* 57 (interview with Steve Carbone).

11. Jacobs et al., *Gotham Unbound,* 76.

12. Selwyn Raab, "Panel Says Mob's Friends Got Teamster Jobs at Javits Center," *New York Times,* May 4, 1995, at B3.

13. Kenneth Conboy, Second Interim Report of the Investigations and Review Officer, Report to Judge Haight, March 13, 1995.

14. James B. Jacobs and Kristin Stohner, "Ten Years of Court-Supervised Reform: A Chronicle and Assessment," 6 *Cal. Crim. Law Rev.* 3 (2004).

15. Government's Memorandum of Law in Support of Its Motion for Preliminary Relief, 12, *U.S. v. New York City District Council of Carpenters,* 90 Cir. 5422 (S.D.N.Y. 1994).

16. *United States v. Maritas,* Cr. No. 81-122 (E.D.N.Y. 1981).

17. Marcelo Svedese Aff. ¶ 12, *United States v. Dist. Council,* 1994 WL 704811 (S.D.N.Y. Dec. 16, 1994) (No. 90 Civ. 5722 (CSH)) (August 9, 1990). "Vinnie

DiNapoli took me aside and told me to do whatever Pat Campbell told me to do."

18. Svedese Aff., August 9,1990, *United States v. Dist. Council*, ¶ 30, ¶ 25.

19. New York State Organized Crime Task Force (OCTF). *Corruption and Racketeering in the New York City Construction Industry: Final Report to Governor Mario M. Cuomo* (New York: New York University Press, 1990), 19. See *People v. O'Connor*, Ind. No. 7953/87 (N.Y. Sup. Ct.N.Y.Co.).

20. Selwyn Raab, "Ex-Union Official Convicted of Racketeering," *New York Times*, July 6, 1990, at B3.

21. Jacobs et al., *Gotham Unbound*, 73.

22. Ibid., 70, 78.

23. Ibid., 85.

24. Stier, Anderson and Malone, *The Teamsters*, 263.

25. Senate Select Committee on Improper Activities in the Labor or Management Field, Report No. 1417, 85th Cong., 2d sess. (Washington, D.C.: GPO, 1958), 328.

26. *United States v. IBT*, 998 F.2d 120, 121–22 (2d Cir. 1993).

27. Rick Cowan and Douglas Century, *Takedown: The Fall of the Last Mafia Empire* (New York: G. P. Putnam's Sons, 2002).

28. Ibid., 214.

29. Ibid., 214.

30. Tom Renner and Michael Slackman, "They Defied Cosa Nostra," *Newsday*, September 24, 1989, at 5; Jacobs et al., *Gotham Unbound*, 88.

31. OCTF, *Corruption and Racketeering in the New York City Construction Industry*, 15–16.

32. Jacobs and Stohner, "Ten Years of Court-Supervised Reform," Table 1.

33. *People v. Bitondo*, Ind. No. 7952/87 (N.Y. Sup. Ct. N.Y. Co.).

34. OCTF, *Corruption and Racketeering in the New York City Construction Industry*, 23.

35. *United States v. Pasquale Parrello et al.*, 01 Crim 1120, Dec. 5, 2001 (S.D.N.Y.).

36. Ibid., indictment at 53–56.

37. OCTF, *Corruption and Racketeering in the New York City Construction Industry*, 27–29.

38. All of the following are referenced in the Final Report of the New York State Organized Crime Task Force, except as noted.

39. *United States v. Amuso*, 21 F.3d 1251 (2d Cir. 1994), Testimony of Peter Savino, June 1992, 3213–17.

40. Ibid., 3323, 3337–40.

41. *United States v. Amuso*, 21 F.3d 1251 (2d Cir. 1994), Testimony of Peter Chiodo, 1467.

42. District Attorney, New York County, News Release, September 6, 2000: http://manhattanda.org/whatsnew/press/2000-09-06.htm.

43. Barbara Ross, "2 Guilty in Union-Bribe Probe," *New York Daily News,* April 28, 2004, at 18.

44. District Attorney, New York County, News Release, September 6, 2000: http://manhattanda.org/whatsnew/press/2000-09-06.htm.

45. Ibid.

46. Michele McPhee, "Building Biz Bust Nets Mob, Unions," *New York Daily News,* Feb. 27, 2003, at 10.

47. *United States v. Amuso,* 21 F.3d 1251 (2d Cir. 1994), Testimony of Peter Chiodo, 1571–72.

48. Herman Benson, *Rebels, Reformers, Racketeers: How Insurgents Transformed the Labor Movement* (Bloomington, Ind.: AuthorHouse, 2004).

49. *United States v. Local 1804-1 et al., International Longshoremen's Association,* complaint, No. 90 Civ. 0963 (LBS) (S.D.N.Y. 1990).

50. Tim Golden, "U.S. Sues Longshoremen's Local and 44 People, Citing Ties to Mob," *New York Times,* Feb. 15, 1990, at A1.

51. Elizabeth Canna, "ILA Talks Go on Beneath a Cloud," *American Shipper,* 32, no. 4 (April 1990), at 50.

52. Office of New York State Attorney General Eliot Spitzer, Press Release, "17 Associates of the Gambino Organized Crime Family Indicted," June 3, 2002, http://www.oag.state.ny.us/press/2002/jun/jun04a_02.html.

53. Ronald Sullivan, "Officers of Dock Union, Linked to Mafia, Agree to Quit," *New York Times,* Dec. 19, 1991, at B2.

54. National Legal and Policy Center, "More Details Emerge on Gotti Clan's Extortion of Longshoremen," *Union Corruption Update* 5, issue 13, June 24, 2002. Available at http://www.nlpc.org/olap/UCU3/05_13_13.htm.

55. Golden, "U.S. Sues Longshoremen's Local and 44 People, Citing Ties to Mob."

56. Karen Tumulty, "U.S. Files Suit to Oust Mob From N.Y. Waterfront," *Los Angeles Times,* Feb. 15, 1990, at A1.

57. See *United States of America v. Local 1804-1, International Longshoremen's Association, AFL-CIO,* 44 F.3d 1091 (2d Cir. 1995).

58. Arnold Lusbasch, "Convicted Mobster Called Key Dock Rackets Boss," *New York Times,* June 22, 1980, at A35.

59. *U.S. v. Michael Clemente et al.,* 640 F.2d 1069, 1071 (2d Cir. 1981), and Permanent Subcommittee on Investigations of the Senate Committee on Governmental Affairs, *Waterfront Corruption* (Washington, D.C.: GPO, 1984), 80–81.

60. Ibid., 82.

61. Press Release, Office of the N.J. Attorney General, New Jersey Division of Criminal Justice, "Division of Criminal Justice and Waterfront Commission

of New York Harbor Target Mob-Run Shake-Down on New Jersey Docks," March 7, 2002. Available at http://www.state.nj.us/lps/dcj/releases/2002/mob0307.htm.

62. National Legal and Policy Center, "NJ Mob Associate Gets Nearly 6 years in Prison, Ordered to Start Repaying $805K," *Union Corruption Update*, vol. 6, issue 15, July 21, 2003. Available at http://www.nlpc.org/olap/UCU4/06_15_02.html.

63. *United States v. Local 1804-1 et al., International Longshoremen's Association*, complaint, No. 90 Civ. 0963 (LBS) (S.D.N.Y. 1990).

64. National Legal and Policy Center, "N.Y. Boss Linked to Org. Crime." *Union Corruption Update*, vol. 1, issue 11, November 2, 1998. Available at http://www.nlpc.org/olap/UCU/01_11_06.htm.

65. Selwyn Raab, "Report Ties Union Official to the Gambino Crime Family," *New York Times*, Oct. 29, 1998, at B7.

66. U.S. Department of Justice, Press Release: "17 Members and Associations of the Gambino Crime Family Indicted for Corruption on the New York Waterfront." June 4, 2002, 6.

67. President's Commission on Organized Crime (PCOC), *The Edge: Organized Crime, Business, and Labor Unions* (Washington, D.C.: GPO, 1986), 35.

68. See, e.g., Joseph P. Fried, "Movers Included in Charges of Bid-Rigging and Payoffs," *New York Times*, June 14, 1985, at B3.

69. Steven Malanga, "How to Run the Mob Out of Gotham," *City Journal* 11, no. 1 (winter 2001): 44–55.

70. Jonathan Kwitny, *Vicious Circles: The Mafia in the Marketplace* (New York: W. W. Norton, 1979).

71. Ibid., 9–11.

72. Ibid., 87–88.

73. *People v. The Newspaper and Mail Deliverers' Union of New York and Vicinity*, 250 A.D.2d, 207–10 (1st Dep't 1998).

NOTES TO CHAPTER 5

1. See Sidney Lens, *The Labor Wars: From Molly Maguires to the Sitdowns* (New York: Doubleday, 1973).

2. Harold Seidman, *Labor Czars: A History of Labor Racketeering* (New York: Liveright, 1938), 54; Paul Buhle, *Taking Care of Business: Samuel Gompers, George Meany, Lane Kirkland and the Tragedy of American Labor* (New York: Monthly Review Press, 1999), 96.

3. Seidman, *Labor Czars*, 57; Bernard Mandel, *Samuel Gompers* (Yellow Springs, Ohio: Antioch Press, 1963), 506.

4. Seidman, *Labor Czars*, 57.

5. Andrew W. Cohen, *The Racketeer's Progress: Chicago and the Struggle for*

the Modern American Economy, 1900–1940 (Cambridge: Cambridge University Press, 2004).

6. Mandel, *Gompers*, 506–7.

7. Buhle, *Taking Care of Business*, 96.

8. John Hutchinson, *The Imperfect Union: A History of Corruption in American Trade Unions* (New York: Dutton, 1972), 37; Mandel, *Gompers*, 507–8; Seidman, *Labor Czars*, 70.

9. Mandel, *Gompers*, 508.

10. Ibid., 508.

11. Ibid., 15–16.

12. Ibid., 6–7.

13. Philip Taft, *Organized Labor in American History* (New York: Harper and Row, 1964), 686; Mandel, *Gompers*, 509.

14. Seidman, *Labor Czars*, 54.

15. Ibid.; Mandel, *Gompers*, 510; Taft, *Organized Labor in American History*, 47; Philip Taft, *Corruption and Racketeering in the Labor Movement*, 2d ed. (Ithaca: Cornell Industrial and Labor Relations Press, 1970), 47.

16. For a revisionist and more favorable view of Gompers as a progressive labor leader, see Neville Kirk, "Peculiarities Versus Exceptions: The Shaping of the American Federation of Labor's Politics During the 1890s and 1900s," 45 *International Review of Social History* 25–50 (2000).

17. Seidman, *Labor Czars*, 242.

18. Taft, *Corruption and Racketeering in the Labor Movement*, 47–48.

19. Seidman, *Labor Czars*, 245–46; Taft, *Organized Labor in American History*, 687; Hutchinson, *The Imperfect Union*, 289.

20. Taft, *Organized Labor in American History*, 687, quoting William Green to P. J. Murrin, June 19, 1931.

21. Ibid., 687, quoting Green to Murrin, July 27, 1932.

22. Seidman, *Labor Czars*, 246; Taft, *Organized Labor in American History*, 687.

23. Taft, *Organized Labor in American History*, 689; Seidman, *Labor Czars*, 250.

24. Seidman, *Labor Czars*, 251.

25. Taft, *Organized Labor in American History*, 689.

26. Ibid., 690, quoting *Report of the Proceedings of the Sixtieth Annual Convention (AFL)*, 1940, 505–6.

27. Ibid.

28. Ibid., 690.

29. Hutchinson, *The Imperfect Union*, 292–94.

30. Ibid., 294.

31. Ibid., 372.

32. Ibid., 304–5.

33. Arthur J. Goldberg, *AFL-CIO: Labor United* (New York: McGraw-Hill, 1956), 191.

34. Hutchinson, *The Imperfect Union*, 295.

35. Goldberg, *AFL-CIO*, 189.

36. Taft, *Organized Labor in American History*, 693.

37. Ibid., 693–94.

38. Archie Robinson, *George Meany and His Times* (New York: Simon and Schuster, 1981), 191.

39. Taft, *Organized Labor in American History*, 696.

40. Taft, *Organized Labor in American History*.

41. Hutchinson, *The Imperfect Union*, 439–53.

42. See Lee Bernstein, *The Great Menace: Organized Crime in Cold War America* (Amherst: University of Massachusetts Press, 2002), chapter 7.

43. Michael J. Nelson, "Comment: Slowing Union Corruption: Reforming the Landrum-Griffin Act to Better Combat Union Embezzlement," 8 *Geo. Mason L. Rev.* 527 (2000), 532.

44. Robinson, *George Meany and His Times*, 192–93.

45. Ibid., 193.

46. Hutchinson, *The Imperfect Union*, 333.

47. Robinson, *George Meany and His Times*, 201.

48. Hutchinson, *The Imperfect Union*, 333.

49. Bureau of National Affairs, Inc., *The McClellan Committee Hearings—1957, Special Analytical Report* (1957), 184.

50. Hutchinson, *The Imperfect Union*, 317–18.

51. Ibid., 319–20.

52. Ibid., 320.

53. Ibid., 320–22.

54. Ibid., 323–24.

55. Ibid., 306–7.

56. AFL-CIO, *Supplemental Report of the AFL-CIO Executive Council on Ethical Practices Cases* (1957), 51–52; Hutchinson, *The Imperfect Union*, 164.

57. AFL-CIO, *Supplemental Report of the AFL-CIO Executive Council on Ethical Practices Cases*, 56.

58. Hutchinson, *The Imperfect Union*, 310–12.

59. AFL-CIO, *Supplemental Report of the AFL-CIO Executive Council on Ethical Practices Cases*, 12; Hutchinson, *The Imperfect Union*, 312–13.

60. AFL-CIO, *Supplemental Report of the AFL-CIO Executive Council on Ethical Practices Cases*, 12; Hutchinson, *The Imperfect Union*, 313.

61. Hutchinson, *The Imperfect Union*, 314.

62. AFL-CIO, *Supplemental Report of the AFL-CIO Executive Council on Ethical Practices Cases*, 12.

63. Ibid., 22; Hutchinson, *The Imperfect Union*, 314–15.

64. Hutchinson, *The Imperfect Union*, 333.

65. AFL-CIO, *Supplemental Report of the AFL-CIO Executive Council on Ethical Practices Cases*, 77–97; Hutchinson, *The Imperfect Union*, 334–35.

66. Hutchinson, *The Imperfect Union*, 335.

67. Ibid., 336–37.

68. *Welfare and Pension Plans Legislation, Hearings Before the Subcommittee on Welfare and Pension Plans Legislation of the Committee on Labor and Public Welfare*, Senate, 85th Cong., 1st sess. (1957), 180.

69. Ibid., 299.

70. Ibid., 305.

71. AFL-CIO, *Labor Looks at the 85th Congress*, AFL-CIO Legislative Report, no. 77, 1958, 27.

72. Ibid., 31.

73. Hutchinson, *The Imperfect Union*, 361.

74. AFL-CIO, *Labor Looks at Congress . . . 1959*, AFL-CIO Legislative Report, 1959, 4–5.

75. Ibid., 5–9.

76. Taft, *Organized Labor in American History*, 705.

77. AFL-CIO, *Labor Looks at Congress . . . 1959*, 20.

78. AFL-CIO, *Labor Looks at the 86th Congress*, AFL-CIO Legislative Report, 1960, 5.

79. Hutchinson, *The Imperfect Union*, 302.

80. Ibid., 346.

81. Ibid., 348.

82. Ibid., 348–49.

83. Joseph Goulden, *Meany* (New York: Atheneum, 1972), 261.

84. Ibid., 262.

85. Buhle, *Taking Care of Business*, 165; Trevor Armbrister, *Act of Vengeance* (New York: Warner Books, 1980); Stuart Brown, *A Man Named Tony: The True Story of the Yablonski Murders* (New York: Norton, 1976).

86. Buhle, *Taking Care of Business*, 165.

87. Ibid.

88. Sara Fritz, "Union Corruption: Worse Than Ever," *U.S. News and World Report*, Sept. 8, 1980, at 33.

89. Wallace Turner, "Documents Show Strong Ties Between Organized Crime and 2 Top Teamsters," *New York Times*, Sept. 29, 1980, at D10.

90. Peter Per and Frank Swoboda, "AFL-CIO Chiefs Said to Plan on Readmitting Teamsters," *Washington Post*, Oct. 23, 1987, at A1; Carol Matlack, "Taking on the Teamsters," *National Journal*, Nov. 7, 1987, at 2782.

91. Matlack, "Taking on the Teamsters," at 2782.

92. Warren Brown, "Kirkland Supports Stiffer Penalties in Bill," *Washington Post*, Nov. 4, 1981, at D8.

93. Ibid.; AFL-CIO, *The People's Lobby: An AFL-CIO Report on the 97th Congress,* June 1983, 62; "Racketeering Crackdown Sought," *Engineering News-Record* (McGraw-Hill), February 11, 1982, 62.

94. *Hearings Before the Permanent Subcommittee on Investigations of the Committee on Governmental Affairs,* Senate, 97th Cong., 1st sess. (1982), 163, 164–66.

95. Ibid., 169.

96. Ibid., 174.

97. "President Signs Funding Bill That Includes Labor Racketeering Amendments," *Daily Labor Report,* October 15, 1984, at A11; "Racketeering Crackdown Sought," *Engineering News-Record* (McGraw-Hill), February 11, 1982, 62.

98. David E. Elbaor and Laurence E. Gold, *The Criminalization of Union Activity: Federal Criminal Enforcement Against Unions, Union Officials and Employees* (Washington, D.C.: Connerton, Bernstein, and Katz, 1985), 1.

99. Ibid., 2.

100. Ibid., 66.

101. Kenneth B. Noble, "Unions Support Teamsters in Fight with Justice Department," *New York Times,* Sept. 1, 1987, at A16.

102. "Selected Statements Adopted by AFL-CIO Executive Council at Meeting Held Aug. 18–19," *Daily Labor Report,* August 21, 1987, at E1.

103. Matlack, "Taking on the Teamsters," 2782.

104. Ibid.

105. "Kirkland Sees 'No Justification' for RICO Lawsuit Against Teamsters," *Daily Labor Report,* February 23, 1989, at A3.

106. Jane Connolly, "Purging the Teamsters; Why Not Try Union Democracy?" *Nation,* September 5, 1987, 192.

107. Kenneth B. Noble, "Vote Set to End US Control of a Jersey Teamsters Local," *New York Times,* February 15, 1988, B3; Frank Swoboda, "Racketeering Law Faces Toughest Test; Justice Dept., Teamsters Set for Court Battle Over Control of Union," *Washington Post,* July 4, 1988, at A5; Philip Lentz, "US Sues to Oust Top Teamsters," *Chicago Tribune,* June 29, 1988, 1.

108. Lentz, "US Sues to Oust Top Teamsters," at 1.

109. Paula Dwyer, "Will Going After Unions Bust Up RICO?" *Business Week,* May 30, 1988, 30.

110. "Federal Judge Issues Rules Governing Operation of Teamsters Review Board," *Daily Labor Report,* August 21, 1992 at A8.

111. *Hearings Before the Permanent Subcommittee on Investigations of the Committee on Governmental Affairs,* Senate, 101st Cong., 1st sess. (1989), 108.

112. Ibid., 115–17, 120, 120–23

113. "Witnesses Disagree on Whether Trusteeships Deal with Organized Crime's Ties to Unions," *Daily Labor Report,* April 13, 1989, at A12.

114. *Hearings Before the Permanent Subcommittee on Investigations of the Committee on Governmental Affairs,* Senate, 101st Cong., 1st sess. (1989), 401.

115. Ibid., 115–17, 120, 405–6.

116. "Senate Panel Recommends Limiting the Use of RICO to Impose Trusteeships over Unions," *Daily Labor Report,* August 3, 1990, at A10.

117. "Racketeering: House GOP Leaders Planning Probe of Organized Labor," *Daily Labor Report,* May 17, 1996, at D3.

118. AFL-CIO Web site, http://www.aflcio.org/publ/press1996/pr0711 .htm (visited November 3, 2002).

119. "Sweeney Attacks House GOP Leaders for Staging Union Show Trials," *Daily Labor Report,* July 12, 1996, at D3.

120. "Racketeering: House Panel Announces Hearings on Efforts to Halt Labor Racketeering," *Daily Labor Report,* July 8, 1996, at D8.

121. AFL-CIO Web site, http://www.aflcio.org/publ/press1996/pr0724 .htm (visited November 3, 2002).

122. Ibid.

123. Mark Murray, "Labor on Patrol," *National Journal,* September 4, 1999, 2489.

124. Fritz, "Union Corruption," 33.

125. International Brotherhood of Teamsters, Press Release, "American Labor Movement Demands Lifting of Consent Decree," December 6, 2001, Teamsters Online, http://www.teamsters.com/comm/releases.asp (visited October 17, 2002).

126. "AFL-CIO Convention Delegates Endorse Teamsters' Bid to Lift 1989 Consent Decree," *Daily Labor Report,* December 7, 2001, at C2.

127. "Labor Department: Administration Seeks Hike in Funding for Agency Charged with Monitoring Unions," *Daily Labor Report,* February 7, 2002, at A11.

128. Ibid.

NOTES TO CHAPTER 6

1. See, e.g., Philip Selznick, *The Organizational Weapon: A Study of Bolshevik Strategy and Tactics* (New York: McGraw-Hill, 1952).

2. Title IV LMRDA; *Donovan, Secretary of Labor v. Local 719, United Automobile, Aerospace and Agricultural Implement Workers of America,* 561 F. Supp. 54 (N.D.Ill. 1982).

3. Upheld by the Supreme Court in *United Steelworkers of America, AFL-CIO v. Sadlowski,* 457 U.S. 102 (1982).

4. See Samuel Estreicher, "Deregulating Union Democracy: The Internal Governance and Organizational Effectiveness of Labor Unions," in *Essays in Honor of George Brooks,* eds. Samuel Estreicher, Harry Katz, and Bruce Kaufman (New York: Kluwer Law International, 2001).

5. 29 USC 464(c)).

6. Leslie Velie, *Desperate Bargain: Why Jimmy Hoffa Had to Die* (New York: Reader's Digest Press, 1977).

7. Herman Benson, *Rebels, Reformers and Racketeers: How Insurgents Transformed the Labor Market* (Bloomington, Ind.: AuthorHouse, 2004), 40.

8. *Schonfeld v. Raftery,* 271 F. Supp. 128, 133 (S.D.N.Y. 1967).

9. See Arthur Fox and John Sikorski, *Teamster Democracy and Financial Responsibility: A Factual and Structural Analysis* (Washington, D.C.: PROD, 1976).

10. Dan La Botz, *Rank and File Rebellion: Teamsters for a Democratic Union* (London: Verso Books, 1990); Dan La Botz, *The Fight at UPS: The Teamsters' Victory and the Future of the New Labor Movement.* Solidarity Pamphlet (1997).

11. Carl Biers, "Spotlight on ILA Longshoremen," *Union Democracy Review* (August/September 2001).

12. The Association for Union Democracy can be found on the Web at http://www.uniondemocracy.com.

NOTES TO CHAPTER 7

1. Investigations of So-Called "Rackets" Hearings Before a Subcommittee of the Senate Committee on Commerce, 73d Cong., 2d sess. (1933), vol. 1, Parts 1–5.

2. Ibid., 798.

3. Anti-Racketeering Act of 1934, 48 Stat. 979.

4. *U.S. v. Teamsters Local 807,* 315 U.S. 521 (1942).

5. The Hobbs Act made criminal "whoever in any way or degree obstructs, delays, or affects commerce or the movement of any article or commodity in commerce, by robbery or extortion or attempts or conspires so to do, or commits or threatens physical violence to any person or property. . . ." 18 U.S.C.A. § 1951.

6. *United States v. Green,* 350 U.S. 415 (1956).

7. See, e.g., *United States v. Iozzi,* 420 F.2d 512 (4th Cir. 1970); *United States v. Kramer,* 355 F.2d 891 (7th Cir. 1966), cert. granted and case remanded for resentencing, 384 U.S. 100 (1966); *Bianchi v. United States,* 219 F.2d 182 (8th Cir. 1955).

8. *U.S. v. Enmons,* 410 U.S. 396 (1973).

9. Taft-Hartley Act (Labor Management Relations Act) 29 U.S.C. Secs. 141–97.

10. *U.S. v. Ryan,* 350 U.S. 299 (1956).

11. Ibid., at 307.

12. See, e.g., *U.S. v. Lanni, Sr.,* 466 F.2d 1102 (1972); *U.S. v. Phillips,* 19 F.3d 1565 (1994).

13. U.S. Department of Labor, "Warning Signs that Pension Contributions are Being Misused," *Employee Benefits Security Administration,* April 22, 2005. Available at http://www.dol.gov/ebsa/publications/10warningsigns.html.

14. Barbara J. Coleman, *Primer on Erisa*, 3d ed. (Washington, D.C.: Bureau of National Affairs, 1989).

15. James A. Wooten, *The Employee Retirement Income Security Act of 1974: A Political History* (Berkeley: University of California Press, 2004).

16. Theft, 18 U.S.C. sec. 664; False Statements, 18 U.S.C. sec. 1027; Offer, Solicitation, 18 U.S.C. sec. 1954.

17. 29 USCA secs. 401, et seq.; Clyde Summers, Joseph Rauh, and Herman Benson, *Union Democracy and Landrum-Griffin* (Brooklyn, N.Y.: Association for Union Democracy, 1986).

18. Joseph Rauh, "MRDA—Enforce It or Repeal It," 5 *Georgia L. Review* 643 (1970–1971); Michael Nelson, "Slowing Union Corruption: Reforming the Landrum-Griffin Act to Better Combat Union Embezzlement," *George Mason Law Review* 8:527–86; see also Doris McLaughlin's and Anita Schoonmaker's comprehensive, albeit dated, study of LMRDA enforcement, *The Landrum-Griffin Act and Union Democracy* (Ann Arbor: University of Michigan Press, 1979).

19. *United States v. Bertucci*, 333 F.2d 292, 295 (3d Cir. 1964).

20. Convictions upheld on appeal. *U.S. v. Bertucci*, 333 F.2d at 300. For more examples of criminal prosecutions brought under the LMRDA, see *U.S. v. Roganovich*, 318 F.2d 167 (7th Cir. 1963), and *U.S. v. Kelley*, 545 F.2d 619 (1976).

21. 18 U.S.C.S. 1952.

22. *U.S. v. Altobella*, 442 F.2d 310 (1971).

23. S. Rep. No. 644, 87 Cong., 1st sess. (1961), 4.

24. *U.S. v. Nardello*, 393 U.S. 286 (1969).

25. The 1967 President's Commission on Crime and the Administration of Justice, Task Force on Organized Crime, Task Force Report on Organized Crime (Washington, D.C.: GPO, 1967).

26. 115 *Congressional Record* 5874 (1969) (remarks of Senator McClellan).

27. 18 U.S. Secs. 1962–65.

28. James B. Jacobs, Christopher Panarella, and Jay Worthington III, *Busting the Mob: United States v. Cosa Nostra* (New York: New York University Press, 1994).

29. Robert F. Kennedy, *The Enemy Within: The McClellan Committee's Crusade Against Jimmy Hoffa and Corrupt Labor Unions* (New York: Harper & Row, 1960); Victor Navasky, *Kennedy Justice* (New York: Atheneum, 1971); Steven Brill, *The Teamsters* (New York: Simon and Schuster, 1978); Dan E. Moldea, *The Hoffa Wars: Teamsters, Rebels, Politicians and the Mob* (New York: Charter Books, 1978); Arthur Schlesinger Jr., *Robert Kennedy and His Times* (New York: Ballantine Books, reissue edition, 1996).

30. Ronald Goldfarb, *Perfect Villains, Imperfect Heroes: Robert F. Kennedy's War against Organized Crime* (New York: Random House, 1995).

31. Brill, *The Teamsters*; Moldea, *The Hoffa Wars*; Kenneth C. Crowe, *Collision: How the Rank and File Took Back the Teamsters* (New York: Scribners Sons, 1993).

32. Arthur A. Sloane, *Hoffa* (Cambridge: MIT Press, 1991).

33. Tony Giacalone was heavily involved in labor racketeering. He may have been the LCN member closest to Jimmy Hoffa. For sure, Hoffa granted him all kinds of favors and opportunity to profit from IBT and its pension funds' actions and inactions. See Lester Velie, *Desperate Bargain: Why Jimmy Hoffa Had to Die* (New York: Reader's Digest Press, 1977).

34. James B. Jacobs, Christopher Panarella, and Jay Worthington III, *Busting the Mob: U.S. v. Cosa Nostra* (New York: New York University Press, 1994).

35. Ibid., 6, 14–15.

36. President's Commission on Organized Crime, *The Edge: Organized Crime, Business, and Labor Unions* (Washington, D.C.: GPO, 1986), 100.

37. Permanent Subcommittee on Investigations of the Senate Committee on Government Operations, *Labor Racketeering Activities of Jack McCarthy and National Consultants Associated, Ltd.* (Washington, D.C.: GPO, 1967).

38. Associated Press, "U.S. Jury Acquits Reputed Crime Figure in Union Embezzling Trial," *New York Times*, July 19, 1982.

39. *Teamsters Central States Pension Fund: Hearings Before the Permanent Subcommittee on Investigations of the Committee on Governmental Affairs*, Senate, 95th Cong., 1st sess., July 18–19, 1977 (Washington, D.C.: GPO, 1977).

40. *Donovan v. Fitzsimmons*, consent decree, 90 F.R.D.583 (N.D. Ill., 1981).

41. Inspector General Act of 1978, Pub. L. 95-452, 92 Stat. 1101 (now codified as amended at 5 U.S.C. App. 1–12).

42. Jacobs et al., *Busting the Mob*, 80–82.

43. Ibid., 84–86.

44. This was dramatically illuminated by the famous (Senator Estes) Kefauver Committee hearings in 1951.

45. Mary M. Stolberg, *Fighting Organized Crime: Politics, Justice, and the Legacy of Thomas E. Dewey* (Boston: Northeastern University Press, 1995).

46. Ibid.

47. Ibid., 188; Thomas E. Dewey, *Twenty Against the Underworld*, ed. Rodney Campbell (Garden City, N.Y.: Doubleday, 1974).

48. Barry Cunningham and Mike Pearl, *Mr. District Attorney* (New York: Mason Charter, 1977).

49. Ibid., 102.

50. Jacobs et al., *Busting the Mob*, 89.

51. For a history of the state and local crime commissions, see Lee Bernstein, *The Great Menace: Organized Crime in Cold War America* (Amherst: University of Massachusetts Press, 2002), chapter 5.

52. E.g., Pennsylvania Crime Commission, Organized Crime in Pennsylvania, 1990 Report (1990); Rick Porello's, *Scranton Crime Boss*, AmericanMafia.com, October 8, 2001.

53. Gerald E. Lynch, "RICO: The Crime of Being a Criminal," 87 *Columbia Law Review* 661–764, May 1987; 87: 920–84 (June 1987).

54. Labor Management Racketeering, Senate Committee on Governmental Affairs, Permanent Subcommittee on Investigations, 1978, 77.

55. Peter Vaira and Douglas P. Roller. *Report on Organized Crime and the Labor Unions.* Prepared for the White House (1978). Available at http://www.americanmafia.com/crime_and_labor.html.

56. Sam Nunn, "The Impact of the Senate Permanent Subcommittee on Investigations on Federal Policy," *Georgia Law Review* 21:17–56, at 25.

NOTES TO CHAPTER 8

1. District Council of Carpenters Consent Decree (March 4, 1994); *U.S. v. District Council,* 778 F. Supp. 738 (S.D.N.Y. 1991); 941 F. Supp. 349 (S.D.N.Y. 1996).

2. See generally Tom Robbins, "The Clean-Up Man: Chic Ex-Prosecutor Makes a Bundle Overseeing Teamsters Local," *Village Voice,* April 18, 2001.

3. Stephanie Mencimer, "Ex-FBI Official Pulls at Union's Infamous Roots," National Legal and Policy Center, *Union Corruption Update,* August 16, 1999, at A1.

4. James B. Jacobs and Ellen Peters, "Labor Racketeering: The Mafia and the Unions," 30 *Crime and Justice: A Review of the Research* 229 (2003), 245, 247.

5. See, e.g., *United States v. Local 30 United Slate, Tile and Composition Roofers, Damp and Waterproof Workers Association,* 686 F. Supp. 1139 (1988); *United States v. Laborers' International Union of North America* (Consent Decree, February 15, 1995); see also National Legal and Policy Center, *Union Corruption Update,* January 31, 2000.

6. The Philadelphia Roofers Local 30/30B decree established a "decreeship" with an indefinite term. Judge Bechtle believed that success could be achieved only by convincing the rank and file and the racketeers that court supervision would last as long as necessary to solve the problem. *United States v. Local 30 United Slate, Tile and Composition Roofers, Damp and Waterproof Workers Association,* 686 F. Supp. 1139 (1988).

7. Carl Biers, "Monitor Airs Hotel Union's Dirty Linen," *Union Democracy Review,* no. 121. Robert Luskin, the General Executive Board attorney of LIUNA International and his law firm, received at least $4 million in compensation from November 1994 to June 1998. National Legal and Policy Center, Organized Labor Accountability Project, *Failure of LIUNA "Internal Reform Effort,"* (Jan., 1999).

8. *United States v. International Brotherhood of Teamsters,* 1992 WL 297489 (S.D.N.Y. October 6, 1992).

9. Steven Greenhouse, "Teamsters Push to End Decade of Supervision,"

New York Times, August 14, 1999, at A1 (stating that the trusteeship had cost the IBT $82 million, or about $8–9 million per year).

10. The internal reform process had cost about $35 million by September 1999. Mark Murray, "Labor on Patrol," *National Journal,* Sept. 4, 1999, at 2489.

11. Kurt Muellenberg retired from the Department of Justice and did not plan a full-time second career in the private sector; he agreed to a $190 hourly rate. Interview with Kurt Muellenberg, Nov. 7, 2002.

12. *United States v. Int'l Bhd Of Teamsters Local 851* (consent decree reached before filed) (Sept. 12, 1995).

13. For example, Trustee Robert Bloch in the Chicago Laborers District Council trusteeship negotiated a new three-year labor contract that provided for higher wages, better benefits, and, for the first time, a grievance procedure. Press release, "United States Department of Justice, Consent Decree Allows Federal Court to Supervise Purge of Organized Crime from 19,000 Member Chicago Laborers' Council," August 12, 1999.

14. Eugene Kiely, "Local 560: Proof is in the Vote; Election Is Test of U.S. Efforts to Clean Up Teamsters," *Record,* Nov. 27, 1988, at A2.

15. *United States v. Local 1804-1 et al.,* consent judgment for Local 1804-1, 4–5.

16. *United States v. Int'l Bhd of Teamsters,* 745 F. Supp. 908, 135 L.R.R.M. (BNA) 3079 (S.D.N.Y. 1990), *aff'd,* 941 F.2d 1292, 138 L.R.R.M. (BNA) 2219 (2d Cir. 1991).

17. *United States v. International Brotherhood of Teamsters,* 742 F. Supp. 94, 97 (S.D.N.Y. 1990).

18. Telephone Interview with Robert Welsh, Special Master, Roofers Local 30/30B, in Philadelphia (Nov. 25, 2003).

19. Herman Benson's *Rebels, Reformers and Racketeers: How Insurgents Transformed the Labor Movement* (Bloomington, Ind.: AuthorHouse, 2004) is a compelling account of the frustrations and dangers experienced by dissidents.

20. Interview with Kurt Muellenberg (Nov. 7, 2002).

21. The MTDC had its own Investigations Officer, Michael Chertoff. Consent Decree, *United States v. Mason Tenders District Council of Greater New York,* 94 Civ. 6487 (S.D.N.Y. 1994). The LIUNA International union agreed to "voluntarily" adopt a major reform effort in order to avoid a court-ordered trusteeship. Robert Luskin serves as counsel, prosecuting disciplinary cases; W. Douglas Gow serves as "Inspector General," investigating allegations of member impropriety or fraud; Peter Vaira serves as "Hearing Officer," deciding a member's guilt or innocence on the basis of evidence gathered by the inspector general (as well as hearing the member's defense); and W. Neil Eggleston serves as "Appellate Officer," hearing appeals from rulings by the hearing officer. National Legal and Policy Center, Organized Labor Accountability Project, *Failure of LIUNA "Internal Reform Effort"* (Jan. 1999), 3–4.

NOTES TO CHAPTER 9

1. *United States v. Local 560, Int'l Bhd of Teamsters,* 581 F. Supp. 279, 287 (D.N.J. 1984).

2. Ibid., at 287.

3. Telephone interview with Edwin Stier (July 3, 2000) [hereinafter Stier Interview II]. See generally, Leonard R. Sayles and George Strauss, *The Local Union* (New York: Harper, 1967), 125 (discussing the role of business agents).

4. Sayles and Strauss, *The Local Union,* 48–55 (discussing the steward as a "middle man"); Stier interview II.

5. *Local 560, Int'l Bhd of Teamsters,* 581 F. Supp. at 289.

6. James B. Jacobs, Christopher Panarella, and Jay Worthington III, *Busting the Mob: U.S. v. Cosa Nostra* (New York: New York University Press, 1994), 32.

7. Mike Kelly, "The Legacy of Tony Pro," *Record,* Dec. 13, 1988, Bl. For his services, Konigsberg paid $15,000. *Local 560, Int'l Bhd of Teamsters,* 581 F. Supp. at 307.

8. *Local 560 Int'l Bhd of Teamsters,* 581 F. Supp. at 292.

9. 18 U.S.C. 1951; *United States v. Provenzano,* 334 F.2d 678 (3d Cir. 1964), petition for cert. denied, 379 U.S. 947 (1964).

10. *Local 560, Int'l Bhd of Teamsters,* 581 F. Supp. at 289.

11. 18 U.S.C. 371.

12. *United States v. Provenzano and Bentro,* 440 F. Supp. 561 (S.D.N.Y. 1977).

13. *United States v. Provenzano,* 615 F.2d 37, 39–42 (2d Cir. 1980); *Local 560, Int'l Bhd of Teamsters,* 581 F. Supp. at 289; Laurie Cohen and Herb Greenberg, "The Giura Bombshell, Bizarre Turn for Noted Money Manager," *Chicago Tribune,* Feb. 9, 1986, at C1.

14. *Local 560, Int'l Bhd of Teamsters,* 581 F. Supp. at 311.

15. See generally, *United States v. Provenzano,* 605 F.2d 85 (3d Cir. 1979); *Local 560, Int'l Bhd of Teamsters,* 780 F.2d 267, 273–74 (D.N.J. 1985).

16. *Local 560, Int'l Bhd of Teamsters,* 780 F.2d at 274; Peter Sampson, UPI, July 9, 1981, available in LEXIS, News Beyond Two Years File.

17. Susan Edelman, "100 Attend Low-Keyed Funeral for Tony Pro," *Record,* Dec. 18, 1988, A1.

18. 18 U.S.C. 1964. See Gerard E. Lynch, "RICO: The Crime of Being a Criminal," Parts I and II, 87 *Colum. L. Rev.* 661 (1987) and Parts III and IV, 87 *Colum. L. Rev.* 920 (1987); Michael J. Goldberg, "Cleaning Labor's House: Institutional Reform Litigation in the Labor Movement," 1989 *Duke L.J.* 903 (1989) (hereinafter *Cleaning Labor's House*).

19. *Local 560, Int'l Bhd of Teamsters,* 581 F. Supp. at 287–88.

20. Ibid., at 284.

21. Ibid., at 285.

22. Ibid., at 286.

23. *United States v. Local 560, Int'l Bhd of Teamsters,* 780 F.2d 267 (3d Cir. 1985).

24. *Local 560, Int'l Bhd Of Teamsters,* 581 F. Supp. at 299–301.

25. Ibid., at 318.

26. Ibid., at 318.

27. Ibid., at 317.

28. Ibid., at 324.

29. *United States v. Local 560, Int'l Bhd of Teamsters,* 1987 U.S. Dist. LEXIS 14878, 2 (D.N.J. 1987).

30. See James B. Jacobs, Christopher Panarella, and Jay Worthington III, *Busting the Mob: U.S. v. Cosa Nostra* (New York: New York University Press, 1994), 35–36.

31. *Local 560, Int'l Bhd of Teamsters,* 1987 U.S. Dist. LEXIS 14878 at 3.

32. Ibid., at 6.

33. Ibid., at 6–8.

34. *United States v. Local 560, Int'l Bhd of Teamsters,* 731 F. Supp. 1206, 1206–9 (D.N.J. 1990).

35. See Report and Recommendations of the Court Appointed Trustee for Teamsters Local 560, at 5 (Jan. 1999); *Local 560, Int'l Bhd of Teamsters,* 581 F. Supp. at 279, (D.N.J. 1984) (82–689) (hereinafter Report and Recommendations).

36. Jacobs et al., *Busting the Mob,* 36.

37. Report and Recommendations, at 2.

38. Tom Toolen, "Editor Sheds Light On Union Local," *Record,* Jan. 26, 1988, at B11.

39. Robert D. McFadden, "Teamster Unit is Given Back Local Control," *New York Times,* Feb. 26, 1999 at B1.

40. Plan for Transition to Membership Control of Local 560, Report to Judge Ackerman, at 4 (Feb. 10, 1988); *Local 560, Int'l Bhd of Teamsters,* 581 F. Supp. 279 (D.N.J. 1984) (82–689).

41. Recommendations for Modification of Local 560 Trusteeship After December 6, 1988, Report to Judge Ackerman, at 4–5 (Nov. 21, 1988); *Local 560, Int'l Bhd of Teamsters,* 581 F. Supp. 279 (82–689). Judge Ackerman affirmed Stier's recommendations. See Letter Opinion and Order (November 28, 1988); *Local 560, Int'l Bhd of Teamsters,* 581 F. Supp. 279 (82–689).

42. *Local 560, Int'l Bhd of Teamsters,* 694 F. Supp. 1158, 1184–85 (D.N.J. 1988); see also "Teamster Rallies Called Nazi-Like," *Record,* Mar. 21, 1990 at A5.

43. *Local 560, Int'l Bhd of Teamsters,* 694 F. Supp., at 1185.

44. Ibid.

45. Ibid., at 1158.

46. Ibid., at 1156–66.

47. Ibid., at 1170.

48. Ibid., at 1168–69.

49. Ibid., at 1192.

50. Ibid.

51. *Local 560, Int'l Bhd of Teamsters*, 974 F.2d 315, 324 (3d Cir. 1992).

52. See Eugene Kiely, "Teamsters Leaders Vow Honest Union; Control Shifts to Sciarra Slate," *Record*, Dec. 8, 1988, at A1; Stewart interview. Stier's assessment of the state of the trusteeship and union postelection can be found at Federal Government's Use of Trusteeships under the RICO Statute: Hearings before the Senate Permanent Subcommittee on Investigations, 101st Cong., 1st sess., (1989), at 179–258.

53. Report and Recommendations to Judge Ackerman, at 9.

54. *Local 560, Int'l Bhd of Teamsters*, 736 F. Supp. at 607.

55. *Local 560, Int'l Bhd of Teamsters*, 974 F.2d, at 315.

56. *Local 560, Int'l Bhd of Teamsters*, 736 F. Supp., at 612.

57. *United States v. Local 560, Int'l Bhd of Teamsters*, 754 F. Supp. 395 (D.N.J. 1991).

58. *Local 560, Int'l Bhd of Teamsters*, 754 F. Supp. at 408.

59. *United States v. Local 560, Int'l Bhd of Teamsters*, Unpublished Opinion of March 27, 1991, aff'd, 974 F.2d 315 (3d Cir. 1992).

60. Judgment Order and Permanent Injunction, at 1 (Mar. 27, 1991), *United States v. Local 560, Int'l Bhd of Teamsters*, 581 F. Supp. 279 (D.N.J. 1984) (82–689).

61. *United States v. Local 560, Int'l Bhd of Teamsters* and Mezzina; Conlon, Complaint, at 17–18.

62. Stewart interview.

63. *United States v. Local 560, Int'l Bhd of Teamsters*; Mezzina and Conlon, Complaint, at 16.

64. *United States v. Local 560, Int'l Bhd of Teamsters*; Mezzina and Conlon, Compl., at 16.

65. Report and Recommendations, at 10.

66. Interim Settlement Agreement and Consent Decree at 5 (Feb. 6, 1992); *United States v. Local 560, Int'l Bhd of Teamsters*, 581 F. Supp. 279 (D.N.J. 1984) (82–689) (hereinafter Interim Settlement).

67. Order of Modification of Interim Settlement Agreement and Consent Decree of Feb. 6, 1992, and Sept. 11, 1992, at 3; and May 18, 1994, at 3–4.

68. See Order of Modification of Interim Settlement Agreement and Consent Decree of Feb. 6, 1992, and Sept. 11, 1992, at 3; and May 18, 1994, at 4.

69. *United States v. Local 560, Int'l Bhd of Teamsters*, 581 F. Supp. 279 (D.N.J. 1984) (82–689) (listing the members of the Executive Board).

70. Interim Settlement, at 4.

71. Ibid., at 7–8.

72. Report and Recommendations, at 11; Stewart interview.

73. Modification of Interim Settlement Agreement and Consent Decree of

Feb. 6, 1992, at 1–2 (Sept. 11, 1992), *United States v. Local 560, Int'l Bhd of Teamsters*, 581 F. Supp. 279, (D.N.J. 1984) (82–689) (hereinafter Modification of the Interim Settlement).

74. Modification of Interim Settlement, at 1–2.

75. Stier interview.

76. Report and Recommendations at 13; Order of Modification of Interim Settlement Agreement and Consent Decree of Feb. 6, 1992 and Sept. 11, 1992 at 3 (May 18, 1994), *United States v. Local 560, Int'l Bhd of Teamsters*, 581 F. Supp. 279 (D.N.J. 1984) (82–689) (citing Al Vallee's resignation), and Consent Order Approving Appointment Filling Vacancy to the Local 560 Executive Board (Nov. 14, 1995), *United States v. Local 560, Int'l Bhd of Teamsters*, 581 F. Supp. 279 (D.N.J. 1984) (82–689) (consent order approving appointment to fill vacant Executive Board seat).

77. Ellen Simon, *Newark Star-Ledger*, Feb. 26, 1999. See, e.g., In Re: Onofrio "Fred" Mezzina, Decision and Opinion of the Court Appointed Trustee (Aug. 30, 1995), *United States v. Local 560, Int'l Bhd of Teamsters*, 581 F. Supp. 279 (D.N.J. 1984) (82–689).

78. Report and Recommendations, at 15–16.

79. David Voreacos, "Teamster Leader Set to Ask U.S. to End Control of Local," *Record*, Feb. 25, 1994, at A4.

80. Report and Recommendations, at 19.

81. Simon, *Newark Star-Ledger*.

82. Ibid.

83. Robert D. McFadden, "Teamsters Unit Is Given Back Local Control," *New York Times*, Feb. 26, 1999 at B1; Transcript of Proceedings Regarding Ending the Trusteeship, at 3 (Feb. 25, 1999), *United States v. Local 560, Int'l Bhd of Teamsters*, 581 F. Supp. 279 (D.N.J. 1984) (82–689).

84. McFadden, "Teamsters Unit Is Given Back Local Control," at B1.

85. See ibid.

86. David Voreacos, *Record*, Feb. 26 1999, at A1.

87. Kaboolian testimony.

88. *Local 560, Int'l Bhd of Teamsters*, 581 F. Supp., at 282.

89. Ibid., at 299.

90. Ibid., at 326.

91. *United States v. Local 295, Int'l Bhd of Teamsters*, 1987 U.S. Dist. LEXIS 14878, at 6.

92. *Local 295, Int'l Bhd of Teamsters*, 1987 U.S. Dist. LEXIS 14878, at 4.

93. *Local 295, Int'l Bhd of Teamsters*, 1987 U.S. Dist. LEXIS 14878, at 5.

94. Stier interview II.

95. Robert C. Stewart, "Voice of the Bar: Local 560 Prosecutor Rebuts Criticism of Trusteeship," *N.J.L.J.*, November 15, 1999, at 25.

96. Stier interview II.

NOTES TO CHAPTER 10

1. *United States v. Dist. Council*, 778 F. Supp. 738, 743 (S.D.N.Y 1991).

2. Government's Motion for Preliminary Relief, 12.

3. Second Interim Report of the Investigations and Review Officer, 41–42; *United States v. Dist. Council*, 1994 WL 704811 (S.D.N.Y. Dec. 16, 1994) (No. 90 Civ. 5722 (CSH)) (Mar. 13, 1995) (hereinafter Second Interim Report).

4. Government's Motion for Preliminary Relief, 12–14.

5. Government's Motion for Preliminary Relief, 15; *United States v. Maritas*, Cr. No. 81–122 (E.D.N.Y. 1981).

6. Government's Motion for Preliminary Relief, 15; see also Government's Supp. Compl., 37.

7. See *U.S. v. Salerno*, 505 U.S. 317 (1992).

8. Government's Motion for Preliminary Relief, 16.

9. Ibid.; Svedese Aff., ¶ 3, 2.

10. Svedese Aff., ¶ 30, 13.

11. *People v. O'Connor, Ind.* No. 7953/87 (N.Y. Sup. Ct. N.Y. Co. Sept. 6, 1989).

12. Second Interim Report, 18; Salvatore Miciotta Decl. ¶¶ 3–11, *United States v. Dist. Council*, 1994 WL 704811 (S.D.N.Y. Dec. 16, 1994) (No. 90 Civ. 5722 (CSH)) (Nov. 9, 1994).

13. Svedese Aff., ¶ 30, 13.

14. Government's Motion for Preliminary Relief, 1; Government's Supp. Compl., 1.

15. Government's Supp. Compl., 10.

16. Ibid., 35–49; 29 U.S.C. §§ 401–531 (1976), 73 Stat. 517 (1959). This argument was first used by the government in *United States v. Local 560, Int'l Bhd of Teamsters*, 581 F. Supp. 279 (D.N.J. 1984). But see *Bellomo v. United States*, 2003 WL 22331878 (E.D.N.Y. Oct. 8, 2003), and *United States v. Bellomo*, 263 F.Supp.2d 561 (E.D.N.Y. 2003). For a legal analysis, see Ehren Reynolds, "Protecting the Waterfront," 10 *Cal. Crim. Law. Rev.* 1 (2005).

17. Government's Supp. Compl., 11–49.

18. Ibid., 11–34.

19. Consent Decree (filed on Mar.4, 1994), *United States v. Dist. Council*, 1994 WL 704811 (S.D.N.Y) (No. 90 Civ. 5722 (CSH)).

20. Consent Decree, 5.

21. Interim Report of the Investigations and Review Officer, at 9, *United States v. Dist. Council*, 1994 WL 704811 (S.D.N.Y. Dec. 16, 1994) (No. 90 Civ. 5722 (CSH)) (Oct. 4, 1994) (hereinafter Interim Report).

22. Second Interim Report, 40 (Mar. 13, 1995).

23. Consent Decree, 10.

24. Ibid.

25. Kenneth Conboy, An Open Letter to the Members of the United Brother-

hood of Carpenters and Joiners of America from Judge Kenneth Conboy, *The Carpenter,* Jan./Feb. 1994.

26. *United States v. Dist. Council,* 1994 WL 704811 (S.D.N.Y. Dec. 16, 1994) (No. 90 Civ. 5722 (CSH)).

27. Interim Report, 19.

28. Government's Motion for Preliminary Relief, 16.

29. Ibid., ¶ 22.

30. Second Interim Report, 29.

31. Investigations and Review Officer's Charges at 1–5, *Investigations and Review Officer v. Ruotolo* (Mar. 13, 1995). Investigations and Review Officer's Charges at 1–3, *Investigations and Review Officer v. Schepis* (Mar. 13, 1995).

32. Second Interim Report, 30–36.

33. Third Interim Report, 48–50.

34. Second Interim Report, 23.

35. Jerry Capeci, "Death Returns to 'The Life,'" Gang Land: the Online Column, Nov. 2, 1998, at http://www.ganglandnews.com/column99.htm.

36. Miciotta Decl., 3.

37. Second Interim Report, 8.

38. John Mitchell Aff. Exhibit M, *United States v. Dist. Council,* 1994 WL 704811 (S.D.N.Y. Dec. 16, 1994) (No. 90 Civ. 5722 (CSH)) (Mar. 17, 1995) ("Criminal History and Affiliation of Carpenters on the Javits Center Pool List").

39. Second Interim Report, 14.

40. Third Interim Report, 48.

41. IHC Panel's Decision, at 35–36, *Investigations and Review Officer v. Fiorino,* Sept. 28, 1995.

42. Fifth Interim Report of the Investigations and Review Officer, at 6, *United States v. Dist. Council,* 1994 WL 704811 (S.D.N.Y. Dec. 16, 1994) (No. 90 Civ. 5722 (CSH)) (Sept. 30, 1996) (hereinafter Fifth Interim Report).

43. *U.S. v. District Council of Carpenters,* Appeal from the Decision of the Independent Hearing Panel Disciplining Anthony D. Fiorino. September 12, 1996.

44. Third Interim Report, 39.

45. Third Interim Report, 41.

46. James B. Jacobs, Coleen Friel, and Robert Radick, *Gotham Unbound* (New York: New York University Press, 1999), 185–86.

47. Ibid., 189 (quoting the Office of the State Comptroller praising the reforms at the Javits Center).

48. *United States v. Dist. Council,* 880 F. Supp., at 1060–65 (S.D.N.Y. 1995).

49. *United States v. Dist. Council,* 880 F. Supp. 1051, 1057 (S.D.N.Y. 1995).

50. *United States v. Dist. Council,* 880 F. Supp., at 1066–67 (S.D.N.Y. 1995).

51. *United States v. Dist. Council,* 880 F. Supp., at 1059 (S.D.N.Y. 1995).

52. Final Rules for the 1995 Election of the Executive Committee of the District Council of Carpenters of New York City and Vicinity § 2, ¶ 1 (March 1995).

53. Third Interim Report, 3.

54. Ibid., 23.

55. Ibid., 5.

56. The classic study of union members' apathy is Seymour Martin Lipset, Martin A. Trow, and James S. Coleman, *Union Democracy: The Internal Politics of the International Typographical Union* (New York: Free Press, 1956).

57. Sixth Interim Report of the Investigations and Review Officer, at 24; *United States v. Dist. Council,* 1994 WL 704811 (S.D.N.Y. Dec. 16, 1994) (No. 90 Civ. 5722 (CSH)) (Mar. 4, 1997) (hereinafter Sixth Interim Report).

58. Ninth Interim Report of the Investigations and Review Officer, at 31, *United States v. Dist. Council,* 1994 WL 704811 (S.D.N.Y. Dec. 16, 1994) (No. 90 Civ. 5722 (CSH)) (Mar. 4, 1997) (hereinafter Ninth Interim Report).

59. Sixth Interim Report, 23–24.

60. Ninth Interim Report, 32.

61. Sixth Interim Report, 25.

62. Ninth Interim Report, 31.

63. Ibid., 27.

64. Ibid., 28–29.

65. Fifth Interim Report.

66. Ibid., 3.

67. Ibid., 25.

68. Ibid., 5.

69. Ibid., 26–30.

70. Sixth Interim Report, 13. *Impediments to Union Democracy Part II:* Right to Vote in the Carpenter's Union? Hearing Before the Subcommittee on Employer-Employee Relations of the House Committee on Education and the Workforce, 105th Cong., 1st sess., at § IV, ¶ E (June 25, 1998) (hereinafter Impediments to Union Democracy Part II) (prepared statement of Douglas J. Mc-Carron, General President, United Brotherhood of Carpenters and Joiners of America).

71. National Legal and Policy Center, "New York Union Attorney Loses License," 2 *Union Corruption Update* 13, June 21, 1999, at http://www.nlpc.org/olap/UCU/02_13.htm.

72. Selwyn Raab, "Former Chief of Carpenters' Union Convicted of Stealing Funds," *New York Times,* Mar. 25, 1998, at B3.

73. Ninth Interim Report, 2.

74. Eighth Interim Report, 2–4.

75. Impediments to Union Democracy Part II, § I (prepared statement of Douglas J. McCarron).

76. Tenth Interim Report, 1, n.1.

77. Tom Robbins, "Back to the Mob," *Village Voice,* Sept. 19, 2000, 31.

78. Eighth Interim Report, 21.

79. Barbara Ross and Greg B. Smith, "Mob-Extortion Probe Leads to 38 Arrests," *New York Daily News*, Sept. 7, 2000, at 6.

80. National Legal and Policy Center, "Massive New York Probe Nabs 11 Union Bosses," 3 *Union Corruption Update* 19, Sept. 11, 2000, http://nlpc.org/olap/UCU2/03_19.htm.

81. NYC District Council of Carpenters, "Union Elections 2002," http://www.nycdistrictcouncil.com/unofficial_elections.htm.

82. Fourth Interim Report of the Investigations and Review Officer, at 7, *United States v. Dist. Council*, 1994 WL 704811 (S.D.N.Y. Dec. 16, 1994) (No. 90 Civ. 5722 (CSH)) (Mar. 15, 1996).

83. Sixth Interim Report, 26–27.

84. *United States v. Dist. Council*, 2002 WL 31873460 (S.D.N.Y. Dec. 24, 2002), 171 L.R.R.M. 3031 (S.D.N.Y. Dec. 24, 2002).

85. Stipulation and Order at 1–5, *United States v. Dist. Council*, 1994 WL 704811 (S.D.N.Y. Dec. 16, 1994) (No. 90 Civ. 5722 (CSH)) (Dec. 17, 2002).

86. Ibid., 2.

87. Herman Benson, "At the House Hearings on Union Democracy," 120 *Union Democracy Review*, http://www.thelaborers.net/aud/AUD_hearings.html.

88. Robbins, "Back to the Mob," 31.

89. Indictment at 4–8, *United States v. Parrello*, (S.D.N.Y.) (01 Crim. 1120) (Dec. 5, 2001).

90. Ibid., 53–56.

NOTES TO CHAPTER 11

1. James Neff, *Mobbed Up: Jackie Presser's High-Wire Life in the Teamsters, the Mafia, and the FBI* (New York: Atlantic Monthly Press, 1989).

2. James B. Jacobs, Christopher Panarella, and Jay Worthington, *Busting the Mob: United States v. Cosa Nostra* (New York: New York University Press, 1994).

3. Kenneth Wallentine, "A Leash Upon Labor: RICO Trusteeships on Labor Unions," 7 *Hofstra Labor Law Journal* 341 (Spring 1990).

4. *United States v. International Brotherhood of Teamsters*, complaint, 88 Civ. 4486 (S.D.N.Y. 1988).

5. Ibid., 104–15.

6. Jacobs, Panarella, and Worthington III, *Busting the Mob*; see also Rick Porrello, *The Rise and Fall of the Cleveland Mafia* (Fort Lee, N.J.: Barricade Books, 1995), 218–28.

7. *United States v. International Brotherhood of Teamsters*, consent decree, 808 F. Supp. 279 (S.D.N.Y. 1988).

8. Frederick Lacey, "The Independent Administrator's Memorandum on

the Handling and Disposition of Disciplinary Matters." Unpublished report to Judge Edelstein, October 7, 1992, 5–6.

9. *United States v. International Brotherhood of Teamsters*, 728 F. Supp. 1032, aff'd 907 F.2d 277 (2d Cir. 1990).

10. Ibid.

11. *Investigations Officer v. Senese, et al.*, Decision of the Independent Administrator (July 12, 1990), aff'd *United States v. IBT*, 745 F. Supp. 908 (S.D.N.Y. 1990), aff'd 941 F.2d 1292 (2d Cir. 1991), cert. denied, *Senese v. United States*, 112 S.Ct. 1161 (1992).

12. *Investigations Officer v. Calagna, Sr., et al.*, Decision of the Independent Administrator (June 14, 1991), aff'd *United States v. IBT*, 1991 WL 161084 (S.D.N.Y. 1991).

13. *Investigations Officer v. Salvatore*, Decision of the Independent Administrator (October 2, 1990), aff'd *United States v. IBT*, 754 F. Supp. 333 (S.D.N.Y. 1990).

14. *Investigations Officer v. Wilson, et al.*, Decision of the Independent Administrator (December 23, 1991), aff'd United States v. IBT, 787 F. Supp. 345 (S.D.N.Y. 1992), aff'd in part, vacated in part, 978 F.2d 68 (2d Cir. 1992).

15. *United States v. International Brotherhood of Teamsters*, 803 F. Supp. 767 (S.D.N.Y. 1992), aff'd in part, rev'd in part, 998 F.2d 1101 (2d Cir. 1993).

16. Meagan Kiley, "The International Brotherhood of Teamsters' Disciplinary Procedures: A Look at the Independent Review Board," unpublished seminar paper, New York University School of Law, 2003, 2.

17. Ibid., 14.

18. *United States v. International Brotherhood of Teamsters*, 803 F. Supp. 267 (1992), 770.

19. Dan La Botz, *Rank and File Rebellion: Teamsters for a Democratic Union* (London: Verso Books, 1990); Kenneth C. Crowe, *Collision: How the Rank and File Took Back the Teamsters* (New York: Scribners and Sons, 1993).

20. *United States v. International Brotherhood of Teamsters*, 988 F. Supp. 759 (S.D.N.Y. 1997).

21. Stier, Anderson & Malone, LLC, *The Teamsters: Perception and Reality: An Investigative Study of Organized Crime Influence in the Union* (Washington, D.C.: International Brotherhood of Teamsters, 2001). Additional histories include David Witwer, *Corruption and Reform in the Teamsters Union* (Urbana-Champaign: University of Illinois Press, 2003), and Kenneth Crowe, *Collision*. For further discussion of Project Rise, see James B. Jacobs and Ryan Alford, "The Teamsters' Rocky Road to Recovery: The Demise of Project Rise," *Trends in Organized Crime* 9(1) (November 2005).

22. President's Commission on Organized Crime (PCOC), *The Edge: Organized Crime, Business, and Labor Unions* (Washington, D.C.: President's Commission on Organized Crime, 1986), 76.

23. Ibid., 78.

24. *Brown v. Hotel and Rest. Employees and Bartenders Int'l Union Local 54*, 468 U.S. 491, 494 (1984).

25. PCOC, *The Edge*, 79–80.

26. Robert Mackay, "Washington News," United Press International, August 27, 1984.

27. *United States v. Hanley*, complaint, Civ. No. 90–5017 (D.N.J. 1990).

28. *United States v. Hanley*, 1992 U.S. Dist. LEXIS 22192 (D.N.J. 1992).

29. Ibid.

30. Kathy Seal, "Union Monitor Remains; HEREIU." *Hotel and Motel Management* (1997), 212(6):3–5.

31. Frank Friel and John Guinther, *Breaking the Mob* (New York: McGraw-Hill, 1990).

32. Interview with anonymous DOL official.

33. Department of Labor Office of the Inspector General, 1996 Report, http://www.oig.dol.gov/public/reports/sar/sar0996/olr2.htm.

34. Seal, "Union Monitor Remains."

35. 92 Civ. 7744 (RPP) (S.D.N.Y. 1992).

36. *United States v. HEREIU*, Civ. No. 95-4569 (D.N.J. 1995).

37. Kurt W. Muellenberg, Final Report as Monitor of HEREIU, August 26, 1998, 2. Available at http://www.heretics.net.

38. Ibid., 5–6.

39. Ibid., 14.

40. Ibid., 15.

41. The five locals placed in trusteeship by Muellenberg were Local 122 in Milwaukee; Local 69 in Secaucus, N.J.; Local 4 in Buffalo; Local 57 in Pittsburgh; and AFL-CIO Nursing Home Council in Buffalo. Two (Local 122 and Local 69) held elections and were removed from trusteeship by the end of Muellenberg's term as monitor (Muellenberg 1998, 52–53). These actions in tabular form can be found at http://www.ipsn.org/HEREIU_Table.htm.

42. Daniel Rostenkowski, a consultant, and Robert L. Hickman, Sr., a consultant and business agent for Chicago Local 1, were barred for thirteen years. Nancy Ross (secretary-treasurer of Local 57 and international vice-president) and Vince Fera (Executive Board member) were prohibited from holding positions of trust for three years beginning April 23, 1998 (Muellenberg 1998, 58).

43. Muellenberg, Final Report as Monitor of HEREIU, 59.

44. Ibid., 60.

45. Statement of Kurt Muellenberg, Subcommittee on Employer-Employee Relations of the House Committee on Education and the Workforce, Hearing on the Hotel and Restaurant Employees International Union (HEREIU), July 21, 1999.

46. Statement of John W. Wilhelm, General President of the Hotel Employees and Restaurant Employees International Union, AFL-CIO/CLC, before the Subcommittee on Employer/Employee Relations of the House Committee on Education and the Workforce, July 21, 1999. 106th Cong., 1st sess.

47. William F. Roemer, Jr., *Accardo: The Genuine Godfather* (New York: Ballantine Books, 1995); Gus Russo, *The Outfit: The Role of Chicago's Underworld in the Shaping of Modern America* (New York: Bloomsbury, 2001).

48. The draft complaint, although never filed, is available online at http://www.laborers.org/complaint.html.

49. Michael Bologna and Brian Lockett, "Union President Coia Says He Expects Disciplinary Charges to Be Filed Against Him," *Daily Labor Report*, October 28, 1997.

50. LIUNA Ethics and Disciplinary Procedure. Can be found on the Web at http://www.thelaborers.net/constitutions/constitutions-new-2004/ethics_and_disciplinary_procedure.pdf.

51. Michael Bologna and Brian Lockett, "LIUNA President Arthur Coia Poised to Resign Under Plea Agreement," 189 *Daily Labor Report*, Sept. 20, 1999, AA1.

52. John E. Mulligan, "Coia Resigns as Head of Laborers' Union," *Providence Journal*, December 7, 1999, 1.

53. Carl F. Horowitz, *Union Corruption in America: Still a Growth Industry* (Springfield, Va.: National Institute for Labor Relations Research, 2004), 18–22.

54. GEB Attorney Robert Luskin, "Notice of Trusteeship Proceedings," January 6, 2005.

55. *United States v. Local 1804-1 et al., International Longshoremen's Association*, complaint, No. 90 Civ. 0963 (LBS) (S.D.N.Y. 1990).

56. The complaint did not include the ILA's international union. However, International President John Bowers was named individually, as president of three of the six locals.

57. *United States v. Local 1804-1 et al.*, consent judgment for Local 1804-1, 3.

58. Ibid., 8.

59. *United States v. Local 1804-1 et al.*, consent decree for Local 1814, 2–3.

60. See *United States v. Local 1804-1 et al.*, 44 F.3d 1091, 1094 (2d Cir. 1995).

61. *United States v. Gotti, et al.*, 2002 WL 31946775 (E.D.N.Y.).

62. Ibid.

63. *United States v. DiGilio*, 86 Cr. 340 (D.N.J.)(DRD), aff'd mem., 870 F.2d 652 (3d Cir. 1989), vacated and remanded, 110 S. Ct. 2162 (1990).

64. *United States v. Local 1804-1 et al.*, consent order for Local 1588, 7.

65. *United States v. Liborio "Barney" Bellomo et al.*, Cr. No. 01-416 (S-8) ILG (2002).

66. *U.S. v. Arthur Coffee, Harold Daggett and Albert Cernades*, 04 CR 651 (5-1) (IILG) (E.D.N.Y. 2004).

NOTES TO CHAPTER 12

1. The Organized Crime and Racketeering Section Web site is http://www.usdoj.gov/criminal/ocrs.

2. The National Institute of Justice can be found on the Web at http://www.ojp.usdoj.gov.

3. See Ross Sandler and David Schoenbrod, *Democracy by Decree: What Happens When Courts Run Government* (New Haven: Yale University Press, 2003).

4. Margo Schlonger, "Beyond the Hero Judge," 97 *Mich. L. Rev.* 1994 (1999); Malcolm Feeley and Edward Rubin, *Judicial Policymaking and the Modern State: How the Courts Reformed America's Prisons* (Cambridge, U.K.: Cambridge University Press, 1998). For a valuable theoretical discussion about the production of organizational change, see Michael Dorf and Charles Sabel, "A Constitution of Democratic Experimentalism," 1998 *Columbia Law Review,* 267.

5. For a detailed account of Boyle's reign as head of the United Mine Workers and of the murder of Jock Yablonski, see Arthur H. Lewis, *Murder by Contract: The People v. "Tough" Tony Boyle* (New York: Macmillan, 1975).

6. Robert Fitch, "Union for Sale," *Village Voice,* September 2–8, 1998; can be found on the Web at http://www.laborers.org/Village_FitchDC37_9-2-98.htm.

7. National Legal and Policy Center, Organized Labor Accountability Project, "Jury Convicts Diop, Lubin for Fraud," *Union Corruption Update,* July 31, 2000.

8. Robert Michels, in Oscar Grusky and George A. Miller, *The Sociology of Organizations: Basic Studies* (New York: Free Press, 1970).

9. See Herman Benson, *Rebels, Reformers and Racketeers: How Insurgents Transformed the Labor Movement* (Bloomington, Ind.: AuthorHouse, 2004); Clyde Summers, "Union Trusteeships and Union Democracy," *University of Michigan Journal of Law Reform,* 24:689–707 (1991); Clyde W. Summers, Joseph L. Raub, and Herman Benson, *Union Democracy and Landrum-Griffin* (Brooklyn, N.Y.: Association for Union Democracy, 1986); Mike Parker and Martha Gruelle, "Democracy Is Power: Rebuilding Unions from the Bottom Up," *Labor Notes* (Detroit, 1999).

10. Benson, *Rebels, Reformers and Racketeers.*

11. FBI Director Robert Mueller requested $5.1 billion for fiscal year 2005, approximately 44 percent of which was to be allocated to counterterrorism and counterintelligence. See testimony of Robert S. Mueller III, Director FBI, before the House Appropriations Committee, Subcommittee on the Departments of Commerce, Justice, and State, the Judiciary and Related Agencies, 108th Cong., 2d sess., March 17, 2004.

NOTE TO CHAPTER 13

1. George Kannar, "Making the Teamsters Safe for Democracy," 102 *Yale Law Journal* 1645 (1993).

Bibliography

Abadinsky, Howard. 1994. *Organized Crime.* 4th ed. Chicago: Nelson Hall.

Adamic, Louis. 1958. *Dynamite: The Story of Class Violence in America.* New York: Chelsea House Publishers (first published, 1931).

Armbrister, Trevor. 1980. *Act of Vengeance.* New York: Warner Books.

Aronowitz, Stanley. 1998. *From the Ashes of the Old: American Labor and America's Future.* New York: Houghton Mifflin.

Bell, Daniel. 1951. "Last of the Business Rackets." *Fortune Magazine,* June.

———. 1962. *The End of Ideology: On the Exhaustion of Political Ideas in the Fifties.* New York: Free Press.

Benson, Herman. 2004. *Rebels, Reformers and Racketeers: How Insurgents Transformed the Labor Movement.* Bloomington, Ind.: Authorhouse.

Bernstein, Lee. 2002. *The Great Menace: Organized Crime in Cold War America.* Amherst: University of Massachusetts Press.

Blakey, Robert G., and Ronald Goldstock. 1980. "On the Waterfront: RICO and Labor Racketeering." *American Criminal Law Review* 17:341.

Block, Alan, and Sean Patrick Griffin. 1997. "The Teamsters, the White House and the Labor Department." 27 *Crime, Law and Social Change* 1.

Bonanno, Bill. 1999. *Bound by Honor: A Mafioso's Story.* New York: St. Martin's Press.

Brill, Steven. 1978. *The Teamsters.* New York: Simon and Schuster.

Brown, Stuart. 1976. *A Man Named Tony: The True Story of the Yablonski Murders.* New York: Norton.

Bruno, Robert. 2003. *Reforming the Chicago Teamsters: The Story of Local 705.* De Kalb: Northern Illinois University Press.

Buhle, Paul. 1999. *Taking Care of Business: Samuel Gompers, George Meany, Lane Kirkland and the Tragedy of American Labor.* New York: Monthly Review Press.

Bureau of National Affairs, Inc. 1957. *The McClellan Committee Hearings—1957, Special Analytical Report.*

Cohen, Andrew W. 2004. *The Racketeer's Progress: Chicago and the Struggle for the Modern American Economy, 1900–1940.* Cambridge: Cambridge University Press.

Cohen, Rich. 1998. *Tough Jews: Fathers, Sons and Gangster Dreams.* New York: Vintage.

Coleman, Barbara J. 1989. *Primer on ERISA.* 3d ed. Washington, D.C.: Bureau of National Affairs.

Cooley, Robert, with Hillel Levin. 2004. *When Corruption Was King.* New York: Carroll and Graf.

Cowan, Rick, and Douglas Century. 2002. *Takedown: The Fall of the Last Mafia Empire.* New York: G. P. Putnam's Sons.

Crowe, Kenneth C. 1993. *Collision: How the Rank and File Took Back the Teamsters.* New York: Scribners and Sons.

Cunningham, Barry, and Mike Pearl. 1977. *Mr. District Attorney.* New York: Mason Charter.

Dean, Andrew B. 2000. "An Offer the Teamsters Couldn't Refuse: The 1989 Consent Decree Establishing Federal Oversight and Ending Mechanisms." *Columbia Law Review* 100:2157–94.

Dewey, Thomas. 1974. *Twenty against the Underworld.* Edited by Rodney Campbell. Garden City, N.Y.: Doubleday.

Drucker, Peter. 1976. *The Unseen Revolution.* New York: Harper and Row. (Republished in 1996 as *The Pension Fund Revolution*).

Dubinsky, David, and A. Raskin. 1977. *David Dubinsky: A Life with Labor.* New York: Simon and Schuster.

Estreicher, Samuel. 2001. "Deregulating Union Democracy: The Internal Governance and Organizational Effectiveness of Labor Unions." In *Essays in Honor of George Brooks,* edited by Samuel Estreicher, Harry Katz, and Bruce Kaufman. New York: Kluwer Law International.

Elbaor, David E., and Larry Gold. 1985. *The Criminalization of Union Activity: Federal Criminal Enforcement against Unions, Union Officials and Employees.* Washington, D.C.: Connerton, Bernstein, and Katz.

Foner, Philip S. 1950. *The Fur and Leather Workers Union.* Newark: Norton Press.

Fox, Stephen. 1989. *Blood and Power: Organized Crime in Twentieth-Century America.* New York: Morrow.

Fried, Albert. 1980. *The Rise and Fall of the Jewish Gangster in America.* New York: Holt, Rinehart and Winston.

Friel, Frank, and John Guinther. 1990. *Breaking the Mob.* McGraw-Hill.

Gentry, Curt. 1991. *J. Edgar Hoover: The Man and His Secrets.* New York: Penguin Books.

Goldberg, Arthur. 1956. *AFL-CIO: Labor United.* New York: McGraw-Hill.

Goldberg, Michael J. 1989. "Cleaning Labor's House: Institutional Reform Litigation in the Labor Movement." *Duke Law Journal* 1989:903–1011.

Goldfarb, Ronald. 1995. *Perfect Villains, Imperfect Heroes: Robert F. Kennedy's War against Organized Crime.* New York: Random House.

Goulden, Joseph. 1972. *Meany.* New York: Atheneum.

Harper, Michael, and Samuel Estreicher. 4th edition 1996. *Labor Law: Cases, Materials and Problems.* Boston: Little Brown.

Hatman, Victoria C. 1993. *Labor Visions and State Power: The Origins of Business Unionism in the United States*. Princeton: Princeton University Press.

Hopkins, A. D., and K. J. Evans. 2000. *The First 100: Portraits of the Men and Women Who Shaped Las Vegas*. Las Vegas: Huntington Press.

Hughes, Rupert. 1940. *Attorney for the People: The Story of Thomas E. Dewey*. Boston: Houghton Mifflin.

Hutchinson, John. 1972. *The Imperfect Union: A History of Corruption in American Trade Unions*. New York: Dutton.

Ieromino, Steven T. 1994. "Note, RICO: Is It a Panacea or a Bitter Pill for Labor Unions, Union Democracy and Collective Bargaining?" 11 *Hofstra Labor Law Journal* 499.

Jacobs, James B., and Ryan Alford. 2005. "The Teamsters' Rocky Road to Recovery: The Demise of Project Rise." *Trends in Organized Crime* 9(1) (November).

Jacobs, James B., Eileen Cunningham, and Kimberly Friday. 2004. "The RICO Trusteeships After 20 Years: A Progress Report." 19 *Labor Lawyer* 419.

Jacobs, James B., Coleen Friel, and Edward O'Callaghan. 1997. "Pension Forfeiture: A Problematic Sanction for Public Corruption." *American Criminal Law Review* 35:57–92.

Jacobs, James B., Coleen Friel, and Robert Radick. 1999. *Gotham Unbound: How New York City Was Liberated from the Grip of Organized Crime*. New York: New York University Press.

Jacobs, James B., and Lauryn Gouldin. 1999. "Cosa Nostra: The Final Chapter?" In *Crime and Justice: A Review of Research*, vol. 25, edited by Michael Tonry. Chicago: University of Chicago Press.

Jacobs, James B., and Alex Hortis. 1998. "New York City as Organized Crime Fighter." 42 *New York Law School Law Review* 1069.

Jacobs, James B., and Elizabeth Mullin. 2003. "Congress' Role in the Defeat of Organized Crime." *Criminal Law Bulletin* 39 (3): 269–312.

Jacobs, James B., Christopher Panarella, and Jay Worthington III. 1994. *Busting the Mob: United States v. Cosa Nostra*. New York: New York University Press.

Jacobs, James B., and Ellen Peters. 2003. "Labor Racketeering: The Mafia and the Unions." 30 *Crime and Justice: A Review of Research*, edited by Michael Tonry.

Jacobs, James B., and David Santore. 2001. "The Liberation of IBT Local 560." *Criminal Law Bulletin* 37(2):125–58.

Jacobs, James B., and Kristin Stohner. 2004. "Ten Years of Court-Supervised Reform: A Chronicle and Assessment." 6 *California Law Review* 3.

Johnson, Malcolm. 1950. *Crime on the Labor Front*. New York: McGraw-Hill.

Joselit, Jenna W. 1983. *Our Gang: Jewish Crime and the New York Jewish Community*. Bloomington, Ind.: Indiana University Press.

Kannar, George. 1993. "Making the Teamsters Safe for Democracy." 102 *Yale Law Journal* 1645.

Kefauver, Estes. 1951. *Crime in America*. Garden City, N.Y.: Doubleday.

Kennedy, Robert F. 1960. *The Enemy Within*. New York: Harper and Row.

Kiley, Meagan. 2003. "The International Brotherhood of Teamsters' Disciplinary Procedures: A Look at the Independent Review Board." Unpublished New York University School of Law Seminar Paper.

Kimeldorf, Howard. 1988. *Reds or Rackets? The Making of Radical and Conservative Unions on the Waterfront*. Berkeley: University of California Press.

Kobler, John. 1971. *Capone: The Life and World of Al Capone*. New York: Putnam.

Kwitny, Jonathan. 1979. *Vicious Circles: The Mafia in the Marketplace*. New York: W. W. Norton.

La Botz, Dan. 1990. *Rank and File Rebellion: Teamsters for a Democratic Union*. London: Verso Books.

Lacey, Frederick. 1992. "The Independent Administrator's Memorandum on the Handling and Disposition of Disciplinary Matters." Unpublished report to Judge Edelstein, October 7.

Landesco, John. 1968. *Organized Crime in Chicago*. Originally published in 1929 by the Illinois Association for Criminal Justice. Chicago: University of Chicago Press.

Lens, Sidney. 1959. *The Crisis of American Labor*. New York: Sigamore Press.

———. 1973. *The Labor Wars: From the Molly Maguires to the Sitdowns*. New York: Doubleday.

Lichtenstein, Nelson. 1995. *Walter Reuther: The Most Dangerous Man in Detroit*. Urbana-Champaign: University of Illinois Press.

Lipset, Seymour M., Martin Trow, and James Coleman. 1956. *Union Democracy: The Internal Politics of the International Typographical Union*. Glencoe, Ill.: Free Press.

Lynch, Gerald. 1987a. "RICO: The Crime of Being a Criminal, Part 1." *Columbia Law Review* 87:661–764.

———. 1987b. "RICO: The Crime of Being a Criminal, Part 2." *Columbia Law Review* 87:920–84.

Maas, Peter. 1997. *Underboss: Sammy the Bull Gravano's Story of Life in the Mafia*. New York: HarperCollins.

Mandel, Bernard. 1963. *Samuel Gompers*. Yellow Springs, Ohio: Antioch Press.

McClellan, John. 1962. *Crime without Punishment*. New York: Duell, Sloan, and Pearce.

McLaughlin, Doris, and Anita Schoonmaker. 1979. *The Landrum-Griffin Act and Union Democracy*. Ann Arbor: University of Michigan Press.

Methvin, Eugene H. 1998. "A Corrupt Union and the Mob." *Weekly Standard* 3(48):25–29.

Moldea, Dan E. 1978. *The Hoffa Wars: Teamsters, Rebels, Politicians and the Mob*. New York: Paddington Press.

Muellenberg, Kurt W. 1998. Final Report as Monitor of HEREIU, August 26, 1998. Available at http://www.heretics.net.

Mulligan, John E., and Dean Starkman. 1996. "An F.O.B. and the Mob (Laborers' International Union of North America President Arthur A. Coia)." *Washington Monthly* 28(5):11–13.

Murray, Mark. 1999. "Labor on Patrol," *National Journal*, September 4, 1999, vol. 31, no. 36, 2489.

Navasky, Victor S. 1971. *Kennedy Justice.* New York: Atheneum.

Neff, James. 1989. *Mobbed Up: Jackie Presser's High-Wire Life in the Teamsters, the Mafia, and the FBI.* New York: Atlantic Monthly Press.

Nelson, Michael. 2000. "Slowing Union Corruption: Reforming the Landrum-Griffin Act to Better Combat Union Embezzlement." *George Mason Law Review* 8:527–86.

New York State Crime Commission. 1953. Final Report of the New York State Crime Commission to the Governor, the Attorney General and the Legislature of the State of New York. Albany: State of New York.

New York State Organized Crime Task Force. 1990. *Corruption and Racketeering in the New York City Construction Industry: Final Report to Governor Mario M. Cuomo.* New York: New York University Press.

Nunn, Sam. 1986. "The Impact of the Senate Permanent Subcommittee on Investigations on Federal Policy." *Georgia Law Review* 21:17–56.

Office of the Independent Hearing Officer (LIUNA). 1999. "Executive Summary of IHO Decision re: LIUNA General President Arthur A. Coia." March 8. Available at http://www.laborers.org.

Peterson, Virgil W. 1983. *The Mob: 200 Years of Organized Crime in New York.* Ottawa, Ill.: Green Hill.

Pennsylvania Crime Commission. 1990. *Organized Crime in Pennsylvania: A Decade of Change.* Conshohocker, Pa.: Pennsylvania Crime Commission.

Porrello, Rick. 1995. *The Rise and Fall of the Cleveland Mafia.* Fort Lee, N.J.: Barricade Books.

Powers, Richard. 1986. *Secrecy and Power: The Life of J. Edgar Hoover.* New York: Free Press

President's Commission on Crime and the Administration of Justice, Task Force on Organized Crime. 1967. *Task Force Report: Organized Crime.* Washington, D.C.: GPO.

President's Commission on Organized Crime. 1986. *The Edge: Organized Crime, Business, and Labor Unions.* Washington, D.C.: President's Commission on Organized Crime.

Raskin, A. H. 1954. "Unions and the Public Interest." *Commentary*, February.

Rauh, Joseph. 1971. "LMRDA—Enforce It or Repeal It." *Georgia Law Review* 5:643–86.

Repetto, Thomas E. 2004. *American Mafia: A History of Its Rise to Power.* New York: Henry Holt.

Reuter, Peter. 1984. "Racketeers as Cartel Organizers." In H. Alexander and G.

Caiden (eds.), *Political and Economic Perspectives on Organized Crime*. Lexington, Mass.: D. C. Heath, 49–65.

Reuter, Peter. 1987. *Racketeering in Legitimate Industries: A Study in the Economics of Intimidation*. Santa Monica: RAND.

Reynolds, Ehren. 2005. "Protecting the Waterfront: Prosecuting Mob-Tied Union Officers Under RICO and the Hobbs Act after Schiedler," 10 *Cal. Crim. Law Rev.* 1.

Robinson, Archie. 1981. *George Meany and His Times*. New York: Simon and Schuster.

Roemer, William F., Jr. 1995. *Accardo: The Genuine Godfather*. New York: Donald I. Fine.

Rubin, George. 1988. "McCarthy Selected to Head Teamsters; Developments in Industrial Relations," *Monthly Labor Review*, October 1988, vol. 111, no. 10, at 45.

Russo, Gus. 2001. *The Outfit: The Role of Chicago's Underworld in the Shaping of Modern America*. New York: Bloomsbury.

Russell, Thaddues. 2001. *Out of the Jungle: Jimmy Hoffa and the Remaking of the American Working Class*. New York: Alfred A. Knopf.

Sandler, Ross, and David Schoenbrod. 2003. *Democracy by Decree*. New Haven: Yale University Press.

Schlenger, Margo. 1999. "Beyond the Hero Judge." 97 *Michigan L. Rev.* 1994.

Schlesinger, Jr., Arthur. 1996. *Robert Kennedy and His Times*. New York: Ballantine Books (reissue edition).

Seal, Kathy. 1997. "Union Monitor Remains; HEREIU." *Hotel and Motel Management*, 212(6):3–5.

Seidman, Harold. 1938. *Labor Czars: A History of Labor Racketeering*. New York: Liveright.

Sheridan, Walter. 1972. *The Fall and Rise of Jimmy Hoffa*. New York: Saturday Review Press.

Siciliano, Paul. 2003. "Eyes Wide Shut: Labor Law Textbooks and the Treatment of Organized Crime's Infiltration and Use of Labor Unions." Unpublished, New York University School of Law Seminar Paper.

Sifakis, Carl. 1987. *The Mafia Encyclopedia*. New York: Facts on File.

Sloane, Arthur A. 1991. *Hoffa*. Cambridge: MIT Press.

Stier, Anderson & Malone, LLC. 2001. *The Teamsters: Perception and Reality: An Investigative Study of Organized Crime Influence in the Union*. Washington D.C.: International Brotherhood of Teamsters.

Stolberg, Mary E. 1995. *Fighting Organized Crime: Politics, Justice, and the Legacy of Thomas E. Dewey*. Boston: Northeastern University Press.

Summers, Anthony. 1993. *Official and Confidential: The Secret Life of J. Edgar Hoover*. New York: G. P. Putnam's Sons.

Summers, Clyde. 1991. "Union Trusteeships and Union Democracy." *University of Michigan Journal of Law Reform* 24:689–707.

Summers, Clyde W., Joseph L. Rauh, and Herman Benson. 1986. *Union Democracy and Landrum-Griffin.* Brooklyn, N.Y.: Association for Union Democracy.

Taft, Phillip. 1964. *Organized Labor in American History.* New York: Harper and Row.

———. 1970. *Corruption and Racketeering in the Labor Movement.* 2d ed. Ithaca: Cornell Industrial and Labor Relations Press.

United States Congress. 1933. *Investigation of So-Called "Rackets." Hearings before the Subcommittee of the Senate Committee on Commerce* [commonly known as the Copeland Committee]. 73d Cong., 1st sess. Washington, D.C.: GPO.

———. 1957. *Welfare and Pension Plans Legislation. Hearings before the Subcommittee on Welfare and Pension Plans Legislation of the Committee on Labor and Public Welfare,* Senate. 85th Cong., 1st sess. Washington, D.C.: GPO.

———. 1958. *Senate Select Committee on Improper Activities in the Labor or Management Field,* Report No. 1417, 85th Cong., 2d sess. Washington, D.C.: GPO.

———. 1960. *Final Report of the Select Committee on Improper Activities in the Labor or Management Field* [McClellan Committee Report]. 86th Cong., 2d sess., S. Rept. 1139. Washington, D.C.: GPO.

———. 1977. *Teamsters Central States Pension Fund: Hearings before the Permanent Subcommittee on Investigations of the Committee on Governmental Affairs,* Senate. 95th Cong., 1st sess., July 18 and 19, 1977. Washington, D.C.: GPO.

———. 1978. *Labor Management Racketeering: Hearings before the Permanent Subcommittee on Investigations of the Committee on Governmental Affairs,* Senate. 95th Cong., 2d sess., April 24 and 25. Washington, D.C.: GPO.

———. 1979. *Report of the Select Committee on Assassinations.* 95th Cong., 2d sess., House Report No. 95-1828, Part 2. Washington, D.C.: GPO.

———. 1982. *Hearings Before the Permanent Subcommittee on Investigations of the Committee on Governmental Affairs,* Senate. 97th Cong., 1st sess. Washington, D.C.: GPO.

———. 1983. *Prepared statement of Donald Wheeler, Special Agent in Charge, Chicago Office, Organized Crime and Racketeering Section, Inspector General's Office, Department of Labor. Prepared statement before the Permanent Subcommittee on Investigations of the Committee on Governmental Affairs,* Senate. Chicago, Illinois, March 4. Washington, D.C.: GPO.

———. 1984a. *Hearings before the Permanent Subcommittee on Investigations of the Committee on Governmental Affairs, United States Senate.* 98th Cong., 2d sess., August 27, 1984. Washington, D.C.: GPO.

———. 1984b. *Waterfront Corruption: Report Made by the Permanent Subcommittee on Investigations of the Committee on Governmental Affairs, United States Senate.* 98th Cong., 2d sess., March 27, 1984. Washington, D.C.: GPO.

United States Congress. 1985. *Organized Crime and Labor Management Racketeering: Hearings before the President's Commission on Organized Crime.* 99th Cong., 1st sess., April 24. Washington, D.C.: GPO.

———. 1989. *Federal Government's Use of Trusteeships under the RICO Statute: Hearings before the Permanent Subcommittee on Investigations of the Committee on Governmental Affairs, United States Senate.* 101st Cong., 1st sess., April 4, 6, and 12. Washington, D.C.: GPO.

———. 1989. *Hearings before the Permanent Subcommittee on Investigations of the Committee on Governmental Affairs, United States Senate.* 101st Cong., 1st sess. Washington, D.C.: GPO.

———. 1996. *Testimony of Robert Luskin before the Subcommittee on Crime of the Committee on the Judiciary, United States House of Representatives.* 104th Cong., 2d sess., July 25. Washington, D.C.: GPO.

———. 1997. *Administration's Effort against the Influence of Organized Crime in LIUNA.* House Judiciary Committee, 105th Cong., 1st sess., Jan. 2. Washington, D.C.: GPO.

———. 1999. *Subcommittee on House Employer-Employee Relations, Committee on Education and the Workforce. Hearing on the HEREIU.* 106th Cong., 1st sess. Washington, D.C.: GPO.

United States Department of Justice. 2000. "Justice Department Announces New Agreement Continuing Laborers Union Reforms until 2006." Press release. January 20. Available at http://www.usdoj.gov.

———. 2002. "17 Members and Associations of the Gambino Crime Family Indicted for Corruption on the New York Waterfront." Press release. June 4.

Vaira, Peter, and Douglas P. Roller. 1978. *Report on Organized Crime and the Labor Unions.* Prepared for the White House. Available at http://www.americanmafia.com/crime_and_labor.html.

Velie, Lester. 1977. *Desperate Bargain: Why Jimmy Hoffa Had to Die.* New York: Reader's Digest Press.

Wallentine, Kenneth. 1990. "A Leash Upon Labor: RICO Trusteeships on Labor Unions," 7 *Hofstra Labor Law Journal* 341.

Witwer, David. 2002. "The Landrum-Griffin Act: A Case Study in the Possibilities and Problems in Anti-Union Corruption Law," 27 *Criminal Justice Review* 301.

———. 2001. "Depression-Era Racketeering in the Building Services Union." Association for Union Democracy. *$100 Club News*, no. 82, November.

———. 2003. *Corruption and Reform in the Teamsters Union, 1898 to 1991.* Urbana-Champaign: University of Illinois Press.

———. 2003. "The Scandal of George Scalise: A Case Study in the Rise of Labor Racketeering in the 1930s," 36 *Journal of Social History,* 917.

Wooten, James A. 2004. *The Employee Retirement Income Security Act of 1974: A Political History.* Berkeley: University of California Press.

Index

Page numbers including an asterisk refer to a footnote.

Montalvo, Nick, 103
Moody, James, 23
Morgenthau, Robert, 248
Morrin, P. J., 79
Morrissey, John, 70, 72
Moscatiello, Louis, 30, 72
Motion Picture Operators Union
 (MPOU), 26
MPOU (Motion Picture Operators
 Union), 26
MTA (Master Truckmen of America),
 60, 61
Muellenberg, Kurt W., 138, 146, 159, 213,
 217–221, 294n41
Mueller, Robert S., 296n11
Murder Incorporated, 49
Muscarella, U.S. v., 140*

Nader, Ralph, 111
Natale, Ralph, 214, 215, 216
National Institute of Justice, 240
National Labor Relations Act
 (NLRA/Wagner Act), 6, 9*, 24–25, 25*,
 54, 260
National Labor Relations Board (NLRB),
 6, 9, 53, 54, 119
National Legal and Policy Center (NLPC),
 221–222
*National Organization for Women, Scheidler
 v.*, 140*
National unions, 6–7
Neff, James, xxii, 203
New Jersey Casino Control Commission,
 214
New Jersey Division of Gaming Enforcement, 214, 215
New York City, 57–75; building trades/
 construction, xxi, 57, 59, 68–72, 125–126
 (*see also* New York City District Council
 of Carpenters); crime families in, 4–5,
 57, 58, 127; FBI in, 12–13; fish industry,
 52; Javits Convention Center, 32, 59, 64,
 183, 185, 191–193, 200; meat industry,
 52, 74; parking garage workers, 30;
 poultry industry, 52; U.S. judicial districts in, 16; waste-hauling industry,
 xxii, 44, 59, 67–68; waterfront, xviii–xix,
 49–50, 51, 82, 91, 227
New York City Cartmen's Association, 67

New York City District Council of Carpenters, 183–202; Javits Convention
 Center, 32, 59, 185, 191–193, 200; labor
 racketeering prosecutions, 65–66; presi-
 dents, 125, 184; RICO civil suit, 4, 146,
 185–202; RICO trusteeship, xxv–xxvi,
 146. *See also* UBC (United Brotherhood
 of Carpenters)
New York–New Jersey Waterfront Com-
 mission, 50, 91
New York Shipping Association (NYSA),
 229
New York State Crime Commission, 50
New York State Organized Crime Task
 Force (OCTF), xv, xxi, 57, 69–70,
 129–130, 130*
New York State Teamsters Conference
 Employee Welfare and Pension Benefit
 Plan, 162
Newspaper and Mail Deliverers Union,
 6, 75
Nixon, Richard, 17*, 124
NLPC (National Legal and Policy Center),
 221–222
NLRA (National Labor Relations
 Act/Wagner Act), 6, 9*, 24–25, 25*, 54,
 260
NLRB (National Labor Relations Board),
 6, 9, 53, 54, 119
No-show jobs, 33
Norris-LaGuardia Act (1932), 5*
Nunn, Sam, 93, 93*
NYSA (New York Shipping Association),
 229

O'Connor, John, 65, 185–186, 186*
OCRS (Organized Crime and Racketeer-
 ing Section, U.S. Department of Justice),
 16–17, 17–18, 123, 124, 240
OCTF (Organized Crime Task Force, New
 York State), xv, xxi, 57, 69–70, 129–130,
 130*
O'Dwyer, William, 258
Office of Labor-Management Standards,
 U.S. Department of Labor (OLMS), 98,
 119
Office of Labor Racketeering, U.S. Depart-
 ment of Labor (OLR), 127
O'Leary, Howard E., 218
OLMS (Office of Labor-Management Stan-

About the Author

JAMES B. JACOBS is Warren E. Burger Professor of Law and Director, Center for Research in Crime and Justice, New York University School of Law. A lawyer/sociologist, Jacobs writes widely on criminal justice topics including prisons, corruption, hate crime, and organized crime. This book is the fourth volume in a long-term research project to document and analyze the status of organized crime and organized crime control in the last quarter of the twentieth century and the first decade of the twenty-first century. Each volume stands on its own, offering a particular perspective on different facets of Cosa Nostra's political and economic power and the government's post-1970s criminal and civil remedial efforts.